THE OTHER RENAISSANCE

Also by Paul Strathern

The Florentines
The Borgias
Death in Florence
Spirit of Venice
The Artist, the Philosopher and the Warrior
Napoleon in Egypt
The Medici

THE
OTHER
RENAISSANCE

From Copernicus to Shakespeare

PAUL STRATHERN

Atlantic Books
London

First published in Great Britain in 2023 by Atlantic Books,
an imprint of Atlantic Books Ltd.

1 2 3 4 5 6 7 8 9

A CIP catalogue record for this book is available from the British Library.

Hardback ISBN: 978-1-83895-513-7
Trade paperback ISBN: 978-1-83895-516-8
E-book ISBN: 978-1-83895-517-5

Map artwork by Keith Chaffer

Hardback endpaper image: Chart by Andreas Cellarius
illustrating a heliocentric model of the universe as proposed by
Nicolaus Copernicus, 1661 *(steeve-x-art/Alamy Stock Photo)*

Printed in Great Britain

Atlantic Books
An Imprint of Atlantic Books Ltd
Ormond House
26–27 Boswell Street
London
WC1N 3JZ

www.atlantic-books.co.uk

To
My Brother Mark

CONTENTS

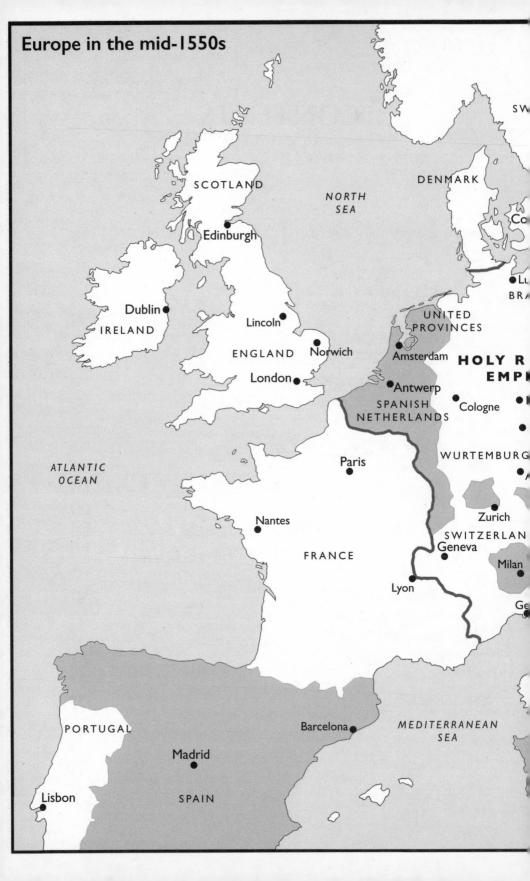

Europe in the mid-1550s

SCOTLAND
Edinburgh

NORTH
SEA

DENMARK

SW

Co

Lu

BRA

Dublin

IRELAND

Lincoln

ENGLAND

Norwich

UNITED
PROVINCES

Amsterdam

HOLY R
EMPI

London

Antwerp

SPANISH
NETHERLANDS

Cologne

ATLANTIC
OCEAN

Paris

WURTEMBURG

Nantes

Zurich

SWITZERLAN

Geneva

FRANCE

Lyon

Milan

Ge

PORTUGAL

Barcelona

MEDITERRANEAN
SEA

Madrid

Lisbon

SPAIN

TIMELINE OF SIGNIFICANT EVENTS
DURING THE NORTHERN RENAISSANCE

1415 Jan Hus, founder of the Hussites, burned at the stake

1432 Van Eyck completes the *Ghent Altarpiece*

1460s Regiomontanus oversees the building of the first observatory in Europe

1464 Death of Nicholas of Cusa

1474 Technique of painting in oils spreads from the Netherlands to Italy

1494 Signing of the Treaty of Tordesillas: Pope Alexander VI draws a line down the Atlantic Ocean, dividing the globe between Spain and Portugal

1497 John Cabot sails from Bristol and reaches North America

1509 Erasmus writes *In Praise of Folly*

1512 Torrigiano is commissioned by Henry VIII to create a Renaissance tomb for Henry VII

1514 Dürer produces *Melencolia I*

1515 Francis I ascends to the throne of France

1517 Martin Luther nails his *Ninety-Five Theses* to the door of Wittenberg Castle Church

1519 The death of Leonardo da Vinci in France

1519 Charles V is crowned Holy Roman Emperor

1525 Death of Jacob Fugger the Rich

1529 The Colloquy of Marburg fails to unite Protestants

1533 Henry VIII breaks with Rome

1536 John Calvin arrives in Geneva; Calvinist missionaries soon begin to spread over northern Europe

1536 French explorer Jacques Cartier brings Chief Donnacona from the New World to see Francis I

1541 Death of Paracelsus

1543 Copernicus is shown the first published edition of his *De Revolutionibus Orbium Coelestium*, describing the solar system, while on his deathbed

1543 Vesalius publishes *De Fabrica*, describing human anatomy

1547 The completion of the Château de Chambord in the Loire Valley

1547 The death of Francis I of France

1553 The death of Rabelais

1553 English explorer Richard Chancellor visits the court of Ivan the Terrible

1558 The death of Holy Roman Emperor Charles V

1569 Mercator publishes his *Atlas*, containing his cylindrical projection map of the world

1572 The St Bartholomew's Day massacre of Huguenots in France

1588 The Spanish Armada fails to invade Elizabethan England

1589 The death of Catherine de' Medici, mother of French kings and ruler of France

1596 Johannes Kepler publishes his laws describing the elliptical orbit of plants

1600 The founding of the East India Company in London

1601 Tycho Brahe dies in Prague

1608 Invention of the perspicillium in Holland, which inspires Galileo to create the telescope

1616 The death of Shakespeare

1642 Cardinal Richelieu dies in France

1648 The Peace of Westphalia ends the Thirty Years' War

THE
OTHER
RENAISSANCE

LIFTING THE LID

PARACELSUS'S REPUTATION HAD SPREAD before him. His grand inaugural lecture in 1526 as professor of medicine at the University of Basel, the oldest and most prestigious in Switzerland, had attracted a large crowd. The front rows of the hall were filled with the city worthies in their robes of office; alongside them were the university professors bedecked in their black gowns with coloured sashes; and amongst them were the city's fashionably attired leading physicians. Ordinary townsfolk, the merely curious, and many students were crammed into the back rows, squatting in the aisles, or spilling out through the open door into the main square.

Enter Paracelsus in his ragged leather alchemist's apron, bearing aloft a covered platter. He began his lecture by announcing to the assembled company that he would now reveal to them the greatest secret of medical science. Whereupon, with a flourish, he lifted the lid from the platter. To reveal a pile of fresh human excrement.

The first rows of the audience, close enough for their nostrils to detect the odour of what lay before them, rose to their feet. Muttering angrily amongst themselves, they began making their way back up the aisles, their scowling faces forcing a path through the squatting students cluttering the exit.

Amidst the rising hubbub, Paracelsus's voice could be heard calling out after them: 'If you will not hear the mysteries of putrefaction, you are unworthy of the name of physicians.' Paracelsus had long understood that fermentation was the most important chemical process to take place in the laboratory of the human body. Here lay the secret of life itself: how the human body functioned, gaining its nourishment and expelling extraneous, often toxic, matter. The students and other townsfolk who had come along for the show were not disappointed, and began applauding and cheering him to the rafters.

When order was finally restored, with intent students now occupying the front seats of the auditorium, Paracelsus resumed his lecture. He informed his audience that these were times of drastic change. That for the good of humanity our view of ourselves and our place in the world had to be transformed.* Elixirs of life, propitious alignments of the signs of the zodiac, and fallacious systems which prescribed a holistic internal balance of 'humours' as the key to human health were all now outmoded – mere things of the past. The world did not ultimately consist of earth, air, fire and water; and the time was over when the physician's task was to relate these elements to the four humours, whose balance was said to control our health – namely, black bile (earth), blood (air), yellow bile (fire) and phlegm (water). The earth contained all manner of chemicals and plants, just as the body suffered from all manner of ailments and diseases. The task of the physician was to learn which of these chemicals and plants were appropriate for curing particular infirmities. Likewise, it was necessary to learn through experience the required dosages necessary to eliminate such illnesses. Suitably diluted quantities, regularly administered, might

---

* Although Paracelsus was here referring to purely medical matters, such feelings were becoming more widespread in many spheres. It is no coincidence that, almost ten years previously, Martin Luther had nailed his Protestant theses to the door of Wittenberg Castle Church; and even as Paracelsus was delivering his lecture at Basel, in faraway Poland, Copernicus was piecing together his idea of the solar system.

cure the patient; excessive doses were liable to be lethal. Here, Paracelsus was laying the foundations of modern pharmacology.

Thus spoke the man whom many regard as the father of modern medicine. Others, by contrast, continue to regard him as no more than a bombastic self-advertising quack. The Renaissance was in many ways a schizophrenic era. A number of its finest pioneering thinkers would frequently retain incongruous remnants of earlier medieval preconceptions, even as their discoveries opened up entirely new fields of knowledge which superseded such ideas. The upheaval in European thought which today we call the Renaissance was also divided in another sense. While many elements of the Renaissance originated in Florence and the city-states of Italy, a quasi-independent 'Other Renaissance' was coming into being north of the Alps. The Swiss physician Paracelsus was a prime, if somewhat uncouth, exemplar of both these processes.

The man we now know as Paracelsus was born on 1 May 1493 in the village of Egg in northern Switzerland, his given name being Theophrastus Bombastus von Hohenheim.* Later in life he would style himself as Paracelsus – meaning 'greater than Celsus', the first-century physician considered at the time to have been the greatest medical practitioner of the Ancient Roman era. For over a millennium, the works of Aulus Cornelius Celsus had been considered lost, their existence only known from admiring references which appeared in the manuscripts of his contemporaries and a number of later sources. Then, in the mid-1400s, a copy of Celsus's *De Medicina* (On Medicine) was discovered by Pope Nicholas V in the Vatican archives. In 1478, Celsus's treatise became one of the first medical works to be printed, immediately gaining a wide circulation and the high reputation it deserved.

Celsus's medical expertise was largely grounded in the knowledge he had absorbed during the practice of his profession, and was for the most part unadulterated by the holistic theory, erroneous beliefs and sheer superstition which had accumulated around this subject during the many

---

* Contrary to popular misconception, the word 'bombastic' does not in fact derive from his name, though it would have been most apt had it done so.

centuries since his death. Paracelsus was deeply struck by what he read of the Roman Celsus's works, and decided to begin as he would go on – rejecting the orthodox traditional teachings of his era as inferior rubbish. This attitude, roundly proclaimed, meant that as a student he found it prudent to absent himself from a succession of German universities, including Heidelberg, Tübingen and Leipzig. Consequently he decided on a course of self-education, and set out to see for himself what he could discover. 'Knowledge is experience,' he proclaimed, an adage to which he would for the most part adhere throughout his controversial career. It would also become one of the central tenets of Renaissance scientific thought.

In the course of Paracelsus's quest for self-education, he claimed to have tramped the highways and byways of Europe from Scandinavia to Constantinople, from Scotland to Sicily. Later, he would even assert that he had gained a medical doctorate at the University of Ferrara in 1515 or 1516 (accounts vary). However, the university records for this period had been lost, a fact of which he was almost certainly aware. During Paracelsus's wanderings through the length and breadth of Europe (and possibly even as far afield as Egypt), he accumulated a vast compendium of medical knowledge, including many old wives' tales, local superstitions and witches' cures. He also sought out alchemists, consulting them on their various laboratory techniques.

Paracelsus became experienced at sorting the wheat from the chaff amongst these 'cures', discovering many genuinely efficacious herbs, plants and other 'elixirs'. Likewise, he learned a number of fundamental principles from the alchemists' experimental methods and materials, arriving at the conclusion that the human body itself operated in the manner of a chemical laboratory. He began developing a form of what became known as iatrochemistry, a medical chemistry using minerals to combat illness or malfunctions in the body's internal workings. Here again, he insisted that practice was the way to knowledge: 'The patients are your textbook, the sickbed is your study.'

On occasion, his successful treatment of a local worthy would result in him being appointed to a post at a nearby university. But his wilful eccentricity would soon become apparent. For a start, he insisted upon delivering his lectures dressed in an alchemist's rough leather apron rather than formal academic robes. Rather than the customary Latin, he chose to lecture in German, so that he would be understood by all the local barber-surgeons, alchemists and itinerant quacks whom he publicly invited to hear him speak. His lectures tended to ridicule orthodox medical learning, in favour of his own revolutionary theories.

As a result, Paracelsus became hugely popular with his students and would frequently be carried off by them to the town's taverns. Here he cut a curious figure amongst his roistering young admirers. His travels had given him the tanned visage of a vagabond. Yet his coarse, curiously hermaphroditic features were beardless. One report describes him as dressed in 'beggar's garb', and he was in the habit of wearing the same scruffy clothes for months on end, not even bothering to remove them before he fell onto his bed in a drunken stupor. Bodily hygiene was evidently not part of his medical practice.

Another habit he developed, unusual for a physician, was to carry around with him at all times a large, ornately carved broadsword. This he claimed had been presented to him by the Grand Vizier of Constantinople, or had been discovered by chance atop a peak in the Alps, or... When enacting his outlandish traveller's tales, he was liable to leap onto a tavern table, enthusiastically brandishing his sword above his head. He even gave it a name: Azoth, the alchemists' term for the creative force of nature. It is said that he took his sword to bed with him. This was his constant and sole sleeping companion, for he is not known to have slept with any human companions, male or female. Impotence was the likely cause of his chastity. But despite this involuntary virtue, his general demeanour meant that his university faculty appointments seem to have lasted little longer than his time as a student at any particular university.

The high point in Paracelsus's career came in 1527, when he arrived in the Swiss city of Basel. At the time, the celebrated Dutch humanist Desiderius Erasmus was residing there. Although Erasmus was generally regarded as the greatest scholar in Europe, he was renowned for the fact that his mind was always open to new ideas.

Erasmus invited Paracelsus to visit him, and was so intrigued by the eccentric physician's novel ideas that he enquired if he knew of any remedy to cure him of his kidney complaint, along with the painful gout from which he had begun to suffer. Paracelsus duly prescribed a course of treatment, and Erasmus was cured of these ailments which had defied the finest medical minds in Europe.

Erasmus was so impressed that he used his considerable influence to get Paracelsus appointed as the city's medical officer, along with a post as professor of medicine at the local university. At the age of thirty-four, Paracelsus stood on the threshold of a great career – as long as he behaved himself. It was now that he delivered his inaugural lecture, in which he lifted the lid on modern medicine.

It comes as little surprise that Paracelsus gained himself many enemies, both within the medical community and beyond. His detractors maintained that he simply stole many of his ideas and mythological 'cures' from others, to say nothing of plagiarizing the works of Celsus himself. Paracelsus claimed that he was merely putting into practice much of the knowledge which had come to light in the recently discovered work of Celsus, at the same time improving upon this with discoveries and remedies of his own. There was method in his hubris of naming himself Paracelsus.

Here was the beginning of modern medicine. So why is Paracelsus not universally acclaimed as 'the father of modern medicine'? Though highly regarded as a Renaissance man in Germany to this day, in Italy many continue to see him as an unscrupulous and opportunistic buffoon. There is more than a grain of truth in this latter assessment. Paracelsus's genuine achievements remain undermined by his occasional recourse to hermetic practices and other esoteric pursuits when the mood took him. To say nothing of his resort to downright fraudulence. As ever, Paracelsus was his own worst enemy. When he found himself in need of cash he was as capable as any quack of cooking up his own bogus 'elixir of life', and then selling bottles of this for a suitably inflated price – before quickly removing himself from the local jurisdiction. In some cases, flakes of gold were introduced to the mixture, in order to impress the gullible and justify the inflated price of a particular elixir.

The wonder is not that he spent so much of his time travelling, but that he got away with continuing to do so.

Paracelsus also developed (or purloined) a number of classic medieval remedies. Typical of these was the popular old wives' tale known as the doctrine of signatures. Each plant was deemed to have its own signature, which indicated the disease that it cured. For example, an orchid resembled a testicle, and was thus ideal for curing venereal diseases; heart-shaped lilacs were perfect for the relief of heart complaints; yellow celandine flowers provided a remedy for jaundice; and so forth...

Paracelsus was a man whose practice, and probably his beliefs too, straddled two ages. He combined the superstitious knowledge of the medieval era with the empirical science of the new age of the Renaissance. Yet it must be stressed that he was far from being alone in such aberration. Lingering strands of medieval waywardness would continue to contaminate scientific practice for centuries to come. And prime examples of this schizophrenic approach were not unique to the Renaissance, either. No less than Galileo Galilei himself, widely regarded as a founder of the modern scientific age – and certainly the finest astronomer of his time – was not above casting the occasional astrological chart for some wealthy dignitary willing to pay off his debts. A century later, Robert Boyle, the Irish 'father of modern chemistry', remained an avid (and convinced) alchemist on the side. But perhaps the most notorious of all was his contemporary Isaac Newton, who lived well into the 1700s and was known to have devoted more of his time and energy to numerology, alchemy, and obscure biblical prophecies concerning the location and proportions of King Solomon's Temple in Jerusalem, than he did on the physical science and mathematical calculus which would revolutionize our knowledge of how the world works.

When Paracelsus lifted the lid on his pile of excrement, he was revealing a profound truth which would prove of lasting benefit to humanity. Yet his dabbling in the 'signatures' of plants, bogus elixirs, and other metaphysical matters was possessed of the same physical quality as the steaming pile on his platter. There can be no denying that originality and ordure coexisted to a remarkable extent in the life of

Paracelsus. We shall hear more of him later. Some of it edifying; some of it less so.

Not all great thinkers of this era were prone to such gross lapses as Paracelsus. Indeed, one might be forgiven for overlooking the odd misstep by some pioneer Renaissance scholar exploring unknown regions ahead of his contemporaries. Yet this was definitely not the case with the exemplary science carried out by Dietrich of Freiberg, whose combination of empirical and deductive thinking remains as clear and perceptive today as it was seven centuries ago.

Sometime during the early 1300s, this middle-aged Dominican friar found himself gazing up at a rainbow in the sky. For centuries the rainbow had presented an insoluble conundrum. It was visible, it contained all colours, and there was no denying its existence. Yet on closer examination it didn't appear to exist at all. It arose from no exact spot on earth and arched down to no precise location; similarly illusionistic was its appearance at different places in the sky when seen from different viewpoints.

Friar Dietrich was well aware that, according to the Bible, the rainbow represented God's promise to Noah that he would never again unleash a cataclysmic flood capable of destroying all life on earth. This multicoloured arch in the sky embodied the divine bridge between Heaven and earth. It illustrated God's grace and his pledge that humanity could gain redemption from life on earth and pass over this bridge into Paradise.

Dietrich had recently been reading a commentary by the tenth-century Arabic scholar Alhazen on the optics of the Ancient Greek geometer Euclid. Writing around the third century BC, Euclid had proposed that the eye gained its sight by emitting rays of light. Alhazen agreed with the gist of Euclid's thesis, but proposed a vital modification. Instead of the eye emitting rays, it was in fact receiving light rays 'from each point of every coloured body... every straight line that can be drawn from that point'. Friar Dietrich noticed how the rainbow only occurred during a concatenation of sunlight and rainstorm, suggesting that these effects were somehow responsible for this seemingly immaterial manifestation

– which had all the appearance of being caused by rays emanating from it into the human eye. Evidently Euclid had got it wrong, and Alhazen's modification was correct.

Dietrich surmised that the sun's rays passed into the drops of rain falling through the sky, and that the water of these droplets somehow refracted and reflected these rays, causing them to emerge as the colours of the rainbow. But how on earth could he discover whether this conjecture was in fact true?

He realized that he could not possibly study the individual droplets of rain. For a start, the rainbow effect always seemed to retreat the closer one tried to approach it. So Dietrich conceived of an experiment that was as ingenious as it was novel. And this is all the more remarkable when one takes into account that, during this period, the whole idea of practical experimentation was for the most part confined to the dubious fume-filled realms of the alchemist's den. More orthodox knowledge was confirmed by appeal to authority – usually a pronouncement in the works of Aristotle, or some similarly acceptable classical scholar, whose interpretation had been sanctified by the teachings of the Church. Such was the learning propagated in the schools and universities of the time: this body of knowledge became known as Scholasticism.

However, Dietrich would take a different approach; one which inspired an utterly original insight. He conceived of one single raindrop, magnified to the size of a volume of water contained in a round glass flask. This would act as a droplet of water falling through the sky. He held his flask up to the sunlight. The light was refracted as it passed through the magnified droplet (the flask of water), producing an exact imitation of the rainbow effect.

Continuing with his experiments, Dietrich of Freiberg was able to demonstrate how the rainbow always produced precisely the same colours, in precisely the same order. He managed to show why the rainbow formed an arc, and sometimes produced a second, fainter arc with its colours reversed, just as he had on occasion observed during an actual rainbow. He was also able to show how two people standing beside each other did not in fact see the same rainbow, and that this had nothing to do with any rays emanating from their different pairs of eyes. It was because the eyes of each observer received different refracted rays from the rainbow itself. Not surprisingly, Dietrich of Freiberg's accomplishment has been hailed as 'probably the most dramatic development of 14th- and 15th-century optics'.

This account of Dietrich's impressive discovery contains many of the characteristic ingredients of the Renaissance. The word *renaissance* literally means 'rebirth' and refers to the rebirth of ancient classical knowledge – much of which had been lost, forgotten or overlooked in Europe during the many centuries after the fall of the Roman Empire. Dietrich of Freiberg had taken as his starting point the classical legacy of Euclid, as re-interpreted by the Arab scholar Alhazen. Also characteristic of the Renaissance was Dietrich's enquiring mind, which was attempting to seek beyond the inadequate description given by medieval 'authority'. Finally, he was willing to conduct an experiment, so that he could discover an explanation which matched his actual experience and did not depend upon divine or metaphysical interpretation.

The only untoward element of this story is that, like the medical revolution which would later be pioneered by Paracelsus, it took place in the German-speaking lands of northern Europe – rather than south of the Alps, the traditional locus of the early Renaissance. There is no denying that many of the first developments of what became known as the Renaissance took place in Italy. Between the thirteenth and fifteenth centuries, the comparative stasis of medieval learning was increasingly disturbed by new knowledge arriving in Italy via trading links with the Arabic world of the Middle East. There, many Ancient Greek and Roman texts lost to Europe had been preserved. These had been read by Arabic scholars, whose understanding of such works had inspired them to create a golden age of learning. This had led to new scientific discoveries, original interpretations of classical philosophy, and some of the finest Arab literature.

Over the centuries, this knowledge would filter back to Italy, largely through trade links with the Arab world. Yet this sense of new knowledge – and a renaissance of ideas – was not unique to Italy. Innovative ideas, new learning, original art and revolutionary science also began to appear across northern Europe. In some cases this was undeniably influenced by the Renaissance taking place in Italy – yet to a large extent this Other Renaissance would transform European culture in its own unique fashion. Our modern world owes at least as much to the Other Renaissance as it does to our traditional conception of the Renaissance which originated in Italy.

Indeed, arguably, three of the most significant events of the entire Renaissance era would take place north of the Alps. These were the invention of a moveable type printing press by Johannes Gutenberg, the instigation of Protestantism by Martin Luther, and the proposal by Nicolaus Copernicus that the earth was part of a solar system. Printing would result in the widespread dissemination of learning, encouraging original interpretations of what had previously been regarded as authoritative texts. Protestantism would shatter the hegemony of the Roman Catholic Church, splitting Europe. And Copernicus would dislodge humanity from its central place in the universe, an event which would provoke a subtle but profound psychological effect on the human psyche.

Admittedly, all three of these developments would contain elements of the very controversy and unoriginality to which Paracelsus was prone. Printing had in fact been invented in China some centuries prior to Gutenberg's invention (though he almost certainly remained ignorant of this fact). Likewise, Christendom had split once before, when in 1054 the Orthodox Church of Constantinople rejected the authority of the Papal Church in Rome. And finally, Copernicus's heliocentric idea had been anticipated well over 1,500 years previously, by the Ancient Greeks – most notably Aristarchus – only to be disavowed and forgotten during the ensuing centuries.

But the crucial point is that these innovations proposed by Gutenberg, Luther and Copernicus would, often after considerable opposition, come to be recognized by the Renaissance world as accepted fact. As such, these three events would play a major role in undermining forever what had previously been the fundamental certainties of western human existence, and would in doing so give birth to a new modern humanity that inhabited an utterly transformed world.

CHAPTER 1

GUTENBERG

S ometime around the year 1450, an event took place in the
Franco-German city of Strasbourg which would have repercussions
far beyond its formative influence on the early Renaissance. The German
inventor Johannes Gutenberg began issuing the first works produced on
his newly invented moveable type printing press. Unfortunately, behind
this simple fact lurks a complex tangle of devious machinations, financial chicanery, bankruptcy, and all manner of commercial double-dealing.
This in no way detracts from the technical ingenuity, beauty and efficacy
of Gutenberg's printing press, though it does suggest that others were
quick to see its ultimate value. As is so often the case, the human element
detracts from the technical purity of our greatest achievements.

Many throughout the ages have boasted of their willingness to lose
everything in a Faustian bargain which would render their name immortal.
Gutenberg was one of the few who achieved this feat – though without
the aid of any Faustian bargain. On the contrary, Gutenberg fought long
and hard to receive just recompense for his ingenious invention. He died
in 1468 in his late sixties, in the town of his birth. He had never married,
and thus had no family to support him. Always a modest man, few people

even knew of his existence – let alone of his era-transforming achievement, which had by then spread across Europe and was making fortunes
for a new type of profession known as a 'publisher'. All that Gutenberg's
neighbours knew was that he was an old man with a gushing grey beard,
who lived on a small stipend provided by the ruling archbishop-elector
and was looked after by his servant. He received few visitors and his
funeral would be a simple affair. The church where it was held has long
since been destroyed; the graveyard where he was buried has vanished,
and with it the location of his tomb. This is the man named by *Time*
magazine in 1997 as being responsible for the most important invention
of the second millennium – an assessment which remains widely held to
this day.

Johannes Gutenberg was born around 1400 in Mainz, on the River
Rhine. This small city was an important harbour for barges trading on the
Rhine between northern and southern Germany. At this time Germany
was divided into dozens of small city-states. Mainz was of some importance, being ruled by an archbishop-elector – one of the seven electors
who between them chose the Holy Roman Emperor.* This election was
of immense significance, for the Holy Roman Empire claimed titular
rule over much of central Europe, including the German states, eastern
France, northern Italy, Austria and the Czech lands (Bohemia). Only
France rivalled its power, though not its territorial claims.

Johannes's father, Friele Gensfleisch zur Laden zum Gutenberg, was
a goldsmith by trade, and is thought to have held an important post in
the ecclesiastical mint of Johann II von Nassau, Archbishop-Elector of
Mainz. Johannes's mother was probably the daughter of a local merchant.
Young Johannes followed his father into the mint, where he gained his
first knowledge of metallurgy, which would play a crucial role in his later

---

* The other six German electors were the Archbishops of Trier and Cologne, the
King of Bohemia, the Count Palatine of the Rhine, the Duke of Saxony and the
Margrave of Brandenburg.

life. During this period the major trading cities of Europe all minted their own currencies, most of which had no official exchange rates with each other. This naturally led to widespread discrepancies of accepted value, in what many have seen as a classic example of muddled medieval practice. However, this very imprecision served a useful commercial purpose (other than simple overcharging). At the time, the Church forbade the sin of usury – the loan of money at a rate of interest. The imprecise exchange rates between the multiple currencies of Europe used at the annual international trade fairs enabled merchants, bankers and traders to extract a covert profit from their loans without attracting the attention of the local religious authorities.* This vital fact enabled trade to thrive throughout the length and breadth of Europe.

In 1411, the citizens of Mainz rose up against the archbishop-elector and his ruling elite. This caused the Gutenberg family to flee some hundred miles up the Rhine to the Franco-German city of Strasbourg. They almost certainly remained in the minting business – or at least some branch of expert metallurgy – which enabled the young Johannes to remain abreast of the latest developments. Sometime in his early thirties, Johannes Gutenberg had a moment of inspiration when all the elements of his metallurgic expertise came together. According to the prolific twentieth-century science writer Isaac Asimov, 'although the concept of printing probably took no more than an instant of time to enter Gutenberg's head, the practical development took at least twenty years'.

As with all such revolutionary inventions, printing relied upon the seemingly fortuitous coming-together of a number of apparently unrelated objects. These included serviceable paper or vellum (made of soft, thin calfskin); moulds that could easily be adapted for the mass production of precise metal type; and a strong pressing machine. One of Gutenberg's vital contributions to printing resulted from his knowledge of metallurgy. It led him to understand that an alloy of tin, lead and antimony would be required for the metal type, rendering it strong enough to retain its

---

* In modern parlance, this practice is known as arbitrage.

precision yet soft enough not to damage the paper of the page that was being printed. His second crucial contribution was the invention of an oil-based ink capable of printing clearly. Existing water-based inks were liable to bleed across the page.

A further stroke of inspiration was to understand that if he cast entire alphabets of smaller metal blocks, and even common words, such moveable metal type could be laid out in a tray to produce an entire line of words. Lines of such trays could be laid out to form pages of coherent sentences. Paper could then be placed over them and pressed hard against the type by a machine which could be wound tight, much like an olive press. This process could be repeated, until such time as the letters needed to be inked once more. Such moveable type could also be rearranged to print an entirely different page of text, until all the separate paper pages of a work were piled up, ready to be placed in order and sewn or bound together as a book. This could then be inserted into a stamped or decorated leather cover for protection.

The only hindrance to this truly original plan was Gutenberg's unique blend of commercial naivety, simple bad luck and general ineptitude. It is difficult to decide which of these was responsible for his first mention in the city records of Strasbourg, when in 1437 he appeared in court charged with breaking his promise to marry a local woman.

By this stage, the details of a moveable type printing press were evidently beginning to come together in his mind. It was time to move from the drawing board to practical construction, which would require a considerable sum of money. In order to achieve this aim, Gutenberg decided in 1439 to invest his modest savings in a commercial venture. This involved a scheme to manufacture polished metal mirrors, for sale at the great exhibition of the emperor Charlemagne's relics that was due to take place at the nearby city of Aachen. The event was expected to attract large numbers of visitors from all over Germany and France, many of whom would doubtless wish for a souvenir. But the mirrors manufactured by Gutenberg and his business partners were to be more than just simple mementoes. According to the accompanying publicity, the mirrors were designed to enable the pilgrims to 'capture holy light radiating from religious relics'.

That summer, the rains were such that the nearby river burst its banks and Aachen was inundated with serious floods. This caused the Charlemagne celebrations to be postponed until the following year. In one fell swoop, Gutenberg's business partners, the few mirrors which had so far been produced, and all of his investment suddenly disappeared. He was forced to return home penniless. The great secret invention which he had hatched in his mind some half a dozen years earlier seemed more unrealizable than ever.

However, Gutenberg was not given to despair. During the following years he is known to have undertaken a number of preliminary trials of his printing idea. One of these produced a pamphlet containing a short work named *Aventur und Kunst* (Adventure and Art). In this he outlined his nascent idea – probably with the aim of attracting a financial backer. He also began work on copper engravings, in partnership with an artist who styled himself 'The Master of Playing Cards'. These engravings and Gutenberg's pamphlet caught the eye of a rich moneylender-cum-entrepreneur named Johann Fust, with whom Gutenberg struck a Fustian bargain. Fust was so impressed with Gutenberg's idea that he loaned him 800 guilders.* Fust also persuaded his future son-in-law Peter Schöffer to join the project. Schöffer was a scribe who had worked in Paris, where he had learned to design typefaces.

By 1452, Gutenberg had set up a workshop in Mainz. At this stage, he either decided – or was persuaded by Fust – to lessen the risk of his enterprise by using his printing press for two separate purposes. Gutenberg's initial idea had been to print meticulously produced high-quality bibles. These would require much time and effort. Each page would contain two columns of forty-two lines each (with wide additional margins to accommodate engraved or hand-drawn artistic decorations). In all, each bible would consist of 1,282 pages. They would be more than just holy books; they would be nothing less than divine art. Properly marketed to wealthy

---

* Equivalent values are notoriously difficult to gauge over the centuries, but contemporary records indicate that an artisan, or skilled worker, could expect to earn around forty guilders a year.

religious institutions, they would take on the status and rarity of sacred relics, and could well achieve prices similar to those of such rare items. Gutenberg's original aim was to produce 300 such bibles, which would take a matter of years to produce.

But Fust was interested in a more rapid return on his investment. He quickly grasped that Gutenberg's moveable type printing machine could be employed for a diversity of tasks. Fust insisted that in between printing pages of the bibles, the machine could be set to work producing cheaper, more readily saleable items. These included Latin grammars, which were always in demand. On top of this, the Church was now in the market for thousands of printed documents which, after they had been authenticated by the papal authorities, could be sold as indulgences.*

By 1455, Johannes Gutenberg had finished printing his first batch of bibles. It is estimated that he completed some 180 copies of these forty-two-line editions – most printed on paper, others on vellum. In order to continue production, he found that he needed further investment and was loaned a further 800 guilders by Fust. However, within a year Gutenberg and Fust had fallen out, with Fust accusing Gutenberg of siphoning off funds for his own private purposes. In fact, Gutenberg's lack of efficient business practice was the more likely explanation for the losses.

Fust now demanded the immediate and complete repayment of his 1,600 guilders, plus 6 per cent interest, amounting to a grand total of 2,026 guilders. Of course, this would not have been expressed as such, on account of the ban on usury. (More likely, the extra money would have been charged as 'late fees'. If money was repaid at once, or within a very short period, no fee was incurred. However, as the length of the loan increased, so did the 'late fees'. This was usury, plain and simple, transmogrified into another form of transaction by the use of different legal terminology.)†

---

* The buying of an indulgence granted the purchaser a reduction of the time they would spend in Purgatory after their death. In Purgatory, the dead sinner underwent painful and appropriate torture for the sins they had committed during their earthly life. Only then could their 'purged' soul arise to take its place in Paradise.

† Modern examples of such financial art can be seen in legal distinctions between 'tax avoidance' and 'tax evasion'; or 'investment' and 'gambling'.

A trial took place at the archbishop-elector's court in Mainz. The verdict went in Fust's favour, awarding him control of Gutenberg's workshop, as well as the stock of more than half of the bibles, complete or otherwise, that Gutenberg had printed. Consequently, Gutenberg was declared bankrupt.

In 1459, Gutenberg left Mainz with the aim of setting up a new business some 100 miles away, in the different jurisdiction of Bamberg. Here he began using some of the moveable type he had retained in order to print some more bibles. How many, and how complete these were, remains debatable. Gutenberg never printed his name or the name of the press on any of his bibles.

Back in Mainz, the new enterprise established by Fust and Schöffer began printing what became known as the Mainz Psalter (a Book of Psalms), a commercially successful work whose frontispiece included the name of the publisher, date of publication and owner of the printing press. No mention of Gutenberg's name.

By 1462 Gutenberg had returned to Mainz, but was soon forced to flee when the latest archbishop-elector, Adolf II von Nassau, was overthrown in a popular uprising. However, within three years Adolf II was reinstated and the ageing Gutenberg was invited to return. By now, Adolf II had been informed of the honour which Gutenberg had brought to Mainz with his new invention (though there was no inkling of its unprecedented importance). Adolf II awarded Gutenberg the minor title *Hofmann* (gentleman of the court), which came with an annual stipend, a ceremonial uniform for him to wear when attending state functions, and a tax-free allowance of 2,180 litres of grain and 2,000 litres of local wine. Gutenberg would have little time to enjoy these benefits. He died three years later, at the age of sixty-eight.

Despite the modest honour bestowed upon Gutenberg by Adolf II, it would be more than thirty years before Johannes Gutenberg was officially recognized as the inventor of the moveable type printing press. By this time, his invention had come into its own. As many as 9 million copies of 30,000 separate titles had been printed on moveable type machines and were in circulation around Europe. They were issued not only in Latin, the language of scholarship, but also in languages ranging from Italian to Flemish, German to Spanish, even English – their information thus being available to all citizens who could read. In this manner, the printed dissemination of knowledge – for anyone who was literate – became arguably the most significant extension of democracy in Europe since the establishment of democracy itself, in Ancient Greece some 1,500 years previously.

CHAPTER 2

JAN VAN EYCK

W HEN PRINTING SPREAD SOUTH across the Alps, it first reached Venice in 1469. By this time the city was well established as a major trading centre, with commercial links extending throughout the Aegean and the Middle East. It was accustomed to the arrival of novelties, and its entrepreneurial merchants were quick to spot the commercial possibilities provided by such innovations. Consequently, within just a few years, Venice had established itself as the publishing capital of Renaissance Italy, and soon developed from the printed word to more accomplished representations. The following is but one example.

In 1500, Leonardo da Vinci and his mathematician friend Luca Pacioli travelled to Venice in order to publish Pacioli's work on geometry, *Divina Proportione*, for which Leonardo had provided a number of etchings of regular three-dimensional solids. These are not quite so simple as they might sound, and they provide a fine example of the 'rebirth' of classical knowledge that was taking place in Italy.

In the third century BC, the Greek mathematician Archimedes had made a list of regular solids, known as polyhedra (meaning 'many faces'). An icosahedron (*ikosi*, 'twenty') has twenty faces that are all equilateral triangles. Cutting off the triangle points on this three-dimensional figure creates twelve new pentagon faces (five sides), and the twenty triangle faces become hexagons (six sides). This is what is known as a truncated icosahedron.

A simple visualization of a truncated icosahedron is an inflated soccer ball with twelve black pentagons and twenty white hexagons. Leonardo's drawing did not contain an inflated truncated icosahedron, but it was given a convincing three-dimensional appearance by having its sides depicted as strips of wood. This had the effect of rendering a surprising visual simplicity to the geometric complexity of the objects he drew. As we shall see, this would have a transformative effect upon one of the finest artists of the northern Renaissance.

The main purpose of Pacioli's work was to demonstrate aesthetic and geometric proportion with particular reference to architecture and painting. By this time, Leonardo was already renowned throughout Italy as one of the finest masters of oil painting. (Three years later he would begin painting the *Mona Lisa*.) Indeed, it is the revolution in art brought about by the new medium of oil painting which is most readily associated with the Italian Renaissance.

Yet, ironically, this new method of painting with oils – which would transform Renaissance art – was not invented in Italy. Like printing, it originated in the Other Renaissance, and would not travel south across the Alps until 1474, some five years after the arrival in Italy of Gutenberg's printing press. But, as with the printing press, the Italians were quick to discover and exploit the multiple complexities of the medium.

Such facts do not denigrate the achievements of the northern Renaissance; they merely indicate an evolving pattern that took place in a number of fields and which came to the fore in the Renaissance. A discovery originally made in the north of Europe would often undergo a dramatic development when it reached Italy, which caused many to mistake the development for the actual discovery itself.

The classic example of this is Galileo's 'invention' of the telescope. Galileo had never seen a telescope, but he had heard of the invention of a device known as a perspicillum in the Netherlands, and had been told how it worked. Magnification of an image could be produced by placing two simple lenses in a tube, and the effect could enlarge a distant object by up to ten times. In the Netherlands, the perspicillum was regarded as a mere novelty, and treated as little more than a toy. However, Galileo quickly understood the huge potential of such a device. He set to work at once, experimenting with various versions of this original idea: different lenses, placed at varying lengths apart in the tube. He quickly managed to construct a perspicillum far superior to the Dutch device – one which was capable of magnifying images over thirty times their original size as seen by the naked eye. Galileo decided that his instrument was so much more effective than the Dutch perspicillum that he gave his own device a new name: 'telescope' (from the Greek, 'see at a distance'). Galileo was soon producing even more powerful telescopes, which were capable of examining the night sky. In this way, Galileo's 'invention' launched modern astronomy, enabling the discovery and identification of phenomena which had never before been observed – such as the craters on the surface of the moon and the rings around the planet Saturn. But while the original perspicillum may have been improved almost beyond recognition, it still remained a northern European invention – despite Galileo's claims (and attempts to patent 'his' new device).

Prior to the arrival of oil painting in Italy, most of the early Renaissance artists used tempera or fresco. In tempera, the ground pigment (colour) is mixed with a water-soluble substance such as egg yolk, and sometimes vinegar as well as water. As the mixture dries, it binds the pigment to the painting surface, such as planed wood or dry plaster. This method can be overpainted, and it was typically used, along with gold leaf, to create Greek icons. However, the method can be slow, as layer upon layer of translucent paint is applied to build up effects such as volume, and the richness of colour which emerges as the painting ages.

With fresco, on the other hand, the ground pigment is mixed with water and applied directly to fresh (*fresco*) damp plaster. This enables the artist to spread the paint over the surface more easily. As the plaster dries, the pigment is absorbed to become part of the plaster, and thus part of the wall itself – achieving a remarkable vividness, typified by Michelangelo's frescoes on the ceiling of the Sistine Chapel. The disadvantage of this method is that the paint soon dries, and cannot then be altered. This means that the artist can only paint a patch of the surface each day, and the method requires a precisely pre-conceived idea that can be painted with relative speed.

The pigment used in oil paint, on the other hand, is blended with linseed oil, poppyseed oil, walnut oil or some such. This ensures that it does not dry so quickly, and thus enables the artist to blend his colours on the canvas (or board). This achieves both a richness and a depth of colour, as well as a far greater range of light, shade and nuanced blends. It also allows the artist to stand back and assess the effect of his brush-work, which can, if necessary, be overpainted. The finished work can be preserved with a transparent glaze, which adds its own radiant effect.

It is now known that the earliest use of oil paint was by Buddhist monks sometime during the mid-600s AD, in central Afghanistan. The monks painted images of the Buddha on mountainsides or cave walls, and these were preserved from wind, sand and rain by the use of glazes. Over the centuries, this method eventually became known in Europe, but it was little used. And when it was, its more subtle qualities were seldom employed. Not until the advent of the Dutch artist Jan van Eyck were the qualities of oil painting fully exploited. For this reason, some continue to credit van Eyck as the inventor of oil painting, and in many ways his numerous innovations and sheer skill lend more than a little truth to this claim.

Jan van Eyck seems to have been born some years before 1390, in the Flemish town of Maaseik. It stands on the eastern border of Belgium, on the banks of the River Maas (Meuse), and the artist took his name from an alternative spelling of the town's second syllable, which means 'oak'. Little is known of his early life, apart from the fact that he quickly mastered the art of painting – especially in oils, which were very much the coming fashion in Flanders during the early 1400s. He was taken on as a court artist by Philip the Good, Duke of Burgundy, the Habsburg ruler of Flanders and the Netherlands. Philip, who spent much of his time in Bruges, had helped develop the city port which lay some ten miles inland, with a canal stretching from the coast to the city's own network of canals. Philip's court at Bruges was one of the most lavish in Europe, largely due to the economic prosperity of the city.

The strategic location of Bruges would establish it as the major commercial city of northern Europe. The sea trade to the east was controlled by the Hanseatic League, an economic and defensive alliance of coastal cities whose ports stretched from Hamburg and thence to the Baltic and as far east as Novgorod in Russia. The extensive and profitable wool trade from England passed through Bruges on its way south to northern Italy. From the early 1300s this trade was also carried from Bruges by Genoese and Florentine galleys, around the Iberian coast to the Mediterranean ports of Italy. At the time, Florence was the main commercial centre for the wool trade and increasingly under the influence of the Medici banking family, who had an extensive network of agents all over Europe and their main northern offices in Bruges.

At the same time, a similarly wealthy German family – the Fuggers of Augsburg in Bavaria – owned mining interests from Hungary to Bohemia and Silesia. In particular, they held a monopoly on the copper trade. Although their business was centred in Augsburg, it had a network of agents throughout eastern Europe, and was strongly represented in Bruges. This concentration of international trade and political interests meant that Bruges soon had representatives from all major European trading nations, a thriving port, and the major bourse (or stock exchange) on the continent.

The original bourse, where merchants met to buy and sell 'shares' to finance joint enterprises, was established as early as 1307 at the tavern run by the Van der Beurze family, hence its name. Similar institutions would soon spring up all over Europe, wherever an enterprise was too costly, or risky, to be undertaken by one owner. The original model for such commercial activity had developed in Venice, well before it became institutionalized in Bruges. However, it was the bourse model that soon spread to major ports and the big annual trade fairs held at such cities as

Lyon, Frankfurt and Geneva. There appear to have been certain elements common to all these early capitalistic exchanges: a thriving commercially minded bourgeoisie, an entrepreneurial ethos willing to take risks in order to achieve gain, and a form of loosely democratic city governance (often corrupt, but giving its citizens a degree of belief in their own liberty).*

The wealth generated by the merchants of Bruges enabled many of them to become patrons of the arts. Originally, paintings were commissioned of religious subjects; but merchants, much like their rulers, soon began employing artists to paint their portraits. Unlike in the Italian Renaissance, where portraits tended to be of aristocrats, princes and Church dignitaries (and their various mistresses), the painters of Bruges found themselves commissioned to paint portraits of a more homely aspect. Instead of palatial or classical settings, patrons tended to prefer domestic interiors, with rather more discreet indications of their wealth. The career of Jan van Eyck typically reflects this social development.

It was in 1425, when van Eyck was in his early thirties, that he became attached to the court of Philip the Good. Besides painting, his duties also included work as a *valet de chambre*, a loosely defined court position which not only secured him a regular income but also involved him in various extracurricular duties. Between 1426 and 1429 he seems to have travelled on a series of well-paid 'secret' commissions for the duke 'in certain distant lands'. It is probable that these were little more than diplomatic tours furthering relations with European trading partners, but they were certainly extensive. According to some sources, evidence for this could be seen in the remarkable accuracy of van Eyck's portrayal of Jerusalem in the background of a painting he completed some years later. Unfortunately, this work is now lost, though a contemporary copy of it suggests a remarkably detailed verisimilitude.

It is thought that Jan van Eyck may well have served his apprenticeship under his older brother Hubert, who was also a talented artist. Yet

---

* By contrast, autocratic centres in Europe tended to lag behind in such activity. Paris would not have a stock exchange until 1720. Vienna, capital of the Austrian Empire, would establish one some fifty years after that. And Madrid would have to wait a further fifty years.

from the outset it was Jan who exhibited exceptional skill and imaginative vision in his use of oils. His first transcendent masterpiece was the *Ghent Altarpiece*, which consists of multiple panels depicting religious scenes and is regarded to this day as one of the masterworks of European art of any period. The sheer immensity of this work, which was to become a polyptych altarpiece for St Bavo's Cathedral in Ghent, indicates that van Eyck was assisted by several other contemporary Flemish artists. Initially, the chief of these was Jan's older brother Hubert, though he is known to have died in 1426. After this, it is speculated that Jan's younger brother Lambert, also a fine artist, acted in a supervisory role over the other artists, as well as making major contributions of his own.

The twelve interior panels are on two levels. Central to the upper level is a depiction of Christ the King, crowned and seated on his throne, and clad in a bejewelled crimson robe. On either side of him are panels of the Virgin Mary and John the Baptist. The two outer panels on this level depict a nude Adam, a fig leaf modestly obscuring his nakedness, and a nude Eve, holding in her right hand a small lemon (indicating the apple containing the knowledge of Good and Evil). These are said to be amongst the first realistic depictions of the human nude during the early Renaissance. (Unknown to any Flemish artists, the Florentine Masaccio was at the same time painting a naked Adam and Eve being expelled from the Garden of Eden.)

In the *Ghent Altarpiece*, the most impressive painting is the large central panel on the lower level. This depicts groups of saints and soldiers, sinners and clergy, all assembled in a rural landscape around an altar on which stands the symbolic Lamb of God, surrounded by a kneeling group of worshipping winged angels.

In all, the painting of the *Ghent Altarpiece* took just over a decade, being started sometime in the mid-1420s and completed in 1432. (An indication of Philip the Good's generosity can be seen in the fact that he allowed his court artist to be employed for so long on this major task.) The work also provides a clue to the social structure developing in Flanders during this period. This vastly expensive work was not commissioned by the head of state but by one Jodocus Vijd, a wealthy merchant who would eventually become the mayor of Ghent. Jodocus and his wife, Lysbette, appear on their knees praying on the back panels, which become visible when the altarpiece is closed.

The use of oil paint in the *Ghent Altarpiece* is immensely sophisticated, entailing full employment of the superior subtleties of hue and density, shading, solidity and overall dexterity of this medium. Oil painting had yet to reach Italy or play any part in the Italian Renaissance. Van Eyck's near-contemporaries living in Florence, such as Botticelli and Piero della Francesca, were still using tempera. Just a few decades later, Botticelli would paint his *Adoration of the Magi* in tempera. Like the *Ghent Altarpiece* its subject is religious, although the figures who appear in the painting are recognizable members of the Medici family as well as other members of the Florentine administration. However, in many other fundamental aspects the two paintings are indicatively different.

In Botticelli's painting, the glimpse of the landscape in the background contains classical ruins. The figures are not separated into panels, but form a coherent group, and their features are imbued with personality. Botticelli even includes an enigmatic self-portrait gazing out at the viewer at the edge of the painting. The *Ghent Altarpiece* may contain some of the finest painting of its own – or any other – period, but it is indubitably medieval in its overall character, despite its emergent elements of Renaissance realism. The portraits of Jodocus and Lysbette Vijd may well be good likenesses, but their attitude in prayer gives away little of their character. By contrast, although Botticelli's self-portrait may be enigmatic, it is very much the face of a knowable person. As are the portraits of the Medici family and other Florentine worthies included in the scene. In the *Ghent Altarpiece* the Gothic elements are beginning to shed their stylized aspect, but have not yet quite taken on the humanistic realism of the Italian Renaissance.

But just one year after completing the *Ghent Altarpiece*, Jan van Eyck would paint a self-portrait which not only utilizes all the advantages of oil, but also depicts with bare-faced realism a strong character who is very much his own man. Above the meticulous and searching gaze of his face, his head is covered with a roughly tied, flamboyant crimson turban.

This is the man who has travelled to Jerusalem, a man of the world, the forthright character who would from now on sign his paintings with a boastful, barely coded, anagrammatic version of his own name: ALS ICH KAN (because I can). He reckoned he was the finest painter of his time, and he wanted everyone to know it.

Despite such arrogance – reminiscent of several Italian Renaissance artists as they grew into the knowledge of their own originality and talent – Jan van Eyck was not entirely free. He remained notionally in the employ of Philip, Duke of Burgundy. And even in the midst of his work on the *Ghent Altarpiece*, van Eyck was obliged to perform an important duty for his master, who was due to be married to Isabella of Portugal, the only surviving daughter of King John I of Portugal. Although this was to be an arranged marriage, with important dynastic and political implications, Philip had never set eyes upon Isabella and was keen to see what his new bride looked like. So, in 1429, van Eyck was despatched to Portugal to paint a portrait of Isabella, a journey which would take him away for nine months.

By this stage, van Eyck was in the process of developing the stark realism which would characterize his 'self-portrait with a crimson turban'. However, on arrival in Portugal, van Eyck realized that his commission was going to present more than a little difficulty. Isabella was no beauty, and he was well aware that his portrait would have to satisfy the expectation of visual truth required by his master, Philip the Good, but without offending Isabella and the royal family of Portugal. Van Eyck's portrait has long since been lost, but it appears that he managed to overcome this all-but-impossible situation with some considerable skill. According to contemporary reports, he succeeded in imbuing Isabella's plain and characterless features with a restrained dignity. This made her likeness both recognizable to Philip the Good and acceptable to her royal parents. (This was some feat. Two later portraits of Isabella, by other artists, do not manage to achieve such a remarkable balance. In one she appears both lean-faced and austere to the point of oddity; in the other the artist simply ducks the problem by giving her girlish features which are too superficial and youthful to be imbued with any mature character.)

No discussion of van Eyck's work would be complete without the inclusion of his masterpiece, usually known as the *Arnolfini Portrait*, which he painted at the age of forty-four, at the height of his powers. This stands alongside the finest works of the entire Renaissance, yet it is unmistakably a work of the northern region of this age of transformation.

Giovanni Arnolfini is known to have been a highly successful merchant from Lucca – the city-state on the northern border of Florence – who lived most of his life in Bruges. In van Eyck's painting, Arnolfini's surprisingly youthful face has a solemn, almost stern expression, and his features betray nothing of his Italian origins. The work is a double portrait depicting Arnolfini laying his outstretched hand upon the hand of his apparently pregnant bride. He is dressed in a fur coat, made of expensive pelts – presumably imported from Russia via the Hanseatic trade. On his head is an exaggeratedly large top hat, which in windy Holland could only have been taken seriously by one who aspired to the highest dictates of fashion. As with so much fashion, it is of course ridiculous, yet the wearer nonetheless sees himself as above such banality. His wife's modestly downcast face is childish and submissive beneath the white crochet of her headscarf. But her voluminous lime-green gown with its long ermine-lined sleeves and their complex brocade is an unmistakable social statement. Such a garment was a demonstrative masterwork of this Flemish craft, and would have cost a fortune.

Around the couple are all the trappings of a typical Dutch interior of the period, with several indications of their wealth. Most noticeable is the ornate chandelier that hangs down above the couple's heads, and the mirror on the wall behind them. More subtle evidence of luxury can be seen on the table and windowsill behind Arnolfini, on which are scattered some oranges (a scarce delicacy). Then there are the strings of pearls hanging beside the mirror. (It has been suggested that van Eyck must have used a magnifying glass to render the precise glint on each of these pearls.)

The perspective focal point of the painting is the central convex mirror behind the couple, in the glass of which can be seen the backs of the couple, as well as the tiny distorted reflections of two figures beyond them

– one of whom is presumed to be van Eyck himself. His florid yet suitably discreet signature is inscribed on the wall beside the mirror: *Johannes de eyck fuit hic 1434* (Jan van Eyck was here 1434). This identification may have been intended to gratify the subjects as much as the artist. By this stage in his professional life van Eyck was a name indeed, perhaps the most prestigious marque in the art market.

At the couple's feet is a fluffy pet dog, probably a Bolognese lapdog, which some have seen as a sign of fidelity. (Fido, always a common dog's name, has connotations of the Latin for 'fidelity'). The dog has also been identified as a symbol of lust, indicating the couple's wish for a child.

The fact that the couple have laid their outstretched hands somewhat formally, one upon the other, suggests this may have been a solemnized blessing of the marriage (with the second tiny figure reflected in the mirror being the official witness). However, the bride in her sumptuous flowing green gown appears evidently far-gone in pregnancy. Though some critics have, somewhat implausibly, insisted that such a bulging dress was very much the fashion of the period.

In fact, the more one inspects the painting, the more it appears replete with enigmatic hints and suggestions – and these have encouraged a multiplicity of critical interpretations. It has even been compared, with its many clues, to a Sherlock Holmes story – only with the final pages left missing. A more straightforward account is given by the twentieth-century American critic Craig Harbison, who refers to it as 'the only fifteenth-century Northern panel to survive in which the artist's contemporaries are shown engaged in some sort of action in a contemporary interior. It is indeed tempting to call this the first genre painting – a painting of everyday life – of modern times.'

The Renaissance, both south and north of the Alps, would be characterized by its humanism. This new way of thinking undeniably had its philosophical underpinnings, as we shall see; however, it was in essence more of an attitude. Where the preceding medieval era viewed our life on earth as a preparation for eternal judgement and the life hereafter, humanism stressed that we should go beyond this spiritual aspect and live out our lives as fully rounded human beings in the present world. In this sense, the *Arnolfini Portrait* is an embodiment of this secular humanism. The painting may be filled with oblique, often ambiguous references, hinting at all manner of readings, but its most satisfying experience is simply itself. This is how people lived. It may have been in Bruges. It may have been over 500 years ago. It may have been only the rich who could have lived like this. And it may be no more than a stylized pose... But it is recognizable – for all its trickery, its subtle artistry, its homely particularity, even – as a resonant generalized indication of who we are. A man and a woman at home.

CHAPTER 3

NICHOLAS OF CUSA

A s the world of art in northern Europe began its drastic transformation, shedding the stylistic formalism and religious subject-
matter of medieval art, so the northern intellectual world underwent a
similar revolution. The origins of the humanistic way of thought and its
empirical attitude to learning were not the sole preserve of the Italian
Renaissance. Indeed, the 'father of humanism' is generally recognized as a
German, born in 1401 in the Electorate of Trier: Nicholas of Cusa.*

The son of 'a prosperous boatman and ferryman', Nicholas was
a precocious student. In his early teens he entered the University of
Heidelberg, the oldest in Germany, which had been established in the
middle of the previous century. Here he studied law, before transferring
to the University of Padua near Venice. He graduated in 1423, but instead
of becoming a lawyer he took up minor holy orders. From the outset,
Nicholas was an imaginative polymath, his mind fecund with novel ideas
on all manner of subjects. Under normal circumstances such ideas would
have been controversial, and might even have put his life in mortal danger

---

* The Latinized form of the German Kues, a small town on the River Moselle.

(almost 150 years later, the Italian philosopher Giordano Bruno would be burned at the stake for expressing similar ideas). However, it seems that the sheer brilliance of Nicholas of Cusa's mind won him friends in high places.

Nicholas first achieved public attention in 1433 with his meticulous research into the *Donation of Constantine*. This was the fourth-century document in which the emperor Constantine (the first Christian ruler of the Roman Empire) acknowledged the superiority of the Church of Rome over the Byzantine Church in Constantinople. In effect, this made the pope the undisputed ruler of all Christendom. However, Nicholas of Cusa's research led him to discover that this document was in fact an eighth-century forgery.

Despite this controversial finding – which pointed to the connivance of Pope Stephen II and several subsequent occupiers of the Throne of St Peter – the present pope, Eugene IV, appeared to welcome Nicholas's findings. The reign of Eugene IV was a time of much difficulty for the papacy, which was both unpopular and threatened with another schism. (The previous Great Schism, which had seen popes in Rome and Avignon both claiming legitimacy, had only been resolved a couple of decades earlier.) Pope Eugene IV's unpopularity was due at least in part to his hysterical fits of anger, directed at clergy and laity alike. At one point he was even forced to flee Rome in a boat, disguised as a monk, as the population pelted him with stones and refuse from the banks of the Tiber.

However, he remained friendly with Nicholas of Cusa, and in 1437 the pope appointed him to head a delegation to Constantinople with the all-but-impossible task of bringing about a reunion of the Roman and Byzantine churches. To the astonishment of many, Nicholas's delegation succeeded. (The fact that this reunion only lasted a year was hardly Nicholas's fault.)

Eugene IV remained Nicholas's protector, enabling him to propagate his most profound, and most astonishing, ideas. In 1450 Nicholas completed a work in the form of dialogues between a layman and a priest. This was entitled *Idiota de Mente* (literally translated as 'An Idiot Speaks

His Mind').* Surprisingly, it is the 'idiot' who puts forward Nicholas's bold proposals, which contrast sharply with the orthodox Aristotelian views proposed by the priest. It should be borne in mind that during this period Aristotle was regarded as the highest authority on intellectual matters: his word was seen as little less than Holy Writ.

In opposition to this, Nicholas proposed a Platonic-mathematical-scientific world view, making such pronouncements as 'Mathematics is the mind of God' and 'Number is the principal clue which leads to wisdom'. Despite this, he regarded knowledge as provisional, forever open to improvement, explaining: 'As a polygon inscribed in a circle increases in number of sides... so the mind approximates to truth but never coincides with it... Thus knowledge is at best conjecture.' Not until the twentieth century would scientists begin to accept this last limitation.

Despite the abstract flavour of Nicholas's mathematical pronouncements, his motives were entirely practical. Delineating discrete parts of the world by measurement was what led to knowledge, which was essentially a practical matter. Such thoughts opened the way to an entirely different method of learning.

In order to understand the magnitude of Nicholas's mode of thought it is necessary for the moment to take the wider view. At this point in the world's history, China was the leading civilization. There was little contact between Europe and China. (Marco Polo's tales of his travels and the wonders of Chinese civilization were taken by most to be mere fables and exaggerations.) Yet it was precisely during these years that China would cede superiority to Europe. The decay in China largely came about because of the separation between the intellectuals of the court (philosophers, poets, theologians) and the common people, whose mercantile practices were leading to ever-greater efficiencies, innovations and wealth. With Confucian theologians influencing the emperor's mind, decrees were issued which curtailed commerce, banned mercantile enterprise, and put an end to sea trade and the arrival of new ideas.

---

* At the time, the word 'idiot' was a general term used to describe any layman or private individual who did not hold public office.

Ironically, it was the very opposite to the process which was taking place in Europe. And it was Nicholas of Cusa who was giving voice to this new direction. Mathematical measurement should be applied to the world. Architecture, commerce, shipbuilding, the very nature of tools and machines – all would undergo major developments during the Renaissance era as a result of this new attitude towards the practical world.

Nicholas himself took to practical science, making a number of suggestions and innovations. Some of these would be acted upon almost immediately; others would take years to reach fruition. Precision of measurement remained his aim and his forte. He found that, by pouring equal weights of water into a cubic container and a spherical container, it was possible to calculate the value of π to three decimal places, i.e. 3.142. Using geometrical methods he attempted to solve the ancient conundrum of squaring the circle. This involves constructing a square with the same area as a circle, which is now known to be impossible. However, in the course of his attempts by pure geometry to solve this problem he managed to calculate the value of π as 3.1423, a figure of greater accuracy than any before – including that calculated by Archimedes, who in fact only worked out its limits of between 223/71 and 22/7 (3.14084 and 3.14285). Nicholas also argued that there was a need to calculate a new calendar, as the seasons were gradually falling out of synchronization with the dates and the months (it would be almost 150 years before his suggestion was taken up by Pope Gregory XIII).

Perhaps Nicholas's most important invention was a new type of spectacle lens. Previously, lenses had been ground to a convex shape. This was an easier process, and it enabled the viewer to achieve long-sightedness. Nicholas tried the opposite method, grinding a lens into a concave shape, and found that it enabled the viewer to achieve near-sightedness. This brought about a revolution. Old men with failing sight could continue reading, learning, making suggestions, discoveries, inventions. It is little exaggeration to say that intellectual life almost doubled over the coming century as a result of Cusa's innovation.

A further revolution was instigated when Nicholas turned his attention to a study of the heavens. Despite the fact that the telescope had yet to be invented, his observations enabled him to reach some highly original conclusions. While several of the Ancient Greeks had speculated on such matters, drawing their own similar conclusions, Nicholas was perhaps the first to put these together into a truly universal structure.

First, he realized that the earth was not the centre of the universe. Indeed, the universe and all the stars had no centre. This meant that there was no 'up' and no 'down' in the universe at large, which was 'interminate'. It is not quite clear how he understood this term. He did not believe that the universe was infinite, yet he felt it had no outer limit or termination. (This is uncannily similar to our modern view of the universe.) More than a century before Copernicus proposed his theory, and Galileo raised his telescope to the night sky, Nicholas wrote:

Since, then, the earth cannot be the centre [of the universe], it cannot be entirely devoid of motion... It is clear to us that the earth is really in motion though this may not be apparent to us, since we do not perceive motion except by comparison with something fixed.

This even contains the germ of the idea of relativity. He continued:

The earth is a noble star... it is not possible for human knowledge to determine whether the region of the earth is in a degree of greater perfection or baseness in relation to the regions of the other stars.

In Nicholas's view, the stars were made of similar material to the earth. They were also inhabited by living beings, who were neither inferior nor superior to humanity, only different from us. He went on to explain:

It does not seem that, according to the order of nature, there could be a more noble or more perfect nature than the intellectual nature which dwells here on this earth as in its region, even if there are in the other stars inhabitants belonging to another genus: man indeed does not desire another nature, but only the perfection of his own.

In 1446, Nicholas was made papal legate to Germany. This meant that he acted as the pope's representative in the German states. His scientific writing and his experiments do not seem to have interfered with this work, as the pope made him a cardinal two years later in recognition of his services to the Church. In 1450 Nicholas would be made Prince-Bishop of Brixen, becoming ruler of the small papal principality in the Tyrol belonging to the Holy Roman Empire.

In 1459, at the age of fifty-eight, Nicholas became vicar-general of the Papal States. He thus became nominal ruler of the territories occupying the region north of Rome, and further north in the Romagna, bordering on the Adriatic Sea south of Venice. These territories were for the most part semi-independent city-states, whose petty-tyrant rulers paid regular 'dues' to Rome in acknowledgement of their vassal status.

There is little doubt that Nicholas of Cusa was able to flourish owing to his residence first in Germany and then at some distance from Rome. The fact that he was for the most part his own ecclesiastical master, and a friend of Eugene IV and then Nicholas V, must also have worked in his favour. He was able to carry out his experiments and theorizing without worrying if this clashed with the strictures of the current Church orthodoxy. However, none of this accounts for the sheer originality of his thinking. Besides the subjects already mentioned, Nicholas made original contributions in fields ranging from biology to medicine. By applying his belief in rigorous measurement to the field of medicine, he would introduce the practice of taking precise pulse rates to use as an indication of a patient's health. Previously, physicians had been in the habit of taking a patient's pulse and using their own estimation of its rate to infer the state of their health. Nicholas of Cusa introduced an exact method, weighing the quantity of water which had run from a water clock during one hundred pulse beats.

The achievements of Nicholas are all the more commendable when one considers that these were troubled times in Europe. From 1439 onwards the French declared their own pope, Felix V. Meanwhile, Eugene IV and the Holy Roman Emperor maintained an uneasy peace. Eugene IV did fulfil the tradition of crowning the emperor Sigismund at a ceremony in Rome in 1433; but the more serious business of uniting Christendom in the face of Ottoman expansion in Asia Minor and the Balkans was not achieved. In 1453 Constantinople was overrun by the forces of Sultan Mehmed the Conqueror, and the Byzantine Empire (the eastern wing of the ancient Roman Empire and the centre of Orthodox Christianity) came to an ignominious end.

Nicholas of Cusa's faith has on occasion been questioned in the light of his scientific world view. In fact his belief in God was unwavering. His spiritual viewpoint was largely mystical, a forerunner of what became known as pantheism. This is the belief that God is the world and the world is God, which certainly aligns with his understanding of the mathematical structure of the world. Thus there was no basic contradiction between his belief in God and his belief in the universality of mathematical science.*

Nicholas's scientific work would go on to influence thinkers of the calibre of the German philosopher-mathematician Gottfried Leibniz, a leading philosopher of the Enlightenment who lived two centuries later. Nicholas's political theorizing was also ahead of his time. He wrote that government should be by the consent of those who were governed, 'since by nature all men are free'. His attitude towards other religions was

---

* In the centuries prior to Nicholas of Cusa, the great Arabic scholars and scientists – whose Golden Age would so influence the Italian Renaissance – maintained a similar belief. In their view of Islam: 'To know the world is to know the mind of God.' And 500 years after the death of Nicholas of Cusa, Albert Einstein would be possessed of a remarkably similar pantheistic faith. He believed that God was the way the world worked: the laws of nature were not only universal but also the laws of God. Such religious thinking has thus produced (or at least accompanied) some of the greatest advances in science. Though it should not in any way be confused with those made by the God-obsessed Newton, whose beliefs were incontestably Christian yet incontestably heretical. (Despite becoming Master of Trinity College Cambridge, Newton refused to believe in the Holy Trinity, one of the central tenets of Christian orthodoxy.)

also astonishingly progressive. During the perilous years after the fall of Constantinople he wrote a work describing a meeting in Heaven between representatives of all nations and all religions. These included Judaism and Islam, which he asserted had a common truth, not least because they all in their own way recognized the Bible.

The work and thought of Nicholas of Cusa is indicative of the wide-ranging re-examination of the human condition which was beginning to take place, especially amongst thinkers of the northern Renaissance. Another leading German scientific thinker from this period, who would become a friend of Nicholas of Cusa, was Regiomontanus, who was born Johannes Müller in rural Bavaria, southern Germany, in 1436.

This adoption of Latin names, especially amongst scholars, echoed the universality of Medieval Latin as the pan-European language of learning – from theology to philosophy, from the law to natural philosophy (the name given to science). Medieval Latin was a somewhat debased form of the Classical Latin spoken in Ancient Rome. In fact, the word 'medieval' would later be coined from the Latin *medium aevum* (middle age). The written Latin of medieval scholars was largely consistent throughout Europe. The spoken Latin of the people was most certainly not. Following the end of the Roman Empire, different spoken dialects began to evolve in different regions. These would later become formalized as the different so-called Romance (i.e. Roman) languages: Italian, French, Spanish, Portuguese and Romanian. There were also more localized languages, such as the Catalan spoken in eastern Spain, and southern French Languedoc (*langue d'oc*, 'the language of *oc*'). Both Catalan and Languedoc are thought to have derived from 'dog Latin', the language spoken amongst the multinational Roman soldiery.

---

* This was spoken in the Occitanie region, which covers most of southern France. The language of *oc* was distinct from the French language of *oïl* (pronounced 'oo-ee') spoken north of the Loire. Both these words are predecessors of the modern word *oui*. Likewise, *oc* and *oïl* have their origins in the Latin word *hoc*, meaning 'this', which in vulgar Latin meant 'yes'.

Regiomontanus was sent to the University of Leipzig in 1437, at the age of eleven. Five years later he was studying at the University of Vienna, where he took a master's degree and began lecturing in optics and classical literature at the age of twenty-one. This certainly reflects his exceptional intelligence, but such disregard for youth was not an uncommon occurrence at the time. In this era, children passed from childhood to young manhood with little heed to any intervening period of adolescence. This was a necessity amongst peasant families, but it also occurred within urban artisan families, where children frequently began their apprenticeships in their pre-teen years. Around this time, Leonardo da Vinci, the illegitimate son of a Florentine lawyer, entered the studio of Verrocchio when he was just fourteen.*

While Regiomontanus was teaching at the University of Vienna, the city was visited by the Greek scholar Bessarion, who would play a significant role in Regiomontanus's subsequent career. As such, it is worth examining Bessarion's unusual background.

Bessarion was born in 1403 at Trebizond, on the Black Sea coast of Asia Minor (modern Turkey). He was educated in Constantinople some thirty years before it fell to the Ottoman Turks. Here his widespread learning would later lead to him being regarded as 'the last of the Hellenes' (i.e. Ancient Greeks), in recognition of his understanding of Ancient Greek philosophy, especially that of Plato. Such was his authority in Constantinople that he was chosen as a senior member of the Orthodox delegation to the ecumenical council which ended in Florence in 1439. This attempt to unite the Orthodox (Eastern) Church with the Catholic (Western) Church followed Nicholas of Cusa's visit to Constantinople in 1437, and its apparent agreement would prove equally fragile.

---

* Such practice would continue for centuries to come. Midshipmen in the English navy, taken on as trainee officers – often for long voyages – were barely into puberty. Horatio Nelson would become a midshipman in 1771 at the age of twelve. During the following decade, Pitt the Younger became prime minister of Britain at the age of twenty-four, after entering Cambridge at fourteen, becoming a qualified lawyer and already having gained considerable political experience as chancellor of the exchequer.

Bessarion strongly supported Pope Eugene IV's wish for unification. This made him unpopular amongst his fellow delegates, but caused him to be made a cardinal by the pope. He would consequently live in Rome, where his palazzo has been likened to Plato's Academy. Although Latin was the western European language of scholarship, Ancient Greek remained largely unknown. Under Bessarion's guidance, many works of Ancient Greece – of which western Europe was ignorant – were translated into Latin. And it was in this way that Regiomontanus learned sufficient Greek for him to be accepted as a member of Bessarion's entourage while he travelled through Italy. During these years, Regiomontanus would complete a new translation of the second-century Greek *Almagest* by Ptolemy. This is the work in which Ptolemy describes the movements of the sun, the moon, the planets and the stars around the earth, which was deemed to be the centre of the universe. For many centuries, such geocentric teaching had been accepted by the early Christians as Holy Writ, and as such its authority lay beyond question.

During the course of his involvement with Ptolemy's text, Regiomontanus initially accepted the Ptolemaic system, believing that if the earth in fact moved then birds would be blown away into space – and there would similarly be a trail of clouds left in the earth's wake. Later he appears to have developed certain doubts about the validity of the geocentric system. Without revealing the full extent of these doubts, he wrote to a friend: 'I cannot get over my amazement at the mental inertia of our astronomers in general who [credulously] believe what they read in the books, tablets and commentaries as if it were divine and unalterable truth. They believe the authors and neglect the truth.' Towards the end of his life, he would write: 'It is necessary to alter the motion of the stars a little because of the motion of the earth.'

Some suspect that Regiomontanus must surely have thought through the obvious implications of these remarks, i.e. that the earth moves around the sun. But there is no evidence for this. On the contrary, despite his suspicions as to the accuracy of Ptolemy's universe, Regiomontanus seems to have continued to use geocentric astronomical mathematics, as well as accepting the authority of Aristotle's pronouncement that 'comets were dry exhalations of *Earth* that caught fire high in the *atmosphere* or similar exhalations of the *planets* and *stars*'. This reliance on 'authority' was certainly the case when he made observations of the comet which remained visible for two months during early 1472. He calculated this comet's distance from the earth as 8,200 miles, and its coma (the diameter at its head) as 81 miles. According to the contemporary astronomer David A. J. Seargent: 'These values, of course, fail by orders of magnitude, but he is to be commended for this attempt at determining the physical dimensions of the comet.'*

However, Regiomontanus would make two contributions of lasting importance. In his work on rules and methods applicable to arithmetic and algebra, *Algorithmus Demonstratus*, he reintroduced the symbolic algebraic notation used by the third-century Greek mathematician Diophantus of Alexandria. He also added certain improvements of his own. Basically, this is the algebra we use today, where unknown quantities are manipulated in symbolic form, such as $ax + by = c$. Here x and y are variable unknowns, and a, b, and c are constants.

Prior to this development algebraic questions were written out in prose form, as in the following epigram which indicates how old Diophantus was when he died:

His boyhood lasted one sixth of his life; his beard grew after one twelfth more; he married after one seventh more, and his son was born five years later. The son lived to half his father's age, and the father died four years after his son.

---

* This comet is visible on earth at intervals ranging from seventy-four to seventy-nine years. Its first certain observation was recorded in a Chinese chronicle dating from 240 BC. When it was observed by the English astronomer Edmond Halley in 1705 it was named after him. The justification for this is that Halley was the first to realize that it was the same comet as had appeared at 74–79-year intervals since time immemorial. Even so, Regiomontanus deserves more than a little credit for his observation of the comet, for in the words of the twentieth-century American science writer Isaac Asimov: 'This was the first time that comets were made the object of scientific study, instead of serving mainly to stir up superstitious terror.'

If we reduce this somewhat opaque information to numbers – apart from the father's unknown age, which we designate as x – we can produce an algebraic formula:

$$\tfrac{1}{6}x + \tfrac{1}{12}x + \tfrac{1}{7}x + 5 + \tfrac{1}{2}x + 4 = x$$

From this we can multiply all terms by the lowest common denominator of all the fractions, which is 84. This gives us:

$$14x + 7x + 12x + 420 + 42x + 336 = 84x$$

Thus: $9x = 756$ and $x = 84$, the age at which Diophantus died.

Regiomontanus also made considerable advances in trigonometry, although it has since been discovered that at least part of this was plagiarized from the twelfth-century Arab writer Jabir ibn Aflah. On top of this, Regiomontanus drew up books of trigonometric tables: these lists provided ready answers in the calculation of angles and lengths of sides of right-angle triangles. In this way trigonometry could be used to discover such things as the heights of buildings, or use the angle of a star above the horizon to determine geographical location for mariners and such. For centuries, prior to computers, such tables were essential equipment for all mathematicians. And it is in these tables that Regiomontanus popularized yet another notational advance. Instead of fractions, which could become increasingly complex, he started using decimal point notation, which was much easier to manipulate. A simple example: the sum of 1/8 + 1/5 is much easier to calculate when these numbers are written as 0.125 + 0.2. The answer in fractional form is 13/40, but in decimal form it is simply 0.325. Furthermore, the decimal answer is much more amenable to further addition, multiplication and so forth with other numbers in decimal form.

After leaving Rome, Regiomontanus travelled around Europe, continuing to compile his tables and frequently constructing ingenious objects for his hosts. In Hungary, for King Matthias I, he created a handheld astrolabe. Such devices were first made by the Ancient Greeks in around 200 BC. They contain many moving parts, which mirror the movements of the planets and the stars. Astrolabes can be put to a variety of uses, including astronomy, navigation, the calculation of tides, and the determining of horoscopes for astrologers.

In Nuremberg, Regiomontanus established a novel type of printing press, the first of its kind devoted entirely to the printing of scientific and mathematical works. He also oversaw the building of the earliest astronomical observatory, in Germany. Finally returning to Rome, he constructed a portable sundial for Pope Paul II. Later he also seems to have re-established contact with his friend and mentor, Cardinal Bessarion, who was in Rome in 1471 for the conclave to elect a new pope after the death of Paul II. Indeed, many amongst the cardinals regarded Bessarion as the man most suited to become the next pope, but his election was blocked by a group of Italian cardinals who were unable to accept the idea of a Greek holding such an office.

Regiomontanus died in Rome during 1476 at the early age of forty. It is now thought that he died of the plague, though at the time many suspected that he had been poisoned by friends of a rival mathematician. These were enemies of Bessarion, and Regiomontanus had exposed the shoddiness of their work – rendering their theories redundant.

CHAPTER 4

FRANCIS I AND THE FRENCH RENAISSANCE

A POPULAR ANECDOTE HAS IT that the Renaissance began in France when the twenty-one-year-old King Francis I offered the ageing Leonardo da Vinci a pension of 1,000 gold écus and a residence near to his chateau if he would come to live in France.

Francis I was an impressive figure. Over six feet tall (an exceptional height during this period) and broad-shouldered, with a powerful nose and a winning smile, he led his army into battle wearing gilded armour. Francis I already knew of Leonardo by repute, and had certainly seen some of his finest work, such as *The Last Supper* in Milan, before later encountering the artist himself at peace talks being held in Bologna in 1515. By this time Leonardo was a stooped old man with a long grey beard, but he remained a charismatic figure. The king and the artist had much in common, especially their polymathic interest in the arts and the sciences. They seem to have taken to each other at once.

Two years later, Leonardo arrived at Amboise in the Loire Valley to take up residence in a small manor house set in its own gardens, beside the extensive royal chateau on its hill overlooking the river. Leonardo brought with him his faithful assistant, Melzi, and a wagon carrying his worldly possessions and several paintings, including the *Mona Lisa*.

It is said that the young Francis I often visited Leonardo, and that they would talk together for hours. Leonardo seems to have been aware of his impending death. According to his biographer Michael White, concerning an entry in his notebook at the time: 'we can discern a distorted reflection of his own fear of death'. This passage in which Leonardo describes the fossil of a fish is indeed resonant:

How many changes of state and circumstances have succeeded one another since there perished in some deep and sinuous crevice the marvellous form of this fish... Now destroyed by time, it has been waiting patiently in this cramped space, and with its bones stripped bare, it has become a prop and support for the mountain rising above it.

Two years after arriving in France, Leonardo fell mortally ill. According to Giorgio Vasari, the renowned chronicler of Italian Renaissance artists, Francis I is said to have made his way quickly to Leonardo's bedside:

Thereupon [Leonardo] was seized by a paroxysm, the messenger of death; for which reason, the King, having risen and having taken his head, in order to assist him and show him favour, to the end that he might alleviate his pain, his spirit, which was divine, knowing that it could not have any greater honour, expired in the arms of the King.*

---

* Doubt has been cast on Vasari's story, as there is evidence that the king was that day signing an act into law some 150 miles away – at Saint-Germain-en-Laye, outside Paris. But three centuries later it was noticed that the act was not in fact signed by the king himself, but by his chancellor *de par le roi* (in the king's name). So there may well be some truth in Vasari's touching story.

France's geographical location places it firmly in both northern Europe and the Mediterranean world. The influences on the French Renaissance would eventually become similarly divided. However, initially French art was dominated by Italian Renaissance painters; though these too would in time have a significant influence on the northern Renaissance.

This is typically reflected in France's earliest Renaissance artists, especially those who formed the First School of Fontainebleau in 1531. These artists were employed at Francis I's royal palace some forty miles south of Paris. There Francis I was busy transforming what had once been a medieval country mansion into a splendid palace fit for the king of Europe's most powerful nation, and there was much work for artists and decorators. As can be gauged from his relationship with Leonardo da Vinci, the French king was possessed of both wisdom and taste, and it can be argued that he personally was responsible for the membership of the First School of Fontainebleau.

One of the leaders of the school was Rosso Fiorentino (a name he had acquired on account of his red hair, and the fact that he came from Florence). In 1523, at the age of twenty-eight, he moved to Rome, where he found himself working alongside (and in competition with) such artists as Raphael and Michelangelo. The sack of Rome in 1527 by an army of unpaid *Landsknechte* (German mercenaries) left Fiorentino bereft of his possessions, the tools of his trade, and any patrons. On hearing of Fiorentino's plight, Francis I invited him to Fontainebleau.

In Italy, the pellucid realism of such artists as Botticelli and Leonardo which had characterized the early Italian Renaissance was now giving way to the expressive distortions of the mannerist style. This can readily be traced in the work of Michelangelo, as he abandoned his initial realism and gradually developed a more mature style, which incorporated certain exaggerations of realism to add expression to his works. A classic example of this is his larger-than-lifesize nude statue of David, which was completed in 1505 when he was thirty years old. This took him five years of obsessive solitude, during which he engaged in the physically daunting task of chipping, carving and smoothing (without the aid of any assistants) a seventeen-foot-high, 12,000-pound block of white Carrara marble in a large shed by Florence Cathedral. The sheer stamina involved in the creation of this work may have been draining, but according to his friend and biographer Condivi the isolation of working alone in this fashion for so long would not have affected Michelangelo 'since he was by nature a solitary and melancholy person, *bizzarro e fantastico*, a man who "withdrew himself from the company of men"'.

The finished statue appears at first sight to be the epitome of realism. Yet on closer inspection it becomes clear that the statue has certain exaggerated features. This was in part due to Michelangelo's original commission, which decreed that the statue would stand on the roof of Florence Cathedral, more than 100 feet above the onlookers below.

Seen from such a perspective, any faithfully realistic statue would have seemed distorted, with its upper body, and particularly its head, appearing unnaturally reduced in size. In order for the statue to retain a realistic appearance under such circumstances, Michelangelo realized he would have to exaggerate the size of David's head. To distract from this, he decided he would also exaggerate the size of the statue's hands. It is here that the *bizzarro e fantastico* element of Michelangelo's character came to the fore. In fulfilling these exaggerations, he quickly saw that this not only harmonized the appearance of the statue when seen from below, but it also gave it an inner power: an aspect of *terribilità*. This word literally means 'terror', but in this context it is better described as 'awe' or 'an air of the sublime'.

Michelangelo realized this mannerism could be used to give a powerful 'presence' to all manner of figures. And he would employ this element to great effect on his next great work: the painting of the ceiling of the Sistine Chapel. Here many figures are foreshortened, twisted or expanded to great effect. His fellow artists in Rome soon saw the advantages of such covert exaggerations – and thus mannerism became established.

This trait is recognizable in the first great work that Fiorentino produced for Francis I – a depiction of Bacchus, Venus and Cupid painted in 1531. In it, the actual nude figures are independently heavy, yet their poses are arranged in such a way that the painting contains an overall element of lightness.

Unlike the Flemish artists of the northern Renaissance, Fiorentino and the other Italian artists whom Francis I imported to Fontainebleau brought with them the light colourful style and flourishes of the High Renaissance as it had evolved in southern Europe. There was no place for modest interiors – even if well furnished – such as those in the *Arnolfini Portrait*. The southern artists were accustomed to painting the palazzi of aristocrats and cardinals, which made them feel quite at home decorating the walls of Francis I's great chateau. Classical and religious scenes with grandiose effects were required for such a palatial setting. Many of the paintings were contained in highly ornate stucco frames. Beside them stood statues of the ancient gods, behind which were walls covered with delicate frescoes. All this gives the remaining Francis I apartments of the palace at Fontainebleau a somewhat oppressive luxury. This work may have been done by some of the finest Italian artists of the age, but it is simply too much for the modern sensibility.*

Towards the end of Fiorentino's life he returned to Tuscany for a brief spell. Even before this, his works had taken on a darker tone, often inhabited by contorted or emaciated figures alongside more exotic faces and characters

---

* The same criticism has been applied to Michelangelo's ceiling of the Sistine Chapel. However, here the sheer magnitude and distance above the viewer of the multitude of frescoes lessens to a certain extent the oppressive and overwhelming effect of such an array of art crammed into one space. Yet it is worth noting that, rather than the ceiling as a whole, it is certain individual images that most inspire our admiration. Our attention is drawn to these, which have been so singled out as to become famous in their own right, quite apart from the overall ceiling. Perhaps the best known of these is God imparting life to Adam, with his finger outstretched towards Adam's hand. Another is the sheer intensity of the powerfully foreshortened figure of God creating the sun and the moon. Also unforgettable is the figure of the damned man being carried down to Hell, his hand half obscuring the look of utter horror at the vision below, which he hardly dares to face. The northern Renaissance was also capable of such excess, as for instance in the *Ghent Altarpiece*. But apart from Church commissions, it soon began evolving its own characteristics, which reflected its emerging, more egalitarian society. Northern art for the most part began concentrating on urban, individual, bourgeois, humanistic elements, such as those in the *Arnolfini Portrait*. It is indicative that the most notable exception comes in the form of the chateaux of the Loire, which were built for royalty and aristocrats.

in fashionable attire. These works retained the power of his earlier paintings but expressed a woeful, often depressive air, as in his masterly *Deposition*. This depicts the emaciated body of Christ being borne away from the cross amidst a crowd of varied figures, including dark-skinned turbaned men, weeping nuns and prostrated women in billowing silken dresses. Later, Fiorentino returned to France, where he continued to be the leading light of the First School of Fontainebleau. However, it comes as little surprise that according to Vasari he took his own life in 1540, though no reason is given for this. He was forty-five at the time of his death.

The artists of the First School of Fontainebleau were almost exclusively Italian imports, but their influence would soon spread eastwards into the Netherlands, causing a number of Flemish artists to adopt what came to be known as Northern Mannerism. And with the advent of the Second School of Fontainebleau in the late 1500s, Flemish and home-grown French artists would prevail, further advancing the style of Northern Mannerism with its unique blend of Italian Renaissance and Gothic art.

One of the most important events of this entire era was the European rediscovery of the New World in 1492 by the Genoese explorer Christopher Columbus, who had been employed by the king and queen of Spain.* Meanwhile, Portuguese explorers had reached the Cape of Good Hope in southern Africa as early as 1488, and were now discovering the extent of the Indian Ocean. Both of these developments were aimed at finding a new way to Asia, in order to break the Venetian hold over the trade in silk, spices and other luxuries along the Silk Routes.

In order to avert a war between expansionist Portugal and Spain, in 1494 Pope Alexander VI drew a line down a map of the Atlantic, decreeing that all land discovered to the west of this line would belong to Spain, and all land to the east would belong to Portugal. Within

---

* The Vikings had reached Newfoundland some 500 years earlier, but were unable to sustain a settlement for more than a few years. The First Americans are now thought to have arrived on the west coast up to 40,000 years prior to this.

three years the English ignored the pope's decree, with King Henry VII sponsoring the Venetian explorer John Cabot (Giovanni Caboto) to sail west in search of a northerly route to China. Cabot made landfall on the coast of what is now Canada. The exact location remains unknown, but it was possibly Newfoundland or Nova Scotia; nonetheless Cabot planted a flag and claimed the land for England.

Francis I was late to wake up to the possibilities intrinsic to such exploration. It was not until 1523 that he hired the Florentine Giovanni da Verrazzano to chart the coast of the New World with the aim of finding a northern route to China. Following various mishaps, Verrazzano's expedition was reduced to a single ship, the three-masted 100-ton *La Dauphine*, by the time it reached Madeira in the mid-Atlantic. With a crew of less than fifty men, and supplies for eight months, *La Dauphine* set sail west in the new year.

After a six-week voyage, in March 1524 Verrazzano arrived at Cape Fear, on an island off the coast of what is now North Carolina. Immediately, he set about exploring, soon discovering the Pamlico Sound lagoon and recording that this was undoubtedly the entrance to the Pacific Ocean. Despite this, he continued north up the coast, mapping his route. Curiously, he appears to have missed the entrance to Chesapeake Bay and the mouth of the Delaware River. He arrived at the mouth of the Hudson River, where he encountered some indigenous people now known to have been Lenape, whose woodland territory extended through the hinterland from Delaware to Long Island.*

Verrazzano decided against venturing into the Hudson River, which he assumed was another lagoon. He then sailed as far north as Narragansett Bay, where he was received by a delegation of Narragansett tribesmen who gave him hospitality for two weeks. By now it was midsummer, so he decided to sail back across the Atlantic before the advent of the winter storms.

---

* The Verrazzano-Narrows Bridge, which spans the stretch of water between Brooklyn and Staten Island at the entrance to New York Harbour, is named after Verrazzano and probably crosses the very stretch of water where his ship first encountered the canoes of the Lenape.

Seen from the hindsight of five centuries, it is easy to criticize Verrazzano's expedition for its lacunae and missed opportunities. These are especially evident when compared with the thoroughness of his fellow Florentine explorer Amerigo Vespucci's Spanish-backed expeditions down the coast of South America two decades earlier. In the light of this, it is only right that the entire New World should be named after Amerigo. Even so, Verrazzano was the first to map almost the entire length of the eastern seaboard of North America. Had it been realized that North and South America were in fact two subcontinents joined by a comparatively narrow isthmus, the northern part might well have been named Giovannia, or even Verrazzania. The discovery of America as a whole – and the realization by Amerigo Vespucci that it was not China, and the West Indies were not offshore islands of south Asia – belongs very much to the Mediterranean contribution to the Renaissance. On the other hand, the discovery and exploration of North America is very much an independent achievement of the Other Renaissance.

At the end of his pioneering voyage, Verrazzano arrived back in France on 8 July 1524. He then travelled to deliver his findings to Francis I, informing him that he had named the land he had explored 'Francesca', in honour of His Majesty.

Verrazzano would undertake two further voyages to the New World, the last of which reached the island of Guadeloupe in 1528. Here he put ashore, only to be encountered by hostile local Caribs, who are reported to have slaughtered and eaten him.

In 1532, the feudal Duchy of Brittany finally became integrated with France. Two years later, Francis I despatched the French-Breton explorer Jacques Cartier on a voyage of exploration across the Atlantic, with the aim of finding a western route to China. It was Cartier's three voyages to the New World that would mark France's first realistic incursions into the continent. These would have lasting consequences, for both France and North America.

Cartier's ambitious yet suitably vague brief from Francis I was to 'discover certain islands and lands where it is said that a great quantity of gold and other precious things are to be found'. This marked a change of the original aim. As the dream of finding a western route to China was beginning to fade, so the dream of finding even greater treasure on the newly discovered continent began to rise.

This last hope was no chimera. Three years earlier, Spanish explorers in South America had been awed by the sight of local people wearing amulets, necklaces and other ornaments made of the finest gold and silver. Enquiries amongst the indigenous peoples had suggested the existence of a man, or a place, which the Spanish translated as *El Dorado* (The Golden One). This name would take on legendary proportions, and inspire Spanish explorers for years to come. And although no actual El Dorado had yet been discovered, in 1421 the Spanish conquistador Hernán Cortés had succeeded in conquering the Aztecs in what is now Mexico, pillaging much treasure in the process. Twelve years later, the conquistador Francisco Pizarro defeated the Incas in what is now Peru, gaining access to gold mines and the fabled 'silver mountain' of Potosí. So Cartier had good reason to believe that similar treasure would be found in North America.

After sailing across the Atlantic in twenty days, Cartier reached the New World in early May 1534. Here he began mapping and exploring Newfoundland and other islands in the Gulf of St Lawrence and the estuary of the St Lawrence River. He also twice made contact with indigenous peoples, almost certainly including the Mi'kmaq who inhabited the woodland near the mainland shore at Chaleur Bay. During these two meetings, some trading took place. Cartier then had a third meeting, this time with members of the more extensive Iroquois people. During the course of the meeting, Cartier's men planted a wooden cross bearing the proclamation 'Long live the King of France', thus laying claim to the territory. The Iroquois grasped what was happening, and relations quickly deteriorated. Cartier then kidnapped two of the sons of their chief, Donnacona, who finally agreed to let them sail with Cartier on the condition that they returned with a quantity of European goods to trade. Despite the lack of any evidence, Cartier returned to France convinced that he had landed in Asia.

The following year, Cartier returned with three ships, 110 men and Donnacona's two sons. This time he sailed along the north of the Gulf of St Lawrence, and then continued over 200 miles up the St Lawrence River, certain that this was the route to China. His passage was halted by rapids at Hochelaga (site of present-day Montreal). Cartier was so convinced that the river led to China that he named these rapids *La Chine* (French for 'China'; this was the site of present-day Lachine). Onshore was an indigenous settlement such as he had never seen before: a thousand people lined the riverbank to greet him. A few days later he sailed back down the river to the smaller settlement of Stadacona (near modern-day Quebec City), where Donnacona had his residence. Here Cartier set up camp on an island which he named *Île de Bascuz* ('Isle of Bacchus', after the Ancient Roman god of wine, owing to its expanse of wild grapes).

By now it was well into October, and Cartier realized that it was too late to return to France. Cartier and his men, with the help of some indigenous locals, built a fort in order to sit out the winter of 1435–6. The French were anticipating cold weather, stacking up logs for fuel and storing quantities of salted fish and game within their fort. However, nothing had prepared them for the ferocity of the Canadian winter in these parts, where the temperature could sink below −30°C for months on end. The river froze over, with ice six feet thick covered by a further four feet of snow. Soon scurvy broke out in Cartier's fort, resulting in the sickness and death of several dozen French and Iroquoians. According to Cartier's log: 'out of the 110 that we were, not ten were well enough to help the others, a pitiful sight to see'.

When Donnacona paid a visit to the fort and saw the conditions to which its inhabitants had sunk, he passed on to Cartier a recipe for a cure made from the bark of the aneda tree, a local evergreen spruce. During the following week, Cartier and his companions consumed the entire bark of one of these tall trees in a medicine concocted according to Donnacona's instructions. Whereupon all those struck down with the disease were suddenly cured, causing Cartier to record this as 'a miracle'.

During Cartier's conversations with Donnacona, he learned of a place called the 'Kingdom of Saguenay', which was said to lie some way to the north. This land was reputedly populated by fair-haired people, and contained much gold, as well as rubies and other jewels. Cartier decided to kidnap Donnacona so that he could personally convince King Francis I of the existence of this fabulous, barely credible land.*

In July 1436, fourteen months after they set sail for France, Cartier and his depleted men arrived back at Saint-Malo. Chief Donnacona was duly taken to see Francis I. Although given the royal treatment by the French king, Donnacona pined for his homeland and his people – to such an extent that he died three years later.

In 1540, Francis I ordered Cartier to set forth on a third expedition, this time with the aim of colonizing the land he had discovered. This Cartier now referred to as 'the Country of Canadas' after the Iroquois word for a village: *kanata*. Francis I instructed Cartier to found a colony in Canada, where he would rule as captain-general in the king's name. On 23 May 1541, Cartier sailed from Saint-Malo with five ships containing more than a hundred settlers and convicts. (The latter were expected to undertake the hard labour while the colonists cultivated the land.)

On arriving at Stadacona, Cartier became suspicious of the welcoming Iroquoians, who cannot have been too pleased to learn of the death of their chief. Consequently, Cartier decided to establish his colony some ten miles upstream, at a propitious spot he had noted on his previous visit. This is the site of present-day Cap-Rouge.

The first settlers, along with the convicts and such cattle as had survived the three-month voyage, now disembarked and began making preparations to establish the colony. Trees were hewn, wooden huts were set up; cabbage, turnip and lettuce seeds were planted in a sheltered garden area; and the colony was named Charlesbourg-Royal.

---

* The Kingdom of Saguenay belongs in the same category as the legendary El Dorado. However, some modern French historians have suggested that these fair-haired people might have been the original Vikings, who are known to have settled to the north in Newfoundland some 500 years previously. The behaviour and wondrous artefacts of the Vikings would have become a folk memory, with descriptions of their curious clothing, medallions and rituals increasingly embellished as the story was passed down from generation to generation.

On the cliff overlooking the riverside settlement, a protective fort was constructed.

By now, the men had begun collecting diamonds and nuggets of gold, which they found as they dug up the earth. Even so, Cartier remained convinced that this was not the real Saguenay, and set off upriver with a party in longboats. They skirted the rapids by portage, and then began rowing their way north up the Ottawa River, a tributary of the St Lawrence. In the end, Cartier found himself unable to proceed any further upriver owing to there being so many rapids, and decided to return to the settlement.

Here he discovered that relations with the local Iroquoians had taken a turn for the worse. They no longer approached the colony in a friendly fashion to trade fish and game; instead they prowled ominously through the surrounding woods. Then one day, without warning, they attacked, killing thirty-five settlers before Cartier and the rest managed to make it up to the safety of the fort. Cartier and what remained of his company survived another bitterly cold winter, able to avoid scurvy by imbibing evergreen-bark infusions.

With the coming of spring, Cartier and his men left the fort and returned to live in the settlement. But he soon decided that this was unsustainable with so few inhabitants. He also decided to abandon the search for Saguenay. It was time to return home. Early in June 1452, the settlers loaded up their ships with the gold and diamonds they had mined, and set sail downriver. As they were crossing the Gulf of St Lawrence, they encountered a flotilla of French ships under the command of Jean-François de La Rocque de Roberval, a senior army officer and friend of Francis I. Cartier was informed by Roberval that the king had despatched him to take charge as the first governor-general of Canada, thus supplanting Cartier's post as captain-general. Roberval specifically forbade Cartier from returning to France, and instead ordered him to join the newly arrived ships to continue the search for Saguenay.

During the night, Cartier and his men silently hauled their anchors and glided away into the dark, raising their sails when out of earshot of

Roberval's ships. By dawn they had made it beyond the nearest headland and were able to hide amongst the offshore islands. When Roberval left to travel up the St Lawrence River, Cartier and his men voyaged back across the Atlantic to France, arriving home in October 1452. Here they began unloading their cargo of treasures. But on examination by mineralogists, the gold was found to be fool's gold (iron pyrite, a mineral whose flecks only resemble gold) and the diamonds were nothing more than quartz crystals.

Cartier and his men had not only lost their 'fortune', but also faced being put on trial when Roberval returned and revealed that they had disobeyed his orders, which had been given in the name of the king.

A year later, Roberval too was forced to abandon his settlement, considering the conditions too harsh and the search for Saguenay futile. On his arrival back in France he found that the nation was at war with Spain, and he was ordered to report immediately to Paris for military duty. Cartier and his men thus avoided any charges. Cartier would live out his days on his estate outside Saint-Malo, where he died in 1557 at the age of sixty-five. Not until half a century later would France eventually establish a colony in Canada – under Samuel de Champlain, who built a settlement near to Stadacona, which he named Quebec. Here the settlers began trading with the local indigenous peoples, exchanging French guns, alcohol and clothing for furs.

This was the first step in the creation of the French Overseas Empire, which over the coming centuries would grow to span all four continents, becoming second only to the British Empire (the largest established empire the world has yet seen).

Francis I would reign over France for over forty years (1515–47), and it was during this period that one of the most lasting and spectacular developments of the French Renaissance took place: the building of many of the chateaux along the Loire Valley. These fairy-tale white castles make a unique contribution to the world's architecture – and have since influenced buildings from Ludwig of Bavaria's Neuschwanstein to the castles of Disney World. They are a development of the classic walled fortresses of the medieval era, blended with a delicate Italianate influence from the Florentine Renaissance. Mostly they are expanded and ornamented castles stripped of their bulky defensive features, intended as fanciful aristocratic residences gracing a peaceful countryside.*

Many of these chateaux feature graceful towers, clusters of turrets, and purely decorative moats. Their surrounding gardens were laid out in symmetrical shapes, with flowerbeds divided by gravel pathways. Artificial lakes, fountains and ornamental grottoes were a frequent feature. Perhaps the finest example, and certainly the largest, is the Château de Chambord, built by Francis I himself. Its façade is over 100 yards wide and contains 800 sculpted columns. From its elaborate roof sprout a host of turrets, which Francis I intended to resemble the minarets of Ottoman Constantinople. Francis I played an overseeing role in much of the design. However, the main architect is known to be the Italian Domenico da Cortona, and many suspect that Chambord also contains features suggested to the young Francis I by Leonardo da Vinci before he died.

The most spectacular interior feature is a double spiral staircase, whose intricate ingenuity is typical of some of Leonardo's designs. The English diarist John Evelyn, who visited Chambord in the following century, described it as follows:

> it is devised with four [sic] entries or ascents, which cross one another, so that though four persons meet, they never come in sight, but by small loopholes, till they land. It consists of 274 steps (as I remember), and is an extraordinary work, but of far greater expense than use or beauty.

---

* Ironically, France would be at war for much of Francis I's reign, though most of the fighting took place in Italy and Spain. Francis I, resplendent in his gold-plated armour, played a brave and active role in many battles, to such an extent that in 1525 he was captured by his great rival the Holy Roman Emperor Charles V, who was also King of Spain. Francis I would spend a year in captivity in Madrid, before his release after being forced to sign a humiliating peace treaty.

The building of Chambord started in 1519, and would still not be completed when Francis I died in 1547. By that time, no less than 1,800 builders, designers, architects and other artisans were employed on its construction, which had by then cost some 444,070 gold livres.*

It is difficult to view such extravagance as being in the spirit of the northern Renaissance. If anything, it matches the excesses of the Renaissance popes in Rome during this period, who were lavishing the vast papal income on such projects as the new St Peter's and the Sistine Chapel.† This may hold true for much of the architecture of the northern Renaissance, but as we shall see, the literature of this era was not necessarily so restrained.

---

* *Livre* is the French for 'pound'. As to this colossal sum, it is impossible to assess its value in present-day terms. Suffice to say that around this time a minor nobleman could expect to derive an annual income approximately equivalent to 400 livres from his estates.

† A century later, Louis XIV, 'the Sun King' – who built the far more extensive Palace of Versailles – would build an extension to Chambord. This was a stable capable of containing 1,200 horses, so that he could use Chambord as a hunting lodge.

CHAPTER 5

A NEW LITERATURE: RABELAIS

T HE ARISTOCRATIC COURTS AT the chateaux along the Loire attracted all manner of poets, troubadours and literary entertainers. Yet the finest writer of the early French Renaissance was undoubtedly François Rabelais, whose presence would hardly have been tolerated at any such self-respecting court.

Ironically, Rabelais was in fact born within the shadow of one of the largest and most ancient chateaux in the Loire Valley, the Château de Chinon, whose origins date from the eleventh century. By the time Rabelais was born around 1490, in the small town of Chinon – beneath the castle walls on the banks of the River Vienne, a tributary of the Loire – the chateau had expanded to become an extensive and palatial fortress, one of the favourite residences of the French kings. It was here in 1499 that Louis XII (predecessor to Francis I) greeted the notorious twenty-three-year-old Cesare Borgia, son of Pope Alexander VI, who had renounced his cardinalate in order to marry into French royalty. This was an occasion of great pomp and ceremony, and would certainly have been witnessed by the young

Rabelais. Borgia's procession up the long ramp to the chateau's entrance included no less than seventy mules bearing gifts and treasures, guarded by armed mounted attendants all decked out in the spectacular red and yellow livery of the Borgia family. We can only imagine the face of young Rabelais gazing in childish awe from amongst the crowds lining the route.

Not much detail is known of Rabelais' life, but what does emerge is a cat's cradle of contradictions. He was both a monk and a writer of ribald tales. His humanist beliefs and Ancient Greek scholarship contrast strongly with his intimate knowledge of the low-life and bawdy behaviour of the taverns. This is not the literature of a man born in the shadow of a royal palace, but of a man who enjoyed the other delight on offer in Chinon – which was then renowned for producing the finest wine in all of France, outshining even Burgundy and Bordeaux.*

Rabelais' father was thought to have been a moderately successful local lawyer; nonetheless, the young Rabelais forswore the family profession and entered the Franciscan order of monks as a novice. Later, he would become a fully fledged friar, making use of his time reading Latin works and learning Ancient Greek. He also seems to have become conversant with natural philosophy (science), law and humanist philosophy. As if this was not enough, he then left to study medicine at the University of Poitiers, in central France. After this he travelled south to settle in Lyon, a major commercial and intellectual centre at the time, as it was an important staging post on the trade route that linked northern Italy to Paris and the Netherlands.

During this period Rabelais wrote to the great humanist scholar Erasmus, sending him a printed copy of a rare Greek manuscript. By now

---

* During the late 1850s, 40 per cent of French vineyards were blighted by phylloxera, a disease carried by tiny aphids inadvertently imported from America. A successful cure for this disease was found by grafting French vines to phylloxera-resistant American roots. The vineyards of Chinon implemented this cure, but it is claimed that the wine never quite recovered its full, rich subtlety. Today, Chinon red wine retains a faint echo of the sophisticated, multilayered richness which once made it the wine of kings, but it has lost the full inner body which supported these rich qualities.

Rabelais had become a friend of the locally based German-born publisher Sebastian Gryphius. Consequently Rabelais began writing pamphlets which included satirical descriptions of local worthies. He also undertook less scurrilous work in the form of translations of ancient classical writers. These included the Greek physician Hippocrates (c. 460–375 BC), the founder of medicine – after whom the Hippocratic oath is named.* Rabelais is also known to have studied Galen, who in the second century AD succeeded Celsus as the finest physician in the Roman era.

It was during these years in Lyon that Rabelais began writing his multi-volume masterwork *Gargantua and Pantagruel*, which is largely devoted to the antics of its eponymous heroes. The escapades and exploits of the giant Gargantua and his all-consuming son Pantagruel include all manner of riotous indulgence. The prologue baldly states: 'Most illustrious drinkers, and *you*, the most precious pox-ridden – for to *you* and *you* alone are my writings dedicated…' Most of this hilarious work is fantastic in the extreme, yet cunningly slipped in between these ridiculous exploits are many snippets of wisdom, allusions to the humanist ideas that were beginning to spread throughout Europe during this period, and general common sense regarding the life we lead.

All this makes a striking contrast to medieval French literature, with its improving parables, the lives of the saints, and the poems of chivalry and chaste love performed by the travelling troubadours. A summary of a characteristic slice of narrative from the first volume of Rabelais' pentalogy gives an indication of its style and content. While Pantagruel is away

---

* To this day, doctors in many countries (including the UK and USA) are required to swear to uphold a version of the Hippocratic Oath before being permitted to take up their profession. This is essentially a solemn promise requiring the newly fledged physician to adhere to certain moral practices. The oath's first requirement is 'to do no harm', but it also goes on to require patient confidentiality and explicitly forbids the use of poison, even when the patient requests this. Besides euthanasia, it also bars the use of a pessary to cause abortion. The oath-taker is further required to swear, 'I will not use the knife, not even, verily on sufferers from the stone [Kidney Stone], but I will give place to such as are craftsmen therein.' This shows the early distinction between physicians (doctors) and surgeons (who performed operations).

at university, he learns that Gargantua has been 'translated to Fairyland by Morgan Le Fay'. (The latter is the enchantress from Arthurian legend, and allows for a word play with the French *fay*, 'fairy'.) Pantagruel and his companions return to reclaim his father's lands and besiege one of its cities. As Rabelais describes it: 'Through subterfuge, might and urine the besieged city is relieved.' During the course of a downpour of rain, Pantagruel sticks out his tongue so that his army can shelter beneath it; meanwhile the narrator takes refuge in Pantagruel's mouth.

This was humanism writ large, with all the foibles, mock-heroics and scandalous behaviour of everyday life which had been missing from much of the respectable literature of the medieval era. The tales of Gargantua and Pantagruel may be vulgar in content, and their prose is hardly elevated in its use of the French language. On the contrary. Yet amidst all the exaggerations and implausibilities it is studded with erudite references, scatological puns, playful neologisms and the like. The first part of this work was published in 1532, and it comes as little wonder that Rabelais chose to give himself a pseudonym: Alcofribas Nasier (an anagram of his name).

In the second book, Gargantua decides to build a monastery: the Abbey of Thélème. An inscription at the entrance gate lists unwelcome guests: 'hypocrites, bigots, the pox-ridden, Goths, Magoths, straw-chewing law clerks, usurious grinches, old or officious judges, and burners of heretics'. The abbey contains both monks and nuns, all of whom are good-looking. They are served superb meals and are free to frolic in a swimming pool as they practise 'Thélémisme', whose only rule is: 'Do what you want.' And so it goes on...

Reaction to Rabelais' work was predictably mixed. Many loved it; others, especially in the Church, were scandalized. So how did Rabelais manage to get away with it? Why was he not charged with pornography, blasphemy, or simply general outrage to public morals? The fact is, Rabelais had a number of friends in high places who so enjoyed his work that he remained under their protection. He is known to have accompanied the aristocratic Cardinal Jean du Bellay on several trips to Rome. And owing to Rabelais' widespread erudition, he managed – with the help of his patrons – to secure posts at various universities. He is recorded as having taught medicine at the universities of Montpellier and Lyon for short periods, and also to have delivered a celebrated public lecture in Lyon using the corpse of a hanged man to reveal the secrets of human anatomy. This was during a period when the dissection of human cadavers was widely prohibited. The authoritative view of human anatomy was taken from the classic works of Galen, who had gained much of his knowledge from dissecting pigs and sheep.

It seems that Rabelais himself was as entertaining, erudite and grotesquely humorous as the characters in his tales, and this must have endeared him to his friends and patrons. Cardinal du Bellay is even thought to have recommended Rabelais' work to Francis I, who certainly both read and enjoyed it. However, when Francis I died in 1547, Rabelais' luck quickly ran out. His books were banned by the French Parlement, and the Church authorities were out for his blood. This was an ongoing problem for Rabelais, and he is known at one stage to have fled across the French border to take refuge in the independent imperial city of Mainz (in what is now German territory). But his friends still managed to secure for him a paid curacy at Meudon, just outside Paris. However, in 1552 Rabelais found it prudent to resign from his post so as to escape the jurisdiction of the ecclesiastical courts. He died the following year, probably in his mid-sixties. The year after that, the final book of his tales of Gargantua and Pantagruel appeared. This features an epic sea voyage, including everything from the killing of a sea monster to feasting on grotesque culinary dishes. Here Rabelais succeeds in echoing the classical voyage of the Argonauts in search of the golden fleece, as well as the modern explorations undertaken by Jacques Cartier in Canada.

As for his critics, he forestalled them in characteristic fashion. Those who dismissed his folly for writing 'such idle tales and amusing twaddle' had only themselves to blame, for 'you are scarcely wiser to waste time reading them'. But in the end he forgave himself and his critics as being 'more forgivable than a heap of sarrabovines, bigot-tails, slimy-snails… lecherous shavelings, booted monks and other such sects who disguised themselves as masked revellers to deceive the world'.

Rabelais' is no ordinary prose, being filled with long lists, neologisms and absurdities, and advising his readers to read his works 'not so much to pass time merrily but wickedly, so as to harm someone, namely by articulating, arse-ticulating, wry-arse-ticulating, bumculating, bollock-ulating, diaboculating...' As a final piece of advice he tells his readers: 'And if you desire to be good Pantagruelists (that is, to live in peace, joy and health, always enjoying good cheer) never trust folk who peer through a hole.'

Rabelais' admirers loved all this; upright citizens remained outraged by it. As was to be expected of a writer who encouraged his readers to 'drink for the thirst that is to come', he advised them, 'If you don't want to see a fool, then break your mirror,' and sympathetically diagnosed their most common illness: 'he suffered from that terrible disease called lack of money'. On top of this he peppered his larger-than-life tales with such oblique insights as 'Wisdom does not enter a malicious mind' and 'A child is not a vase to be filled but a fire to be lit'. His last words were 'I go to seek a Great Perhaps', and he even turned his last will and testament into a parody: 'I have nothing, owe a great deal, and leave the rest to the poor.' This was surely not to be viewed as serious litera-ture. Yet his words remain as divisive today as they were when he first penned them, almost five hundred years ago. It comes as little surprise that controversy has remained integral to Rabelais' reputation through the centuries.

The literary critic Georges Bertrin, writing in *The Catholic Encyclopedia* of 1911, is worth quoting at length for he succeeds in being both outraged and profound in his assessment, calling Rabelais:

> a revolutionary who attacked all the past, Scholasticism, the monks; his religion is scarcely more than that of a spiritual-ly-minded pagan. Less bold in political matters, he cared little for liberty; his ideal was a tyrant who loves peace... His vocab-ulary is rich and picturesque, but licentious and filthy. In short, as [the seventeenth-century philosopher and satirist] La Bruyère says: 'His book is a riddle which may be considered inexplicable.

Where it is bad, it is beyond the worst; it has the charm of the rabble; where it is good it is excellent and exquisite; it may be the daintiest of dishes.' As a whole it exercises a baneful influence.

Later in the twentieth century, the Surrealists and James Joyce were favourably inspired by Rabelais, and sought to emulate aspects of his work. On the other hand, the moralistic George Orwell, who also showed great sympathy for the poor and downtrodden, seems to have missed the point, dismissing Rabelais as 'an exceptionally perverse, morbid writer, a case for psychoanalysis'. Rabelais was as much against tyranny as Orwell's *1984*, yet as Georges Bertrin had perceptively observed, Rabelais' utopia required a 'tyrant who loves peace'.

This raises a profound philosophical question, which had been discussed by the Ancient Greek philosophers but resurfaced during the Renaissance: if there is to be a free society where everyone is permitted to 'do what you want', how can this exist? Two centuries later, the French philosopher Jean-Jacques Rousseau declared that citizens should throw off the constraints of society and be free, and those who refused this opportunity should be compelled to be free. This dilemma would recur in the French Revolution, and again in the Communist Revolution, when ironically it would be used as an excuse for imposing 'freedom' as a form of conformity. The search for Rabelais' 'tyrant who loves peace' continues to this day. Such thought leads to the conclusion that the anarchic freedom found in Rabelais' riotous tales can perhaps only be perpetrated on the page, never in life. Yet paradoxically, it is the exaggerated life that he describes which inspires in us the very spirit of freedom.

But Rabelais can also be seen in another light. The Renaissance was a period of profound human transformation, and his tales can be seen as analogous to this transformation. The medieval constraints on humanity were bursting at the seams, and a new way of living was beginning to emerge. Even the world itself had begun to expand, at least for Europeans, with the discovery of the New World and the opening of a new route around the Cape of Good Hope to eastern

Asia. The distortions and grotesqueries of Rabelais' work, along with his penetrating observations about human life, were merely a reflection of what was taking place around him in Europe. New knowledge, new discoveries, new sciences, new art and architecture – the European world was changing as never before. The truths and behaviours which were emerging during the Renaissance were in their own way as fantastic as the antics of Gargantua and Pantagruel.

Even an etymological analysis of the giants' names and their associations is instructive. Gargantua is gargantuan, huge, monstrous, larger-than-life, elephantine, clumsy and so forth. Pantagruel is similarly illustrative. 'Panta' hints at panting, yearning. Pan is the lecherous half-goat god of Ancient Greece; he is also the god of chaos and 'panic'. 'Pan' suggests all-embracing – as in Panhellenic, pan-American and panorama. Meanwhile 'gruel' was a ubiquitous medieval food (often a thin mixture of ground cereals, like porridge). Pantagruel was thus all-consuming.

Rabelais took his place amongst a new kind of literature that was beginning to emerge. His work was novelistic, episodic, discursive and unbuttoned, rather than adhering to the traditional strictures of poetry, classical writing or myth. Two centuries earlier, the Florentine writer Giovanni Boccaccio had written his *Decameron*, a compendium of bawdy tales and erotic misadventures. And it is not an accident that Rabelais was a contemporary of Leonardo da Vinci. Indeed it is no great stretch to see Rabelais' work as a teeming subconscious underside to the man who committed his fantastic scientific imaginings to the pages of his coded notebooks. And following on from Rabelais came the Spanish writer Miguel de Cervantes and the shambolic adventures of his mock-heroic Don Quixote.

One millennium previously, the Ancient Greek tragedian Euripides had written: 'Those whom the gods wish to destroy they first make mad.' In Rabelais and his like we can see a metaphoric madness which sought to destroy the old and make way for the new.

Something utterly transformative was taking place. Something which continues to this day. Here was nothing less than individuality beginning to emerge and spread through the modern western consciousness. But this was such an unprecedented evolutionary step that initially it could only be understood as exaggeration, as a form of madness.

CHAPTER 6

MARTIN LUTHER AND THE PROTESTANT REFORMATION

WITH THE ADVENT OF Martin Luther, this previously imagined madness took a turn towards reality. Tradition has it that on 31 October 1517, the thirty-three-year-old Martin Luther publicly nailed his *Ninety-Five Theses* to the wooden door of the Castle Church of Wittenberg. Whether or not this act actually took place in quite this fashion, the symbolic force of the tale cannot be denied. This event marked the beginning of Protestantism, and an end to the hegemony of the Holy Roman Church in western Europe. The Reformation of the Church had begun.

Luther's *Ninety-Five Theses* was a comprehensive demand for a reform of the Church. The most significant and divisive idea deriving from the theses was his insistence that believers had direct access to God through prayer, and so had no need of intercession on their behalf through a priest. There was thus, by implication, no need for the Holy Roman Church, the pope, the priesthood, holy relics, or indeed the entire apparatus of the established Catholic religion. Luther's act would divide Europe, plunging the entire western continent into decades of religious persecution and widespread social unrest, finally culminating in the most destructive war Europe had yet witnessed. Nothing would be the same again.

This would, in effect, be the spiritual and secular conflagration which became the background to the northern Renaissance. Just as Ancient Greece had flourished through the upheavals and conflicts between its city-states – even the conquest of Athens by Sparta in the Peloponnesian War – so would the Other Renaissance take on its own distinctive cultural transformation against the background of war. In this way, the loosening of the ties binding the medieval world would enable a freedom in which the Renaissance could evolve.

Martin Luther was born on 10 November 1483, the first of several brothers and sisters. His birthplace was Eisleben, a small town in a copper-mining region of eastern Germany, ruled over by the counts of Mansfeld in the name of the Holy Roman Emperor. Apart from a single visit to Rome on a pilgrimage, Luther would spend his entire life living in and around this region of Upper Saxony.

Luther's father, Hans Luder (later Luther), was a leaseholder of a small copper mine and smelter in the nearby town of Mansfeld, where young Martin moved with his family when he was just one year old. Martin's father was hard-working, with a good head for business, and would end up as one of the town's five ruling councillors. He also harboured ambitions for his firstborn son, whose mother, Margarette (née Lindemann), came from a family of high-ranking officials in the Eisenach administration.

Martin went to a good local school, studying the three traditional subjects of medieval education – grammar, rhetoric and logic – with the aim that he should become a lawyer. Luther would later describe this education as 'purgatory and hell'. Martin's mother was a conscientious woman who did not believe in having servants perform tasks she could perform herself. But she was not physically strong, and from an early age she developed a stooped back from carrying loads of wood into the house, bearing pails of water from the well, and helping scrub the floors.

At the age of seventeen, Martin entered the nearby University of Erfurt, which he would later describe as 'a beerhouse and a whorehouse'. Each day he was woken before dawn for 'a day of rote learning and often wearying spiritual exercises'. In 1505 he duly received his master's degree and entered the legal profession in accordance with his father's wishes.

Within months he had abandoned the law, declaring it to be nothing but uncertainty. He returned to the university and began attending lectures in philosophy and theology. Here he gradually began to discover a new certainty. His lecturers imbued in him a healthy scepticism, which was to be applied even to the greatest philosophers. He was taught that the only certain knowledge came from his own experience. Such empiricism was ahead of its time, and ran contrary to the orthodox acceptance of 'authority' (found in the likes of Aristotle and Galen).

Luther's mother had given him a Latin Bible, which he read avidly. This alone was sacrosanct and not open to doubt. He came to believe that knowledge of God came only from the indubitable pages of the Bible, and through divine inspiration.

In July 1505, Luther was returning to university on horseback when he was overtaken by a violent thunderstorm and came close to being struck by a lightning bolt. This inspired in him a sudden fear of death, and provided the divine revelation for which he had been waiting for so long. On the spot, he swore to himself, 'Help! *Saint Anna*, I will become a monk!'*

Luther now abandoned his studies and entered St Augustine's Monastery at Erfurt, telling his university friends that they would see him 'not ever again'. His father was outraged, and his friends bewildered. Luther entered into his new monastic life with fervour, spending hours on end in prayer, fasting, and going to confession. Despite this, he would later describe this period as one of deep spiritual despair.

Two years later Luther was ordained in Erfurt Cathedral. As a student of theology he had proved to be a prodigy, and this, together

---

* St Anna is first mentioned in the apocryphal Gospel of St James, and is also referred to, but not named, in the Quran. She is the mother of Mary, and thus the maternal grandmother of Jesus.

with his exemplary behaviour, led to him being noticed by Johann von Staupitz, vicar-general of the Augustinian friars. Staupitz had recently been instrumental in establishing the University of Wittenberg, and he invited Martin Luther to become a lecturer in theology there.

In Wittenberg, Luther entered a new world. This was the seat of the Elector of Saxony, Frederick III (the Wise) and his court, which included scholars and artists as well as the elector's renowned collection of 17,443 holy relics. These included a thumb from St Anne, a twig from Moses's burning bush, hay from the holy manger, and milk from the Virgin Mary. Both pious and worldly, Frederick III jealously protected the interests of the citizens under his authority. His court painter was Lucas Cranach the Elder, certainly the most successful German artist of his time. In part, this was due to his prolific output, which would eventually amount to more than 13,000 paintings.

Cranach the Elder was born in 1472 and probably received his apprenticeship in southern Germany, where the influence of the Italian Renaissance had long since spread across the Alps. Cranach was chosen as Frederick III's court artist in 1504, and is best known for his realistic portraits. These have a clear, almost photographic likeness, which at the same time succeeds in hinting at the inner character of his subject. They are also distinctly German in style. Cranach's portraits have a solidity which is quite distinct from the more flamboyant or mannerist aspect of his Italian counterparts. (Botticelli, Leonardo and Michelangelo were all contemporaries.) Cranach's portrait of Frederick III depicts a broad-shouldered man with a large but neat grey beard. The plain honesty of the elector's features reflects what we know of his personality. Later, Cranach would paint a portrait of the middle-aged Luther. His simple black cap and plain black clothes frame a stolid face of evident intelligence, also suggesting a certain rooted honesty and self-belief.

In Wittenberg, Luther soon gained the respect of Frederick III and formed a friendship with Cranach. Later he would form a close friendship with Philip Melanchthon, professor of Greek at the university. However, prior to coming close to such secular friends, Luther had to be taught a lesson by his vicar-general, Johann von Staupitz.

Staupitz became Luther's confessor, and soon found himself enduring hour-long confessions from his earnest young protégé, who insisted upon pouring out the long litany of sins he had committed during the twenty-one years of his life. Staupitz was descended from an ancient family of high standing, and as such he had been brought up to believe in a more worldly approach to the priesthood. He enjoyed the good things of life such as intellectual conversation, and dining at the table of Frederick III.

Gradually, in paternal fashion, Staupitz began encouraging the young Luther to turn aside from his insistence upon spiritual perfection. Instead of obsessive introspection, Luther was guided towards a more outward-looking spirituality. God had need of men of intelligence, such as Luther, but such men were of little use if they did not mingle with others, passing on their wisdom. By means of gentle teasing, Staupitz encouraged Luther to ignore his obsessive thoughts of inadequacy. To gain self-confidence was not the sin of pride but the embracing of a sense of outward purpose. Luther's character was being coaxed into a subtle transformation. Later, he would declare, 'If it had not been for Dr Staupitz, I should have sunk in hell.'

Staupitz inculcated in Luther the idea of the 'sweetness' of God, and how he should take pride in his holy calling. In 1510, Luther was entrusted to travel to Rome, along with a companion, on business concerned with the Augustinian order. Luther and his companion set forth with high expectations on the 750-mile journey which led across the Alps, through Italy, to the Holy City. For the first and only time in his life, Martin Luther would travel more than sixty miles from his place of birth.

Although Luther had by now relaxed into a more mature and rounded personality, he had not wavered from his profound faith. On the long walk south, Luther and his companion would put up at monasteries for the night. In many of these institutions he found himself shocked at the laxity of morals, disregard for spiritual matters, and the luxurious living he encountered. Nonetheless he arrived in Rome with the highest expectations, which were quickly dashed. In the words of the twentieth-century American theologian George Wolfgang Forell:

The city, which [Luther] had greeted as holy, was a sink of iniquity; its very priests were openly infidel, and scoffed at the services they performed; the papal courtiers were men of the most shameless lives; he was accustomed to repeat the Italian proverb, 'If there is a hell, Rome is built over it.'

On the long walk home, Luther became more and more uneasy about his relationship with such a Church, and turned to his Bible for reassurance. In Rome, beset by his horror at the depravity of the city of St Peter, a voice had arisen within him, telling him: 'The just shall live by faith.' As he trudged back to Wittenberg, these words kept repeating themselves in his mind.

Five years after his visit to Rome, Luther was promoted to vicar of Saxony and Thuringia, a post that charged him with overseeing the eleven Augustinian monasteries in the province. It was during the course of his travels between monasteries that he came across a Dominican friar called Johann Tetzel, who had been commissioned by Pope Leo X in Rome to sell indulgences throughout Saxony.

The selling of indulgences was an increasingly widespread means of raising money for the Church during the late 1400s and the ensuing years of extravagant popes. This was the era in which such buildings as the Sistine Chapel and the new St Peter's Basilica were being constructed in Rome, and even the huge income which the papacy received from all over western Christendom was proving insufficient to support such ambitious and expensive projects. On top of this, the interior decoration of these buildings by the finest Italian Renaissance artists and sculptors only added to the need for increased papal income. Tetzel had proved so talented at selling indulgences that the pope had even appointed him Grand Commissioner of Indulgences for Germany.

In the course of his work Tetzel introduced certain refinements, intended to increase this form of income. He announced that an indulgence not only reduced one's period spent in Purgatory, but worked on a sliding scale. The more one paid, the less time one spent in Purgatory. Then he announced that indulgences could also be purchased for relatives who were already dead. This gave rise to his habit of rattling the coins in his collecting box and chanting:

As soon as the gold in the casket rings,
The rescued soul to heaven springs!

Tetzel's theological-financial ingenuity knew no bounds. He even came up with a special, highly expensive indulgence which could be purchased for a sin which one had not yet committed. This led to an incident which has all the hallmarks of a classic German folktale, though according to reliable contemporary sources it actually took place.

In Leipzig, Tetzel was approached by a nobleman who wished to purchase one of the special indulgences for a sin not yet committed. Tetzel agreed to sell him this expensive document, but only if he paid in full, and at once. The nobleman agreed, paid the sum, and was then presented with his indulgence, together with its seal of authenticity. However, after Tetzel set off down the highway from Leipzig, bearing with him all the money he had collected throughout the city, the nobleman despatched a band of his men to chase after him and rob him of every coin in his possession. This was the sin for which he had purchased his special indulgence.

Needless to say, Luther found nothing amusing in Tetzel's practice of selling indulgences, and sending such iniquitous money to Rome in order to finance the extravagant behaviour of Leo X.* This was the final straw, and Luther now sat down to make a list of all that he considered to be wrong with the current practices of the Church. The list would end up as the celebrated *Ninety-Five Theses* which Luther is said to have nailed to the door of Wittenberg Castle Church on 31 October 1517. Luther's dramatic

---

* Leo X was the first Medici pope. His father, Lorenzo the Magnificent – head of the Medici banking family that ruled Florence – had purchased a cardinal's hat for him at the unprecedented age of thirteen. This ensured that he would inevitably rise to become a senior cardinal with a good chance of becoming pope. Cardinal Giovanni de' Medici's elevation to Pope Leo X duly took place when he was just thirty-seven years old. He would die some eight years later, bloated from overindulgence and almost certainly poisoned.

act is seen as the beginning of the Reformation, which would split the Church into two factions: on the one side the Roman Catholic Church; and on the other a host of differing Protestant religions. As we shall see, the Reformation would prove a gradual but highly disruptive process.

However, the veracity of Luther's original act remains unclear. It was later recorded that, on 31 October 1517, Frederick III had a night of troubled dreams while staying at his residence in Schweinitz, some thirty miles away. These featured a monk writing on the door of Wittenberg Castle Church, in letters large enough for Frederick III to read even though he was so far away. The pen with which the monk wrote these words was so long that its end reached as far as Rome, and caused the pope's triple crown to shake on his head.

Decisive events of this nature frequently attract omens and imaginative confirmation. The words of Andrew Pettegree of St Andrews University would seem to be the most appropriate response. He has described Luther's act as 'a very good example of history being made because of a current need to create a historic event'. Indeed, the first references to the supposed incident at Wittenberg Castle Church do not start appearing until some thirty years later, and even Luther himself makes no reference to it.

The incident itself may be mere legend. Yet what is undeniable is the fact that Luther, or one of his supporters, ensured that the document containing his *Ninety-Five Theses* was printed so that Luther could circulate a few copies amongst his friends. The gist of the theses is apparent from the outset. The first thesis states: 'When our Lord and Master Jesus Christ said, "Repent", he willed the entire life of believers to be one of repentance.' Ensuing theses elaborate on this concept: repentance concerns the believer's inner struggle with sin, rather than involving any external confession and absolution from a priest.

Apart from a denial of the power of the pope and the Church, Luther specifically asks in Thesis 85: 'Why does the pope, whose wealth today is greater than the wealth of the richest Crassus,' build the Basilica of

---

* Marcus Crassus, an unscrupulous Roman general who lived in the first century BC, was widely renowned as having been 'the richest man in Rome', and his name became a byword for excessive wealth.

St Peter with the money of poor believers rather than his own money?'

Such was the sensation caused by Luther's *Ninety-Five Theses* that 'in just two months they were known all over Germany'. The following year they were spreading across Europe. In March 1518, Erasmus sent a copy to his fellow humanist Thomas More, who would become the Lord High Chancellor of England under Henry VIII. Later in the same year a German translation was undertaken. Naturally, word soon reached Rome of what was taking place. This caused more than a little irritation, yet such reformist heresies were not without precedent. Two centuries previously the English theologian and scholar John Wycliffe had seriously questioned the authority of the priesthood, attacking the profligacy of the Church. In pursuance of his views, he had translated tracts of the Bible into English, so that his followers could read for themselves the actual words of Jesus's preaching. Some years later, Pope Martin V declared Wycliffe to be a heretic, ordering his books to be burned. By this time Wycliffe had died, but it was thought necessary for his body to be exhumed and publicly burned.

Wycliffe's example later inspired the Czech theologian Jan Hus, who embarked upon a similar campaign against the corruption of the Church, inspiring an entire movement known as the 'Hussites'. Hus was similarly excommunicated, but he was burned at the stake while he was still alive – in 1415, just two years before Luther posted his *Ninety-Five Theses*.

Luther was summoned to Rome to explain himself, but Frederick III managed to persuade Pope Leo X that Luther should be 'examined' by the papal legate Cardinal Cajetan at Augsburg, where the Imperial Diet was taking place.* For three days in October 1518, Luther defended himself with such conviction that the 'examination' degenerated into confusion, with both sides shouting and haranguing each other. Luther appeared by now to be in some peril, but with the aid of a sympathetic local monk he managed to slip out of Augsburg under cover of darkness before he could be detained by the Church authorities.

By this time, the fundamental danger of Luther's preaching had been

---

* This was essentially the non-legislative advisory council of the Holy Roman Emperor, which during this period met on an irregular basis, every few years.

realized by the influential theologian Johann Eck, who was determined to silence him. Luther claimed his authority in dismissing the power of the Church could be found in the Bible itself. Namely, in Matthew 16:18–19, in which Jesus states:

> And I say to thee: That thou art Peter; and upon this rock I will build my church, and the gates of hell shall not prevail against it. And I will give to thee the keys of the kingdom of heaven. And whatsoever thou shalt bind upon earth, it shall be bound also in heaven: and whatsoever thou shalt loose on earth, it shall be loosed also in heaven...

In Luther's view, God may have made St Peter the rock upon which the Church was built, but it did not confer on his successors (i.e. the popes) the sole right to interpret scripture. Luther thus denied one of the central doctrines on which the pope's authority rested: papal infallibility. In the eyes of Eck, this made Luther another Hus, who had to be destroyed utterly.

By now Luther's teachings were beginning to spread beyond intellectual circles, and word of his inflammatory theses was reaching congregations in France, Italy and even England. Many students travelled for miles on foot to hear his sermons at Wittenberg. Luther defended faith as simply the righteousness of Christ: 'That is why faith alone makes someone just and fulfils the law.' Luther saw faith as a gift from God; the experience of being justified by faith was 'as though I had been born again'.

In 1520, Luther was warned in a papal bull that he would be excommunicated unless he renounced his teachings, especially the *Ninety-Five Theses*. Luther ignored this, and was consequentially summoned to appear before the Diet of Worms (the small city on the Rhine where the latest Imperial Diet was being held in the presence of the Holy Roman Emperor, Charles V). Frederick III of Wittenberg had taken Luther under his protection, and he now used his influence as an elector to ensure that Luther was allowed safe passage both to and from the Diet.

At the Diet, Luther's arch-enemy Eck insisted upon Luther's heresy, backing up his argument with his own theological quotations, chapter and verse, from the Bible. Luther still refused to recant, causing Charles V to issue the Edict of Worms, which declared Luther to be an outlaw and a heretic. This made it a crime to meet Luther, to give him shelter or food or in any way assist him. He could even be murdered with impunity. Fortunately, Luther remained under the protection of Frederick III, and made his way under the guarantee of safe passage back towards Wittenberg.

As Luther passed along the highway through a forest, he was ambushed and kidnapped by masked robbers. But it soon became clear that these 'masked robbers' were in fact soldiers acting under the instructions of Frederick III, and Luther was whisked away to the impregnable clifftop Wartburg Castle.

Here Luther was given shelter, and during his isolation he set about the mammoth task of translating the New Testament into German. It was his intention to make the Bible and its teachings accessible to all – not just priests and scholars. When read out aloud it would even be understood by those who could not read. At the same time, he began issuing tracts condemning the Catholic interpretation of the Mass, the worship of relics as idolatry, and the act of confession to priests. He declared: 'Every Christian is a confessor.'

During this period of comparative safety and isolation, Luther began broadening and deepening his definition of faith and his explication of the Bible. He specifically identified the pope as the Antichrist mentioned in St Paul's Epistles to the Thessalonians.

Luther's opposition to the corrupt practices of the Church struck a chord with many throughout Germany, resulting in a more widespread undercurrent of political turmoil. In 1521 Wittenberg was visited by a company calling themselves the Zwickau Prophets. They preached the equality of all men and the imminent return of Christ, signifying the End of Times. Word was sent to Luther, begging him to return and resolve the increasingly volatile situation.

That year, Luther secretly made his way to Wittenberg. As he wrote to Frederick III, justifying this move: 'During my absence, Satan has entered my sheepfold, and committed ravages which I cannot repair by writing, but only by my personal presence and living word.' Luther immediately embarked upon a series of Lenten sermons, preaching the Christian values of love, compassion and charity, and warning his listeners to trust in God's will rather than join the outbreak of violence which seemed imminent. Luther's preaching prevented an uprising, and the Zwickau Prophets were chased out of the city. But this still left Luther in a difficult position. The people were vociferously demanding political reform. Meanwhile, on the other front, he remained under attack from the established Church.

In 1525 things came to a head with the outbreak of a widespread peasants' revolt, which soon spread through the central-southern German provinces of Swabia, Thuringia and Franconia. But Luther remained firmly against such uprisings: 'Therefore let everyone who can, smite, slay, and stab, secretly or openly, remembering that nothing can be more poisonous, hurtful, or devilish than a rebel... For baptism does not make men free in body and property, but in soul...'

When the peasant rebels found that Luther did not back them, there was consternation amongst their ranks. At Luther's bidding, many laid down their arms. Consequently the revolt was savagely put down. In 1526, he wrote: 'I, Martin Luther, have during the rebellion slain all the peasants, for it was I who ordered them to be struck dead.' Yet far from being an admission of guilt, this put the blame on the peasants for their blasphemy against Christ's teachings in the Gospels. Christ did not teach violence; on the contrary his message was that we should love one another with compassion.

The consequence of Luther's actions resulted in two gains for him – one public, one private. Publicly he was now trusted by the German rulers, who were sympathetic to his religious teachings against Rome. Privately, it led to a more radical step for Luther the priest. In 1523, Luther had facilitated the rescue of twelve nuns from a Cistercian convent under attack – secretly arranging for them to be smuggled out in herring barrels. One of these nuns was the twenty-six-year-old Katharina von Bora. The forty-one-year-old Luther became smitten with Katharina, writing in a letter to one of his followers: 'Suddenly, and while I was occupied with far different thoughts, the Lord has plunged me into marriage.'

Already a number of former priests belonging to religious orders had begun to marry. Luther had frequently condemned the vows of chastity as irrelevant to living the true life of Christ, but many of his followers were shocked when they heard news of his marriage. Previously, Luther had been so driven by his work that he had lived off scraps of simple food, and the neglect of his domestic circumstances had often resulted in squalor. As he himself admitted, his 'mildewed bed was not properly made for months at a time'.

Now, all this changed. The married couple moved into a monastery gifted to Luther by the new elector, John the Steadfast, who in 1525 had succeeded Frederick III upon his death at the age of sixty-two. Despite his protection of Luther, Frederick III had never formally renounced his Catholic faith, though it is claimed that he affirmed his adherence to Lutheranism on his deathbed. Whether or not this was so, Luther's safety was guaranteed: John the Steadfast had converted to Lutheranism some years before he became elector. From now on, although Luther continued to be driven by his work, he was surrounded by a happy domestic family life, and his wife Katharina would produce six children.

Meanwhile, the Reformation started by Luther was well underway, with his ideas beginning to take root all over the continent, especially in northern Europe. This was strongly facilitated by the use of Gutenberg's invention. New printing presses had long been established in Germany and Italy, and by the early 1500s these could be found from Stockholm to Sicily, from Lisbon to Vienna. The outpouring of pamphlets and religious works in the vernacular tongues was soon producing a groundswell in favour of Protestantism of various varieties.

The first state to adopt Protestantism as its official religion was Prussia in north-eastern Germany, where in 1525 Duke Albert declared the 'Evangelical Faith' to be the official state religion. By now Catholics were referring to the new religionists as 'Lutherans'. In the German lands, the Prussian example was soon followed by numerous imperial free cities and other more informal entities (i.e. smaller pockets of territory nominally part of the Holy Roman Empire). The larger, mainly northern and eastern, German states soon began following suit, with Hesse becoming Protestant in 1526, Saxony in the following year, and then Electoral Palatinate and Württemberg.

Meanwhile, there was a parallel development in the neighbouring Swiss Federation, with the Protestant teachings of Huldrych Zwingli holding sway in Zurich, the leading city of the Swiss Federation. Although Zwingli claimed that he had never read Luther's work, his teachings were remarkably similar (even including his own theses in the form of *Sixty-Seven Articles*). However, it soon became evident that Zwingli's teachings were more socially radical than those of Luther, who had drawn back from outright revolt.

In an attempt to form a united Protestant Alliance, Prince Philip of Hesse assembled the Colloquy of Marburg in 1529, with the various leaders gathering at his castle. However, instead of uniting the Protestant movements, this meeting only served to highlight their differences – especially concerning theological doctrine. The discussions eventually centred on the doctrine of Holy Mass, which derives from Christ's pronouncement at the Last Supper that the wine was his blood and the bread was his body. Luther insisted that this was literally the case at every Mass, a view strongly opposed by Zwingli. Luther became so enraged that he carved into the table Christ's pronouncement as it appeared in Latin in the Bible: *hoc est corpus meum* (This is my body). Zwingli persisted in his view that this was not literally the case, insisting that *est* merely meant 'signifies'.

The other leading Swiss theologian was John Calvin, whose influence soon prevailed in the Swiss city of Geneva. By the mid-1500s this had become the most influential city in the entire Protestant movement. 'Calvinist' missionaries from Switzerland and Germany soon spread over Europe, becoming responsible for the Huguenots in France, and the Calvinists in Scotland under the leadership of the fiery John Knox. Meanwhile, in Hungary, Lutheranism prevailed amongst the German-speaking minority, with Calvinism spreading amongst the ethnic Hungarians. In Scandinavia, Lutheranism became predominant, with German fishermen spreading it as far afield as Iceland.

In France, traditionally regarded – by both itself and the papacy – as the 'most Catholic' nation, the humanist Francis I initially chose to tolerate the growing Huguenot movement. On the other hand, both Italy and Spain would remain fervently committed to Catholicism. After the newly united Spain had driven the Moors (Muslims) from the Iberian peninsula in 1492, the Inquisition had been set up to root out any backsliding amongst the *conversos* (the Muslims and Jews who had remained and converted to Christianity). By the time Lutheran Protestantism arose in Germany, the Spanish Inquisition already had forty years of practice in enforcing Catholic orthodoxy and dealing with heresy. The consequent flood of gold arriving in Spain from the New World transformed the country into the leading Catholic power in Europe. In England, the arrival of Protestantism would soon provoke a unique political situation, involving both Spanish and Scottish claimants to the English throne.

Medieval Europe had been used to wars, whose outcome had done little to alter the status quo. But now the northern Renaissance was beginning to experience deeper divisions, which threatened to tear the continent apart.

CHAPTER 7

THE RISE OF ENGLAND

Eɴɢʟᴀɴᴅ's ɪɴᴠᴏʟᴠᴇᴍᴇɴᴛ ɪɴ ᴛʜɪꜱ potentially explosive situation would prove both symptomatic and unique. Such a paradoxical role can in large part be ascribed to the country's insular nature and the character of its rulers during this period. England may not have been central to the birth of the northern Renaissance, as Florence was to the birth of the Italian Renaissance, but its drastic transformation would be echoed by similarly drastic changes in countries from France to Spain, the Netherlands to Bohemia. For this reason it is worth outlining England's situation in a little more detail.

The foundation of England's role in the Other Renaissance was laid by Henry VII, who became king by defeating Richard III at the Battle of Bosworth Field in 1485. This put an end to the civil war known as the Wars of the Roses, which had dragged on intermittently for the previous quarter of a century. Henry VII was leader of the Red Rose House of Lancaster, and united the country by marrying Elizabeth of York, of the White Rose House of York. Henry VII thus established the House of Tudor as a royal dynasty. Having ascended the throne at thirty-eight, he would reign for twenty-four years, during which the ravaged medieval land was transformed into a country capable of playing a vital role in the northern Renaissance.

Henry VII put England on a firm economic footing by promoting the cross-Channel wool trade with the Netherlands, from whence this product was transported to such cities as Florence in northern Italy. Here the raw fleece was transformed into fine cloth. It was this trade, financed by the Medici Bank of Florence, which provided the financial stimulus for the Italian Renaissance.

Henry VII may have introduced a period of comparative peace and prosperity, but the English nobility would pay heavily for this in the form of the king's extensive and avaricious tax policy. This was administered by his chancellor, Archbishop Morton, with his notorious 'Morton's Fork', an early catch-22. Parsimonious noblemen who spent little were deemed to be saving much, and were taxed accordingly; whereas those who spent their money more freely evidently had enough to pay higher taxes... They couldn't win. Much of this income found its way into the royal coffers, and Henry VII's seventeenth-century biographer Francis Bacon would go so far as to claim that Henry VII was diligent about keeping detailed records of his personal finance down to the last half-penny. Records show that he also personally initialled every single page of the National Exchequer account ledgers.

During the early 1500s, Henry VII's health went into decline. He died of tuberculosis in 1509, aged just fifty-two, leaving his kingdom transformed – and the succession guaranteed to his eldest surviving son.

One of Henry VII's major legacies, whose significance was not fully realized at the time, was his sponsorship of voyages to the New World. In 1496, just four years after Columbus's rediscovery of America (and some thirty-eight years before Francis I of France despatched Jacques Cartier for the first time), Henry VII granted letters patent to a certain Giovanni Caboto (anglicized to John Cabot) giving him the right to explore 'whatsoever islands, countries, regions or provinces of heathens and infidels, in whatsoever part of the world placed, which before this time were unknown to all Christians'.

The forty-six-year-old John Cabot had probably been born in Genoa, but for reasons unknown he moved to the rival Venice to ply his trade as a merchant mariner, sailing to the eastern Mediterranean and Egypt. Later he even went so far as to claim that he had visited the Islamic holy city of Mecca, which was forbidden to all infidels (i.e. non-Muslims). However, this exaggeration appears on a par with his entries in the ledgers he presented to his Venetian sponsors after a Mediterranean voyage in 1488. That same year he fled the city, with debtors pursuing him from port to port as far as Spain. He finally managed to elude his pursuers and reached London in 1495, where his nautical abilities – rather than his ledger-keeping – were brought to the notice of Henry VII.

Cabot's first attempt to cross the Atlantic was in 1496, when he sailed from Bristol on a fifty-ton caravel with triangular lateen sails, manned by a crew of less than twenty men. A contemporary commentator reported: 'he went with one ship, his crew confused him, he was short of supplies and ran into bad weather, and he decided to turn back'. Subsequent voyages would prove more successful.

After setting sail from Bristol on 2 May 1597, Cabot first made landfall after fifty days, possibly at Cape Bonavista, Newfoundland – thus becoming the first European since the Vikings, some 500 years previously, to set foot on North American soil. Cabot planted a flag, claiming this new-found land for the King of England. He went on to map the entire rugged west coast of Newfoundland, covering over 600 miles. On an ensuing voyage he would travel with five ships laden with cheap merchandise, suggesting that he had previously made contact with the indigenous peoples and wished to establish trade. It was probably during this later trip that he left behind in America some friars, whose aim was to found a missionary station. (Archaeological findings supporting this have been discovered, but it is disputed whether these are the remains of a mission, or indeed whether Cabot was even responsible for landing the friars.)

In 1508–9, John's thirty-two-year-old son, Sebastian Cabot, undertook a somewhat more ambitious and successful expedition, travelling north past Labrador and into Hudson Bay. He then travelled south, as far as Chesapeake Bay. Sebastian Cabot traversed back and forth across as much as a thousand miles of the North American coastline.

Such voyages, and those undertaken later by Cartier, would result in two developments whose significance would remain for five centuries. First: the French contesting of the English claim to Canada, which prompted further English exploration and settlement to concentrate on the lower eastern seaboard of North America. And second: the division of the New World into a southern subcontinent retaining a southern European character, and a northern subcontinent which developed the northern European characteristics of its earliest colonists – the English, the French and later the Dutch. This division would prove crucial to the development of the New World, and remains indelible to this day.

However, it should be noted that the effects on the indigenous peoples of both subcontinents would be catastrophic. European colonization of the Americas was very much a one-way process. The arrival in Europe of chocolate, tobacco, potatoes and syphilis would hardly compensate for the near (or actual) extinction of peoples ranging from Inuit tribes in the frozen north to the fierce Aónikenk giants of Patagonia.*

All the developments which took place in England during the reign of Henry VII can with hindsight be viewed as preparing the ground for the glories of the English Renaissance to come. At the time, however, England was hardly regarded as one of the major players on the European scene. France, Spain and the Holy Roman Empire were indubitably the leading powers. Meanwhile, in the Italian city-states, such as Florence, Venice and Rome, the Renaissance was already at its height. The Renaissance in England can be said to have begun with the arrival in London of the Italian sculptor Pietro Torrigiano around 1510.

Pietro Torrigiano was born in Florence in 1472 – three years before the birth of Michelangelo, and when the twenty-year-old Leonardo da

---

* At the time the first European explorers reached the southern tip of South America, the average European was only just over five feet tall. It is unlikely that the Aónikenk were 'ten feet tall or even more' as contemporary European explorers claimed; even so, anyone even six or seven feet tall would have appeared as a Goliath to contemporary European eyes.

Vinci was just starting his career. Thus, Torrigiano grew up in Florence amidst the finest flowering of the Italian Renaissance. Having shown early talent, his education and artistic apprenticeship were sponsored by Lorenzo the Magnificent, the flamboyant Medici ruler of Florence at the pinnacle of its Renaissance splendour.

There is no doubting Torrigiano's talent, but along with this came an intense pride, ambition and a violent temperament. It was this potent mix that led to his downfall in Florence. One day during his apprenticeship, while drawing a copy of a fresco in a chapel alongside his close friend Michelangelo, an exchange of words appears to have ignited Torrigiano's hidden jealousy of his friend's superlative talent. What began as an argument quickly escalated into a fist fight, during the course of which Torrigiano punched Michelangelo so hard in the face that he broke his nose (a disfigurement which would remain noticeable for the rest of Michelangelo's life).

When Lorenzo the Magnificent heard what had happened he was furious, and Torrigiano was so frightened that he fled from Florence to Rome to escape Lorenzo's wrath. In Rome he was able to find work on the stucco decorations of the Borgia apartments. After this, his luck appears to have run out, and he ended up volunteering as a mercenary soldier for a succession of small city-state armies. Quite how he ended up in London in 1510 at the age of thirty-eight remains something of a mystery, but he seems to have arrived well recommended.

By now Henry VII had been succeeded by his seventeen-year-old son Henry VIII, a handsome young man of exceptional intellect, taste and athletic ability. Henry VIII commissioned Torrigiano to make a tomb for his recently deceased father. Torrigiano also created a superb terracotta bust of Henry VII, which was taken from the former king's death mask and was said to be an uncanny likeness. It depicts a serious long-faced man with an air of unmistakable self-possession. Torrigiano's tomb can still be seen in Westminster Abbey, and was judged by the influential twentieth-century art critic John Pope-Hennessy as 'the finest Renaissance tomb north of the Alps'.

Henry VIII had not expected to succeed to the throne, and only became heir apparent after the death of his elder brother, Arthur, in 1502.

Henry VII had become reclusive in his later years and passed on little advice to the future Henry VIII, who ascended to the throne in 1509 'untrained in the exacting art of kingship'.

By 1519, the Habsburg Charles V had succeeded to both the throne of Spain and then the imperial throne of the Holy Roman Empire, making him the most powerful figure in Europe. Four years earlier, the young Francis I ascended to the throne of France. Some years previously, England had once again been at war with France, but Francis I now wished to ally himself with England. He needed to counteract the threat from Charles V, whose Spanish territory threatened France from the south, while the Habsburg Netherlands and the German states threatened from the east.

Henry VIII was in favour of such an alliance, but did not wish it to be perceived that England occupied the lesser role in this partnership. A meeting between the two dashing young monarchs was arranged to seal the treaty in 1520 in northern France. Henry VIII was determined to impress Francis I, and the English camp mounted a dazzling display of feasts, jousting, entertainments and golden ornaments, along with an array of tents and attendants clad in cloth of gold (fabric woven with gold thread). Not to be outdone, Francis I mounted a similarly golden display, and this joint royal meeting became known as the Field of the Cloth of Gold.

Francis I and Henry VIII greeted one another amicably, and the meeting was a success. Thus Henry VIII ensured that from now on England would be viewed with respect amongst the body of European nations.

The following year, Henry VIII further advanced the cause of England in Europe by offering Pope Leo X English soldiers to fight for the Holy League against the Ottoman Turks, whose advance through the Balkans was beginning to threaten western Christendom. In confirmation of his loyalty, Henry VIII wrote a book dedicated to Leo X which contained an erudite defence of Christianity, stressing the duty of all European monarchs to rally to the pope's cause against the Ottomans, and also fiercely attacking the spread of the new Lutheran heresy which opposed the Catholic faith. Leo X was so impressed by Henry VIII's book that he bestowed upon the king the official title *Fidei Defensor* (Defender of the Faith).[*]

We now come to the vexed and intricate question of Henry VIII and his succession of six wives. From the outset, it was considered imperative that Henry VIII produce a legitimate male heir to ensure the Tudor succession. Within two months of him ascending to the throne, the teenage Henry VIII was married to the twenty-three-year-old Catherine of Aragon, daughter of the king and queen of Spain. Catherine had in fact previously been married to Henry VIII's elder brother, Arthur, until his death in 1502. This seemingly heartless business of passing on the previous heir's wife was for purely dynastic purposes, reinforcing the link between a comparatively unimportant England and powerful Spain, which was growing ever richer through the continuing import of South American gold.

As the years passed, Catherine suffered a succession of miscarriages and stillbirths, with but one daughter surviving. By 1525 it became clear that the forty-year-old Catherine would never produce a male heir. By now the thirty-four-year-old Henry VIII had become infatuated with one of Catherine's royal attendants, an intelligent and attractive twenty-three-year-old called Anne Boleyn. As it happened, Henry VIII had previously seduced, and then cast off, Anne's older sister, Mary. Anne was determined that this should not happen to her, and she informed Henry VIII that she would not submit to his desires unless they were married. Henry VIII appealed to Pope Clement VII to annul his marriage to Catherine on the grounds that, as she had been his brother's wife, the marriage was invalid. Clement VII refused this appeal, so Henry VIII decided to take matters into his own hands. He declared himself 'sole protector and Supreme Head of the Church and clergy of England', annulled his own marriage to Catherine of Aragon and married Anne Boleyn. England's break from Rome meant that it now became part of the increasing Protestant movement spreading throughout Europe.

---

[*] Despite ensuing history, this title has never been revoked, and the words *Fid Def* or the abbreviation *F D* (*Fidei Defensor*) still appear after the monarch's name on British coins.

Opposition to Henry VIII's declaration of an independent Church of England was widespread, both at home and abroad. In order to protect growing Protestant England from invasion, Henry VIII decided to build up the English navy. At the beginning of his reign, he had inherited a navy of just fifteen ships. Thirty years later, after establishing a naval dock at Portsmouth, England boasted a navy of forty-five ships manned by experienced sailors drawn from ports throughout England. This would prove an auspicious move. (England's investment in naval power would, over the coming centuries, enable the country to build up and defend the seaways of an overseas empire, as well as ensuring its ability to defend its island homeland from invasion by more powerful European rivals. Henry VIII's decision to place England's fortune in the hands of his Royal Navy was arguably the most defining moment in this island's history since the Norman invasion of 1066 and the civil rights granted by the Magna Carta of 1215.)

Meanwhile, at home Henry VIII faced Catholic opposition, especially amongst powerful and senior clergy. So, in 1536, in order to confirm the break with Rome and assert the independence of his new church, he ordered the dissolution of the monasteries. Such centres of papal power existed all over the country, attempting to influence local opinion against the king's declaration. Abbots, monks and nuns were driven from their abbeys, monasteries and convents, many of which were destroyed or left in ruins.

This put an end to the payment of papal dues, indulgences and the like, stemming a considerable outflow of money from England to Rome. Henry VIII also seized many of the monasteries' treasures. But there was more to this than plain robbery. In line with Protestants on the continent, Henry VIII disliked the traditional worship of holy relics, and exposed many of these as fraudulent. A typical example of this was the phial of Christ's blood which was held at Hailes Abbey in Gloucestershire. This was investigated and found to contain 'honey clarified and coloured with saffron'.

Henry VIII also encouraged the spread of humanist ideas, which had already begun to take root in England before he ascended to the throne. Erasmus had paid three extended visits to England between 1500 and 1514, residing in London and teaching at Oxford and Cambridge universities.

The court of Henry VIII attracted an array of creative talent that would initiate a process which in the years to come would make London a rival of Renaissance cities throughout northern Europe. In 1518 the king commissioned Torrigiano to create for him in Windsor Castle an original tomb of greater proportions and artistic splendour than that of his father. The paperwork containing a commission to 'Peter Torrisany' (as the Florentine had now become known) and indentures for various expenses involved has survived. But the building of the tomb was never completed, and the fate of most of its intended components remains something of a mystery.*

Torrigiano is known to have left England around this time and travelled to Spain. Here his violent temperament put an end to a promising career. He unwisely clashed with the Spanish Inquisition and ended up in prison in Seville, where he died in 1528, aged fifty-five.

Several other foreign artists would travel to ply their trade in London, attracted by the possibility of lucrative work at the English court. In the years to come, these would mainly be Flemish, in flight from the religious troubles across the Channel in their homeland.† At the same time, a number of Italian artists followed in the footsteps of Torrigiano, introducing the new mannerist style to England. But by far the most significant artist of the English Tudor period was the German Hans Holbein the Younger.

---

* Apart, that is, from the magnificent black marble sarcophagus, which now contains the body of Lord Nelson in the vault of St Paul's.

† By now the whole of Europe, including England, was very much beset by the increasingly complex Catholic–Protestant conflict. In 1547, Flanders would become a Catholic colony of Spain under the Holy Roman Emperor Charles V, though by that time many of its inhabitants were Protestants. Meanwhile, England's relations with Spain had deteriorated after Henry VIII's divorce of the Spanish Catherine of Aragon and the break of the English Church with Rome. Such was the troubled background to the emergent Renaissance in England (and indeed the whole of northern Europe). It is worth stressing once again how reminiscent this was of the divisions which marked the emergence of both Ancient Greece and the Italian Renaissance. Major advances in so many civilizations throughout history seem to have taken place against a background of similarly deep divisions and widespread conflict: an age of uncertainty giving birth to a profound transformation of all aspects of cultural life.

Holbein was born at Augsburg in southern Germany in 1497, where his father Hans Holbein the Elder ran a large studio. Hans the Younger learned his trade from his father, but at the age of eighteen he struck out on his own for Basel, some 200 miles away in Switzerland. In 1519 Holbein was admitted to the painters' guild in Basel, and that same year he married an older widow named Elsbeth Binzenstock, by whom he later had a son and a daughter. During the ensuing years Holbein travelled, seeking work in the Swiss city of Lucerne as well as at the court of Francis I, but with little success. His wife remained behind in Basel, running her former husband's tannery business.

Despite Holbein's setbacks, we have a clear indication of his ambition and self-belief during this period. Contrary to the rules of his guild forbidding such practice, Holbein began signing his name on his paintings. At some stage in his travels, Holbein's name came to the attention of Erasmus, and in 1523 he painted an exceptional portrait of the celebrated humanist philosopher, capturing the likeness of a cultivated scholarly figure.

At the age of twenty-nine, on the advice of Erasmus, Holbein travelled to England, where his realistic style and sheer talent were fully appreciated – to the extent that he was elevated to the post of King's Painter to Henry VIII. After the break with Rome, the taste for religious paintings all but died overnight in England. Unlike in Italy, classical scenes were not favoured, and in consequence portrait painting flourished. Holbein's often spare but always realistic talent was particularly suited to portraiture. His paintings are indubitably influenced by the northern Renaissance, but on occasion retain a lingering element of the medieval era. This lends his style an element of strength and originality. He also had an uncanny ability to catch the temperament of his sitter. His self-portrait of 1543 depicts a burly bearded figure with a distinctly medieval aspect: this is the image of a strong personality with little time for the exaggerated refinements which often grace the works of other Renaissance artists. His 1536 portrait of the forty-five-year-old Henry VIII conveys both the power and intelligence of his sitter, as well as seeming to hint at the paranoia and dissipation to come. With hindsight, we can see that this was the period when Henry VIII was on the cusp: the brilliant powerful monarch was on the point of descending into the bloated megalomaniac riven with suspicion.

Holbein also drew a plain but enigmatic sketch of Anne Boleyn, and painted a brooding portrait of Henry VIII's chancellor Sir Thomas More, but managed to elude any connection with their downfall and execution. However, his luck nearly ran out in 1539 when his patron Thomas Cromwell, Henry VIII's chief minister, became involved in finding Henry VIII a new wife.

Following the death of his third wife, Jane Seymour, the king found himself in pressing need of a fourth. The twenty-five-year-old Anne of Cleves was suggested by Cromwell, on the grounds that marriage to her would cement an alliance with her brother, Duke Wilhelm of Cleves, the most powerful Protestant ruler amongst the German states. Cromwell spoke highly of Anne's physical beauty, but when Holbein arrived in Germany to paint her portrait for Henry VIII's approval, he found himself faced with an undeniably plain young woman. Holbein did his best to steer a middle course, capturing her lack of glamour but somehow making her face merely demure when framed by her sumptuous crimson and gold robes and the rich intricacy of her lace headwear.

Henry VIII appeared satisfied with the portrait, yet when he actually saw Anne on her arrival in England in January 1540, he was more than disappointed, referring to her as a 'fat Flanders mare'. But it was too late to call things off without incurring the wrath of her powerful brother. The ceremony went ahead, though Henry VIII found himself unable to consummate the marriage owing to a 'very evil smell about her' as well as 'the looseness of her breasts and other tokens'.

After six months the marriage was annulled, apparently without rancour on either side, and Anne of Cleves went to live at Hever Castle in Kent, where she was referred to as 'the king's beloved sister'. Cromwell did not escape so lightly, and was executed for treason the following month. Holbein, sensing that he too stood in danger, made himself scarce. Indeed, many thought he had fled back to Basel, to the company of his neglected wife Elsbeth and their children. But it is now known that he hid out in a house near the church of St Andrew Undershaft – a district of London inhabited by many foreign residents, where his presence would not have been noticeable.

Despite this, Holbein did in fact return to Basel on a fairly regular basis during these years. By now Basel had become a leading centre of the Reformation, renowned for its printing presses, which disseminated the works of Luther. Even before leaving Basel, Holbein had created a woodcut of 'Luther the German Hercules', depicting a giant figure of Luther attacking Pope Leo X and battering other celebrated Catholic figures, such as Aristotle and the great medieval theologian Thomas Aquinas, with a spiked club. Yet despite the turn in Basel's fortunes, Holbein invariably found himself longing to return to the teeming alleyways and fine palaces of London, which was now beginning to rival Antwerp as a commercial hub, with a population of around 70,000.*

Holbein always returned alone to England, where he resumed his post as the King's Painter. In contrast to his master Henry VIII, most of Holbein's love life remains something of a mystery. It is known that he always stayed with Elsbeth on his return to Basel, and these visits resulted in at least one miscarriage. But by now he also had two young children in England, being looked after by a nurse. There is no mention of their mother(s?). As the King's Painter, with many important commissions on the side, Holbein was now making a good steady income. He appears to have regularly sent money back to Elsbeth, and also some fine clothes, which she wore. Though it is known that she sold the portrait he painted of her.

During Holbein's later years, his painting expanded its range. Following the English trend, he took up the fashionable genre of painting miniature portraits. In the other direction, his scope broadened to large portraits in more detailed settings. These were filled with iconic objects intended to convey or symbolize the character and activities of the sitter.

---

* Paris, with a population of over 150,000, was the leading city of Europe during this period.

Typical of such works is his portrait of Georg Geise, a merchant who lived in the Steelyard, the London headquarters of the Hanseatic League.* Geise is dressed in the sumptuous distinctive clothing which would have marked him out as both German and wealthy. It is known that Geise's father had been mayor of Danzig, and Copernicus may have been one of his cousins. Holbein's painting places Geise in the slightly cramped conditions of his working office, and depicts many of the implements of his trade. Behind him are some delicate weighing scales, a hanging seal stamp, and various letters tucked into the woodwork of the wall, as well as shelves containing ledgers and boxes. The desk before him is covered with a Turkish rug on which are standing goose-feather quills (pens), an inkstand and a sand shaker (to dry the ink), as well as sealing wax on which he would stamp his personal seal to close the letter. There is also a round tin, its lid half open to reveal the worn gold and silver coins inside. Most significant of all is a Venetian glass vase containing carnations. These flowers were symbolic of Geise's engagement, the occasion which had inspired the portrait.

All of this is conveyed with vividly realistic exactitude. Only on closer examination does the deeper artistic deception become apparent. The corner of the wooden wall behind Geise is not a right angle, and likewise the table does not quite form a rectangle. Also, the letter above Geise's head, affixed to the wall with sealing wax, is an optical illusion given the positioning of the ledger; and the nearby hanging scales are unbalanced. All this has led the modern art critic Stephanie Buck to comment: 'The apparently splendid world of the rich merchant Gisze [sic] is thus by no means as sound and stable as it appears at first.'

---

* As we have seen, the Hanseatic League was the powerful trade confederation which controlled international commerce through the Baltic region and the North Sea coast of Europe. Its residence in London was at the Steelyard (*Stalhof*), a separate walled community on the north bank of the Thames, by the mouth of the River Walbrook. The Steelyard contained warehouses, accommodation, banking facilities, its own guildhall and chapel, wine cellars, and even beer halls which served German beer and sausages. This enclosure had virtual diplomatic immunity. Its inhabitants did not have to pay local taxes, and were bound by the edicts of the Hanseatic League.

This leads us to the question: what precisely was Holbein attempting
to do here? Was he perhaps trying to hint at the hazards and decep-
tions of Geise's commercial activity? Several of the celebrated figures in
Holbein's earlier portraits had also occupied precarious positions, though
the younger Holbein did not presume to portray this. His art had not
yet developed this suggestive symbolism. And besides, such comment
on political figures, no matter how covert, would certainly have been
dangerous. It is difficult to decide whether the later Holbein was playing
tricks on the likes of Geise, or simply imbuing his art with secrets for
his own satisfaction. This is quintessentially a Renaissance problem.
Humanity was expanding its self-understanding, and the individual was
beginning to explore the limits of what he or she could do. The artist, as
representative of our imagination, was beginning to suggest that there
was more to the reality around us than we had previously been led to
believe. Holbein's painterly 'tricks' – of which he would go on to produce
several more – are emblematic of what can best be characterized as the
psychological expansion that was taking place during the Renaissance, in
both northern Europe and Italy. Human consciousness was opening up
to embrace the innovativeness of a new age.

Towards the end of Henry VIII's reign, having divorced two wives
and executed two others (including Anne Boleyn), the king became a
very different man from the dashing young scholar and athlete of his
youth. The young king who had been both a nimble dancer and an able
composer degenerated to a figure of gross ugliness. He became heavily
overweight, and his previously sharp intellect degenerated to the point
where he became a boorish, lascivious, ever-suspicious tyrant.

Holbein painted a portrait of Henry VIII in his later years that is
now lost, but well-documented copies of it remain. Here again, Holbein
employed his 'tricks', but this time they were tricks of necessity. In order
to mask the man that Henry VIII had become, Holbein painted him in an
aggressive pose and wearing a large protruding codpiece, his legs spread
apart, his hands on his hips, his body slightly angled to give it added
power. This portrait was intended as a strong propaganda statement. Yet
despite the expensive, ermine-collared, excessively broad-shouldered

half-cloak, it is possible to read the tell-tale signs beneath the veneer. There is no avoiding the king's bloated middle-aged girth or the fold of skin beneath the bearded chin, and even though Holbein has exaggerated the length of his white-stockinged legs, this is but a facsimile of the giant character it was intended to portray. Holbein the realist could only do so much to mask the reality which stood before him.

Henry VIII died in 1547 aged fifty-five, his eyes compressed to narrow slits by his bloated face. Eleven years later, the throne would be inherited by his twenty-five-year-old daughter (by Anne Boleyn), who would assume the title Elizabeth I.

CHAPTER 8

THE RISE AND RISE
OF THE FUGGERS

I N ITALY, PARTICULARLY IN Florence, it was the Medici banking family
who played a leading role in sponsoring the works of art, architecture
and learning that constituted the Italian Renaissance. No such family
dominated the northern Renaissance, which was sponsored by a range of
rulers and up-and-coming merchants.

However, there was one family who made even more money than the
Medici, and whose business interests extended far further. This was the
Fuggers of Augsburg, the dominant commercial family across much of
northern and eastern Europe throughout the Renaissance period. They
would also use their wealth to sponsor a number of cultural projects, even
if they were no match for the Medici in this aspect. Wealth and behind-
the-scenes influence seem to have been the Fuggers' main ambitions,
as distinct from the Medici's role as cultural benefactors and eventually
rulers of their home city. However, as supreme exemplars of the rising new
merchant class, the Fuggers illustrate the gradual shifting of social power
away from the landed royalty and powerful Church figures, towards a

newly emerging bourgeoisie. And increasingly, this middle class would also provide both the sponsors and the audience for the creative products of the northern Renaissance.

It is no accident that the Fuggers came from the same city as the Holbeins. From the outset, the Renaissance rode the new wave of prosperity that was transforming Europe. By the time of the northern Renaissance, Augsburg was the third city of Germany – after the Hanseatic port of Lübeck, and the Rhineland city of Cologne. (Cologne had a population of around 40,000, and Augsburg something over half of this figure.) Augsburg's great advantage was its geographical location. It lay on the banks of the River Lech, a tributary of the upper Danube, and stood at the foot of the Alps on the main trading route between Venice and Cologne. As such, it was one of the first cities in Germany to feel the influence of the Italian Renaissance. Augsburg's magnificent town hall (*Augsburger Rathaus*) and the impressive interior of the grand Fuggerhäuser family residence would be amongst the first examples of Renaissance architecture north of the Alps.

Augsburg's unique geographical position had long been recognized. The Romans had founded a city there in 15 BC, naming it after the Emperor Augustus and making it the capital of the important Roman province of Raetia. This territory covered much of Bavaria, Switzerland and the Tyrol; to the south it adjoined northern Italy, while to the north its border marked the limit of the Roman Empire in Germany. This was strategic territory – both in Roman times and through the following eras.

For centuries Augsburg was a free imperial city, ruled over by its own prince-bishop under the auspices of the Holy Roman Emperor. The town merchants were in the habit of setting out their stalls in the square near the prince-bishop's palace, but they became increasingly exasperated by their ruler's interfering edicts, which they felt were limiting their trade. In 1276, the merchants drove the prince-bishop out of Augsburg, and he took refuge in a castle some distance from the city. From then on, the city's de facto rulers were the main merchant families. Half a century later, when the Black Death swept through Europe, Augsburg somehow evaded this scourge, which some estimate killed up to a third of Europe's population. Augsburg's miraculous escape enabled its weavers to steal a march on its Italian competitors in such cities as Florence, and Augsburg's leading merchant families prospered accordingly.

The Fugger family came from the village of Graben, some twenty miles upstream of Augsburg on the Lech. In such villages it was tradition for each family to stick to their own trade: the millers, the foresters, the weavers, the smiths and so forth. Often they even took on the name of their trade – such as Müller, Forster, Weber (weaver), Schmidt. And for the most part they remained in their home location, where they could be sure of work.

The first member of the Fugger family to take the adventurous step of leaving to strike out on his own was Hans Fugger, a weaver by trade who set out for Augsburg in 1367. He had heard that the city was much in need of weavers, and he was not disappointed. No sooner had he entered through the gate in the city walls than he noticed that there was coloured bleached cloth hanging out to dry on racks, giving the narrow cobbled streets a colourful air of festivity. As required by law, Hans Fugger duly registered himself for residency and tax purposes at the city hall. The clerk evidently misheard Fugger's rural accent, for he registered him under the name of 'Fucker'.

Hans Fugger proved an industrious worker, and soon rose from being a mere weaver of cloth to becoming a dealer in cloth, with a premises and workers of his own. And it was Hans who instigated what would become a Fugger family tradition: he married into wealth. His bride was Clara Widolf, a daughter of the head of the weavers' guild. The weavers were not only wealthy, but wielded considerable power in the city. In 1378 they used their influence to depose a city mayor who had begun distributing taxpayers' money amongst the poor, and ensured that he was executed for this pernicious activity.

When Clara died, Hans married a woman called Elizabeth Gfatterman, who was also the daughter of the head of a guild. And it was here that the exceptional element appears to have entered the Fugger family. Where Hans had been merely industrious, his new wife was possessed of an exceptional business acumen. When Hans died in 1408,

Elizabeth took over the Fugger accounts, and began putting the business on a firm economic footing. It was she who now executed the deals, buying merchandise and contracting loans taken on by the company. This was no mean feat for a woman in an exclusively male commercial world, but Elizabeth was evidently possessed of the supreme confidence of a guild leader's daughter, and she ensured that the business established by her dead husband's sheer industry was directed in a more purposeful fashion. Determined to retain full control of the family business, she rejected all suitors. And the contemporary tax records reveal the extent of her commercial abilities. When Elizabeth took over the running of the family business in 1408, the Fuggers' 'property assessment' stood at 2,020 florins.* In the year following her death in 1441, the Fugger property was assessed at 7,260 florins – a massive increase of well over 200 per cent in just over thirty years. By the time of Elizabeth Fugger's death, she had become one of the city's leading taxpayers.

Elizabeth's son Jakob (now usually known as Jakob the Elder) was born in 1398, and from an early age Elizabeth had made sure that he was thoroughly educated in her business methods. He and his elder brother, Andreas, were apprenticed into the goldsmiths' guild before they inherited the business on the death of their mother. Together they ensured that the Fugger enterprise continued to flourish. Just eight years

---

* The gold florin, *fiorino d'oro*, was first minted in Florence in 1252 and quickly gained Europe-wide recognition as a standard currency owing to its undeviating gold content. Each coin was guaranteed to contain 54 grains of 'fine' gold. (At present, a grain of 100 per cent gold is worth just under $4.) The word 'grain' as a measure of fine metal derives from the Bronze Age, where it was assessed as the mass of a single ideal grain of wheat or barley. Unlike the florin, locally minted currencies in other cities were liable to have their precious metal content surreptitiously downgraded during times of economic difficulty. As for assessing the modern equivalent-worth of a florin, this is all but impossible as prices for houses, livestock, food, cloth, a labourer's wage and so forth have fluctuated wildly in uncoordinated fashion over the centuries. Suffice to say that in Augsburg during this period a middling merchant's family townhouse with servants could probably have been maintained for around 200 florins a year. And an artisanal worker would have been lucky to earn a tenth of this sum.

after Elizabeth's death the business was worth 10,800 florins, making it the fifth biggest in the city. Although younger than Andreas, Jakob the Elder appears to have been the more talented of the two, and there is evidence that he began expanding the business abroad, with some lengthy periods of absence from the city residents' register. Evidence for both his business acumen and his travels can be gleaned from the fact that his name appeared on an edict issued by the town council in 1442. This followed a warning from Duke Otto of Bavaria that merchants should cease from bypassing the road leading through his territory so that they could avoid paying tolls.

The surviving portrait of Jakob the Elder depicts an undeniably ugly man with a suspicious, miserly sneer: the embodiment of a scrooge-like character. How much this cartoonish aspect is due to the artist, and how much of this may be ascribed to the prevailing medieval style, is difficult to discern. However, despite his unprepossessing appearance, Jakob the Elder was able to continue the family tradition of marrying into wealth. In 1440 he wed Barbara Bäsinger, the daughter of local mint-keeper Franz Bäsinger.

Like many of Europe's leading commercial cities, Augsburg minted its own currency, and Franz Bäsinger had made a fortune melting down imported silver ingots and casting them into coins that were then stamped with the city's coat of arms, which depicted a pine cone.* However, within four months of Jakob's marriage it came to light that his father-in-law was a sham. His apparent wealth had been accumulated by covertly debasing the city's silver currency. This was a serious offence, undermining faith in both Augsburg's currency and the reputation of the city itself. Such a charge might even have resulted in Bäsinger's execution had his son-in-law not stepped in. Jakob the Elder volunteered to pay off all the debts incurred by Bäsinger's criminal activities, and the Augsburg authorities agreed to this generous offer. Whereupon Franz Bäsinger fled

---

* In later years the silver for these coins would come from the mines at Joachimsthaler in Bohemia, which provided silver for coins all over Germany and Austria. Such currency became known as Joachimsthalers, which became shortened to thalers – the origin of the word 'dollar'.

the city in disgrace – though he still managed to remain in the same business, eventually becoming master of the mint in the small Tyrolean city of Schwaz, across the Alps in Austria.

Financial expertise may have been brought into the Fugger family by women like Elizabeth Gfatterman, but in the view of some, Franz Bäsinger may have contributed a certain element of his own to later generations. Namely, the willingness to take risks and cut corners when necessary – a useful ability for any ambitious businessman.

By now the Fuggers had moved into a fine three-storey house which stood on the corner opposite the hall of the weavers' guild. On one side of the house was the commercial heart of the city, and on the other was the Jewish quarter, with a street called Jew Hill running down to a canal. According to the Fugger biographer Greg Steinmetz: 'The Romans had dug canals and lined them with wooden beams. At night, when all was quiet, one could hear water running through.' These canals had once formed a moat around the city walls, and the fact that one could hear the tinkling flow of water in the silence of the night gives an indication of how close even a city such as Augsburg remained to the surrounding countryside during this period. From the woodland and fields across the River Lech, one would have heard the owls and other night birds calling through the darkness. Otherwise the silence of the streets at night would only have been broken by the lantern-bearing nightwatchman calling out the hours as he passed on his rounds. And at dawn the bell would have rung out from the Perlachturm, the tenth-century former watchtower rising 200 feet above the city rooftops, its toll heralding the opening of the city gates and the beginning of a new day.

In 1455, the Fugger business was divided in two, with Andreas and Jakob agreeing to go their different ways. According to the records, Andreas took with him 4,440 florins, while Jakob kept 5,697 florins – a fair indication of their differing talents. Andreas died two years later, leaving a modest legacy. Jakob the Elder, on the other hand, continued to flourish, branching out into the gold trade as the scope of the Fugger business spread ever wider, beyond the city, with dealings in places ranging from Venice to Cologne.

Jakob the Elder seems to have been fortunate in that his wife, Barbara, proved as able as his mother had been when it came to looking after the company affairs, especially when he was away on his travels. Even more auspicious was the fact that his father's two wives had come from leading families in Augsburg. By the time Jakob was in his sixties, his wealth and the family's connections by marriage meant that he was permitted entry to the *Herrentrinkstube* (Gentlemen's Drinking Hall). This was an exclusive club that formed the 'social centre of gravity of the economic and political elite'. The Fuggers had arrived, and were generally recognized as a new addition to the dozen or so patrician families in Augsburg. This was no mean feat in such a rich trading city.

Jakob the Elder died in 1469, at the age of seventy-one. He had always driven himself hard, and was renowned for his industry, but he seems to have found time to father eleven children with his wife. Like her mother-in-law Elizabeth, Barbara took over the running of the family business after the death of her husband. She too proved an exceptionally astute businesswoman, and her guidance of the Fugger family enterprise ensured continued success and profits, until she gradually delegated the running of the company to her sons.

It was fortunate that the crabbish and miserly-looking Jakob the Elder proved such a productive father, for it was his highly talented tenth child – later to become known as Jakob the Rich – who eventually took over the reins of the family business. With the aid of two of his older brothers, Ulrich and Georg, Jakob the Rich would guide the Fugger family business from provincial riches to a Europe-wide industrial concern, the likes of which has not been seen before or since.

An indication of Jakob the Rich's prodigious abilities can be seen from the fact that in 1473, at the age of fourteen, his older brothers despatched him to Venice to represent the family business. At the time, Venice was the major trading city in Europe. Its galleys ventured north and east as far afield as Crimea and the Levant – terminals of the Silk Routes from China – bringing back silk and spices. Meanwhile, other galleys travelled west, trading with the silver mines of southern Spain, the Cornish tin mines in England, as well as Flemish and English wool on the Bruges market.

Yet the juvenile Jakob the Rich would have had more to contend with than Venetian traders being dismissive of his youth. For some decades now Germans had been distrusted in Venice. After taking out loans from local bankers, some unscrupulous Germans had rapidly departed the city and made their way back across the Brenner Pass, disappearing into northern Europe. Indeed, such was the bad name attached to German traders that the Medici Bank – the main banking enterprise in Europe at the time – had expressly forbidden the managers of its Venetian branch from conducting any business involving Germans. Despite this edict, one trusted senior manager of the bank in Venice, Neri Tornaquinci, had been tempted into giving a large high-interest loan to a German merchant, who promptly absconded. For months Tornaquinci frantically juggled the books in an attempt to disguise his loss, until eventually his misdeed was detected and he lost everything – his prestigious position, his house, and any prospect of being trusted ever again by fellow bankers.

Despite such German misdemeanours, the young Jakob the Rich was soon heavily involved in Venetian trade. He seems to have charmed his way in with the Italians, adapting his name to Jacobo and quickly picking up a wide knowledge of Italian. Most importantly, it was in Venice that Jakob the Rich learned the art of banking.

The Italians had invented banking in Europe during the previous century.* Indeed, the very word 'bank' comes from the Italian *banco*, meaning 'bench', where the first bankers set up their counters on the street. *Credito* and *debito* are also Italian words. These were the terms at the top of the columns in the account books, which by the time Jakob the Rich arrived in Venice featured a new, highly efficient mode of recording transactions: double-entry bookkeeping, whose methods would first be set down in writing by the Italian monk and mathematician Luca Pacioli in 1494.

---

* Earlier forms of banking had of course evolved elsewhere, especially in China, India and Judea (where the Bible records Christ driving the 'usurers' from the Temple in Jerusalem).

However, long before Pacioli's public instruction manual, any skilled Italian banker worth the name had taken to using this method in his *libro segreto* (secret account book). It was simple, but highly advantageous. Essentially, it involved two columns. The left-hand column recorded debit, and the right-hand figures recorded credit. Each transaction was entered in both columns. Thus a loan of ten florins to a customer was recorded in the debit column as an outgoing sum, and also in the credit column as a potential asset. Income against expenses was similarly recorded in both columns. By adding up both columns – literally 'balancing the books' – the bank's total assets and liabilities could quickly be read. Similarly, 'mistakes' could easily be detected.

Young Jakob the Rich quickly grasped this sophisticated accounting method. Meanwhile, back in Germany many traders were still simply jotting down numbers on scraps of paper, with little means of knowing, from moment to moment, how great were their total assets – or losses.

However, while Jakob the Rich was making his way in the banking world of Venice, Ulrich and Georg made a connection that would prove even more auspicious for the Fugger family business. In 1473, Frederick III passed through Augsburg on a diplomatic mission to the Duke of Burgundy. Frederick III was a figure of Europe-wide status. He was the King of Germany and the Duke of Austria, as well as being the first of the Habsburg family to become Holy Roman Emperor, a post whose fluctuating fortunes dated back to Charlemagne in the eighth century.

The Habsburg family originated from Switzerland, where in the eleventh century they had built a castle called Habsburg (literally 'Castle of the Hawks'). Four centuries on, Frederick III dreamed of uniting the far-flung Habsburg 'heritage lands' and restoring the Holy Roman Empire as a force to be reckoned with throughout Europe. But such vast ambitions seemed well beyond the scope of Frederick III, who was notorious for his indolence and indecisiveness. And on top of this, he was also notorious for running up debts and refusing to pay his bills.

When Frederick III arrived in Augsburg, a city which as we have seen was known far and wide for its weaving industry, he approached the local merchants. He needed to impress the Duke of Burgundy, and the uniforms of his somewhat frayed, underpaid entourage were hardly a presentable sight. One by one the merchants of Augsburg made their excuses and slipped out of the city. Ulrich Fugger, on the other hand, saw this as his opportunity. Within no time the emperor and his entourage were measured up and presented with outfits of the finest cloth and silk fabrics the Fugger workshops could provide. Inevitably, no payment was forthcoming, but the grateful Frederick III bestowed upon Ulrich Fugger a coat of arms featuring a lily. This branch of the family was now permitted to use the upper-class title Fugger von der Lilie (of the lily).

While Ulrich and Georg extended the Fugger business throughout Germany, Jakob the Rich remained in Venice. His banking expertise was soon put to good use providing loans to independent silver mine operators in the Salzburg region of Austria. These small concerns were constantly in need of capital to develop and extend their mines. Instead of payment for the loans, Jakob took the novel step of taking a partnership in the mines. Within a few years he had a controlling interest and had cornered the market, insisting that the miners sell their silver directly to him rather than deal through intermediaries.

On another front, Jakob the Rich extended his business interests to Rome, where he began taking on accounts for the Curia (the papal government). Here the Medici had once held sway, but by now the Medici Bank was going into decline as the family shifted its interest from banking to ruling the Republic of Florence and placing their members in senior clerical positions. By this time the Medici ruler known as Lorenzo the Magnificent had taken over Florence. The family would now use its influence with the popes to get two of their younger members appointed as cardinals, each of whom would go on to be elected as pope.

When Jakob the Rich eventually returned to Augsburg in 1487, his extreme wealth and influence meant that he became the de facto head of the family business. The Medici had taken over as rulers of Florence out of necessity, to prevent rival families from stripping them of their wealth with punitive taxes or by more violent means. The Fuggers certainly used their wealth to influence the city council of Augsburg, but they had no wish to emulate the Medici and establish themselves as rulers – even

Above: Part of the *Ghent Altarpiece* by Jan and Hubert van Eyck and others, 1420s.

Right: *The Arnolfini Portrait* by Jan Van Eyck, 1434.

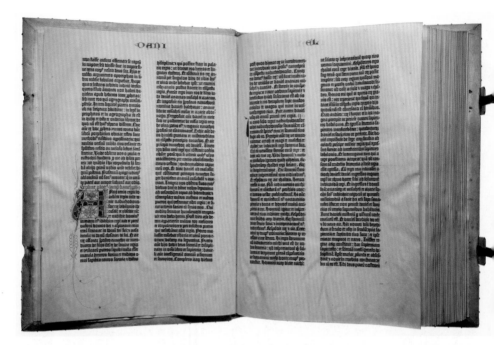

A copy of the Gutenberg Bible, mid-fifteenth century.

A view of the magic double-helix staircase at the Château de Chambord in the Loire Valley, built from a design by Leonardo da Vinci.

Above: The Protestant
reformers with Martin
Luther (*front left*), after
a painting by Cranach
from 1558.

Right: Pietro Torrigiano's
terracotta bust of Henry
VII, c. 1510.

Above: *The Field of the Cloth of Gold*, c. 1545.

Left: Portrait of François I by
Jean Clouet, c. 1530.

Right: Henry VIII as depicted by Hans Holbein the Younger, 1540.

Above: Portrait of Georg Giese by Hans Holbein the Younger.

Left: Albrecht Dürer's portrait of Jakob Fugger, who was known as 'The Rich', 1518.

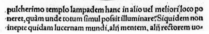

Above left: Copernicus's
heliocentric diagram of
the universe, from *De
Revolutionibus Orbium
Coelestium*, 1543.

Above right: Nicolaus
Copernicus.

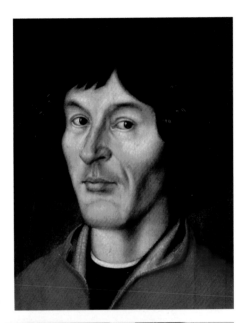

Right: Portrait of
Erasmus by Hans
Holbein the Younger,
1523.

Albrecht Dürer's *Melencholia* I, 1514.

when their immense wealth stirred a natural envy amongst the poorer citizens. For a start, their family and business interests were scattered throughout Europe, and taking power in Augsburg would be largely irrelevant to their commercial activities. A succession of loans to Holy Roman Emperors also ensured their protection.

Although their riches were resented by many, there remained those who were grateful to them – especially amongst the poor. An indication of the Fuggers' attitude towards their fellow citizens can be seen in the fact that they built the Fuggerei. This was a walled district in the city containing streets of well-constructed housing for the poor; initially this included fifty-two family dwellings, but it would soon expand. The Fuggerei still stands to this day, and sociologists claim it as the earliest social housing project in the world. Here was a unique aspect of the northern Renaissance which was well ahead of its time.

When the twenty-eight-year-old Jakob the Rich moved back to Augsburg he introduced many aspects of the Italian Renaissance to the city, and thence to southern Germany. The prime example of this can be seen in the Fuggerhäuser, a vast row of linked buildings which extended along the main Via Claudia (now Maximilianstraße). When it was first constructed, the façade of this building contained a mural by the local artist Thomas Burgkmair, who was related by marriage to the Holbein family. His characteristic portraits – especially one of Emperor Frederick III – were undoubtedly influenced by the Renaissance artists of Italy, which Burgkmair may well have visited. They also bear a certain resemblance to those of his fellow Augsburger and contemporary, Holbein the Younger.

The long façade of the five-storey Fuggerhäuser hides delightful inner gardens which originally contained many Renaissance elements, including pillars and water features. These and the interior decor of the residential quarters were the work of the Flemish mannerist Friedrich Sustris, who was actually born while his father was in Venice working on the decor of the house where Jakob the Rich had taken up residence during the 1480s. The huge interior of the Fuggerhäuser in Augsburg contained the family home, offices, and large warehouses. This was a palace fit for a king, and in time Jakob the Rich would indeed entertain royalty here, most notably the Holy Roman Emperor Charles V, who was also King of Spain.

For some time after his return to Augsburg, Jakob the Rich maintained a mistress by the name of Metchtild Belz, by whom he had a daughter. But he showed no inclination to marry Metchtild, later seeing that she married a local doctor. Jakob quietly made sure that his daughter was well brought up and even educated. He would then arrange for her to marry Gregor Lamparter, the rector of the University of Tübingen, the oldest in Germany. Later he would secure for Lamparter a post as counsellor to the Holy Roman Emperor Maximilian I (the son of his old friend Frederick III), whose succession had been enabled with the aid of Fugger money. Well aware that Maximilian I owed a fortune, much of it to the Fugger family, Jakob even paid Lamparter a generous 8,000 florins a year out of his own pocket.

Not until Jakob the Rich was thirty-nine would he finally decide to get married. Following in the family tradition, he took as his wife a daughter of one of the city's leading families – the eighteen-year-old Sybille Artzt, a blonde and gregarious young woman. However, in the marriage portrait, painted by Burgkmair, neither the bride nor the groom appear in any way happy. They are standing apart, though Jacob's hand can be seen reaching up under her elbow.

Jakob had in mind an heir who could take over his business, but Sybille remained childless. He made a habit of giving her pieces of exceptionally fine jewellery when he returned from his business trips. Amongst these was a ring containing one of the world's largest diamonds, which would be sold on to King Edward III of England. (Later it would appear in a portrait of Elizabeth I.) Regardless of such lavish gifts, Jakob the Rich's marriage remained childless, and it is known that Sybille took a lover, whom she would go on to marry a month or so after Jakob died.

By the early 1500s, the Fugger empire – with Jakob at the helm – reached the length and breadth of Europe. An indication of their hold on the market can be seen from the fact that he tried, and for a short time was successful, in monopolizing the entire European copper market.

In 1500, Jakob the Rich had begun lending large sums to the extravagant Leo X, the first Medici pope. These loans helped fund the building of the new St Peter's Basilica, as well as the interior decoration of the Sistine Chapel, in Rome. (The Italians may have given their artistry, architecture and design to this aspect of the southern Renaissance, but it was at least in part funded by the Fuggers of the northern Renaissance.) Later, Jakob the Rich would assist in Leo X's sale of indulgences, incurring the wrath of Martin Luther.* Around the same time, Jakob the Rich was able to provide large loans to a succession of Holy Roman Emperors, culminating in the vast sum of 543,585 florins – which he loaned to Charles V to 'influence' his election as Holy Roman Emperor.

An indication of the relationship between Jakob the Rich and Charles V can be gauged from a contemporary painting of Charles V as a guest at Jakob the Rich's dinner table, where his host is demonstrating his generosity by tossing into the fire the emperor's signed documents relating to debts said to have totalled some 500,000 guilders (approximately 250,000 florins). In a reciprocal gesture, Charles V granted Jakob the Rich the concession to the fabled silver mines of Seville and Guadalcanal.

So who was this Fugger with the Midas touch, the man some claim to have been the richest private citizen in history? There is a portrait of Jakob the Rich by Albrecht Dürer dating from 1518, when the fifty-nine-year-old Fugger was at the height of his powers. The painting depicts a man with no outward marks of his excessive wealth, set against a plain background. He has hard lean features, their austerity enforced by his thin lips. There are no smile lines in his face, and his intense stare is directed beyond the scope of the canvas. Yet with his lack of facial hair, and his head cropped under his plain cap, his features present a surprisingly contemporary aspect. Dressed in a plain modern suit, this

---

* When Augsburg officially became a Protestant city in 1555, the rights of the Catholic minority would still be represented on the city's ruling council. The rich and powerful Fuggers would remain Catholic, retaining their close links with the Holy Roman Emperor and the Habsburgs. However, Augsburg's transformation was not without its disturbances. At one stage an angry mob of around 1,300 poor working men (just over 10 per cent of the population at the time) marched on the city hall to vent their anger at Jakob Fugger, claiming that 'they lived on oats and he ate pheasant, that he wore furs and they wore rags'.

could be the face of a contemporary banker, or a mogul such as Getty or Rockefeller.

On top of his banking, mining, financing and other mercantile interests stretching from Hungary to Spain to Sweden, Jakob Fugger would also enter the overseas trade. His commercial might was such that he even sought to break the Hanseatic League's hold over the Baltic. With the powerful backing of Pope Leo X and the Holy Roman Emperor Maximilian I (his two largest debtors), Jakob tried to take over the rich Bergslagen mining region of northern Sweden, but was thwarted when the Hanseatic League placed the powerful Protestant Gustav Vasa on the Swedish throne.

Even more ambitious was his participation in a joint venture with other German merchants to finance a fleet of twenty-two Portuguese galleons that sailed for India in 1505. However, income from this large expedition was severely diluted when it returned the following year and King Manuel I of Portugal claimed a third of the profits. Later, Jakob the Rich would single-handedly finance an expedition to the Maluku Islands, the 'spice islands' of the East Indies (now part of Indonesia). Following the success of this expedition, King Manuel I declared the spice trade a monopoly of the Crown of Portugal. Had this not been the case, it is possible that the spice-rich archipelago between Borneo and New Guinea would have become the founding colony of a German overseas empire.

Recent research has also suggested that Fugger may have been the majority investor (through Charles V) in the expedition led by the explorer Ferdinand Magellan, which embarked in 1519 westward around Cape Horn, across the Pacific, and returned to Europe in 1522, having completed the first circumnavigation of the globe.

Intriguingly, the only other family remotely comparable to the Fuggers during this period was the Welsers, who also came from Augsburg and specialized in banking, becoming merchants and venturing into the overseas trade – initially under the auspices of Spain before branching out on their own. Yet unlike the Fuggers they would achieve some success in these last enterprises, being granted land rights in the New World by Charles V on payment of some of his debts. In this way the Welsers became owners and rulers of an entire colony on the northern coast of South America. Because the indigenous inhabitants lived in fishing villages built on stilts above the water, the Welsers named their colony Klein-Venedig (Little Venice). Branching out from this colony, the Welsers established sugar plantations at Santo Domingo on the large Caribbean island of Hispaniola (now divided between Haiti and the Dominican Republic). Sugar was the new gold in northern Europe, where the main source of sweeteners had previously been honey. In order to work these plantations, the Welsers would enter the slave trade.

Like Jakob Fugger's potential trading station in India, and his prospective ownership of the Maluku Islands, Klein-Venedig could have been the founding colony of a German overseas empire. However, the Welsers proved inept administrators of their distant colony, which soon succumbed to an outbreak of civil disorder. In the end Charles V despatched an armed Spanish flotilla to take back control. Klein-Venedig was thus transformed into the Spanish colony of Venezuela (Spanish for 'Little Venice').

The failure of the Fuggers and the Welsers to found overseas colonies poses one of the great might-have-beens of history. The effect of German trading posts – in India and the East Indies, in South America and the Caribbean – and the consequent spread of a German empire across the globe, is all but impossible to gauge. Yet one thing is undeniable: it would certainly have had some effect, indeed probably a major effect. The British, French, Portuguese, Dutch and Spanish empires would not have developed as they did, had they been forced to compete against rich and determined Germans.

Apart from almost establishing a German overseas empire, the Welsers – and later members of the Fugger family – used their immense wealth to play an increasing role in sponsoring the northern European Renaissance. As indicated earlier, this was not done directly, as with the Medici in Italy. The Fuggers were comparatively minor patrons of the arts. But the entire merchant class which benefitted from the Fuggers' success, rising on the tide of commercial enterprise led by the Fuggers and their like, would transform northern Europe – especially in cities such as Bruges, and later Antwerp, Ghent and many smaller German city-states.

As with the Medici bankers in Italy, such wealth was part of the necessary capital which paid for the artists, architects, thinkers, writers and scientists who provided the intellectual framework for another Renaissance, the northern Renaissance, which in turn would give birth to the modern European age. Meanwhile, by comparison Italy and the southern Renaissance had begun to languish. Papal power was diminished by the Reformation. Venice was reduced to a comparative backwater, its trade by way of the Silk Routes superseded by overseas trade around the Cape of Good Hope. And the creative impetus of Florence inspired by the Medici bankers was gradually declining as the Medici transformed themselves from imaginative patrons into a ruling aristocracy.

Following Luther's 1517 proclamation, the princes and rulers of many small German states had switched to Protestantism – often for purely mercenary reasons since, as Protestants, they no longer had to pay taxes to Rome. The slogan of Luther's followers – 'German money for a German church' – had stirred up great enthusiasm in such states. At the same time it also raised expectations amongst many of the peasants and serfs, who had endured little more than subsistence living for well over a century.*

Luther's sermons calling on his faithful flock to resist the power and iniquity of Rome had led many of the poor to believe that he held their interests at heart. In fact, as already indicated, Luther was more concerned with the proper way to live a Christian life, and humanity's relationship with God, than he was with social justice. When a peasants' revolt broke out in 1524, Luther was quick to condemn the outbreak of violence and

---

* Following the Black Death of the 1320s, labour had been in short supply. Employers who wished to retain their peasants, miners, serfs and servants had been forced to grant more favourable conditions, or their employees were liable to seek higher recompense elsewhere. Therefore, for a few decades many of the lower orders had been able to rise above mere subsistence living. Over the generations, the situation reverted to the previous harsh conditions. But there remained, in the folk imagination, the memory of an almost legendary golden era when times had not been so hard and they had enjoyed respect from their employers.

lawlessness as un-Christian behaviour. Despite this, by early 1525 the revolt had spread across a large swathe of southern Germany and into Switzerland and Austria, even reaching Hungary. Angry bands of peasants armed with scythes and makeshift pikes had formed anarchic armies, roaming the countryside and looting all they could lay their hands on. When they attacked settlements, the peasant leaders ransacked the homes of the rich, seeking out silver and valuables, while the rest piled into the kitchens and cellars, gorging themselves and guzzling down wine. According to a contemporary eyewitness, '[a] more drunken, more full-bellied, more helpless folk, one had hardly seen'. It was difficult to decide whether this was 'a carnival's jest or a war... and whether a peasants-war [or] a wine war'. Yet there was no mistaking the rape, mayhem and murders, to say nothing of the burned-down residences it left in its wake.

Luther desperately continued to appeal for peace and order. But his words fell on deaf ears. The people now had a new leader in the form of the theologian Thomas Müntzer, whose radical preaching was as implacably opposed to Luther as it was to the Catholic Church: 'If someone wants to properly reform Christendom, one must throw away the profiteering evildoers.' More than anything, Müntzer was out to get Jakob Fugger. As Fugger's biographer Steinmetz succinctly put it: 'The contrast between Fugger and Müntzer could not have been greater. One was the archcapitalist and the other the archcommunist.'

Such remarks may appear anachronistic. After all, it would be more than three centuries before Karl Marx wrote his *Communist Manifesto*. Yet here was Müntzer preaching, 'All things are to be held in common, and distribution should be to each according to his need' – the very words of Marx himself! Meanwhile, capitalism may have been in its infancy, but as we have seen Fugger could be quite the equal of any nineteenth-century American robber-baron when he wished to gain a monopoly and impose his will upon the market. Steinmetz reckons that Jakob the Rich would come to 'own 2.2% of all Europe's economic output'.* So perhaps

---

* By comparison, John D. Rockefeller, the richest American of all time, owned 1.5 per cent of US GDP in 1937.

it's not too extravagant to claim that communism and capitalism, as we know them, were at the very least nurtured by the northern Renaissance.*

During the peasants' revolt, Jakob the Rich was able to take refuge in the Fuggerhäuser, which was guarded by hired mercenaries. Augsburg would experience only passing turmoil, existing as it did at the very edge of the main region initially affected. Even so, it was enough to panic Jakob Fugger, who now saw all Protestants as his enemy – writing in a letter to his Polish agent in Kraków: 'The new priests are telling the people to disobey the law... I don't know what is going to happen.'

He was by this time sixty-six, and severely ill. Contemporary descriptions of a swelling in his stomach suggest that he may have had a tumour. However, he refused to let any doctor operate on him. Some fifteen years earlier his oldest brother, Ulrich, had died after an operation. Medicine was only just beginning to make advances out of the medieval era, but with figures like Paracelsus emerging, many had little trust in medicine as a science. This was especially the case with surgeons, who often conducted their operations armed with primitive devices that were not sterilized. Overcome with pain and weakness, Jakob the Rich took to his bed. On 30 December 1525, he died in the Fuggerhäuser at Augsburg.

In keeping with the double-entry bookkeeping style which he had so favoured, his account books revealed that his total assets came to 3,000,058 guilders. His liabilities were assessed at 867,797 guilders. Jakob the Rich died without direct descendants. On learning of his death, his wife Sybille absconded with as much jewellery as she could gather. Seven weeks later she would marry her lover and convert to Protestantism.

The Fugger family business was inherited by Jakob's cousin Anton, who had the good sense to change little and made sure that the business continued as before. Building on the foundations laid by his predecessor, Anton would double the firm's assets by the time of his retirement in 1546 – benefitting in part from the expanding slave trade. The family business

---

* Support for this claim can be seen in the fact that, during the Cold War, a West German stamp featured Jakob Fugger. By contrast, in communist East Germany, Thomas Müntzer appeared on a five-mark note.

was now taken over by Anton's sons. After the death of Charles V in 1556, the Fuggers would finance the election of his successor, Ferdinand I, as Holy Roman Emperor. For this the family would be granted the freedom to colonize the western coast of South America, from Chincha in Peru as far south as the Straits of Magellan. However, on seeing the large financial losses accumulated by the Welser family in Klein-Venedig, the Fuggers decided against taking up this option and the prospect of a German colony occupying 3,000 miles of the western South American coastline was let slip. In the opinion of the Fugger family biographer Mark Häberlein: 'Anton Fugger's abandonment of this undertaking may well have been a wise decision.' On the other hand, this caution extinguished any real hope of establishing a competitive German overseas empire.

CHAPTER 9

COPERNICUS

PERHAPS THE GREATEST RENAISSANCE, in its literal form of the rebirth of ancient learning, took place in the field of astronomy. During the third century BC, the Ancient Greek Aristarchus of Samos was a mathematician in the greatest centre of learning in the ancient world – namely Alexandria, in northern Egypt. His only surviving work is *On the Sizes and Distances of the Sun and Moon*, which assumes a heliocentric world view. And his contemporary, the supreme mathematician Archimedes, elaborated on Aristarchus's ideas as they appeared in his lost works: 'His hypotheses are that the fixed stars and the sun remain unmoved, that the earth revolves about the sun on the circumference of a circle, the sun lying in the middle of the orbit.' Aristarchus proposed that the stars were merely other suns, which despite their fixed motions did in fact move relative to each other and the earth. Unfortunately, the telescope had yet to be invented, which meant that he was unable to prove or demonstrate in any way his seemingly non-intuitive hypotheses.

Nearly four centuries later, the Ancient Roman astronomer Claudius Ptolemy, who also worked in Alexandria, wrote *The Almagest*, which proposed an alternative astronomical picture that appeared to accord more closely with human observation. This was a geocentric model, placing the earth at the centre of the universe. Using observations and mathematical expertise, Ptolemy proposed a system which followed the movements of the moon, the sun and the planets through the heavens. Although these motions consisted of complex epicycles, with variations in speed, direction and apparent distance from the earth, they largely matched observational reality. According to Ptolemy, the stars beyond the planets themselves were part of an outer sphere, which revolved outside the epicycles of the moon, the sun and the planets.

Ptolemy was also able to write tables which predicted, with considerable accuracy, the future movements of the planets and the stars. In accord with his system, Ptolemy wrote a comprehensive four-part work on astrology, which 'enjoyed almost the authority of a Bible among the astrological writers of a thousand years or more'.

Ptolemy's geocentric system was in time accepted by the Roman Catholic Church, and thus became part of theological doctrine. This meant that throughout the Middle Ages the Ptolemaic system could not be contradicted. Anyone who did so was committing heresy. This fact is central to the life and conduct of Nicolaus Copernicus, the man who is credited with resurrecting the ideas of Aristarchus. The importance of Copernicus's feat is all but impossible to exaggerate. Nearly three centuries later, the German poet and polymath Goethe would write in an oft-quoted passage:

Of all discoveries and opinions, none may have exerted a greater effect on the human spirit than the doctrine of Copernicus. The world had scarcely become known as round and complete in itself when it was asked to waive the tremendous privilege of being the centre of the universe. Never, perhaps, was a greater demand made on mankind – for by this admission so many things vanished in mist and smoke! What became of Eden, our world of innocence, piety and poetry; the testimony of the senses; the conviction of poetic-religious faith? No wonder his contemporaries did not wish to let all this go and offered every possible resistance to a doctrine which in its converts authorized and demanded a freedom of view and greatness of thought so far unknown, indeed not even dreamt of.

The man we know as Nicolaus Copernicus was born Mikołaj Kopernik in February 1473.* His birthplace was the provincial city of Thorn on the River Vistula in Poland, some 100 miles south of the Baltic Sea. Thorn (now Toruń) had been founded as a city in the 1200s by the Teutonic Knights. Its strategic position on the Vistula had prompted the Knights to build high defensive walls around the city, with guard towers and a central castle. Later it had become a member of the Hanseatic League, before reverting to Polish rule in 1411, by which time it had a thriving population of 10,000.

Nicolaus's father was a merchant from Kraków, and his mother came from a prosperous local family. His father and mother, along with their servants, occupied an elaborate three-storey house, which had been inherited by Nicolaus's mother. This contained large, high-ceilinged main rooms warmed by extensive fireplaces, their walls decorated with murals. Nicolaus was the youngest of four siblings, and grew up amidst an ambiance of considerable but unostentatious luxury.

When Nicolaus was just ten years old, his father died. All the children were then taken into the care of their maternal uncle Lucas Watzenrode the Younger, an intellectual who moved in humanist circles. Besides being a wealthy man, Watzenrode was also a canon – a member of the clergy who took 'first orders', including the vow of chastity. This post was often, but not always, held prior to taking full 'higher orders' and becoming an ordained priest. Watzenrode had ambitions: he was a canon of Frombork Cathedral, and within six years he would become Prince-Bishop of Warmia, a district of north-eastern Poland abutting the Baltic Sea.

In 1491, at the age of eighteen, Nicolaus and his older brother Andreas were despatched by their uncle Lucas to study at the University

---

* As was common practice amongst scholars, Kopernik would adopt the Latinized form of his name, i.e. Copernicus, in later life.

of Kraków, the main university in Poland. Founded in 1364, this was the second-oldest university in eastern Europe, after the Charles University in Prague. Nicolaus and Andreas travelled the hundred miles up the River Vistula by barge, the main means of public transport in this region during the period. In Kraków they entered an entirely new world. The city was over twice the size of Thorn, and was located at the crossroads between two of eastern Europe's major trade routes. It was here that the route between the important Hanseatic port of Gdańsk and southern Europe met the route between Prague and Crimea, the major terminus of the Silk Routes on the Black Sea. Such extensive commercial connections gave the city a cosmopolitan air. Besides the native Germans and Poles, the population also included Italians, Lithuanians and Hungarians, and the city had one of the largest Jewish populations in Europe. Until recently, the Florentine Medici Bank had retained an agency here, and by now the Fuggers had a well-established branch dealing with trans-shipments from their Hungarian and Transylvanian mines. The university was attended by students from as far afield as Scandinavia and Italy.

At the time, most students enrolled in university at around thirteen, so the eighteen-year-old Nicolaus and Andreas, in his early twenties, would have stood out amongst their contemporaries. Throughout their time in Kraków, they almost certainly lived in the same dwellings, remaining close. However, their temperaments were utterly disparate. The first indication of this comes from studying the university records, where Nicolaus is registered as paying his university fees in full. However, Andreas's name is noticeable by its absence. He appears to have kept the money loaned to him by his uncle Lucas and used it for the traditional student pastimes of wine, women and song.

Nicolaus was enrolled to study canon law,* with the aim of following his uncle's path to an important clerical post. Quite apart from the

---

* This was the body of ecclesiastical law which in general governed ordained members of the Catholic Church. Those outside the Church – the lay population – were governed by what is known as civil or common law. This system of dual jurisdiction prevailed throughout the medieval era, but generally fell into abeyance following the Reformation.

ever-evolving Renaissance, this was a time of world-changing discovery. In 1493, Columbus returned from his first transatlantic voyage to what he thought was Cathay (China). Ironically, it was this mistake which meant most to the natural philosophers (scientists) of the time. To them it proved, once and for all, that the world was round. Nicolas Copernicus became swept up in the excitement of this discovery, and other advances taking place in the northern Renaissance. He attended lectures by Albert Brudzewski, who taught Aristotelian philosophy; however, aside from these Brudzewski also gave private lectures on astronomy, which soon became of consuming interest to Copernicus.

There was a thriving school of mathematics and astronomy at the University of Kraków, and Copernicus became a part of this, proving himself adept in both mathematics and astronomical calculation. Brudzewski was a charismatic figure and highly attuned to the new learning that was spreading through Europe as part of the renaissance of classical thought. Brudzewski had read Regiomontanus and shared his belief that the geocentric Ptolemaic model had its flaws. He had also read the work of the Austrian Georg von Peuerbach, who had lived during the earlier years of the century (1423–61). Peuerbach had been taught by Regiomontanus and had collaborated with him, using instruments which he invented to measure the passage of the stars in the heavens. In 1454 Peuerbach completed his *Theoricae Novae Planetarium* (New Theories of the Planets), which presented a more simplified form of Ptolemy's system. Three years later, using his new instruments and his new ideas, Peuerbach discovered that an eclipse of the sun occurred eight minutes earlier than predicted by previous Ptolemaic tables. This led him to produce a new *Tabulae Eclipsium*, with revised predictions.

Back in Kraków, Bradzewski made a point of keeping abreast of the latest developments, and was especially interested in Peuerbach's ideas, which inspired him to undertake further research of his own. In the course of this he made a number of discoveries. Noticing that the dark marks on the face of the moon (the 'Man in the Moon' of popular mythology) always remained the same, he concluded that the moon did not spin on its orbit, but maintained the same face towards the earth.

His observations of the moon's changing size also convinced him that its passage around the earth was not circular, but elliptic. Copernicus was enthralled, and dreamed of making discoveries of his own.

In 1495 Copernicus left the University of Kraków without a degree, and returned to stay with his uncle Lucas Watzenrode who had now become Prince-Bishop of Warmia. Watzenrode intended to make his nephew a canon, a sinecure which would have supported him during his ensuing studies, but this appointment was held up over a dispute concerning another candidate. So Watzenrode decided to send Copernicus to study in Italy, with the aim of furthering his career in the Church. Two years later, while he was away in Italy, Copernicus would be appointed a canon by proxy, thus guaranteeing him an income.

Copernicus studied at three universities during his stay in Italy, which lasted from 1496 to 1503 and included a number of journeys back across the Alps to see his uncle. Although Copernicus was still supposed to be studying canon law, at the University of Bologna he so impressed the authorities with his astronomical knowledge that he was able to become an assistant to the renowned astronomer Domenico Maria Novara da Ferrara. Together, Copernicus and Novara observed a lunar occultation of Aldebaran. Put simply, this is when the moon eclipses the light of Aldebaran, a bright star in the zodiacal constellation of Taurus, the bull. This prompted Copernicus to start revising his ideas concerning the measurement of distance between the bodies he was observing in the night sky.

The year 1500 saw huge celebrations in Rome, marking one and a half millennia since the birth of Christ. Copernicus was present in the Holy City, as his uncle had arranged for him to undertake an apprenticeship at the Curia. He took this opportunity to deliver a number of lectures in Rome, casting doubt on the mathematical calculations of Ptolemaic astronomy.

Later, Copernicus would study at the universities of Padua and Ferrara, between times making further visits back to his uncle in Warmia. During one of these visits, Uncle Lucas instructed Copernicus to broaden his studies by learning medicine at Padua, which was a renowned centre of medical studies at the time.* In 1503, Copernicus also completed a doctorate in canon law. All this gives an indication of the depth and breadth of Copernicus's learning. It was also during this time that Leonardo da Vinci's wide variety of pursuits made him the epitome of what came to be known as a Renaissance man. One of the great distinctions of this period was the ever-expanding breadth of knowledge of those who contributed to its discoveries. Ideas from one field were likely to inspire breakthroughs in other fields. The greatest advances in Renaissance thought, literature, ideas, science and the arts all took place in the field they referred to as the humanities. Nowadays the humanities are contrasted with the sciences, but in the Renaissance the humanities included the sciences. In accord with its name, this was the study of humanity in all its manifestations, and anything to do with it – in contrast to religious studies.

By the time Copernicus returned home to Warnia he was thirty years old. Apart from brief visits to Kraków, Thorn and Gdańsk he would remain in Warmia for the rest of his life, living as a canon of Frombork Cathedral. He would characterize this spot as 'the remotest corner of the world'. Despite Copernicus's great learning, he was not an ambitious man in any way. According to his biographer Jack Repcheck, 'He was a retiring hermitlike scholar who wanted nothing more than to be left alone.' His uncle's intention that he should one day succeed him as Prince-Bishop of Warmia was politely declined, and he lived out the rest of his days as a lowly canon, fulfilling just the minimum of duties for which he was being paid, and occasionally being called into service as his uncle's physician.

During the ensuing decades Copernicus put together his revolutionary conclusions concerning the solar system. These conclusions, and how they

---

* One of the medical textbooks which Copernicus is known to have studied here was by leading Italian physician Michele Savonarola. He was the grandfather of Friar Girolamo Savonarola, whose fundamentalist preaching had put an end to Medici rule in Florence, until he was burned at the stake for blasphemy in 1498 on orders from Alexander VI, the Borgia pope. These were hardly propitious times for proposing ideas contrary to Catholic orthodoxy. However, the University of Padua was, and would remain, a centre of Renaissance learning. A century later, Galileo would be teaching there, and the English physician William Harvey, who discovered the circulation of the blood, was a student.

were reached, would be poetically described some 500 years later by the
Hungarian writer Arthur Koestler, in his work *The Sleepwalkers: A History
of Man's Changing Vision of the Universe*. Koestler gave his book this title
because it was his opinion that many of the great scientific discoveries of
the Renaissance were in fact achieved almost by accident. The scientists
of this new age were blundering forward, towards they knew not what.

To a greater or lesser extent, this is true of all great ages of discovery.*
Each new addition contributes its part in the construction of a world
which was previously inconceivable. In the case of the Renaissance, this
was very much so. Although the Ancient Greeks and Romans had known
much of what was rediscovered during the Renaissance, the medieval
world had persisted for centuries in a kind of Aristotelian dream. No
matter that many of Aristotle's findings did not in fact accord with reality:
his words and his ideas, together with all the ideas which had accrued to
his vision of the world (such as the Ptolemaic view of the cosmos), were
simply not permitted to be questioned, any more than it was permissible
to question one's faith in God.

Koestler's description of Copernicus's rediscovery of the heliocentric
system has a metaphoric beauty that is experienced by most scientists but
seldom accessible to the non-specialist. Koestler states that Copernicus
'was undoubtedly the first to develop the idea [of a heliocentric arrangement of the planets] into a comprehensive system. This is his lasting
merit, regardless of the inconsistencies and shortcomings of his system.'
He then illustrates this with a superb image, describing Copernicus as a
'crystallizer', before going on to explain what he means by this:

---

* The 'mistakes' made during the Renaissance era often contributed almost as
much as the genuine discoveries. Columbus reporting his arrival in 'Cathay' is but
the most glaring example. And as history makes clear, even 'genuine' discoveries
would in time come to be regarded as 'mistakes', requiring modification. This is
how human knowledge – especially in science – progresses. In later centuries, the
discovery and creation of the Newtonian world view would prove inadequate in
the light of Einstein's theories of relativity. Likewise, around the same time the
utterly basic and ultimately deterministic atomic world would come to be seen as
a façade covering the realm of sub-atomic particles which obey the quasi-random
mechanics of quantum theory.

If you put kitchen salt into a glass of water until the water is 'saturated' and will dissolve no more salt, and suspend a thread with a knot at its end in the solution, then after a while a crystal will form round the knot... [Copernicus] was the patient knot, suspended in the solution, who enabled it to crystallize.

Newton famously characterized his great discoveries by claiming that he had only made them 'by standing on the shoulders of giants'. In the case of Copernicus, we have seen how he stood on the shoulders of Aristarchus, Nicholas of Cusa, Peuerbach and Regiomontanus (to name but a few).

However, Copernicus was by temperament no bold revolutionary, and was never one to rush into presenting his ideas. It was 1514 before he wrote out in his own hand an untitled anonymous essay in which he described in non-technical terms how the Ptolemaic system had 'defects' which led to 'no small difficulties'. He then went on to state: 'I often considered whether there could perhaps be a more reasonable arrange-ment... in which everything would move uniformly about its proper centre, as the rule of absolute motion requires.'

In the manner of Euclid, he then proposed a number of basic axioms. These included: 'The centre of the earth is not the centre of the universe, but only of gravity* and the lunar sphere.' The latter part of this axiom explains how it is the moon, and only the moon, which revolves around the earth. A further axiom stated: 'All the spheres revolve around the sun as their midpoint, and therefore the sun is the centre of the universe.' This was followed by: 'The earth... performs a complete rotation on its fixed poles in a daily motion.' This explained how the surface of the earth passed from the light of day (when half of its surface was exposed to the light of the sun) into the darkness of night (when that same region revolved away from the sun's light and faced the darkness of space).

---

* As will be evident from the ensuing passage, Copernicus's use of this word does not contain the sense of it as a physical force which Newton would later understand.

This essay would come to be known as the *Commentariolus*. Copernicus painstakingly made several copies in his own hand, and sent them to a number of friends from his student days in Kraków and Italy. These friends understood the import of the pamphlet, and made their own copies, passing them on to their own friends. In this way, Copernicus's revolutionary ideas slowly began to spread amongst the cognoscenti. But apart from this, little happened. No outrage, no heated condemnations. And over the years Copernicus's ideas appeared to be overlooked, or simply forgotten. A few of his friends patiently waited for the 'mathematical demonstrations' which Copernicus promised would follow in a 'larger work'. Yet, as the decades passed, nothing further appeared and they gradually lost interest in his fantastical unproven ideas. There were other things to think about.

In 1517, Luther's theses burst upon Europe, creating turmoil throughout western Christendom. Meanwhile Copernicus continued painstakingly setting down his 'larger work', making the requisite mathematical calculations based upon astronomical observations he had made in Italy, and further observations which he now continued to make despite the cloudy northern nights of Warmia. Occasionally he would be summoned to become part of his uncle's retinue on state visits to cities such as Kraków or Gdańsk, as well as the other occasions when his uncle would call on him for medical advice. But Copernicus's wealth of knowledge was such that he was soon being summoned by the authorities to advise on matters of state.

The breadth of knowledge and wisdom possessed by the scholarly canon soon began to spread further afield. In 1519, King Sigismund I of Poland became distressed at the sheer economic muddle which had overtaken his kingdom. Trade was clogged, and no one seemed to know what to do about it. For a start there were no less than three currencies in circulation: that of Royal Prussia, the Polish currency, and the currency minted by the Teutonic Order of Knights. In an attempt to retain the Order's wealth and status, the last of these three currencies had been systematically debased. (Similar practices prevailed amongst the other currencies, though on a lesser scale.) Meanwhile, citizens had begun hoarding more valuable coins for their higher true-metal content, and only using debased or 'clipped' coins.*

Copernicus wrote a paper for King Sigismund I, suggesting a reform of the currency situation, with the maintenance of a single uniform currency. This could then be used to impose some measure of control over the currency in circulation, and thus the turnover of the economy itself. To achieve this, Copernicus proposed what has come to be known as the quantity theory of money. He demonstrated that the price for goods varied directly according to the amount of money in circulation. Limiting or increasing the circulating supply of money could thus be used to control prices and restore a measure of order to the economy. In Copernicus's paper, he stated: 'We in our sluggishness do not realize that the dearness of everything is the result of the cheapness of money. For prices increase and decrease according to the condition of money.'

The fact that King Sigismund I largely chose to ignore this advice, or found himself simply unable to implement it in any effective fashion, does not detract from the radical originality of Copernicus's idea.

Indeed, the quantity theory of money has now taken its place in the economic canon as Gresham's Law, named after Sir Thomas Gresham, the Tudor English financier who became an adviser to Queen Elizabeth I. Gresham's best-known slogan with regard to 'his' law is 'bad money drives out good', referring to the fact that people tended to hoard good money for its valuable metallic content, withdrawing it from circulation or even melting it down, while passing on debased or clipped coinage. Gresham was born in London in 1519, around the time that Copernicus sent his paper to King Sigismund I. All Gresham's fundamental and revolutionary ideas are basically laid out in Copernicus's paper.

---

* A common ruse was to clip away the edges of a coin, and when enough clippings were accumulated one could then melt or hammer these into another coin. Such practice was only overcome when mints began milling their coins – a process which could involve stamping the coins so that their outer edges were raised, or containing the coins in an incised collar so that when they were stamped and expanded their edges became ribbed with regular indentations, or 'milling'. Clipped coins could thus be readily identified by their lack of milling.

However, a reference in a drama by the Ancient Greek comic playwright Aristophanes suggests that the idea behind Gresham's Law was already well understood in his time. It is just possible that the well-read Copernicus was aware of this, which would make the idea behind Gresham's Law yet another rebirth of classical knowledge during the Renaissance. Though if, as is more likely, Copernicus came up with this idea independently, it would be another example of how the new Renaissance outlook had begun to spread through all aspects of European intellectual life – gradually overturning many long-held medieval certainties, and introducing novel concepts of its own. Such change now ranged from humanistic ideas to Luther's *sola fide* (direct access to God through 'faith alone'), and would soon embrace the drastic transformation of Copernicus's heliocentric astronomy.

Copernicus spent the last decades of his life conducting the exacting calculations and putting the final touches to his 'larger work', which would become *De Revolutionibus Orbium Coelestium* (On the Revolution of the Celestial Spheres). At the same time, he continued with his observations, especially with regard to Mars and Saturn. One by one these fell in line with Copernicus's meticulous calculations, confirming his central thesis of positing the heliocentric motion of the planets. The sun lay at the centre of a solar system, surrounded by the nested concentric orbits of the planets. Closest to the sun was the orbit of Mercury, which was completed in eighty days. Then came Venus, with a nine-month orbit. Outside this was the annual orbit of the earth, which was itself orbited by the moon. Beyond the earth was Mars, whose revolution around the sun took two years. Then Jupiter, whose orbit was completed in twelve years. The furthest planet was Saturn, which returned to its place every thirty years. And beyond this lay the stationary sphere of immobile stars, which only appeared to us to move across the sky because they were observed from the earth moving on its orbit.

Copernicus's heliocentric system also explained certain anomalies. As the earth orbited on its circular path around the sun, it tilted slightly on its axis. This accounted for why certain eclipses took place a few minutes before or after their predicted time. Copernicus's system also accounted for why at certain times the outer planets – Mars, Saturn and Jupiter – appeared to move backwards on their orbit. This was because the earth's inner orbit occasionally overtook the larger planets in outer orbits.

As he grew older, Copernicus began to attract a number of visiting intellectuals, keen to hear his latest ideas. One of these was the twenty-five-year-old Austrian-born Lutheran scholar Georg Joachim Rheticus, who would remain with the ageing Copernicus as his assistant.

Rheticus, as well as others, kept urging Copernicus to publish his work, but Copernicus demurred. Being a canon of the Church he was loath to promulgate ideas which might be mistaken for heresy. However, in other matters he does not seem to have been such a stickler for Church discipline. As a canon, he was committed to a life of celibacy. But for several years Copernicus had been sharing his bed with his live-in housekeeper Anna Schilling, believed to have been the daughter of a Dutchman who had settled in the port of Gdańsk, some thirty miles to the west. Such lax disregard for their vows was at the time quite frequent amongst lower-order canons in the region.

Indeed, Copernicus's indiscretion might have been overlooked while his uncle Lucas was prince-bishop, but this was not the case with some of his successors. Prince-Bishop Johannes Dantiscus was particularly upset when in 1537 he succeeded to the bishopric, and wrote to his predecessor Tiedemann Giese, whom he knew was a friend of Copernicus, remonstrating about his canon's behaviour: 'In his old age... he is still said to let his mistress in frequently in secret assignations. Your Reverence would perform a great act of piety if you warned the fellow privately and in the friendliest terms to stop this disgraceful behaviour.' And not only was Copernicus living with his mistress, he was also entertaining in his house Lutherans such as Rheticus.

Prince-Bishop Giese, who had influence at the royal court and was senior to Prince-Bishop Dantiscus, proved a true friend. Not only did he protect Copernicus from censure, but in league with Rheticus he persuaded Copernicus to part with a copy of *De Revolutionibus Orbium Coelestium*, allegedly so that they could study it in greater detail. Between the two of them, Giese and Rheticus then contrived to have Copernicus's work published in Nuremberg in 1543.

They intended Copernicus's work to be judged on its own merit; and wished, as far as possible, to avoid any controversy. Unfortunately, Rheticus was called away from supervising the publication in Nuremberg, and this task was taken over by a Lutheran theologian called Andreas Osiander, who had ideas of his own. Osiander was a reformer of considerable influence; indeed, some years previously he had been instrumental in Nuremberg becoming a Protestant city. Purely on his own initiative Osiander inserted an anonymous preface of his own into *De Revolutionibus Orbium Coelestium*, giving the impression that the preface had in fact been penned by Copernicus himself. In doing so, Osiander managed to undermine the two most important principles which Copernicus wished to uphold: the avoidance of controversy, and the certain truth of his system. Not only did Osiander make a show of how offensive Copernicus's system was to long-accepted orthodoxy; at the same time he stated that the author believed its contents to be a mere hypothesis. At a stroke, he left Copernicus open to a charge of heresy yet simultaneously implied that he did not believe in the truth of what he was saying. As Osiander wrote in his appended preface:

I have no doubt that some learned men have taken serious offence [at Copernicus's ideas]… these men undoubtedly believe that the liberal arts, established long ago as a correct basis, shall not be thrown into confusion… It is the duty of an astrologer [sic] to compose the history of the celestial motions… [but] since he cannot attain to any true causes… these hypotheses might not be true or even probable.

Osiander eventually concluded:

So far as hypotheses are concerned, let no one expect anything certain from astronomy, which cannot furnish it, lest he accept as the truth ideas conceived for another purpose, and depart from this study a greater fool than when he entered it. Farewell.

Fortunately, Copernicus would never see these words. By now he was seventy and lay on his deathbed, having suffered a stroke. However, according to legend, the final printed pages of Copernicus's masterpiece were delivered to him in Warmia, where he still lived in an isolated tower outside Frombork, whereupon he is said to have woken briefly from his coma. In the words of his friend Giese: 'For many days he had been deprived of his memory and mental vigour; he only saw his completed book at the last moment, on the day he died.'

Initially, Copernicus's *De Revolutionibus* caused little controversy, and was even quietly accepted by many astronomers throughout Europe. But, as we shall see, this would not last. The earth was moving; the world and the universe would never be the same again.

CHAPTER 10

ERASMUS

Desiderius Erasmus was probably the leading intellectual figure of the northern Renaissance, as most who encountered him, or corresponded with him, agreed. He is best known for his humanist philosophy, his secular writings, his translations of the Bible, and his general intellectual influence, which was felt all over Europe. Indeed, the name Erasmus is to many all but synonymous with Renaissance humanism, which placed emphasis on humanity rather than medieval spirituality. A gauge of the pervasiveness of Erasmus's influence can be seen from the remarkable fact that in the 1530s (the decade of his death) some 10–20 per cent of the books in circulation throughout Europe were written by him, or plagiarized from his works.

As we have seen, Nicholas of Cusa is generally regarded as the 'father of humanism'. It was he who said:

> The greatest danger against which most men have warned us is that which comes from communicating intellectual secrets to minds become subservient to the authority of an inveterate habit, for such is the power of a long-lasting observance, that most men prefer death to giving up their way of life.

And in this aspect, Erasmus was certainly his true successor. Where Nicholas of Cusa was mystical in his faith – which bordered on pantheism – yet rational in his scientific thinking, Erasmus's core beliefs are more difficult to identify, or even analyse. He was scientific, in that he thought scientifically, or rationally, but he did not think about science. He was a scholar, deeply versed in classical learning, who brought his knowledge to bear on how humanity should conduct itself; yet he refrained from open opposition to the Church. As such, he chose the middle road (*via media*) which earned him the animosity of both sides in this divisive age. Yet as he said, 'Human affairs are so obscure and various that nothing can be clearly known. This was the sound conclusion of the Academic sceptics, who were the least surly of [ancient] philosophers.' And he himself was certainly the least surly amongst modern philosophers. Rather, he preferred to echo Nicholas of Cusa, proclaiming, 'In humility alone lies true greatness, and knowledge and wisdom are profitable only in so far as our lives are governed by them.' And for this he would remain admired, even by friends who became his enemies.

In many ways, Erasmus remains best known today for his pithy remarks and epigrams. But as he put it: 'In no kind of verse have I had less practice than in epigrams; yet sometimes while out walking, or even over wine, I have at different times thrown off a certain number… put together by my friends.' Fortunately for posterity, Erasmus spent a good part of his life on solitary walks or refreshing himself with a jug of wine. Several of his remarks have even become part of our language. We all know such epigrams as 'Prevention is better than cure', 'Ignorance is bliss', and 'Fortune favours the audacious'. Many of these are echoes of remarks he first read in the ancient classics. Yet there can be no doubt that it was Erasmus who first used the phrase 'To call a spade a spade' – because in fact this particular remark was only original by accident: while translating, he mistook the Ancient Greek word for 'pot' as meaning 'spade'. Similarly, Erasmus gave us the term 'Pandora's box' – which when opened would unleash all manner of evils upon the world. In the original Ancient Greek, Hesiod had written *pithos*, which does not mean 'box' but is in fact a large earthenware jar for storing wine or olive oil.

Such nitpicking may seem irrelevant, but Erasmus's life was to pivot on many such ambivalences. For instance, his best-known saying is: 'In the land of the blind, the one-eyed man is king.' This appears profound, yet remains paradoxical under examination. We may be blind to the truth, but how do we identify this one-eyed king who sees a reality beyond our defective vision? Another saying of his which remains with us to this day is 'Women, can't live with them, can't live without them' – a curious remark for a man who was ordained as a priest, and may well have been homosexual.

There is no doubt that Erasmus's father would have sympathized with his son's view of women. Erasmus was probably born in 1466 (just two years after the death of Nicholas of Cusa) in Rotterdam, which was in the territory ruled by the Duke of Burgundy. His father, Gerard, was an ordained priest whose parish was in nearby Gouda. His mother, Margareta Rutgers, was the daughter of a physician and almost certainly Gerard's live-in housekeeper. Erasmus was the second of their illegitimate children.

Despite such inauspicious beginnings, his life at home as a child appears to have been happy enough. But Erasmus would be devastated by the death of both of his parents during the plague in 1483, when he was seventeen. It is claimed by his biographer Cornelis Augustijn that this event caused him to view his life as 'a stain, and [it] cast a pall over his youth'. How much this was the case is difficult to judge. Details of Erasmus's adolescent years are vague and often contradictory. Diligent researchers leafing through such contemporary local records as have survived provide various versions of his life at this time, most of which are contradicted by Erasmus's own unreliable autobiographical writings. Thus, what follows is – of necessity – selective.

It seems that sometime after their parents' death, Erasmus and his elder brother were placed with the Brethren of the Common Life at 's-Hertogenbosch. At school, Erasmus was no prodigy, but appeared to suffer from 'the bewilderment of an over-talented child whose hunger for knowledge remained unsatisfied'. Unusually, this school taught Ancient Greek, which was generally only available at university. Erasmus took refuge in reading, devouring the mostly sacred works in the school library. He dreamed of going to university, but his teachers would have none of this. Poverty and pressure from the Brethren forced him and his brother to enter a seminary for canons near Stein in south Holland, where he would remain for almost half a dozen years. Here the library contained classical Greek works by authors ranging from the poet Homer to Demosthenes, the great orator of Athens, as well as Roman works by the likes of Virgil, Terence and Cicero.

Yet Erasmus was no solitary bookworm. As he himself wrote: 'Life without a friend I think no life, but rather death; or, at least a friendless life, if life it may be called, is first of all unhappy and, secondly fit for beasts and not for men.' He would become friends with many of the priests whom he encountered during his education and beyond, often maintaining contact for many years through correspondence. Most of these friends had inclinations towards the new humanism, many of whose ideas were derived from 'pagan' (i.e. secular) authors such as Cicero and Ovid.

It was in Stein that Erasmus fell in love with a fellow canon, Servatius Rogerus, writing poems to him as well as passionate letters: 'I have wooed you, both unhappily and relentlessly.' As this letter suggests, Erasmus's advances appear to have been rejected physically, if not emotionally. This relationship had all the hallmarks of a motherless and fatherless young man seeking love and solace that was otherwise missing from his life – though surprisingly its ending would cause no major or lasting upset in his life.

Not long after his ordination, Erasmus's superior learning and intellectual abilities attracted the attention of the Bishop of Cambrai, who offered to appoint him as his secretary. In order to accept this post, Erasmus had to be granted temporary dispensation from his priestly duties, though he remained a priest. (This dispensation would in time be made permanent by none other than Pope Leo X.) Erasmus was not only making a wide circle of close friends, but a number of those impressed by the promising young priest appear to have had influence in increasingly high places. Such a dispensation would have enabled Erasmus to live the life of an independent scholar, and it is clear that this was his aim even at this early stage of his life. Erasmus had a gift for friendship, but institutional life – such as in a monastery, with its hierarchy and discipline – would always irk him.

Evidence of Erasmus's ultimate aim soon became clear. In 1495 he succeeded in persuading the Bishop of Cambrai to grant him a stipend so that he could travel to study at the University of Paris. During the medieval era this city had been the European centre of Scholasticism, attracting the finest theological scholars in Europe. Great luminaries of the age such as Duns Scotus, Albertus Magnus and Thomas Aquinas had all taught there. The ultimate authority of Aristotle still held sway in Paris in the Latin Quarter (so named because it was inhabited by students who spoke Latin). However, even in such a bastion of orthodoxy there was a small but growing interest in the new humanism, led by the Italian 'professor of humanity' Publio Fausto Andrelini, who would become another long-term friend of Erasmus.

In order to support his modest stipend, Erasmus undertook some private tutoring. His biographer Léon-Ernest Halkin paints an idyllic picture: 'His letters and his exchanges with his pupils breathe an air of shared affection and, in their company he took long walks in the vineyards around Paris or shared simple and cheerful meals.' There has been a suggestion that all was not quite as innocent as it sounds. At one point Erasmus was abruptly dismissed by the guardian of Thomas Grey, one of his young English pupils.

Four years after arriving in Paris, Erasmus was invited to join the entourage of the Englishman William Blount, a wealthy humanist who had great influence at the court of Henry VIII. Thus, in 1499 Erasmus arrived in England, a country which was to become 'a second homeland'. As ever, he began with a charm offensive: according to modern Cambridge historian Thomas Penn, Erasmus was 'ever susceptible to the charms of attractive, well-connected and rich young men'.

It is difficult to know what to make of these and other suggestive remarks concerning Erasmus's sexuality. There is no doubting his infatuation with Rogerus, but as he grew into maturity he appears to have taken his vows more seriously. As the contemporary Erasmus scholar Erika Rummel points out: no personal denunciation was made of Erasmus during his lifetime, and he took pains in later life to distance himself from these earlier episodes by condemning *sodomy* in his works and praising sexual desire in marriage between men and women.

In London, Erasmus was befriended by Thomas More, a leading English humanist, who would become a lifelong friend. More was a man of many contradictions, and would go on to become a tragic chancellor under Henry VIII. But at this stage he was a young lawyer, vacillating between an ambitious legal career and becoming a simple monk. During this period he would resolve his problem by choosing to enter parliament yet retaining his ascetic habit of wearing a hair shirt. His conversations with Erasmus may well have been instrumental in guiding him to this decision. It would have been characteristic: the inner life of Erasmus was constantly tipping between his own ambivalences.

Erasmus also befriended the English humanist John Colet, whose interest in education would lead him to found St Paul's School, which remains to this day one of London's leading educational establishments. Erasmus's conversations with Colet were fruitful in many ways. Colet introduced him to the new Platonism which had begun to spread through Europe, after previously unknown works of Plato had been carried west by Orthodox monks fleeing Constantinople following its fall to the Ottoman Turks in 1453. For Erasmus, these new ideas were a pleasant contrast to the pall of stale Scholasticism which still hung over Paris.

Discussing education with Colet also led Erasmus to write *On the Method of Study*, offering an enlightened humanist approach to education. In this progressive work Erasmus suggested that pupils should not be subjected to learning by rote, or forced to master boring grammar when learning Latin. Instead they should be encouraged in the art of making conversation: 'For since young children can pronounce any language, however barbarous, within months, is there any reason why the same thing should not occur in Greek or Latin?'

Colet was so impressed by Erasmus's ideas that he would go so far as to offer him a teaching post at his new school. But this was far from what Erasmus had in mind: 'I have not come to these shores to teach literature, in verse or prose. Literature ceased to have charms to me as soon as it ceased to be necessary to me.' Where literature is concerned this is patently untrue: he simply did not wish to become tied down to a job as a teacher. However, in the light of such remarks, it comes as some surprise that during this period he took up a teaching post at Oxford University. The fact was, he needed to support himself. His loyal friends were for the most part not only wealthy but generous, yet Erasmus longed for independence, and he was loath to accept more 'gifts' than he found necessary.

Later, he would take up a longer spell of teaching at Queens' College, Cambridge (where the room he occupied can still be seen on the first floor of 'I' staircase of Old Court). Here Erasmus was appointed a professor of divinity, a post which he could have held for the rest of his life. But Erasmus hardly felt at home in Cambridge. He had never been in good health, and was severely affected by the bitterly cold east winds of winter. Also, he was used to wine, and developed a deep distaste for English ale. However, his duties were light, and he consoled himself that he was not just teaching students: his conversations with his peers meant that he was in fact also teaching teachers.

Ever eager for new experiences, during his long stay in England Erasmus also travelled – making visits of varying length to Paris, Louvain in his native Netherlands, Madrid, and several German cities. His visit to Basel in Switzerland led to the meeting with Paracelsus, where his perceptive understanding of Paracelsus's learning led to the maverick physician being appointed, for a brief period, to the university. Erasmus also visited more than a dozen cities in Italy, acquainting himself with all the latest developments in humanism, as well as making his own contributions.

Erasmus's biographer Halkin maintains: 'In Erasmus's life there was no dominant external event. All his activity was of an intellectual order; it was developed to research; it was translated into his books and letters.' There is of course a deep truth in this. However, Erasmus was no mere intellectual. His extensive travels certainly broadened his horizons. The cities he visited invariably contained well-established universities, where he would be made welcome and add to his ever-growing circle of friends. In this way he encountered all manner of scholars – from the crass, outrageous Paracelsus to the sophisticated, independent-minded More. Erasmus, with his wit and breadth of knowledge, was usually able to engage with and learn from them all. And what he learned would be passed on to others, increasingly in the distilled form of his works. At the same time, he was not above tourism, and made a point of visiting the sights, learning their history.

Erasmus's works and letters are crammed with all manner of erudition, references, examples from the ancients, and the wisdom of great men. Such a diet would cloy, were it not for the fact that his writings are peppered with wit, proverbial stories and the occasional amusing anecdote.

For instance, there is the tale of the unknown Irishman who walked into the king's palace and sat himself down for breakfast. The servants enquired what office he held at the court: none, said he, but I want one. Ordered to leave, he replied: 'I will, but only after breakfast.' The courtiers' indignation turned to laughter, and they asked how he had the face to do such a thing. 'Why,' replied the Irishman, 'I knew the king was rich enough to stand me breakfast.' Other witty observations feature the foibles of fashionable young Venetians, Englishmen abroad and the like. As is evident, these are more than just jokes: they indicate a wide experience of European characters, pinpointing their traits.

Erasmus's best-known work is *In Praise of Folly*. The idea for it came to him when he was crossing the Alps on horseback with a group of fellow travellers. In the introduction he describes the genesis of this work to his friend Thomas More, to whom he dedicated *In Praise of Folly*:

Not wanting to waste all the time I was obliged to be on horseback on idle gossip and small talk, I preferred to spend some of it thinking over some topic connected with our common interests…

Erasmus wrote his original draft of this work in Latin, giving it the title *Moriae Encomium*. This has a double meaning: 'In Praise of Folly' or 'In Praise of More', After assembling the contents of the book in his mind as he journeyed back to London, Erasmus finished writing it in just a few days while staying at the house of 'his finest friend' Thomas More. The result is a work of sharp satirical brilliance, especially with regard to the Church. Yet it always seems to draw back at the last moment, thus avoiding any accusation of heresy.

At the outset, Folly is characterized as a woman. Yet this has no simple sexist intent. Folly praises herself in a piece of skilful tomfoolery: 'I am myself wherever I am, and no one can pretend I'm not – especially those who lay claim to be called the personification of wisdom.' Erasmus's depiction of Folly is blatant, satirical and slippery. Folly may be responsible for human error, but without her very spontaneity we would have no social life or happiness. No one is free from Folly, especially those whose self-importance leads them to claim otherwise.

Worst of all are the popes, who claim to be the successors of St Peter. How could a man in such a position lay claim to secular power? A pope riding into battle to defend his patrimony makes a mockery of his office, and all that goes with it: 'A grain of the salt Christ spoke of would suffice to rid them of all their wealth and honours, their sovereignty and triumphs, their many offices…' Erasmus then goes on to list the pope's vast army of supporters:

Countless scribes, copyists, clerks, lawyers, advocates, secretaries, muleteers, grooms, bankers and pimps (and I nearly added something more suggestive, but was afraid of being too blunt for your ears) – in short, an enormous crowd of people now a burden on the Roman see (I'm sorry, I meant 'now an honour to') would be left to starve. A monstrous abominable crime!

Erasmus's attack is pointed enough, but the parenthesized afterthoughts lend a somewhat arch flavour, at least to modern ears. Yet it is worth remembering what Erasmus was attacking, and the risk he ran in doing so. Here was an ordained priest, whom the Church had released from his pastoral duties so that he could pursue a life of scholarship, making so bold as to criticize the very Church to which he still belonged.

Later in the short book (or long essay, it is that brief), Erasmus goes on to attack kings, princes and their administrators, who are portrayed as no better than their long train of hangers-on. He offers some plain and blunt advice to such leaders:

> Once he is at the helm of government he has to devote himself to public instead of his personal affairs, and must think only of the well-being of his people. He can't deviate by so much as a hair's breadth from the laws he has promulgated and set up himself.

And furthermore, the leader should fearlessly investigate the probity of all the magistrates and officials of his administration, ensuring their integrity. Such was the responsibility of public office: 'the exercise of true sovereignty'. Here Erasmus was far ahead of his time, yet he was also in tune with the spirit of his age. However, he gives no specific prescription – no early form of communism, as proposed by Müntzer against the capitalist Fuggers.

Erasmus's words were inspired by the direct honesty and decency which he had found in his reading of the classics. This was how Cicero would have spoken, how Demosthenes had addressed the citizens of Athens. He proposed true nobility, rather than empty noble promises; he demanded only an end to the hypocrisy which had by now pervaded all levels of office.

Yet in this work Erasmus does of course have a message. It is a plea for decency and for the rule of law to be applied to all citizens. It is a plea for human honesty. Only when he starts to attack the philosophers does he wander off course somewhat. Here he is undeniably *out* of tune with his age:

> Philosophers, cloaked and bearded to command respect... insist that they alone have wisdom... a pleasant form of madness, which sets them building countless universes, and measuring the sun, moon, stars, and planets by rule of thumb or a bit of string.

In this way, these misguided seekers after wisdom attempt to explain 'thunderbolts, winds, eclipses and other inexplicable phenomena'. This is not merely an attack on the empty rhetoric of sophists, but also an attack on the natural philosophers. In Erasmus's view, nature derided such endeavours. These philosophers were not only ignorant of themselves, but insisted that 'all other mortals are but fleeting shadows'. Erasmus endorses Socrates, whose central message was 'Know thyself'. On the other hand he remains a realist, denying the idealism of Plato, who depicted humanity as staring at the fleeting shadows of mere appearance playing across the wall of a cave, when they should turn around to face the light of day outside the cave – the ideal reality of truth.

As we have seen, one of the most vital aspects of the Renaissance was the reawakening of scientific enquiry. After centuries of quasi-stasis, investigators were now trying to work out how the world worked, the nature of the heavens, the extent of the earth. And it was such enquiry which was leading to new, or newly rediscovered, inventions – along with the spread of such knowledge throughout the continent. Gutenberg's printing press, and the transformative industry it spawned, would help release a new spirit of enquiry into all realms of human knowledge. As indeed it would help spread the works of Erasmus.

In Praise of Folly was concerned with the state of the Church, of Christianity in general and the behaviour of individual Christians in particular. It was a social work, which satirized humanity; and, as such, should not really have been concerned with science. Ironically, this work ends with a perceptive – if double-edged – psychological remark: 'No man is wise all the time.' Erasmus's work too had its blind spots.

In Praise of Folly was first published in 1511; and to the astonishment of Erasmus and his friends, who had advised him against publication in the light of its controversial contents, the work was an overnight success. Soon it was being translated from its original Latin into French, then Czech, then German. This meant that its readership was expanding far beyond the circle of scholars for whom it might originally have been written. Now anyone who could read their own language had access to Erasmus's ideas. Holbein himself was in London at this time, and he added his own witty illustrations to the margins of Erasmus's personal copy.

But how could such a book be written by someone who had spent his entire life avoiding controversy? Who had apparently gone out of his way not to outwardly oppose the prevailing orthodoxy? Erasmus had evidently taken a calculated risk, banking on the narrow-minded view which characterized entrenched intellectual and theological authority. He made sure that his criticism appeared to lampoon only historical figures. Far be it from him to suggest that this was a satire on the present establishment... And astonishingly, Erasmus got away with it: he had correctly understood the nature of his readers. At least, those amongst his audience who mattered to him.

When copies of *In Praise of Folly* reached Rome, the book was immediately read by the erudite and fun-loving Medici pope Leo X, who expressed himself highly amused by its contents. It was evident that he thought the references to the popes applied only to previous occupants of the Vatican, especially his immediate predecessor, Julius II, who was known as the Warrior Pope. They had nothing to do with him... However, historians have consequently pinpointed the book's most immediate effect. In the words of the modern medieval historian Hunt Janin: 'Although Erasmus himself would have denied it vehemently, later reformers found that *In Praise of Folly* had helped prepare the way for the Protestant Reformation.'

The modern Lutheran scholar A. Brian Flamme perceptively points out:

> Classical humanism, championed by the likes of Erasmus [and] More... was not progressive in the modern sense, but conservative and restorative. Christianity was not the enemy. She was the precious jewel that had lost her lustre in the grime of scholastic neglect and clerical corruption.

It would seem only natural that Luther and Erasmus would find common cause in their work. However, nothing of the sort took place. To generalize, Luther was concerned with doctrine. Erasmus, on the other hand, was against doctrine: his concern was with ethics. For all his wish to see reform, Erasmus also wished to remain *within* the Church:

> There are some things which God has willed that we should contemplate, as we venerate himself, in mystic silence; and, moreover, there are many passages in the sacred volumes about which many commentators have made guesses, but no one has finally cleared up their obscurity.

Luther, for his part, would have no truck with such contradictions. His love was for theology and doctrine. The Bible was not filled with obscurities: 'God has caused the Word to be published and proclaimed, in which he has given the Holy Spirit to offer and apply to us this treasure, this redemption...'

Where Erasmus had an abhorrence for conflict, Luther insisted upon it. *In Praise of Folly* was not the kind of material to be nailed defiantly to the door of a cathedral. In the end, Erasmus became so exasperated by Luther that he was drawn into penning a *Diatribe* against him, condemning Luther for denying the existence of free will, insisting that our nature was all part of God's plan. Luther replied with his famous dismissal: 'You are not pious.' Erasmus would remain in the Church until his death; Luther's ideas would tear Europe apart.

The Renaissance was a time of increasing change, extending into all spheres of life. So it comes as little surprise that politics should come under discussion. Erasmus and his friend Thomas More would both make important contributions to political theory. However, the first major Renaissance work in this sphere would be by the Florentine diplomat and writer Niccolò Machiavelli, who in 1513 wrote *The Prince*. This contains, with reference to past and present political figures, advice on how a leader can attain power and then hang on to it. Machiavelli's advice is amoral and cynical, but above all realistic. This is realpolitik before the name was even coined. No deed or scheming is too underhand, as long as it succeeds in its aim. And the aim for any leader should be absolute power, which should be maintained as such. It is much safer for a prince 'to be hated than to be loved', writes Machiavelli. 'Fear preserves you by a dread of punishment that never fails.' Although he does add that a leader 'ought to avoid making himself hated' if he can. However, much of his advice on how to succeed in politics would seem to indicate that inspiring hatred was the best course.

Machiavelli's recommendation was that a leader should only appear to be a paragon of moral virtue insofar as it furthers his aims, so that the people favour him. Enemies should be eliminated – covertly, or overtly if an example is necessary. Strictly speaking, Machiavelli's *The Prince* belongs to the southern Renaissance, though its effect, and the outrage it provoked, would be pan-European. Within ten years of its publication, Henry VIII is known to have read a copy. Machiavelli's very name would become a byword for iniquity, to such an extent that some years later Shakespeare would have one of his characters protest, 'Am I a Machiavel?' – confident that his audience would understand precisely what he meant. *The Prince* also serves as a useful contrast to the political ideas which would develop in the northern Renaissance.

It is certain that neither Erasmus nor Thomas More read Machiavelli's work before they wrote their own works on politics, some three years later than *The Prince*. (Though written in 1513, *The Prince* would not be published until 1532.) Yet the works written by both Erasmus and More sound uncannily like a general riposte to Machiavelli's highly pessimistic view of human nature.

Erasmus's *Education of a Christian Prince* is dedicated to the sixteen-year-old prince who would eventually become the Holy Roman Emperor Charles V. Erasmus's advice contained within this work was the very opposite of Machiavelli's brutal, uncivilized approach. A ruler should command the respect of his people by living a Christian life. As ever, Erasmus harks back to classical writers, advising his prince to absorb and analyse the idealism of Plato, the inspiring rhetoric of Cicero and the stoicism of Seneca. Though, he warns that these are not Christian writers.

A leader should attempt to emulate the wisdom of Solomon, yet most of all he should 'test everything against the standard of Christ'. This is an uplifting and exemplary work, attempting to set out the positive lessons to be learned from history.

However, it was his friend Thomas More's political book which would attract the most attention. So much so that the word he coined for the title – *Utopia* – has entered the language. More's work describes an imaginary island off the coast of South America, named Utopia. This name contains a skilful double entendre. Utopia derives from the Greek *eu* (meaning 'good') and *topos* (meaning 'place'). But it can also be read as *ou-topos*, which means 'no place'. Utopia is both ideal and non-existent.

More's *Utopia* contains a dialogue between More himself and a sailor called Raphael Hythloday, who has lived on Utopia for seven years and wishes to pass on the wisdom of this marvellous place. Raphael's description of Utopia is in some ways similar to the ideal Republic described in Plato's political work of the same name.* In common with Plato's Republic, Utopia has no such thing as private property. Plato believed that the public good can only flourish when everything is held in common. This is communism, pure and simple. More objects to Raphael, pointing out that such a state would lead to public idleness and a lack of respect for the magistrates charged with administering the law.

The description of Utopia in More's work is so precise and detailed as to make it sound almost like a parody. The island of Utopia has fifty-four towns, one of which is the capital. All these towns have the same plan. Every street is precisely twenty feet broad, and all the houses are identical: they have flat roofs, a front door leading onto the street, and a back door leading into the garden. There are no locks on the doors, and anyone may come in. Citizens must change houses every ten years, to avoid their inhabitants from regarding them as their own private property. There are also farms, each looked after by an elderly wise man and his wife. Every

---

* Plato's title in the original Greek was Δημοκρατία (*Dimokratia*, i.e. 'democracy, rule by the people'. Our word 'Republic' derives from Latin: *res* (thing) and *publica* (belonging to the public).

farm contains forty people, including two 'bondsmen' (i.e. slaves). These bondsmen are convicted criminals, or foreigners who have been sentenced to death in their own country; and their duty is to perform 'vile service'. They are the ones who kill the animals, so that free citizens do not acquire the habit of cruelty.

Everyone works six hours a day, and goes to bed each night at eight o'clock. In the early morning there are public lectures, which are attended by many of the citizens, though they are not compulsory. These lectures are delivered by citizens who have elected to become men of learning and are excused from working at other tasks. There are no beggars, there is no idle work to provide useless luxuries for the rich... and so on.

It is easy to see Utopia as a liberal socialist heaven; and equally easy to see it as a communist hell. It is enlightened, and at the same time insufferably disciplined and boring. Bertrand Russell, who himself often inclined to liberal quasi-communistic views, offered a profound critique: 'Diversity is essential to happiness... This is a defect of all planned social systems, actual as well as imaginary.'

Elements of all three of these Renaissance political handbooks are easily recognizable in the modern world. It comes as little surprise to learn that both Mussolini and Saddam Hussein kept *The Prince* on their bedside reading table. And Erasmus's prescription for leaders to absorb Christian learning and the humanities, at the expense of the sciences, would cast a long and snobbish shadow over learning for centuries to come. Only now are 'nerds' beginning to emerge blinking into the full light of public adulation and vast fortunes. Meanwhile, something in our nature seems to inspire in us the hankering for a utopia – either in the future or a supposed 'golden era' of the past, or worst of all the present. However, even as an unattainable aim, the idea of utopia has undeniably inspired many reforms, righted all manner of injustices, and often encouraged individual liberalization in general. Difficult though it may be for us to accept, the majority of people in the advanced countries of the so-called free west inhabit what all our antecedents throughout history would have regarded as a utopia.

CHAPTER 11

DÜRER

THERE IS NO DOUBT that the southern Renaissance preceded in some ways and some fields the advances which took place in the north. As we have seen, Dutch artists may have gifted Italy with oil painting, but in art itself, southern influences spread northwards in the form of artists such as Torrigiano, who arrived in Tudor London in 1510, and Fiorentino, who led Francis I's First Fontainebleau School in 1530.

Perhaps the best-known artist to travel in the opposite direction was the German Albrecht Dürer, who as early as 1494 – at the age of twenty-three – travelled south across the Alps to see the Italian Renaissance for himself. Dürer would make two trips to Italy, where he admired and studied works by Leonardo da Vinci, Bellini and Raphael, as well as absorbing as much of the Italian Renaissance as his superlative talent could grasp. Initially it all but overwhelmed him. His early masterpiece *Self-Portrait at 26* stands alongside Raphael or Bellini in its self-confident brilliance, sensitivity, finery – and influences. Yet just two years later he would paint his first self-portrait that was unmistakably in his own style. This portrait is darker, in both colour and psychology. It is the sombre portrayal of a complex, fully mature man, his mask-like face and mesmeric gaze barely able to contain the anguish within. Not for nothing does it bear a striking resemblance to many contemporary representations of Christ. Such were the extremes of which the most talented and original artist of the northern Renaissance was capable.

Albrecht Dürer was born in May 1471 in the Free Imperial City of Nuremberg in southern Germany, a nearby rival to Augsburg in the transalpine trade to Venice and Italy. This was a prosperous manufacturing city with a population of 50,000; best known for its clocks, paper mills and publishing. Although it had no university, its numerous printing presses attracted a circle of intellectuals. For the first four years of Dürer's life, the mathematician and astronomer Regiomontanus lived in Nuremberg, there setting up the world's first scientific printing press and observing the comet of 1472.

Albrecht was the son of a prosperous goldsmith from Hungary. He was the third son of eighteen children, of whom only three brothers survived. Such circumstances were not unusual in Nuremberg: being a hub of trade routes exposed the city to imported epidemics.

After a brief schooling, during which young Albrecht learned to read and write, he was removed at the age of ten so that his father could instruct him in the goldsmith's trade. It was around this time that Dürer picked up the rudiments of drawing and the delicate technical skill of engraving. The sight of Dürer drawing at this stage must have been a wonder to behold, if one is to judge from the truly remarkable skill exhibited in a self-portrait he drew at the age of thirteen, copying his image from a mirror. This captures Dürer's somewhat sad youthful expression with no little expertise, and apart from a couple of minor awkward features this could well be the work of a highly talented mature artist. The unnatural straightness and length of his pointing forefinger, along with the slightly faulty rendering of the far edge of his face – which is at an oblique angle (in part disguised by the added extra lines of his falling hair), – are understandable when one realizes that this portrait was done in the unforgiving medium of silverpoint. This medieval technique was developed by scribes and copyists and uses a silver stylus on paper or vellum that has been coated with a mixture of glue water and lead white and then burnished. The fine tip of the stylus leaves a delicate line, which undergoes a chemical change over time, producing a fine precision that is ideal for rendering detail. This method has but one snag: when it has been drawn, a line cannot be changed. Artists must be fully aware of the effect they wish to produce before their stylus touches the parchment.

In the words of Dürer's biographer Jane Campbell Hutchison: 'The work is a tour de force and a clear indication of the type of inborn talent for drawing which has rarely been seen in the history of art.' Two years later, Dürer's father reluctantly agreed that his son could abandon his training as a goldsmith and be apprenticed to the artist Michael Wolgemut, whose studio was at 16 Bergstraße, just two doors away from the family home.

Wolgemut was hardly a distinguished painter, but what he lacked in artistic ability he more than made up for in entrepreneurial skills – winning as many commissions as he could, and passing on to subcontractors those he was unable to fulfil himself.

Dürer was older than the other apprentices in Wolgemut's studio, and his precocious skill (he could already draw better than his master) made him unpopular – the butt of 'unpleasant [and] merciless teasing' from his jealous fellow apprentices. However, regardless of this, Dürer was able to broaden his skills, learning how to treat surfaces, mix paints, and quickly grasping the technique of how to carve woodcuts. Here Wolgemut was a pioneer, dealing directly with Nuremberg publishers to produce woodcuts to illustrate their printed books. Practice soon established Wolgemut, and his studio, as one of the most technically accomplished producers of woodcuts in the trade.

On completing his apprenticeship in 1490, the nineteen-year-old Dürer set off on his *Wanderjahre* (literally 'wandering years'), a German tradition which encouraged newly qualified craftsmen to travel and gain experience – especially from masters living in other regions. Dürer seems to have taken a roundabout route to Colmar, a small town in Alsace in the Upper Rhine Valley. This was the home of Martin Schongauer, generally regarded as the finest engraver in northern Europe – an indication of Dürer's inclination towards this form of art. Unfortunately, by the time Dürer arrived in 1492 Schongauer had died. Little else is known for certain of Dürer's travels during this period, though he is thought to have visited Frankfurt and the Netherlands.

By 1493 he was in Strasbourg, where he painted the earliest of his mature self-portraits. This has neither the self-confidence of his 1498 self-portrait nor the inner turmoil of his 1500 work. It depicts a somewhat straggly-haired young man, with a serious, slightly uncertain expression on his face. In his right hand he holds the stalk of a type of thistle, called in German *Mannestreue* ('loyal man'), indicating that this is a betrothal portrait. While Dürer was away, his father had arranged for him to marry Agnes Frey, the daughter of a prosperous master brass-worker. Such arrangements were traditional, and while on his *Wanderjahre* Dürer would have been expected to sow his wild oats, thus not disgracing his family or ruining his marriage prospects in his home city. The portrait was sent back to Nuremberg for his fiancée and her family.

Dürer returned to Nuremberg in 1494, where at the age of twenty-three he was duly married to the nineteen-year-old Agnes, receiving a handsome dowry of 200 florins. A rapid sketch by Dürer depicts his bride, 'Mein Agnes'. In the words of Campbell Hutchison: 'Still wearing her hair in a virginal braid down her back, she appears heavy-eyed, slightly sullen, and very young... A less radiant bride has seldom been recorded for posterity.'

Just three months after his wedding, Dürer used some of his dowry to finance a trip to Italy. Agnes was left at home. Explanations (or justifications) for this trip run the entire range of emotion and plausibility. It is true that there was an outbreak of plague in Nuremberg at this time, and Agnes may well not have wished to leave the comparative luxury and safety of her parents' home (where the young couple had been living). At the other end of the scale, commentators point out that this trip would in many ways transform Dürer's art – the Italian experience enabling him to see for the first time, with his own eyes, the full range of the Renaissance which was coming to its peak in Italy. Here he would witness examples of all that art was capable of achieving, firing his ambition as never before.

Dürer did not travel on his own. He is thought to have been accompanied by an ebullient rugged-faced companion named Willibald Pirckheimer, whose appearance belied his acute intelligence and thirst for learning. Pirckheimer came from a distinguished family in Nuremberg, was a year older than Dürer, and was filled with patrician self-confidence. He was studying law at Padua, and during the course of their friendship Pirckheimer would fill the huge gaps in Dürer's education, introducing him to the humanist ideas he had picked up at university and amongst his father's intellectual circle in Nuremberg. Apart from becoming a close lifelong friend of Dürer, Pirckheimer would soon become one of the most influential humanists in Germany. He would write an important history of the country, and become a close friend of Erasmus and other well-known humanists. An indication of his wide influence can be seen from the fact that Thomas More would dedicate the first Swiss edition of *Utopia* to Pirckheimer.

On his first visit to Venice, Dürer met the local artist Jacopo de' Barbari, amongst whose many talents was the painting of miniatures, which would pique Dürer's interest in the rendering of the tiniest fine detail. He also met Andrea Mantegna, one of the pioneers of Renaissance painting in Italy, who excelled in rendering human anatomy and also landscape in perspective. Dürer dutifully concentrated on making detailed copies of works by both these masters.

When Dürer returned to Nuremberg in 1495 he opened his own workshop. He was now beginning to make some money and could afford a couple of assistants. In the ensuing years he began to develop many of the techniques and effects which he had absorbed in Italy, making them utterly his own.

Dürer and Pirckheimer corresponded regularly when they were apart. Their letters show the robust closeness of their friendship and there is no reticence in their contents. 'You stink so much of whores that it seems to me I can smell it from here,' Dürer writes. It is clear that they had both enjoyed sexual adventures during their time in Italy. The prostitutes of Venice were renowned throughout Europe, though there are indications that Pirckheimer – and possibly Dürer as well – enjoyed the odd dalliance with 'handsome Italian soldiers'. Though both friends also shared their worries over contracting 'the French Disease'.*

In their correspondence Pirckheimer is not afraid to make rude remarks about Agnes; he seems to have taken an instant dislike to Dürer's wife. And Dürer himself was not above the occasional slighting comment about her, either. His marriage seems to have remained little more than an 'arrangement' between the two families involved. Agnes and Albrecht were incompatible characters; there would be no children.

Such openness in correspondence was hardly standard practice at the time, especially between members of different classes. But the friendship which developed between Pirckheimer and Dürer seems to have been informed by classical models – in particular the witty and observational correspondence of Cicero. Here we can see how aspects of Renaissance humanism were beginning to penetrate the entire range of human behaviour.

An idea of how much Dürer had learned in Italy can be seen in his 1498 engraving *The Sea Monster*. This large and detailed engraving focuses on a nude woman being carried away by a 'monster' whose top half is a bearded male (with a single jagged antler protruding from his head) and lower body covered in scales. The woman is gazing back towards the shore where her companions are fleeing from the water in panic, and their servant is crying out towards the abducted woman, his arms raised. Behind them the steep hillside rises towards a castle that resembles the Kaiserberg in Nuremberg, with further towers on a distant peak. The nude subject is conveyed with anatomical verisimilitude, while her turned face looks back at her companions with a longing yet surprisingly calm expression. The art critic Jonathan Jones has characterized this as a 'troubling,

---

* This was syphilis, which is widely thought to have been brought from the New World to Europe by crewmen on Columbus's ships when they arrived back in Spain in 1493. From here the disease quickly spread to Naples. The French king Charles VIII conquered Naples in 1494, and when he marched his large French army back north towards France, the disease was spread throughout the Italian peninsula. Consequently it became known as the French Disease. Its effects were physically grotesque and painful, going through worsening stages and frequently ending in death. There was no cure at this time.

wondrous image of the erotic', and the bare black-and-white shades of the etching seem to reinforce this aspect. Here Dürer fully expresses the detail and perspective he assimilated in Italy, while the medium gives it an unmistakably northern aspect in its very colourlessness.

However, it is two works completed a few years later that begin to show Dürer at his finest: the consummate artist who has completely absorbed all that he has learned and informed it with something as unmistakably his own as was the drawing he did at thirteen. The first of these is his 1502 gouache and watercolour depiction of a young hare. The realism of this portrait (it deserves no less a title), with the fine lines of the hare's spreading whiskers and the differing flows of fur across its body, is all but quivering with life. How could Dürer have painted such a vividly alive animal in such meticulous detail without it moving or hopping away? This secret lies in the tiny, meticulous reflection in the hare's right eye. The consensus amongst art critics is that this miniscule touch of realism reflects the bar of a window frame in Dürer's studio. This could be the case, but more likely it reflects a bar of the cage which contained the hare. The animal must have remained crouched in his studio, almost certainly in a cage where it felt at home and unafraid, remaining utterly still as Dürer silently continued painting, the deft flicks of the ends of his brushes offering no more threat than stalks of grass shifting in the breeze. Here Dürer far surpasses the miniaturist's art that he first learned from Barbari, expanding such exceptional detail to full size. But he did not want to create a portrait of a caged animal; so he left out the obscuring bars, merely hinting at them in the hare's eye.

The second masterpiece of this period is equally stark and straightforward. It is a watercolour named *Great Piece of Turf*. And this, quite simply, is all that it is: a masterfully rendered depiction of various (identifiable) plants growing from a clod of earth. Seemingly devoid of composition, of artistic order, it somehow succeeds in capturing its own super-realist order, with the greenness of the stalks and leaves of the plants rising from the rough tumble of earth against a blank background.

Just before Dürer painted these transcendent yet ultra-simple masterpieces, he was visited in Nuremberg by his Venetian artist friend Barbari, who was on his way to take up an appointment at the court of the Holy Roman Emperor Maximilian I. Though Barbari was not one to give away the hard-earned secrets of his art, he must have shown Dürer some of his sketchbooks, especially those with preliminary drawings for his miniatures. Dürer evidently understood how to extend such techniques to achieve an utterly new and beguiling – almost supernatural full-sized – realism.

Between 1507 and 1509 Dürer paid a second visit to Italy, passing beyond Venice to Padua and maybe even Mantua. He certainly visited Bologna, for it was here that he met Luca Pacioli, the friar mathematician and friend of Leonardo da Vinci. It was Pacioli who had taught Leonardo mathematics, and it seems that Dürer too studied with him. Dürer's meticulous and exact art inclined him to mathematics, and it would play an increasing role in both his painting and his other intellectual interests. Pacioli is known to have taught Dürer linear perspective, which was by now widely developed amongst Italian Renaissance artists. But Pacioli probably taught Dürer much more than this useful mathematical–artistic device, for Dürer would continue to study mathematics over the coming years.

Returning to Venice, Dürer met Giovanni Bellini, who despite approaching eighty years old was still considered the finest artist in the city.* Dürer was more than flattered when Bellini asked him if he could buy some of his work. For Dürer this was a sign that he had 'arrived' at last!

Dürer and Bellini certainly met quite a few times, and there is an anecdote recounted by the classical scholar Joachim Camerarius that one day Bellini implored Dürer to give him 'one of those brushes that you draw hair with'. Bellini was astonished when Dürer informed him that he did it with ordinary brushes, no different from the ones Bellini used.

By the time Dürer returned home from his second visit to Italy, he was known by reputation throughout Europe. In 1512, the Holy Roman

---

* Average life expectancy throughout Europe in 1500 was between thirty and forty years. Those who survived beyond this were frequently infirm. Despite Bellini's failing strength, he would continue painting until within a few years of his death aged eighty-six in 1516.

Emperor Maximilian I became one of his patrons. Despite this, Dürer found that he was making insufficient income from his paintings, and even abandoned this art form for several years in favour of making woodcuts and engravings – which could be reproduced and thus sold many times over. He may not have been the best painter in Europe, but his engravings were unsurpassed.

In 1515 a ship arrived in Lisbon from India carrying on board a rhinoceros. This caused a sensation: such a beast had not been seen in Europe since Roman times. It was but one of several exotic creatures to arrive in Europe during the period. As a modern commentator has pointed out with regard to the rhinoceros: 'In the context of the Renaissance, it was a piece of classical antiquity which had been rediscovered, like a statue or an inscription.' King Manuel I of Portugal decided to send the rhinoceros as a gift to Pope Leo X. Unfortunately the ship was wrecked on the Italian coast and the rhinoceros drowned. However, a Nuremberg merchant named Valentim Fernandes, who was working in Portugal, sent a letter home to a group of Nuremberg merchants describing in some detail the beast he had seen. At the same time, another letter arrived from Portugal with a sketched drawing.

Dürer quickly realized the commercial potential of these descriptions, and used them to recreate an amazingly detailed and lifelike etching of this beast which he had never in fact seen. The finished work is as remarkable for its accuracy as it is for its minor inaccuracies. The most notable of the latter is the natural armour plating with which he covered the beast's body. These plates appear to be held together by regular lines of natural rivets. In real life, especially to the uninitiated eye, the folds in the thick skin of a rhinoceros may well have been mistaken for armour plating. However, the addition of scaly legs and a second horn at the back of the animal's neck could only have been the added touches of an imaginative artist. Nonetheless, such was the authority of Dürer's etching that it continued to be used in German biology textbooks as a true depiction of a rhinoceros well into the twentieth century.

Such additional flourishes were part of a long tradition of depicting imaginary creatures and places – one which saw a resurgence in the

Renaissance. European legends have since time immemorial been replete with references to exotic beasts. Even Aristotle wrote of such 'monstrosities', describing them as 'a mistake of purpose in Nature'. And Dürer, like his contemporary Leonardo da Vinci, would also draw a number of highly imaginative apocalyptic scenes depicting the end of the world. Leonardo tended to see such scenes in terms of huge deluges, like the biblical Flood; whereas Dürer's portrayals tend to feature figures such as the Four Horsemen of the Apocalypse, or Death and the Devil.

As we have seen, the year 1500 marked one and a half millennia since the birth of Christ, and there was a widespread belief around this time that it heralded the Second Coming of Christ, which is mentioned in the Bible: 'This same Jesus, which is taken up from you into heaven, shall so come in like manner as ye have seen him go into heaven.' Such an event would precede the Last Judgement, after which our souls would be despatched to Purgatory, Hell or Heaven.*

Dürer created a number of works for his most important patron, Maximilian I. Amongst these is a large, highly complex woodcut of a triumphal arch, which measures almost ten feet by ten feet. Dürer spent over two years – on and off – busying himself with this work, which includes 195 separate woodcuts printed on 36 sheets of paper. The intention was that it should be hung in princely palaces and city halls throughout the Holy Roman Empire. Indeed, Maximilian I made a habit of giving away copies of this work with this intention.

---

* The human inclination to belief in future apocalyptic events would seem to be perennial. This appears to be more than a simple tendency to gullibility, and is frequently linked to our indelible human inclination to believe in an exotic unknown. From the Ancient Greek Pegasus (half-man, half-horse) to the modern-day Yeti (a hairy near-human giant who lives amidst the snows of the Himalayas), belief in mythic beasts persists. In the space age such myths have even transmogrified to UFOs and aliens. The surrealist artist Salvador Dalí, an aficionado of the bizarre, grew up in a house where a reproduction of Dürer's *Rhinoceros* hung on the wall. He is said to have become obsessed with this image from the age of nine, and even decades later he would frequently incorporate elements of this beast into his own work, justifying their presence with mathematical theories every bit as spurious as Dürer's imaginative additions.

The work itself is a suitably grandiose hotchpotch of styles – resembling, if anything, an example of Indian architecture rather than any classical triumphal arch (such as Marble Arch in London, or the Washington Square Arch in New York). It stands more as a monument to Dürer's indefatigable technical expertise than any aesthetic achievement. Such a work made him rich, allowing him independence – even if it contributed nothing to his artistic attainment and was otherwise a complete waste of his time.

During his adult life, Dürer kept a *Gedenkbuch* (memorial book) in which he made occasional entries recording major family events. These entries may have been sporadic but he recorded events in meticulous detail. His father died in 1502; yet many years later, when Dürer made the requisite entry, his memory was clear:

So the old woman [presumably Dürer's mother, Barbara] helped him up, and the nightcap on his head became suddenly wet with great drops of sweat. Then he asked to drink, and she gave him a little Reinfell [sweet Italian wine]. He took a very little of it and then wanted to get into bed again, and thanked her, and when he had gotten into bed again he fell at once into his last agony. At once his old wife lit the candle and repeated St Bernard's Prayer to him: 'Lighten mine eyes, lest I sleep the sleep of death...'

After her husband's death, Barbara appears to have slipped into a life of near destitution: a fact which she must have hidden from her son out of pride. When Dürer at last discovered his mother's true state of affairs, he moved her into his own home, so that she could be looked after properly. He seems to have grown closer to her during this period. Even so, the charcoal portrait he made of her in 1514 is unsparing. We see a lean, hard-faced woman, her features indicative of idiosyncratic character: difficult, wilful, but above all the mother he loved. All this shines through the utter frailty of her old age.

She would die that same year, aged sixty-three. Dürer's long entry describing her death in the family chronicle is heart-rending. A short extract gives the flavour:

> She feared death very much, but she said that she was not afraid to come before God. Also she died hard, and I noticed that she saw something frightening; for she asked for the holy water and then said nothing for a long time...

During these years Dürer began to suffer from an illness which made him fear that he was 'losing my sight and freedom of hand'. This had a deeply depressive effect on Dürer, whose art depended so much upon exactitude of observation and technique. And it was now that he produced what many consider to be his most quintessential work, an engraving named *Melencolia I.*

This work succeeds in being both deeply moving (or disturbing) and profoundly puzzling. Its main figure (a personification of melancholy) is a large seated, winged angel, her elbow resting on her knee, her face resting against her clenched fist. Her features are darkened, an indication of the black bile said to cause melancholy. This was the same sad pose which Dürer had depicted in his first sketch of his wife, Agnes. The expression on the angel's face is both serious and pensive, rather than overwhelmingly sorrowful. In Dürer's time, 'melancholy' was seen as a necessary affliction of artists. Such depressive episodes helped deepen and inform their creative expression. At least, such was the story.

The brooding angel is surrounded by all manner of emblematic objects, which have made this one of the most interpreted (and over-interpreted) works of European art. In the background, beyond the direction of the angel's blank gaze, the sky is filled with a rainbow and a comet (or the planet Saturn). Beneath the rainbow flies a bat whose spread wings contain the inscription 'Melencolia I'. Around the angel and at her feet are scattered a host of enigmatic objects. At her back is a windowless building from whose walls hang an hourglass (time) and a pair of scales (justice). Set into the wall above the angel's head is a four-by-four magic square, indisputable evidence of Dürer's continuing mathematical interest. The numbers in each column of this square add up to thirty-four. The same is true of each row, as well as both diagonals of the square. The square also contains other significant features. The bottom row includes the digits 15 and 14, indicating the date of the etching, and other numbers are thought to depict the date of the death of Dürer's mother. Resting against the far side of the building is a ladder, whose top rungs are concealed, making it lead to an unseen place. Its bottom rungs are similarly obscured, by a large multifaceted block of stone which is placed in such a way as to make its precise shape and number of faces impossible to determine. Avid symbol-hunters have detected all manner of further mathematical references in this etching – some ingenious and illuminating, others simply preposterous.

What does it all mean? What did Dürer intend it to mean? Being a consummate artist, Dürer leaves such puzzles to the spectator. As in life itself, there is no ultimate interpretation which explains the whole scene. It is an object of contemplation, intended to provoke thought. The profundity and philosophical nature of such thought is a reflection of the eye of the beholder. Though mathematics, especially geometry (Plato's favourite), underlies much of the scene.

In the words of the twentieth-century Hungarian art critic Iván Fenyő the work is also 'a lyric confession, the self-conscious introspection of the Renaissance artist... [a] spiritual self-portrait'. There is no denying the autobiographical element. Dürer was pressingly aware of his failing powers. Facing despair, prior to creating *Melencolia I* he had written 'what is beautiful I do not know'. But as well as providing a complex inner picture of the artist himself, the work is incontestably intended to provoke reflective introspection in the viewer. Description and interpretation of this work are no substitute for simply looking at it and losing oneself in it.*

---

* Amongst its numerous puzzles, the work may also have had a simple exhortatory meaning for Dürer. Many explanations have been given for the inclusion of the letter 'I' in the title. Intriguingly, *I* is the second person singular of the Latin verb *eo*, meaning 'go away'. Dürer undoubtedly suffered from frequent bouts of melancholy during this period, and the title may well have been intended as an admonition: 'Melancholy, go away!'

After the death in 1519 of Dürer's main patron, the emperor Maximilian I, the artist set out on an extended trip to the Netherlands. The ostensible reason for this was to re-establish his imperial patronage with the new Holy Roman Emperor, Charles V. Interestingly, Dürer took along his wife, which suggests that their relationship may have mellowed over the years – or maybe that he wished to present himself before the new emperor as an upright family man. Agnes may well by now have also been acting as Dürer's carer. Around this time, Pirckheimer wrote to a friend: 'Dürer is in bad shape'. Though the twentieth-century art scholar Erwin Panofsky was inclined to the opinion that this referred to the forty-eight-year-old Dürer's spiritual problems. Inevitably, the life of Dürer – as well as that of his home city, Nuremberg – was drawn into the conflict which erupted after Luther nailed his theses to the door of Wittenberg Castle Church in 1517. Three years after this event, Dürer wrote in his diary: 'And God help me that I may go to Dr Martin Luther; thus I intend to make a portrait of him with great care and engrave him on a copper plate to create a lasting memorial of the Christian man who helped me overcome so many difficulties.'

The following year, Pope Leo X issued a papal bull excommunicating Luther. It soon emerged that Pirckheimer's name had been added to the names of other 'heretics' condemned in this bull. All this would certainly have been preying on Dürer's mind as he travelled to the Netherlands to present himself before Charles V. Turning to Luther would have meant his rejection by the Holy Roman Emperor and no further work from any Catholic patrons, in all likelihood leaving him penniless. Despite this, he remained very much in sympathy with Pirckheimer and his humanist circle, and made little secret of this amongst his friends.

Dürer always had wide-ranging interests, and would undertake some extensive travelling during his trip to the Netherlands. Amongst the many and varied sights he saw were Charles V's grand entry into Brussels after his coronation in Cologne, a pair of conjoined twins, wondrous gold and silver Aztec artefacts from the New World, and the bones of an eighteen-foot giant. He also accepted an invitation to dine at the Fugger mansion in Antwerp, and on a visit to the aristocratic Count Nassau's home in

Brussels he saw 'the great bed wherein fifty people can lie', which the count provided for his guests who were unable to withstand the heavy drinking that took place at his grand banquets.

Ever on the lookout for novelties, Dürer was determined to see a beached whale that had been reported on the sands of the North Sea at Zeeland. During the course of the trip to Zeeland, in the midst of a bitter Dutch winter, the ship on which he was travelling broke from its moorings and was blown out into the open sea in a gale. As Dürer recorded:

> Then the skipper tore his hair and cried aloud, for all his men had landed and the ship was unmanned. Then we were in fear and danger, for the wind was great and there were only six people in the ship. So I spoke to the skipper and said he should take heart... and think over what was to be done. He said, if we could haul up the little sail he would try [to see] if we could come to land. So with difficulty we helped one another and got it at least halfway up and went on again toward land... the people on the shore... had already given us up for lost.

By the time Dürer reached his destination at Zeeland, the beach was empty, the whale was gone, and with it the opportunity for Dürer to add to his repertoire of intricate animal drawings. While on this trip, the ailing Dürer caught what appears to have been a severe chill, and the debilitating effects of this would remain with him to the end of his days.

During the course of Dürer's travels in the Netherlands he also met Erasmus, who was working as an adviser to the new emperor. Dürer dined with Erasmus on several occasions. Naturally, Erasmus was keen to have his portrait done by the greatest northern European artist of the age, and Dürer duly agreed to this. But something seems to have taken place between them. After a few sittings and a number of preliminary sketches, Dürer shelved the project. Only after much prodding from the great humanist and his friends would Dürer complete this work six years later. The finished engraving depicts Erasmus in his study, standing at his desk writing. Beside him are a number of books and a vase of flowers. In the background, occupying almost the entire upper left quarter of the portrait, is a framed inscription which reads (in translation from the Latin): 'The Image of Erasmus of Rotterdam was drawn from life by Albrecht Dürer'. Below this, in Ancient Greek, is: 'A better portrait is contained in his writings'.

In keeping with this modest claim, Erasmus's head is covered with a large cloth cap: his features are imbued with little character, and occupy no more space than do his hands, one writing with a pen, the other holding an eyeglass. Dürer's trademark signature – a large flat-topped 'A', containing within its base a smaller 'D' – blatantly occupies the centre of the engraving. Erasmus may well have slighted Dürer, or at least attempted to lord it over the artist with his superior knowledge. Dürer had taught himself a great deal for a man who had not completed his formal education – in this, as in several aspects, he resembled Leonardo da Vinci. Erasmus was, if anything, overeducated, his scholarship often all but overwhelming his writing. Perhaps this was what Dürer was alluding to with his 'better portrait in his writings' remark, which was indicatively written in Greek (indicating to the sitter: 'I too know Greek').

In 1524 Nuremberg was the first imperial city to become Protestant. Despite being excommunicated, Pirckheimer, along with his humanist friends, is said to have prevented any excesses and forestalled widespread disturbances and the destruction of Catholic churches. But despite the change in the city's alliances, Dürer remained – outwardly at least – a Catholic.

With Dürer's eyesight fading, he devoted less of his energies to his art. Instead he concentrated on writing treatises on such subjects as 'human proportions' and 'fortifications'. However, his most important work was his *Four Books on Measurement*. These contain the wealth of mathematical knowledge he accumulated during his life – including the geometrical construction of shadows in prints (projective geometry), as well as several ideas by the Tuscan artist Piero della Francesca which had not yet been published. (These Dürer had almost certainly learned from Luca Pacioli.) Very little of this vast compendium of work is original, but it was written in the vernacular German rather than in Latin. This established Dürer as the first figure of the northern Renaissance to outline in German Euclidean geometry and demonstrate the construction of the five Platonic solids, other Archimedean semi-regular truncated solids, and a number of constructed figures which are thought to have been of his own invention. His treatises were the first printed north of the Alps to view art in a scientific fashion, exposing the mathematical bones upon which much artistic flesh is based.

After the outbreak of the German Peasants' Revolt in 1525, Dürer, like Erasmus, broke off with Luther, as such violence was utterly abhorrent to him.* Dürer died three years later in Nuremberg at the age of fifty-six. Always careful with his money, it was found that his estate was worth 6,874 florins, a considerable fortune for a man of his class. The five-storey *Fachwerkhaus* (traditional timber-framed dwelling) where he lived can still be seen in Nuremberg.

Despite all that Dürer learned from his visits to Italy, he remains to this day a uniquely northern artist. His influence on the northern Renaissance and consequent northern European artists was lasting. Meanwhile the southern Renaissance remained devoid of Dürer's influence, moving away from his all-but-transcendent realism into the distortions of mannerism and the ornamentation of the baroque.

---

* As we have seen, Luther too was against this revolt, but its aims were widely regarded as Lutheran by the Catholic Church, and thus the revolt became indelibly associated with him by many – whether for or against his ideas.

CHAPTER 12

STRADDLING TWO AGES: PARACELSUS AND BRUEGEL THE ELDER

One step forwards, one step backwards. The northern Renaissance, especially in some aspects of science and art, still retained a strong medieval element, which could both inform and undercut its progress in the humanities. Nowhere is this more evident than in Theophrastus Bombastus von Hohenheim, the figure we know as Paracelsus. To expand on his short appearance at the start of this work is highly instructive. The man's character – to say nothing of his great advances, and great disgraces – warrants nothing less.

Paracelsus's fame and notoriety are evident across a wide range of disciplines. As a chemist he played a major role in the discovery and isolation of no less than four elements: zinc, arsenic, bismuth and cobalt (a feat which would remain unsurpassed for two centuries – until the advent of the Swedish chemist Carl Wilhelm Scheele, who isolated five elements). On the minus side, Paracelsus remained throughout his life an inveterate alchemist, at one stage claiming that he had discovered the 'elixir of life'.

Yet even this practice led indirectly to one of his greatest achievements: the preparation of laudanum (opium dissolved in alcohol) – which he used for both pharmaceutical and recreational purposes.

As a pioneer psychologist, his enlightened ideas saved several poor demented souls from being stoned to death for being 'possessed by demons'. In the field of medicine he became notorious for burning books by the ancient classical physician Galen and the Persian-born Avicenna (Ibn Sina), the greatest practitioner of the Islamic Golden Age, proclaiming that much of their work was rubbish. He insisted that his own understanding of medicine far surpassed these historical 'authorities'. And arguably, it did. In other guises he made notable contributions as a lay theologian, a philosopher and a prophet (his 'prognostications' were still being taken seriously by seventeenth-century Rosicrucians).

So, where to begin . . . ? At the end is perhaps most appropriate in this case. As with so much of Paracelsus's life, the circumstances surrounding his death remain obscure. Having spent the night of 21 September 1541 in the White Horse Tavern in Salzburg, the bloated ageing figure staggered down the narrow street towards his lodgings before collapsing onto the cobbles. On being found, he was carried to his bed, where he died three days later aged forty-seven.

Some claim that he had in fact been attacked by a gang of thugs hired by local physicians and other worthies, outraged by his continuous attacks on their probity while enjoying the protection of the local ruler, Duke Ernst of Bavaria. Others claim that he took an excessive potion of his elixir of life, which put him to sleep, and was wakened prematurely, causing a fatal shock to his system.

A wealth of information concerning Paracelsus was gathered by his nineteenth-century biographer, Franz Hartmann, a well-known esotericist and one-time chairman of the Theosophical Society.* According to

---

* Highly popular in the nineteenth century, this society followed a religion whose secret masters lived in remote locations throughout the world, but mainly in Tibet. These superhuman figures possessed great wisdom and occult powers derived from western Neoplatonism and eastern mysticism, as well as a melange of the ancient religions of India.

Hartmann, prior to his death Paracelsus left instructions for his cadaver to be buried in a dung heap, whose fermenting warmth would bring his body back to life. In this way, Paracelsus would be reincarnated in an 'astral body' which would take up residence in 'a certain place in Asia, from whence he still – invisibly, but nonetheless effectually – influences the minds of his followers, appearing to them occasionally even in visible and tangible shape'.*

From rebirth to actual birth. Thus we come to the arrival of Theophrastus Bombastus von Hohenheim on earth in 1493 in the village of Egg, near Einsiedeln, close to a small lake beneath the high Alps of central Switzerland. According to Paracelsus,† he was born the son of a local bondswoman (indentured servant or serf) attached to the nearby ancient Benedictine monastery. He claimed that his father was the illegitimate scion of the aristocratic Bombastus von Hohenheim family from southern Germany. Others have claimed that his father was a mere

---

* The inclusion of such apparently superfluous posthumous metaphysics is intended to illustrate that the strain of irrationality is not confined to the remnants of medieval thought which lasted on into the Renaissance. The human mind throughout history has thrived on metaphysical beliefs – from the pyramids where the mummified pharaohs would rise to enter their 'after life', to the enjoyment of modern movies featuring exorcism, zombies, body-changing and the like. Humanism and the Renaissance may have inspired the human mind on its path to the modern world view, but even this latter also contains its seemingly necessary undercurrent of esoteric thought. From Faust to Frankenstein to Count Dracula, this never-ending cast of figures rises from our subconscious mind to march on beside us, at the edges of our vision. As with Paracelsus, such thought can, and still does, inform all manner of genuine scientific discovery. Today, research into AI (artificial intelligence) has brought huge technical advances, despite its quixotic striving to create 'consciousness'. Likewise the many advances effected by Elon Musk, fuelled by his belief that humanity will escape this polluted earth to thrive on barren planets.

† He would not take on his self-aggrandizing classical name until he was thirty-six and had so blotted his aristocratic moniker that he was no longer able to get away with practising as a physician under the name Theophrastus Bombastus von Hohenheim. I have used the name Paracelsus for the opposite reason – in order to avoid any misidentification such as he sought to perpetrate.

physician from eastern Switzerland, but consequent research has surprisingly tended to confirm Paracelsus's unlikely story.

Paracelsus was a sickly child, and his mother died when he was just nine years old. By this time he must have developed a more robust physique, for his father now chose to up sticks and travel with his juvenile son to Villach, in the province of Carinthia in southern Austria, a journey which would have involved a trek of more than 200 miles through the mountains. This early adventure, passing through Alpine valleys and across high passes beneath snow-capped peaks, evidently sparked in Paracelsus a lifelong love of travel. Likewise, watching his father converse with the locals, seeking out their medical lore and peasant cures, inspired in him a hunger for homespun local knowledge.

On arrival at Villach, Paracelsus's father became attached as physician to the local Benedictine monastery, with his son acting as his assistant and apprentice. At the same time, Paracelsus also took lessons from the young local monks, who had a surprisingly humanistic approach to education.

Following the discovery of silver in the nearby mountains, Carinthia and the nearby Tyrol had become successful mining regions. As security for a loan to the Emperor Maximilian I, Jakob Fugger had been granted local mining rights over this area. Paracelsus's father soon became attached as a roving physician to the local mines, once again taking along his son as his assistant. These mines were dangerous, and the local miners had developed all manner of superstitions. An example of this can be seen in the word 'cobalt', which derives from the German word for 'goblin'. Malicious goblins were said to be responsible for many deaths in the mines, and this particular miners' superstition had more than a grain of truth. Cobalt ore contained much of the silver found in the mines, but it also contained arsenic – which when smelted released toxic arsenic oxide gas.

The young Paracelsus would have learned this and many similar superstitions when accompanying his father to the mines. It soon became clear that he had an exceptional grasp of such knowledge, as well as the more conventional learning he had been taught by the priests. Consequently, at the age of sixteen he was encouraged to take up the study of medicine at the University of Basel. Within a year Paracelsus had become disillusioned with the teaching and had moved on to the University at Vienna. There he learned that the most advanced medical teaching was to be found in Italy, so he travelled to Ferrara, and it was here that he may (or may not) have gained qualification as a medical doctor in 1515.

It was now that Paracelus's *Wanderjahre* began, crossing all over Europe (if he is to be believed), from Lisbon to Moscow, from Jerusalem to Ireland. During part of his travels he enlisted as an army surgeon, which accounted for his visits to Venice, Holland and Denmark. Throughout this entire period he 'sought a universal knowledge... that was not to be found in the books or the faculties'. His collecting of local cures for particular diseases established him as a medical pioneer. Instead of seeking which of the four humours had become unbalanced in his patient, he sought out a clinical diagnosis – and to remedy this issue he would administer a specific medicine. Here lay Paracelsus's groundbreaking technique which would revolutionize medicine: empirical science, based on experience. It utterly contradicted the medieval appeal to authority such as Aristotle or Galen. As such, Paracelsus's medical practice would have been regarded as nothing short of academic heresy.

Paracelsus was aware of his iconoclastic role, and was not above comparing himself with Martin Luther on this score. Although he was well aware of the dangers involved in such a comparison: 'I leave it to Luther to defend what he says, and I will be responsible for what I say. That which you wish to Luther, you wish also to me: you wish us both in the fire.'

His biographer Philip Ball emphasizes Paracelsus's holistic approach to such matters: 'The simple reason for this is that in both cases the arguments were at root theological. No one could divorce beliefs about nature from beliefs about God and the spiritual life of humankind.'

In 1524, after more than ten years on the road, Paracelsus returned to Villach and re-joined his father. It was now that he began writing down his voluminous findings with a view to their publication. And despite his antagonism towards universities, he also began trying to find an academic post. As we have seen, his meeting with Erasmus in Basel resulted in just that: he became a professor of medicine.

Yet after many battles with the authorities (university, civil, religious and legal), numerous escapades, libels and so forth – interspersed with a number of spectacular cures – the authorities finally lost any last vestige of tolerance for their local professor of medicine. A warrant was issued for his arrest. Fortunately, Paracelsus was tipped off, and managed to ride out of town in the nick of time.

Over the coming years, Paracelsus would continue to demonstrate his remarkable skills. By now syphilis had become the scourge of the age and had spread throughout Europe. In these early days the manifestations of this disease were both hideous and extremely painful; it appeared to be incurable and was frequently fatal. The infected found their skin bursting with pustules, which soon became weeping sores. At the same time their flesh began to rot and they stank of putrefaction.

When Paracelsus arrived in Nuremberg in 1530 he soon learned some interesting facts. The first was that the local Fugger family had apparently discovered a miracle cure for syphilis. This involved guaiac, a brown resin obtained from the guaiacum tree, which grew in the Caribbean region. They had immediately obtained a monopoly on the import of this product from the King of Spain, who also happened to be their indebted friend the Holy Roman Emperor Charles V. By now the Fuggers were making a fortune out of the sale of guaiac through their many company outlets, and it had even been blessed by the Church.

The second interesting fact which Paracelsus learned was that, despite this miracle cure, there had been an outbreak of syphilis in Nuremberg. Fearful of the disease spreading, the authorities had quarantined victims in a wooden stockade outside the city walls.

For once, Paracelsus seems to have kept his suspicions to himself – at least for the time being. At considerable risk to his health, he volunteered to cure the syphilitics using his own method. The answer lay in mercury: 'What is a poison if taken in excess... may be a medicine if taken in moderation, and in a form carefully prepared by the physician so that its toxicity is minimized.' Here was a classic case of the science of toxicology which he did so much to found. Administering strictly limited dosages of mercury compounds, taken internally at regular intervals, Paracelsus managed to cure nine of the fourteen victims – a fact confirmed in the city records.

Having effected his cure, Paracelsus decided to write a book about syphilis. In it, he described the symptoms, how the disease was transmitted, and the recipe for the cure which he personally had discovered.* The Fuggers were soon informed of what Paracelsus was doing. Aware of the harm it could inflict on their lucrative guaiac monopoly, they immediately used their powers to supress Paracelsus's book, having the manuscript seized at the local printers and destroyed.

But what is once known is almost impossible to make unknown. Paracelsus simply sat down and rewrote his manuscript from memory, and soon found a publisher who was willing to take the risk of defying the Fuggers. Thus Paracelsus eventually published his *Treatise of the French Disease*. In his usual brazen fashion, Paracelsus made sure that he exposed imposters such as those peddling the guaiac cure and other fraudulent medicines.

In fact, Paracelsus's *Treatise of the French Disease* was a model scientific work, one of the first to appear in the Renaissance. At this time the notion of patent laws was extremely limited and all but unenforceable. A patent protected by an edict issued by the authorities in the city of Nuremberg could be circumvented with little difficulty by merely publishing in the city of Frankfurt. Consequently, scientists of all kinds – from mathematicians to alchemists – were loath to reveal the secrets

---

* Despite this typical claim, Paracelsus had almost certainly heard of the cure while travelling in Italy. The cure is known to have been discovered by Fracastoro of the University of Padua, who was the man who named the disease syphilis – after a mythical shepherd, Syphilus, who was said to have been stricken with the disease after insulting the god Apollo. The mercury cure was a painful treatment, frequently causing almost as much pain as the disease itself. And it was certainly toxic. The skill lay in assessing the correct dosage, depending upon the stage reached by the disease and the general health of the patient. Those who did not die of this treatment usually experienced a remission of the symptoms, often for long periods. In fact, the mercury cure (of one kind or another) would remain the standard medical prescription until the Salvarsan treatment of 1909 which was substituted for arsenic compounds.

of their discoveries. Such secrets, often covertly sold on for considerable sums, were the discoverer's main means of earning a living. In publishing his *Treatise*, Paracelsus set a template for experimental treatises to come.

From now on, the essence of this method would gradually be adopted, step by step, in all sciences – and remains standard practice to this day. First, the disease was described, along with its various symptoms. This was followed by the best methods of cure, along with how to perform or administer such cures. The treatise also explained the general course the disease could take during the period of treatment, and when it was safe to declare the patient cured and restored to health.

Paracelsus was now in his forties, and beginning to feel the effects of his constant travelling and carousing, as well as his penurious, generally scruffy way of living. With the earnings from his *Treatise* he decided to settle down and commit to paper his huge range of medical knowledge. This he modestly entitled *Die Grosse Wundartzney* (The Great Surgery Book). This proved to be a huge success, and was published in Ulm, Augsburg, Frankfurt and beyond. Soon Paracelsus was in demand with dukes, princes and bishops, all willing to pay high fees for his services.

Paracelsus would go on to publish numerous original works, spread over a wide range of scientific knowledge and advances. It was in this way that he outlined such successes as his discovery and isolation of zinc, which he personally named. (This element's crystals are pointed, or *zinke* in German.) Other pioneering works described his original investigations into magnetism, digestion, dietary cures and so forth. His poetic contributions to philosophy were also original, both in their poetry and their philosophy. Alas, in between these exemplary works he could not restrain himself from publishing fantastical tracts on prophecy, all manner of hermeticism, and meandering metaphysical musings on magic and alchemy. As a match to his true masterpiece *The Great Surgery Book* he produced a vast work entitled *Astronomia Magna*, which contains a potent mix of astrology, demonology, esoteric lore, divination and much more.

As a scientist, Paracelsus was far ahead of his time; as a magus (or magician) his beliefs stretched far back, to the superstitious beginnings of human history. Not for nothing would elements of Paracelsus's life appear in the story of Faust, who bargained his soul with the Devil in exchange for all human knowledge and worldly pleasure. As such he would inspire masterworks by the English Elizabethan playwright Christopher Marlowe and giants of German literature from Wolfgang Goethe to Thomas Mann.

If science could be schizophrenic, how much easier it was for art. Paracelsus picked up his medical knowledge tramping through the highways and byways of Europe. In remote villages still inhabiting a medieval past, he learned medicinal folklore which had seemingly been practised by peasants since time immemorial. Much of this folklore would be absorbed into later medicine by way of the iatrochemistry which preceded our use of pharmaceuticals. But who were these people who passed on their knowledge to Paracelsus? Where did they live? And how did they live?

Fortunately we know precisely what these villages looked like, and the features and foibles of their inhabitants – as well as the countryside which marked the boundaries of their existence. They appear in the vivid and detailed rural scenes painted by the Dutch artist Pieter Bruegel the Elder, who not only captured these landscapes but also the behaviours and rituals of the characters and animals who inhabited them. The scenes themselves may be quintessentially medieval in character, but the realism and perspective with which they are portrayed is unmistakably that of a Renaissance artist.

Pieter Bruegel the Elder was born around 1525 in the southern Netherlands in a tiny village named Bruegel outside the city of Breda, in southern Holland. Judging from the precision and exactitude with which Bruegel painted his pastoral scenes, his life must have been deeply rooted in such rural circumstances. There is only one snag: no such village as Bruegel, or any spot resembling that name, ever existed. And according to his biographer Alexander Wied: 'There is, in fact, every reason to think that Pieter Bruegel was a townsman and a highly educated one, on friendly terms with the humanists of his time.' This suggests that Bruegel may in fact have been born in Breda.

Bruegel probably mixed with the educated humanists of Breda, but his biographer Nadine Orenstein insists that 'he had not mastered Latin', which would have been highly unusual amongst such circles. Indeed, she goes as far as to suggest that the Latin inscriptions which appear on some of his paintings were in fact written by another hand.

What is known with more certainty is that the young Bruegel travelled the thirty miles from Breda to Antwerp to begin his five-year apprenticeship in the studio of the artist Pieter Coecke van Aelst, whose paintings of religious scenes exhibited an eclectic blend of Gothic and Italian Renaissance influences. Coecke van Aelst would later be appointed court painter to the Holy Roman Emperor Charles V, who spent time in Antwerp in his capacity as Lord of the Netherlands and Duke of Burgundy. At the time Antwerp was the great commercial hub of northern Europe, having taken over from Bruges after the waterway linking the port of Bruges to the sea began silting up. The port of Antwerp lay at the mouth of the River Scheldt, where the inland canals of the Netherlands linked the Rhine to the North Sea. As a financial centre it also had Europe's largest bourse.* Antwerp had a population of 100,000, a tenth of whom were foreign merchants. With Venice in decline after the discovery of the sea route to Asia around the Cape of Good Hope, and trade with the New World concentrated on ports with more direct access to the Atlantic, Antwerp was now the most cosmopolitan city in Europe.

This plunge into the overwhelming world of sophisticated reality had a profound psychological effect on the young Bruegel. Moored up along the quayside he would have seen lateen-sail barques from Portugal, three-masters which had voyaged from ports as far afield as Zanzibar and Stavanger, their cargoes loaded onto barges from Delft or Mosel, barrels being rolled across the cobbles by sailors in ragged and exotic garb, marking them out as Finnish, Scottish or Moorish. Lined

---

* This may have operated much like a stock exchange, but was in reality a commodity exchange. Financial instruments such as stocks and shares as we know them had not yet come into common usage.

up for sale would have been opened crates of currants from Cyprus, tulip bulbs from Constantinople, reeking salted hides from the eastern Baltic, barrels of sweet wine from Sicily. He would have come across cramped groups of buyers and curious onlookers watching the auction of chained black African slaves, huddles of young mountain girls imported from the Caucasus... Yet all this went deeper than mere impressions and appearances. How could he absorb and express the sheer variety of teeming life he found milling around him amongst the vast cobbled space of the *Grote Markt*, overlooked by windowed cliffs of many-storied houses, with the great unfinished Gothic tower of *Onze-Lieve-Vrouwekathedraal* (the Cathedral of Our Lady) reaching into the sky above the rooftops? How could he render such scenes without being overwhelmed by the sheer teeming multiplicity and variety of it all?

It was now that Bruegel discovered the work of another Dutch artist who seemed to have been similarly overawed by life in much the same way as he himself now felt. Yet somehow this artist, who had died just a decade or so before Bruegel's birth, had managed to express his feelings – at the same time conveying a facsimile of the jumbled life and the discombobulated spirits of both himself and the souls around him. This artist was Hieronymus Bosch, whose crammed canvases – such as his highly charged and ambiguous triptych *The Garden of Earthly Delights* – conveyed everything from the carnival-esque to the grotesque, to such an extent that it was frequently difficult to separate the two. Here, in many ways, was Heaven, Purgatory and Hell – an utterly medieval conception of the afterlife which awaited all souls, yet conveyed in realistic detail; a life in death where reality as we know it has been swirled and sliced into a dreamlike posthumous existence. It was as if Bosch were depicting an image of the mischievous unconscious mind which had swelled up to cloud the clear scientific vision of Paracelsus. Here was the world as it would be inhabited in the years to come by the likes of Faust, Frankenstein, Dracula and their multifarious descendants and dreamers.

The modern analyst Julian Horx captures Bruegel's conundrum when faced with Bosch's *The Garden of Earthly Delights* – the condition which faces us all:

The decision on how to engage with it falls on the observer. The act of engagement allows one to find one's own narratives, representations of anxieties and occurrences familiar to them. The observer is trusted to navigate the chaos of the painting, and by extension the overwhelming complexity of its source material on their own terms.

Bruegel was initially overwhelmed by Bosch's vision of chaos, and it would take him many years before he learned how to 'navigate' such 'overwhelming complexity' on his own terms.

Meanwhile, at the age of twenty-six he qualified as a member of the Guild of Saint Luke (the painters' guild) in Antwerp. He was now a fully fledged and independent artist. He at once set out on an adventurous journey across Europe, passing through France and crossing the Alps to Italy, where he ventured as far south as Sicily. While in southern Italy he witnessed the devastating effects of a Turkish raid on the city of Reggio Calabria. His drawing of this event captures the city on fire, as seen from a safe distance across the bay, with two tiny figures in the foreground throwing up their hands in horror at what they are witnessing. Bruegel here begins to grasp the full scope of landscape painting.

While in Rome, Bruegel briefly found employment as an assistant to the fifty-three-year-old Croatian artist Giulio Clovio, the finest miniaturist of his time. This enabled him to master the art of detail. And later, while passing through Florence, it seems likely that Bruegel was able to see, or study a copy of, Paolo Uccello's *Battle of San Romano*, which he probably completed in the late 1440s. In the foreground, this work depicts lifelike fighting between mounted soldiers. But what seems to have caught Bruegel's interest was Uccello's depiction in the far background of a number of small distant figures moving amidst a countryside of hills and fields.

Bruegel was beginning to assemble the ingredients of his mature masterpieces. Alas, when he returned to Antwerp in 1555 after some four years in Italy he seems once again to have fallen under the influence of Bosch. His 1556 etching *Big Fish Eat Little Fish* depicts a monstrous fish stranded on the shore, spewing from its open mouth a cascade of smaller marine animals that it has swallowed. Meanwhile, a dwarfed human figure in a helmet slashes open its belly with a large serrated knife, causing a cascade of fishy grotesques to pour out onto the sand.

But Bruegel had not entirely forgotten what he learned in Italy. In the background one can see across a wide stretch of water the skyline of a distant city, whose church tower is recognizable as that of Antwerp. And behind the big fish, on the left of the painting, is a fishermen's hut with large gutted fishes hanging from the branches of a tree. There is also a Bosch-like figure – half-human, half-fish – carrying off a smaller fish in its mouth.

The title of *Big Fish Eat Little Fish* is of course proverbial, with the subject matter intended to illustrate this fishy adage, which is thought to date from the twelfth century. And here is the final ingredient for Bruegel's mature works, many of which depict similar proverbs that were just as much a part of everyday peasant life as the old wives' remedies collected by Paracelsus.

Such homespun wisdom also prevailed amongst city folk, especially in Antwerp. Unlike the resplendent figures of the Italian Renaissance, the people of Antwerp:

> spent more attention to making and saving money than they did to spending it 'on showy things', wrote one contemporary visitor, who could not conceal his shock at how bad the food was. It was so awful, he noted, that 'it would be hard to live more poorly'. Even the beer was pretty ghastly, thanks to the city's water.

Ironically, it was this way of life which fostered a new element of egalitarianism that was beginning to emerge in the Netherlands. During the 'glory years' of Antwerp in the sixteenth century, when Bruegel flourished:

> 'Commerce was its identity... the energy which held it together.' Fundamental to that was a very 'pragmatic kind of tolerance': Antwerp's 'business depended on foreign traders, so it had no interest in abolishing the heresies to which so many of those traders were attached'. In Antwerp, money mattered, not God.

And it was this down-to-earth attitude which would permeate Bruegel's masterworks, though in a secular rather than a mercenary sense.

In 1563, Bruegel was engaged to be married to Mayken Coecke, the daughter of his former apprentice-master Pieter. Bruegel now moved to Brussels at the insistence of his future mother-in-law, who had learned that he had formed a liaison with a local servant girl.

However, despite this move, Bruegel would remain in close contact with the Antwerp publisher Hieronymus Cock, who ran the printing presses and distribution network of prints known as *Aux Quatre Vents* (To the Four Winds). As its name suggests, this firm had widespread international contacts, and would play a major role in disseminating copies of Bruegel's drawings and etchings throughout northern Europe. More importantly, Bruegel was now entering the period during which he would produce his best-known paintings.

As was so often the case, especially during the Renaissance era, many of Bruegel's masterpieces were produced against a background of political turbulence. Antwerp may have been the commercial hub of the Netherlands, but Brussels was the political capital – the centre of its regional government within the Holy Roman Empire.

By now the situation in this far-flung Europe-wide empire was beginning to undergo a transformation, largely owing to the declining health of the emperor. Charles V had chosen to establish his main residence in Spain now that his family connections had led to him inheriting the Spanish crown. By this time, the Habsburg family had spread far and wide over Europe, and interbreeding in the family in order to retain dynastic power was beginning to have debilitating genetic effects. Most notably, Charles V had inherited the famous overlapping 'Habsburg Jaw'.*

---

* Technically known as *mandibular prognathism*, this deformity projected the lower jaw so that its teeth overlapped the teeth of the upper jaw, which hindered chewing, affected speech and gave an odd facial appearance. The Habsburg habit of intermarriage between cousins and other close relatives may have extended their European territories, but it also resulted in additional defects, including a tendency to gout, epilepsy and the reinforcing of other genetic flaws.

Owing to increasing ill-health, Charles V felt obliged to divest himself of some of the territories over which he ruled. In 1555, the emperor appeared at a public ceremony held at the Palace of Coudenberg in Brussels. With tears streaming down his face, and forced to lean on his adviser William the Silent* for support, Charles V announced what became known as the Abdications of Brussels. This ongoing process gradually divided the Habsburg Empire into the Spanish line and the Austro-German succession. One result of this was that Charles V's son became King Philip II of Spain and Lord of the Seventeen Provinces of the Netherlands. Philip II was determined to stamp out Protestantism, which had already taken a strong hold in many parts of the Netherlands, especially in the northern provinces. A rumour spread amongst the Protestants that he was planning to introduce the Spanish Inquisition, which in 1566 provoked a revolt led by the Calvinist William the Silent. The revolt led to the Eighty Years' War, during which the Protestant northern provinces of the Netherlands gradually separated from the southern provinces. This division would eventually result in the establish-ment of the Dutch Republic (loosely modern Holland) and the Spanish Netherlands (loosely modern Belgium and Luxembourg). Subsequently, the Dutch Republic would enter its 'Golden Age', during which Dutch traders established an overseas empire from the Americas to Indonesia, while the sciences flourished in the homeland as never before.

Although the ructions of the Eighty Years' War did not involve continuous fighting – there was even a Twelve Years' Truce signed in 1609 – they provided a troubled background to the later years of Bruegel's life, as well as to the ensuing Golden Age of the Dutch Republic. Once again we see a turning point in human history, similar to that of Ancient Greece or the Italian Renaissance, taking place against a background of squabbling city-states and internecine warfare.

---

* Also known as William of Orange. The House of Orange was named after the principality of Orange in southern France, which his family had inherited through marriage in 1530. A later William of Orange, together with his wife Mary, would be invited to take over the throne of Britain in 1689. The present Dutch and British royal families are both directly descended from the House of Orange.

The mature masterpieces which Bruegel would produce during the last years of his life barely hint at the political turmoil unfolding around him. Yet the clues are there if one looks hard enough. His several panoramic winter scenes paint an evocative picture of countryside under snow; these are as spectacular as they are chilling. In one, his well-muffled skaters slither over an ice-bound waterway beneath the watchful eye of dark winter birds perched on the branches of the bare trees. His scenes of the snow-blanketed countryside may be magnificent in their vision of bleakness, but they do not depict a happy or an easy way of life.*

Other paintings by Bruegel during these years depict a wide range of disparate subjects, yet still manage to convey the troubled zeitgeist. Perhaps the most blatant of these is *The Blind Leading the Blind*, which is a nightmarish scene of medieval misery, yet its peasant faces and the literal helplessness of its subjects are rendered with a Renaissance realism and composition that conveys all too well its proverbial content. Here allegory and actuality are blended with supreme artistry. Even the comparative ease of the recumbent figures in his celebrated *The Land of Cockaigne* contains ominous Bosch-like images in the background. This is not just a clerk, a peasant and a soldier lying sprawled out in the afternoon countryside, snoozing after a pleasant bibulous lunch. The clerk's eyes are open, his features frozen in a blank expression. Cockaigne is the mythical land of plenty and these supine figures are gluttons overcome by sloth; it is a vision of spiritual emptiness.

Similarly, Bruegel's brilliantly realized scene in *The Peasant Wedding*, for all its witty observation and feasting plenty, is hardly a joyous spectacle. The plethora of superbly characterized individual figures feature mainly dour faces that are all but expressionless. Yes, this is what it was *really* like...

In the last years of his life Bruegel would paint two versions of *The Tower of Babel*. These depict vast intricate constructions whose

---

* The Little Ice Age, which affected Europe to a more or less degree between 1300 and 1800, was approaching its most severe stage. The depiction of winter scenes became a genre at this time, but the paintings of Bruegel outshone all others in their atmospheric intensity.

incompleteness enables us to gain an insight into the complex engineering involved, and which were inspired by the ruins of the Colosseum – which Bruegel had seen while in Rome during his twenties. Indeed, he is known to have painted an earlier miniature version of this scene while he was working for the maestro Giulio Clovio, though this is now lost. Even so, the larger versions contain a miniaturist's eye for detail – from the tiny silhouettes of the builders against the sky at the uppermost level, to the stonemasons bowing in servile reverence at the foot of the tower as they are approached by the visiting king and his entourage. The building of the Tower of Babel is a biblical symbol of humanity's hubris, even megalomania. It was intended to reach as high as heaven, and this purpose was only frustrated when God inflicted upon its builders the confusion of different languages so that they could not communicate with each other. At the same time, the echoes of the Colosseum in Bruegel's depictions hint at the persecution of the early Christians. As with all great art, this is a fully realized image of aesthetic wonder as well as being an instructive object of contemplation. How tiny and frail is humanity in comparison with its overweening ambitions.

Pieter and Mayken Bruegel would have two sons, who both became artists. Pieter Bruegel the Younger would grow up to build a successful artistic career copying his father's style (and in doing so increase his father's reputation). His other son, Jan Bruegel the Elder, would become an important artist in the Flemish Baroque style which flourished during the Dutch Golden Age.

Pieter Bruegel the Elder himself became old before his time. A self-portrait from 1565 when he was in his early forties depicts a somewhat scruffy bearded figure with an old man's features. He would die just four years later, leaving his mother-in-law Mayken Coecke to instruct his sons in the art of painting. Mayken Coecke, who painted under the name of Mayken Verhulst, is known to have been a highly skilled artist in her own right, though her works have yet to be reliably identified.

And what of Bruegel the Elder's lasting reputation? The great sixteenth-century Italian historian of the Renaissance, Giorgio Vasari – whose *Lives of the Artists* bring so much of this period to life – barely acknowledges the northern Renaissance. Though he does find time to denigrate Bruegel as 'essentially a comic successor to Hieronymus Bosch'. During Bruegel's lifetime he achieved renown largely as a genre painter of peasant scenes – for the most part more popular with the emergent merchant class than with connoisseurs and art critics. During the century after his death he influenced a number of less-talented artists who attempted to imitate him; yet at the same time his true talent was recognized by the Austrian Habsburg emperor Rudolf II and the great Baroque artist Peter Paul Rubens (who collected a dozen of his paintings). Many of Bruegel's most successful works may have featured typical medieval rural scenes, but his painterly skills incorporated a vivid realism against a backdrop of imaginary landscapes (there were no mountain vistas in the Netherlands). Such accomplishments ensured that he is now regarded as one of the most significant northern Renaissance artists – a master whose skills on occasion aspire to the likes of van Eyck and Dürer.

CHAPTER 13

VERSIONS OF THE TRUE: MERCATOR AND VIÈTE

W E NOW COME TO two figures who used ingenious mathematical techniques to unravel their own versions of the truth. These were Gerardus Mercator and François Viète, both of whom lived exciting lives (though not always pleasantly so), and whose works would play a part in transforming the world in which we live. Both of them were contemporaries of Bruegel the Elder, and Mercator was even a fellow citizen of the Habsburg Netherlands who grew up in a village just outside Antwerp. However, Mercator would outlive Bruegel and witness the birth of the Dutch Golden Age – in which his work would play a formative role.

Gerardus Mercator was born Gerard de Kremer* in the village of Rupelmonde, some seven miles south-west of Antwerp, on the left bank of the River Scheldt. At the time of his birth in March 1512, Gerard's

---

* The Dutch-German word Kremer means shopkeeper or trader. When Gerard took on his Latinized academic name, he adopted the slightly more prestigious Mercator, meaning merchant.

German father, Hubert de Kremer, and his wife Emerance already had six children, and were on an extended visit to Hubert's uncle Gisbert, a locally influential priest. Hubert's home town was Gangelt, almost 100 miles east, in Germany, where he plied his trade as a not very successful cobbler. Hubert and his family may have taken refuge with their prestigious relative to escape an outbreak of the plague, or possibly to avoid their debtors in Gangelt. At any rate, after six months Hubert was able to return to his home in Germany, and young Mercator spent his first years in the rural backwater of Gangelt.

During Mercator's youth, two historic events took place which would change Europe forever. Mercator was just five when Luther instigated what would become the Reformation, and he was ten years old when the survivors of Magellan's three-year expedition to circumnavigate the globe arrived back in Seville. By this time young Mercator's father had died, and his uncle had taken on the role of his guardian. Discerning an element of promise in young Mercator, Gisbert used his influence to gain his protégé a place as a pupil at the school of the Brethren of the Common Life in the Dutch city of 's-Hertogenbosch. Despite its name, this was the finest school in the region. As we have seen, forty years previously Erasmus had been educated there, and several of the brethren were known to have been favourably impressed by his humanist texts. Even so, the main curriculum was still based on the traditional scholastic trivium of grammar, logic and rhetoric, all of which were of course taught in Latin. However, in a gesture towards the renaissance of classical knowledge, the curriculum had been extended to include Ptolemy and his *Geography*. The Ancient Greek polymath had written this work in Alexandria around AD 150. The fact that it was written in Ancient Greek meant that it had remained unknown to Europe during the medieval era, as scholars only knew Latin. It was not translated until 1406, when its appearance created a great stir. Meanwhile Ptolemy's geocentric cosmology, which Aristotle had passed on, would not be refuted by Copernicus until 1543, when Mercator was in his thirties. But much of Ptolemy's *Geography*, especially his map of the world – consisting of a chart which stretched from the Atlantic coast in the west to Sinae (China) in the east – had come as a revelation to the young Mercator.

During his time at the school of the Brethren, a leading member of the staff was Georgius Macropedius, regarded by many as the greatest Latin dramatist of the sixteenth century. Indeed, his plays were so widely known that they would later influence the young William Shakespeare. Some of Macropedius's works were adaptations of Ancient Roman comedies by Terence and Plautus, and he staged performances of these works with his pupils as actors. According to Mercator's biographer Nicholas Crane: 'In one of the more raucous works, *Aluta*, the audience was warned against halitosis and flatulence, and then subjected to heavy drinking, vomiting, undressing and a comedic exorcism.'

Not surprisingly, the local audiences were both shocked and entertained by these performances. Macropedius disingenuously explained that such 'images of debauchery were sound educational material, as long as purity and truth prevailed by the end of the play'. The school's plays were frequently sold out, and Macropedius made sure that the takings were distributed amongst the more impecunious members of the cast, which included Mercator. Such drama opened his eyes to another aspect of the Renaissance, introducing him to a more humanistic approach to life.

In 1530, at the age of eighteen, Mercator travelled to the similarly prestigious University of Leuven. Here he passed the entry matriculation, where his name appears in the Latin form he had adopted at school followed by the classification *pauperes ex castro* (poor students of the castle). This indicated that he was given lodgings in one of the communal dormitories set aside for unprivileged students in the castle by the fish market. Rich students lived separately in their own rooms in a more salubrious quarter of the city. Despite such domestic segregation, all students mingled freely, attending the same lectures, and it was here that Mercator formed a friendship with one of his more privileged contemporaries, named Andreas Vesalius, of whom we will hear more later. Suffice to say that Vesalius would become one of the great luminaries of the northern Renaissance, on a par with Mercator himself, with whom he retained a lifelong friendship.

Mercator graduated as a Magister (Master) in 1532. Normally he would now have enrolled for further study in theology or canon law, with the ultimate aim of entering the priesthood and achieving a senior appointment. This was the career plan which his uncle Gisbert doubtless had in mind for him. But by now Mercator had become increasingly troubled by discrepancies between the Bible, allied to the teachings of Aristotle, and observations of the real world which were beginning to circulate, especially in the rapidly expanding realm of geography. The recent discovery of the New World by Spain, followed by Magellan's first circumnavigation, had transformed this field, inspiring the young Mercator. As he would later write: 'Since my youth geography has been for me the primary subject of study... I liked... not only the description of the earth, but also the structure of the whole machinery of the world'.

Mercator's disputations on this subject with his fellow students, in which he frequently put forward his anti-Aristotelian ideas, had come to the notice of the university authorities, and it may have been this which persuaded Mercator to remove himself to Antwerp. Here he made contact with the controversial Franciscan friar Franciscus Monachus, who broadened Mercator's knowledge concerning the latest geographical discoveries and the effects they were having upon the world.

As we have seen, in 1494 Pope Alexander VI had brokered the Treaty of Tordesillas, which aimed to avert a dangerous clash between the two Catholic countries most involved in exploration – namely, Portugal and Spain. The pope had drawn a line north–south through the middle of the Atlantic Ocean: all land discovered to the west of this line (i.e. the New World) would belong to Spain, while all land discovered to the east of it (Africa and Asia) would belong to Portugal. Illustrating this ruling, as well as making allowances for consequent discoveries, Monachus drew two circular maps. One depicted the western hemisphere of the Americas, and the other outlined the eastern hemisphere: Africa, India and the lands to the east, which he named Alta India (in effect 'Beyond India'). In the light of Magellan's circumnavigation, the next obvious step was to create a model of the world in the form of a globe.

Monachus was not the first to do this. Indeed, in line with the rebirth of classical knowledge, it was known that the Ancient Greek philosopher Crates of Mallus (now south-east Turkey) had produced a globe as early as the second century BC. Owing to the state of knowledge at that time, this had necessarily been both incomplete and highly speculative. This illustrated Crates's belief that the world consisted of five distinct climactic zones. Four of these were large land masses, the most detailed of which was the north-eastern land mass that contained an indented sea of recognizably Mediterranean shape, as well as a small offshore north-western island (presumably Britain). The other three land masses, occupying the south-east, south-west and north-west sectors of the globe, had less distinct shapes, and all four were separated by a cross-like 'torrid zone' of sea.

A rather more accurate representation appeared during the Arab Golden Age, when in 1267 the Persian astronomer Jamal al-Din travelled to Beijing and created a terrestrial globe for Kublai Khan. This is thought to have expanded upon the flat map drawn by Ptolemy, including a more accurate delineation of Cathay (China) and the islands of south-east Asia. Just prior to the geographical revolution which had taken place during Mercator's childhood, the German navigator, merchant and map-maker Martin Behaim constructed the *Erdapfel* (earth apple), the earliest-known surviving globe, which followed the prevailing ideas held by Columbus, omitting any large land mass between western Europe and China. This appeared in 1492, and over the coming years it inspired a number of more accurate globes. One, constructed out of two glued-together lower halves of an ostrich egg, was among the first to include the New World. Another, cast in copper, imitated medieval maps which illustrated undiscovered regions with dragons, monsters or mythical beasts. It also labelled the unknown region to the south of China *Hic sunt dracones* (Here be dragons), which would become a popular appellation covering unknown regions in later maps.*

However, the most significant feature of these globes for Mercator

---

* Consequent ingenious scholarship has cast doubt on the accuracy and origin of this imaginative designation, suggesting that it may well have arisen from a copyist's error. In the thirteenth century Marco Polo had described this region as being occupied by 'Dagroians', people who 'feasted upon the dead and picked their bones'.

was that, unlike with previous medieval maps, their geographical features were drawn or painted upon solid round surfaces. A map on a globe represented the actual size and shape of its geographical features, whereas a continuous map on a flat rectangular chart was bound to distort shapes, stretching them the further they were from the Equator. The understanding of this fundamental distinction would be the making of Mercator. But first of all he would have to understand the complexities of maps and globes.

These he learned from a curious character by the name of Gemma Frisius, who took his Latin name from the flat, remote northern province of Friesland, where he had been born into a poor family. Frisius had been orphaned at an early age, and malnourishment had left him stunted in growth, with legs so weak and crooked that he could only walk on crutches. When he was six, a relative took him on a pilgrimage to the nearby shrine of St Boniface in Dokkum, where he underwent a miraculous cure. (Possibly effected by improved diet and the sheer physical exercise required for walking to the shrine.) It soon became apparent that Frisius was of superior intellect, and he was admitted to the University of Leuven, where he stayed on as a teacher after his graduation. Although only four years older than Mercator, at this stage he may well have taught Mercator mathematics.

Around 1530, when Frisius was in his early twenties, a local goldsmith called Gaspar van der Heyden produced 'an ingenious all-in-one terrestrial/celestial globe'. This incorporated a geographical map of the world, on which were also inscribed the main stars of the heavens. Such was the complexity of this muddled enterprise that it required a three-part booklet to explain how to understand it. The task of writing this was assigned to Frisius, and its title gives an indication of the difficulties involved: *On the Principles of Astronomy and Cosmography, with Instruction for the Use of Globes and Information on the World and on Islands and Other Places Recently Discovered.*

Within this cornucopia of often extraneous knowledge were to be found the sound principles which Frisius would later pass on to Mercator. Most importantly, these involved such vital cartographic elements as the principles of longitude and latitude, which form a network covering the surface of the globe. The lines of longitude are drawn down the surface of the globe at regular intervals from the North Pole to the South Pole.* As long as a 'meridian' or middle point (line zero) is established, it is possible to record how far one's position lies east or west of this line from pole to pole. By this time, navigators were beginning to carry shipboard clocks. As a rough-and-ready method for discovering how far east (or west) they had travelled from their home port, they could measure the time discrepancy between noon on the shipboard clock (i.e. noon at their home port) and noon at their current location (the sun's zenith).

The lines of latitude are drawn around the globe, beginning at its widest girth (the Equator), and then ascending in regular diminishing circles towards the North Pole, and also descending at regular intervals to the South Pole. In order to establish their longitude, navigators had learned to measure the precise location above the horizon of stars in the sky. This also could be compared to their location when at the home port. Such measurements were taken with an astrolabe (literally 'star taker'), the forerunner of the sextant.

Van der Heyden's golden globe, and its accompanying booklet, proved so popular that he and Frisius soon set to work producing copies, and it was now that Frisius invited Mercator to join them in this lucrative work – which would provide Mercator with an income for some years to come. At the same time it also enabled him to gain a thorough grounding in the mathematics and methods of cartography.

Van der Heyden's later globes would incorporate the most up-to-date geographical discoveries, using the coastal maps that mariners and voyagers of discovery were bringing back from their travels to many distant regions of the globe. Along with these maps were numerous and varied descriptions of different locations from merchants and inland

---

* Both of these were of course theoretical concepts at the time, conjectured from the fact that a globe must have a top (northernmost point) and a bottom (southernmost point.) It would be some five centuries before the existence of the actual poles was confirmed by discovery.

explorers, whose journals frequently included drawings and route maps of their overland travels. In order to prepare the maps for incorporation on the globe, they first had to be copied to a uniform scale so that they could be aligned with other maps. All this required a sophisticated under-standing of the maps involved, and required the use of geometry, trigo-nometry and especially triangulation.

This last method enabled the map-makers to calculate the precise location of a distant geographical feature – such as a mountain, town or river mouth – using the known location of two other features. The modern version of this method was invented by Frisius in 1533, and worked as follows. First a line of known length was drawn between two features (Brussels and Antwerp in Frisius's early experiment). Then the surveyor would draw a line from each end of the known line directly towards the unlocated feature (Middelberg, in Frisius's case) and measure the angles between these lines and the ends of the known line. This gave him a triangle with a base of known length, and two base angles. From these it was a simple matter of geometry to 'triangulate' the distances to and position of the unlocated feature.

During Mercator's years working with Van der Heyden and Frisius, he mastered practical techniques for engraving on globes, as well as the many mathematical skills involved in transferring and collating maps of differing scales and accuracy. This work not only provided him with financial security, but also enabled him to accumulate some savings. Years of near penury had taught him not to squander his money, and he still slept in one of the poor students' dormitories at the university.

However, Mercator's natural inclination to parsimony soon began to conflict with feelings he had long kept hidden. The early deaths of his parents meant that he had barely any experience of family life; secretly he craved the warmth and company which domesticity seemed to provide.

In 1536, Mercator encountered Barbe Schellekens, 'the daughter of an eminently respectable Leuven widow'. She too knew what it was like to lose a parent, and Mercator was immediately drawn to her. Although Mercator was only twenty-four years old, he proposed to Barbe and they were soon married.

Up to this point, Mercator had lived a protected life almost entirely devoted to his scholarly obsession with maps and the making of globes. According to some sources, his attitude towards women had been much influenced by his schoolmaster Macropedius. Despite the boisterous plays which Macropedius produced, Mercator's favourite teacher held vehemently misogynist views, describing women as 'more dangerous than fire, ocean, wild animals or an evil spirit'. Such opinions were widespread during this time in northern Europe. However, the anomaly between Macropedius's publicly expressed views on women and his riotous dramatic works – which featured much spanking of young boys as well as women – hint at a deeper psychological conflict. And the widespread opinion that Mercator shared Macropedius's prejudices is contradicted by the attitude Mercator adopted towards the two boys his wife soon produced. Later in life Mercator's sons would remember their father with deep affection.

It was around the time of Mercator's marriage that he began to branch out, producing high-quality maps of his own. He quickly established a fine reputation with a highly detailed engraved map of the Holy Land, which would be reproduced many times and earn him a considerable income, much of which was spent on furniture and other improvements to his home.

A year later, in 1538, he produced his first etched map of the world, *Orbis Imago*. This map is highly ingenious in its representation of the globe on a flat surface. The map is in two parts, which join at a tangent. The first part views the world from above the North Pole, the second from above the South Pole. But instead of showing two semicircles, each view is a rounded heart-shape with an indentation curving in towards the pole. This tearing-apart of the semicircle enabled Mercator to represent the land masses without the distorted exaggeration which would have occurred if the maps had stretched to contain two semicircles. A cut-out of these two-dimensional shapes can be twisted and folded into a semblance of a three-dimensional globe, and there is no doubt that Mercator had something similar in mind. When presented in this form, a flat map of the world did not distort the land masses; however, it also did not provide an accurate picture of the distances between various geographical features so was of little use to mariners.

Apart from its geometric ingenuity, Mercator's *Orbis Imago* has two other features of note. The view over the South Pole includes a large-scale representation of Antarctica, which he named *Terra Australis Incognita* (Unknown Southern Land). According to historical records, neither Australia nor Antarctica had yet been discovered by Europeans; however, the existence of such a land mass had long been a theoretical supposition – considered a necessary counterbalance to the land masses of the northern hemisphere. Mercator's map also included the word 'America' as a name for the large land mass to the west of Europe.

The German map-maker Martin Waldseemüller had been the first to use the name 'America' on a map, in 1507. This labelled a large island, straddling the Equator, which he had named after Amerigo Vespucci, the Florentine explorer whose voyages had provided extensive mapping of the south-east coast of this territory which Vespucci first named the New World.

However, in later maps new evidence had led Waldseemüller to take a more tentative view of Vespucci's claims, and he replaced 'America' with the inscription '*Terra Incognita*', suggesting that the Terra de Cuba discovered by Columbus was in fact an eastern part of Asia. Mercator's labelling of America, as well as his clear outlining of the northern and southern parts of this landmass, confirmed once and for all this name.

Mercator's map-making career, delineating his ever-evolving theoretical world on paper, was now interrupted by the invasion of the real world. In 1542 the army of the Duke of Cleves, a powerful member of the Protestant League, laid siege to the Catholic city of Leuven. The spreading turbulence following the Reformation had now reached the Low Countries, causing Mercator's map-making business to collapse.

The siege would be over within months, but Mercator now faced an even greater threat. As we have seen, he had early had his doubts concerning the Aristotelian teachings of the Church. Such doubts had been deepened during the course of his map-making, a project which was clearly inspired by scientific ideas and the new humanism. In fact,

Mercator's small circle of friends in Leuven all viewed with distaste the corrupt behaviour of the popes in Rome, and regarded Luther's new ideas with some sympathy – even though they remained devout Catholics. Although Mercator certainly did not entertain the drastic step of becoming a Lutheran, he indicated his views by dedicating his *Orbis Imago* to his friend Johannes Drosius, who had been a fellow student at the local university. Drosius had gone on to take holy orders, but remained a close friend of Mercator and his quasi-humanist circle. Despite being a priest, Drosius was not afraid to speak his mind; and his increasingly outspoken comments had turned him into a controversial local figure.

Following the siege of Leuven, the Catholic authorities decided that it was time for the city to rid itself of heretics. The campaign to enforce this view was led by the Faculty of Theology at the university, which included two advisers to the Inquisition. One of these, Ruard Tapper, made plain his views, especially on torturing suspected heretics to death:

> It is no great matter whether they that die on this account be guilty or innocent, provided we terrify the people by these examples; which generally succeeds best, when persons eminent for Learning, Riches, Nobility or High Stations, are thus sacrificed.

A list of suspected heretics was drawn up. Amongst the fifty-two names was a wide range of suspects, including a former rector of the university, several priests, a number of local artists... as well as Mercator, who was evidently now considered sufficiently 'eminent'. All those on the list were immediately arrested, apart from Mercator, who happened to be away in Rupelmonde, dealing with the estate of his recently deceased uncle Gisbert.

Mercator's absence only contributed to the inquisitors' suspicions. Mercator was arrested in Rupelmonde and confined to a cell in the town's moated castle. The fact that Mercator was imprisoned some thirty miles from Leuven may well have saved his life. In Leuven his house was searched, and his wife Barbe was interrogated, along with his adolescent sons Arnold and Bartholomeus. Despite uncovering no evidence,

the authorities remained convinced of Mercator's guilt – but he was to be
spared by a technicality. Mercator was, for the time being, domiciled in
a town beyond the jurisdiction of Leuven, whose authorities could order
the arrest of a fugitive from justice but were unable to try him. Others
on the list were less fortunate. Some were tortured and executed, others
burned at the stake, another beheaded, and two women were buried alive.

After seven months in Rupelmonde Castle, Mercator was released.
On his return to Leuven, his only known comment on this entire affair
was a passing remark in a letter to a friend that he himself had suffered
'unjust persecution'. From now on Mercator buried himself in his work.
His ambition was no less than to produce a complete map of the world
which could be used by navigators.

Throughout history, large-scale maps had usually been centred
upon a known location. For instance, Ptolemy's map was centred on the
Mediterranean. Later maps, such as the large round medieval Mappa
Mundi,* had Jerusalem as their centre, with the known world radiating
outwards from this central holy point. Mercator decided that his map
would have no centre. Instead it would be projected onto a grid of longitude
and latitude lines – which would become known as Mercator's projection.
On a globe these lines are curved, but on Mercator's flat surface they were
rectilinear straight lines. This inevitably stretched the scale of the map the
further it moved from the Equator. For instance, on Mercator's map the
Scandinavian peninsula appeared to be three times the size of the Indian
subcontinent, whereas in fact India is one and a half times larger than
Scandinavia. But this would in no way hamper navigation, which relied
upon location established by lines of latitude and longitude. A ship could
sail across an ocean following a constant compass bearing. This may have
appeared curved on Mercator's flat map, but owing to the bulge of the
globe it did in fact represent the most direct route.

Yet what happened when a ship travelled beyond the edge of the
map? If a ship set sail from China, heading east across the Pacific Ocean,
it would soon reach the limit. But if the navigator rolled the map into a

---

* This remains on public display at Hereford Cathedral in England.

cylinder, with the eastern edge of the map attached to the western edge, the solution to this problem was obvious. The navigator could simply continue from the eastern border of the map across the Pacific to the west coast of America. In this he would also be aided by corresponding map references on lines of longitude and latitude.

From now on navigators would adopt Mercator's projection, both for continental and for local charts. The entire world had become 'orientated'. Originally this word meant 'aligned to the east'; on Mercator's projection the world was aligned north, south, east and west, by means of longitude and latitude. And any point on this flattened globe could be pinpointed, as if on a graph, by reading off its precise position in numbers along the lines of longitude and latitude. Dangerous shoals, rocks, river mouths, cities and towns, mountains, borders and even entire countries could be mapped and 'orientated'. Mercator completed his task in 1569, and to this day Mercator's projection is how we envisage the world when it is mapped onto a flat surface.

But Mercator's task was not complete. For the next twenty-six years he painstakingly created more than a hundred maps, all scaled according to his projection. During the final years of his life he started binding these together with the intention of making them into a book. For the front cover he planned to have an engraving of the Ancient Greek Titan named Atlas, kneeling, with the world balanced on his shoulders. Hence the name which would come to be attached to such compilations of maps.

At the age of forty, Mercator had left strife-torn Leuven for the more peaceful Rhineland city of Duisberg in Germany, where he continued his obsessive map-making – collating and adding new cartographic features as European explorers returned from their travels and passed on their discoveries. Mercator also continued to produce globes, as these were more popular with prosperous urban clients who had little need for nautically practical maps. Globes were used as ornaments, emblematic of knowledge and power, while their complex construction also provided Mercator with a greater income. According to his friend and biographer Walter Ghim, Mercator went on living a pious and sober life entirely devoted to the creation of globes and maps. He died in 1594, at the exceptional age of eighty-two. His *Atlas* would appear the following year.

The second member of the mathematical duo featured in this chapter is the Frenchman François Viète. His pioneering work would pave the way for the great French mathematical generation to follow, which would include such figures as Descartes, Fermat and Pascal.

Viète was born in 1540 in Fontenay-le-Comte, near the mouth of the River Loire in western France. His father was an attorney, and his mother came from an important legal family connected to the powerful Catholic League. Not surprisingly, when young Viète went to the University of Poitiers he studied law; however, at the same time he began developing an exceptional facility in mathematics. Upon graduating in 1559 he became an attorney. Through a combination of family connections and intellectual talent, Viète was soon handling important legal matters, such as the Poitou estate inherited by the widow of Francis I.

By this time, France was becoming increasingly divided between the Catholics and the Protestant Huguenots, who inclined to Calvinism. In 1564, Viète's mathematical skills led to him entering the service of the Parthenay family, so that he could act as tutor to the twelve-year-old mathematical prodigy Catherine de Parthenay. Together they wrote a number of treatises on astronomy and trigonometry. In these, Viète used decimal notation several decades before this was introduced to the northern Renaissance by the Dutch mathematician Simon Stevin.*

In a significant advance on Copernicus's heliocentric solar system

---

* Decimal fractions had in fact been invented in Baghdad as early as AD 952 by the Arabic scholar known as al-Uqlidisi. The decimal system was introduced to southern Europe in the thirteenth century by Leonardo Fibonacci, where it found use in accountancy and banking. However, the explicit use of decimals in the mathematics of the northern Renaissance was first introduced by Stevin. His notation may appear a little cumbersome to modern eyes, but it was the first in northern Europe to avoid unwieldy fractions. An example: in Stevin's notation, the number 184.54290 appears as 184⓪5①4②2③9④0.

of 1543, Viète proposed elliptic orbits for the planets some forty years before Kepler's definitive proof of this idea.

In 1571 Viète moved to Paris. The following year the city erupted in the St Bartholomew's Day massacre, during which a Catholic mob went on the rampage, slaughtering several thousand Huguenots. News of this quickly spread across France, resulting in more massacres of thousands of Huguenots. During these violent years Viète was obliged to take on a number of controversial legal cases involving disputes between Catholics and Huguenots, where he was liable to be hired by either side. This eventually led to him falling foul of the Catholic League, whereupon he was taken under the protection of the Duke of Rohan, a leader of the Huguenots. France was descending into an anarchy of warring religious factions.

In 1589 Viète took refuge in Tours with the Catholic King Henry III, who was beset by enemies on all sides: Huguenots, his own brother, and the Catholic League amongst others. Henry III now employed Viète as a codebreaker, with the task of deciphering intercepted messages between the Catholic League and others amongst the king's enemies. Viète had barely embarked upon this task when Henry III was assassinated by a monk. This put an end to the Valois royal line, and the first Bourbon king – already King of Navarre (in northern Spain) — ascended to the throne as Henry IV. Viète's services were retained by the new king, and he was set to work trying to crack the 'Spanish cipher' being used by the king's enemies.

This was a complex scrambling of words involving some 500 characters, but Viète used mathematical techniques which eventually enabled him to decipher the messages. The Spanish cipher used monoalphabetic substitution, with any one of twenty characters for each letter. The cryptographers naively believed that such a complex substitution code was indecipherable. However, after working night and day, Viète finally succeeded in breaking the code using frequency analysis. (The letters of the alphabet, and even common words, appear with more or less predictable frequency in any text.)

When King Philip II of Spain learned that Viète was reading his secret messages that were being smuggled through France to his forces in the Spanish Netherlands, he could not believe it. He immediately contacted the Vatican, claiming that Viète was an 'archfiend in league with the Devil' and should be tried for heresy before a court of cardinals. Pope Sixtus V dismissed Philip II's plea; he was well aware that his own cryptographers had been reading the Spanish cipher for some years, and was more than a little irritated that Viète too now had access to the code. Unwittingly, Philip II had been lucky to escape a charge of heresy himself, for implying that the Vatican employed heretics in league with the Devil.

This was not the first time Viète had been involved in a brush with the Vatican. As early as 1582, Pope Gregory XIII had ordered all Catholic kings throughout Europe to adopt his new revised calendar, which he had even named the Gregorian calendar, after himself. This replaced the Julian calendar, which dated from the time of Julius Caesar in 45 BC. Over the centuries, the Julian calendar had become so seriously out of sync with the seasons that the date of the spring equinox was now almost two weeks behind the actual equinox (equal night and day).

Viète had become involved in a dispute over the new calendar with the Jesuit monk Christopher Clavius, who had been charged with overseeing its compilation. Such was the subtlety of Viète's mathematical argument that it was not until more than twenty years later (after his death) that a flaw was discovered in Viète's calculations.

Viète finally left the French king's service in 1602, exhausted by overwork, and he died the following year at the age of sixty-three. There is some suggestion that he was poisoned on account of his codebreaking exploits. What is more surprising is that, during the course of his hectic royal employment, he managed to produce a body of transformative mathematics. In this, Viète attempted to give algebra a foundation as rigid as that of the geometry of Euclid, whose theorems were built upon a number of self-evident axioms. At the same time he advocated the viewing of geometry in a more algebraic fashion. Instead of the necessarily inexact measurement with a ruler of lines, curves and figures drawn on paper, these were to be reduced to algebraic formulas, thus enabling them to be calculated in algebraic fashion, giving precise numerical answers.

As we have seen, in the previous century Regiomontanus had attempted a similar standardization of algebra – but this had not become

widely accepted. Now Viète would attempt his own fundamental transformation of algebra. This branch of mathematics still largely consisted
of a number of algorithms: rules of thumb to be followed in order to find
the answer to a calculation. These had been set down in prose form – as
indeed had all algebraic formulas. For instance: 'In order to obtain the
cubic power, multiply the unknown by its quadratic power.' In modern
notation, this can be simply put:

$$y \times y^2 = y^3$$

Unfortunately Viète was hampered by the lack of an agreed symbol for
'equals' (=), as well as agreed symbols for 'multiplication' (x) and 'division'
(÷) – which had also hampered acceptance of Regiomontanus's notation.
However, although Viète's attempt to rationalize algebraic notation failed
to gain widespread acceptance, it made many realize that such reform was
long overdue. More ambitiously, Viète pressed ahead with his attempt to
unite algebra and geometry, though here too any general answer eluded
him. But Viète's efforts were not to be in vain. The very fact that he had
attempted such innovations would reinforce the movement of maths in
the direction of its modern incarnation, where solutions to both these
problems would be found.

It would be the following century when Descartes managed to solve
such problems, with the introduction of Cartesian coordinates: two lines
at right angles, one representing the x-axis and the other the y-axis. Here
the answers to an algebraic formula could be transformed into a line on a
graph; likewise geometric lines could be seen as algebraic formulas.

The resemblance between these coordinates and the lines of latitude
and longitude which Mercator drew on his maps is indicative. It was
in this way that Mercator, and to a certain extent Viète, enabled the
northern Renaissance to lay the foundations for our present world view.
It was they who sought to devise a coordinated representation of our
modern physical world in geography, and pointed the way to our modern
theoretical world of multidimensional mathematics.

CHAPTER 14

VESALIUS

AFTER THE PYROTECHNICS OF Paracelsus, medicine was in need of a more sober appraisal. This appeared in the form of Vesalius, who would do much the same for medicine as Mercator and Viète did for their separate fields. He would prepare the ground for advances in medical science during the coming centuries, and in doing so can justly lay claim to being the father of modern anatomy and his work the beginning of modern medicine. Vesalius would achieve this feat by embarking upon a comprehensive anatomy of the human body.

The dissection of human bodies had been a religious taboo in the western world since well before the birth of Christ. This taboo extended through all Abrahamic religions – i.e. Judaism, Christianity and Islam – as well as most of the heterodox sects and cults which pervaded the Mediterranean region and the rest of Europe. The second-century Greco-Roman physician Galen performed dissections on sheep and pigs, as well as Barbary apes (though he is said to have abandoned work on the apes because their smiles and grimaces reminded him too much of human expressions). From these animal dissections he drew anatomical analogies to the human body. He did also have real – though limited – access to human anatomy, during an early period when he worked as a physician to the school of gladiators in his native Pergamon, a prosperous Greek city in western Anatolia (modern Turkey). Here his job involved treating severe wounds and even amputations which the gladiators had inflicted upon one another during their public combats. Consequently, Galen would describe these wounds as 'windows into the body'.

It was the analogies he drew from his animal dissections that sometimes let him down. For instance, in the necks of sheep he found a network of veins which he named the *rete mirabile* (wonderful network). He surmised that human beings also possessed a similar network beneath the brain which transmuted 'vital spirits' in the blood into 'animal spirits', the imaginative and intellectual powers that occupied the empty spaces in the brain. Despite such mistakes, Galen's 'authority' on medical matters reigned supreme throughout the medieval era, alongside that of Aristotle. Not until the Renaissance would his errors come to light.

A century prior to Vesalius, Leonardo da Vinci's obsessive curiosity led him to carry out dissections of human cadavers, which he recorded in his notebooks. By now the prohibition of such activities had become somewhat more relaxed, though they remained frowned upon. Initially, Leonardo's investigations were relatively piecemeal, much like they were for the other topics which crowded the pages of whatever notebook he happened to be carrying with him (usually tied to his belt). Despite this haphazard aspect of Leonardo's enquiries, there was nothing haphazard about his superbly accurate anatomical drawings. As his biographer Walter Isaacson notes: 'With his left-handed curved hatching lines, he gave shape and volume to the form of bones and muscles and with light lines added the tendons and fibers. Each bone and muscle was shown from three or four angles...'

These might be depicted in layered form or occasionally magnified, much as if he were illustrating the mechanics of one of his fantastic machines. Leonardo also devised ingenious techniques to assist him in his researches. On discovering that the eyeball changed shape when cut, he recorded the following advice to himself: 'One should place the whole eye in an egg white, boil it until it becomes solid, and cut the egg and the eye transversely in order that none of the middle portion of the eye be poured out.'

Later in life, Leonardo would visit a hospital in his native Florence, where he engaged in conversation with a frail old man who was said to be more than a hundred years old. Upon hearing on the following day that the old man had passed away peacefully, he obtained permission to dissect his cadaver. This he carried out in meticulous fashion, systematically recording his progress over thirty pages of drawings, accompanied by verbal descriptions. This was a remarkable feat – only possible for someone utterly dedicated, and similarly un-squeamish – considering that, in the interests of science, he refrained from any recourse to damaging preservatives or any attempts to halt the ongoing putrefaction of the centenarian's cadaver. At one point he even describes his motive, and his conclusion:

> I made an autopsy in order to ascertain the cause of so peaceful
> a death, and found that it proceeded from weakness through the
> failure of blood and of the artery that feeds the heart and the
> other lower members, which I found to be very dry, shrunken and
> withered.

But why this diversion? What possible relevance does such work by Leonardo have to the northern Renaissance? In fact, none. And that is the point. By recounting these pioneering anatomical experiments – unique in their breadth, depth and explication – we gain an insight into the immense difficulties involved in human dissection during this period. We can also witness the birth of a new, forbidden science coming into being. Or apparently so. For this infant body of learning would not survive its premature birth – stillborn before it could draw breath – largely through the procrastination of Leonardo himself.

Alas, Leonardo's meticulous work and all his effort proved in vain, at least where science was concerned. Despite his repeated admonitions to himself, he would not live to arrange his notebooks in any semblance of order or delineation according to subject matter. His writings and drawings would be left in a jumble of pages and notebooks, filled with a cornucopia of ideas which merely follow the serendipitous curiosity of his thoughts rather than any systematic study. After his death, his devoted assistant Francesco Melzi left France and travelled back to Italy, accompanied by a handcart crammed with 'some 13,000 pages of notes, many tied with string and ribbon, others gathered in leather-bound notebooks and folders'. Back home, Melzi would make sporadic attempts to order this clutter of material, all in vain. After Melzi's death, members of his family would occasionally pass on, for small remunerations, individual pages torn from the notebooks, or even entire notebooks, to distinguished visitors. Working a century later, Vesalius would remain unaware of Leonardo's pioneering work, which remained lost to history.

Such a lacuna leads one to speculate on how much more, of genuine worth, was lost during this period. Such discovery and progress had little place in the medieval era. The Renaissance would have to find its own way of accommodating and preserving the innovations it produced. All we know are the successes which eluded loss or destruction: Copernicus's revolutionary work published by his friends and gifted to him on his deathbed; Paracelsus's haphazard discoveries, and superstitious lapses, disseminated by means of Gutenberg's invention, which was itself wrested from the hands of its creator. In this aspect, more than most, no history can be any more than an incomplete account. Fortunately for history, Vesalius would do his utmost to gainsay this fact, his work being both painstaking and thorough from the outset. And his motives throughout his long and arduous task would be single-mindedly focused on public recognition and public reward.

Vesalius was born Andries van Wesel in Brussels in December 1514. The Van Wesels were a distinguished medical family, Andries's grandfather having served as Royal Physician to the Holy Roman Emperor Maximilian I. Andries's father, who was illegitimate, became the emperor's apothecary, and was later appointed as the *valet de chambre* to his successor, Charles V. The term *valet de chambre* covered a multitude of positions, ranging from a mere servant in the emperor's bedchamber to a valued personal adviser. Owing to his illegitimacy, and the fact that he was a mere apothecary (compared to his father's far grander post), it seems that Andries's father never quite emulated his own father, and may even have gained his posts only as a favour to the Royal Physician. Either way, Andries's father was almost certainly away from home much of the time, especially after Charles V succeeded to the throne of Spain when Andries was two. This meant that Andries was largely brought up by his mother, Isabel – whose maiden name was Crabbe, indicating that she was probably an English immigrant. At any rate, she was certainly not as intellectually distinguished as the other members of the Van Wesel family, and is said to have been a particularly superstitious woman.

Despite this, Vesalius's mother had very realistic ambitions for her young offspring. At the age of six Vesalius was sent to the Brussels school of the Brethren of the Common Life. His mother may have been unlearned, and possibly looked down upon by other members of the distinguished Van Wesel family, but her husband had inherited – and she occupied – the grand family mansion. This had once been the home of Vesalius's grandfather and contained a well-stocked library of medical books, some of which had even been written by Vesalius's grandfather himself. Isabel, hoping that her son would follow in her husband's footsteps and become an apothecary, encouraged young Vesalius to read in the library, and he soon became fascinated by the wealth of medical lore contained in its volumes. At the age of fourteen, he went to study at the University of Leuven, some twenty miles east of Brussels. And it was here that Vesalius would meet and befriend Mercator, whose work would bear an uncanny metaphorical resemblance to that of Vesalius. (As we have seen, Mercator would go on to map and describe the 'anatomy' of the earth.)

Vesalius's entry into the university was a matter of some pride to his mother, as his father had been excluded from such an establishment owing to the stigma of his illegitimacy. Surprisingly, Vesalius did not register at the school of medicine, but instead chose to study the arts and human-ities, which included learning Latin and Greek, at which he thrived. (The books in his grandfather's library would mostly have been written in

Latin, and Vesalius almost certainly had extended his schoolboy Latin by reading these works.) After young Vesalius graduated with a good arts degree in 1532, he was accepted to study at the prestigious University of Paris, where he entered the school of medicine. Only now did he begin the formal study of this subject.

Despite its reputation, the University of Paris remained firmly committed to the teachings of Aristotle, and its school of medicine was still dominated by the 1,300-year-old ideas of Galen. Lectures in practical anatomy were a comparatively rare novelty, having only recently received limited Church dispensation.

Regardless of such innovation, the entire approach to education in the school of medicine remained rooted in old medieval practices, especially with regards to anatomy. During a typical lesson, the students would be seated in the rising semicircular rows of the lecture hall, peering down at the naked dead body laid out on the dissection table below. The dissection itself was carried out by a barber-surgeon, who would cut into the cadaver with a knife. The lecturer, in his academic gown, stood at a high lectern above the dissection table, reading out the relevant passages from Galen. An assistant would indicate with a staff the revealed organ. As Galen's words were the Holy Writ, no questions were permitted.

The professor of anatomy in Paris at the time was Jacobus Sylvius, whose belief in the teachings of Galen was absolute. If a cadaver was shown to have a different organic structure to that described by Galen, the fault lay in the cadaver itself rather than Galen. After all, the cadavers dissected in front of students were mostly those of recently hanged criminals, where degenerate or warped anatomical features were only to be expected. For similar reasons there was no question of the students taking any active role in dissection. Owing to the depraved nature of the cadavers, 'it was considered degrading for educated people to handle such contemptible specimens'.

Fortunately for Vesalius, one of his anatomy lecturers was Johann Winter von Andernach, a German humanist scholar who disagreed with his colleagues' rigid interpretation of Galen. He pointed out that although Galen's actual practice had involved genuine, though limited, observations of human anatomy (mostly on wounded gladiators), he had garnered most of his actual anatomical knowledge from privately conducted experiments (on animals such as pigs and sheep). Andernach allowed Vesalius and a chosen few of his other students to perform, under his own guidance, a number of their own dissections on such few cadavers as he was able to obtain.

Vesalius quickly became obsessed with anatomy, to the point that he decided to do some original research on his own. He recorded how he 'spent long hours in the Cemetery of the Innocents in Paris turning over bones'. Such a morbid pursuit of learning had its dangers. Interfering with bodies in a graveyard was viewed as sacrilegious, leaving the perpetrator open to a charge of heretical behaviour. And, as Vesalius also recorded, 'Once with a companion, I was gravelly imperilled by many savage dogs.' The religious authorities were not the only ones concerned with people stealing collections of bones.

At the same time, Vesalius began composing his graduation thesis. Interestingly, he chose for his subject the tenth-century Persian physician and alchemist known in the west as Rhazes. (In the Arabic world his full name was Abu Bakr Muhammad ibn Zakariya al-Razi.) The important fact about Rhazes was that he not only based his science upon the experiments he conducted himself, but he also wrote these out in detail, step by step. This meant that they could be precisely repeated by other scientists. Here, reliance upon the word of a universal and unchanging 'authority' was skilfully circumvented.

This important lesson would soon begin to permeate the world of science in both the northern and the Italian Renaissance. The days when scientists – from mathematicians to alchemists – kept their discoveries secret in order to gain advantage over their rivals were coming to an end. Science was entering the public domain. Experimenters would publish their work in books, and their results could be verified (or shown to be faulty) by their peers.

Andernach must have been highly impressed with Vesalius's knowledge and the talents he was beginning to display. Soon, he went so far as to invite his twenty-one-year-old student to assist him with the magnum opus he was writing. This four-volume work would be published as *Institutiones Anatomicae* (The Fundamentals of Anatomy) in 1536, and its introduction includes fulsome praise for Vesalius, whom Andernach described as 'a young man... of great promise, possessing an extraordinary knowledge of medicine, proficient in Latin and Greek, and very skilled in dissection of bodies'.

Unfortunately, in the very year that Andernach's masterwork was published, war broke out between France and the Holy Roman Empire. Vesalius's status changed overnight from being an acclaimed student to that of an enemy alien, and he was forced to flee back to home territory in imperial Brussels.

There is now a difference of opinion as to what precisely Vesalius did next. According to some sources he served for a spell as a military surgeon. This would have enabled him to gain a similar experience with soldiers as Galen had gained with gladiators. However, hostilities during the two-year war between the Empire and France mainly took place in southern Europe, especially in Piedmont in northern Italy, far from the Spanish Netherlands. What most seem to agree on is that eventually Vesalius returned to the University of Leuven, where he entered the medical school and completed his thesis.

At the same time, Vesalius continued with his anatomical obsession. He described how he would ensure that he was 'locked out of [Leuven] so that, alone in the middle of the night, I might take away bones from the gibbet to prepare a skeleton'. Occasionally, the authorities would allow him to perform a forensic autopsy, so that he could determine the cause of death. An insight into the nature of this work can be gained from Vesalius's own meticulous description:

> In the course of a dissection when an injured ovary is first compressed, like an inflated bladder it usually squirts forth this humor with a crackling noise and to an astonishing height, not unlike a fountain. In women that humor is white, like very thick whey, but I have also found it yellowish like somewhat thickened egg yolk.

There is no doubting Vesalius's scientific dedication, which led to almost pathological attempts to discover the truth. And it is here that the full extent of Vesalius's ambition began to emerge. He wished to uncover the anatomical structure of the entire human body, no less. Where Leonardo had been un-squeamish in his somewhat-whimsical curiosity, Vesalius was hell-bent on building up a systematic scientific picture, following the experimental method first set down by Rhazes.

Vesalius's reputation as a talent of great promise seems to have spread far and wide, almost certainly aided by Andernach's description of him in *Institutiones Anatomicae*. Immediately upon his graduation from Leuven, Vesalius received an invitation to become a professor of anatomy and surgery at the University of Padua, one of the finest centres of scientific research in Italy. (Galileo would take up the chair of mathematics here some fifty years later.)

Vesalius began at Padua as he meant to go on. Ensuring that he made no explicit refutation of Galen, he nonetheless encouraged his students to carry out their own anatomical investigations. More importantly for Vesalius, Padua was just twenty miles from Venice, the commercial and cultural capital of the region, and it was here that he met the German-born artist Jan von Calcar, who had served his apprenticeship under Titian. Calcar's particular talents were his ability to imitate the works of others and his supreme skill with woodcuts.

In 1538 Vesalius collaborated with Calcar on the production of his first anatomical text, *Tabulae Anatomicae Sex* (Six Anatomical Charts.) Three of these charts were produced by Calcar, taken from a full-scale skeleton of the human body which Vesalius had put together. The other three made use of charts which Vesalius himself had drawn for lectures to his students. These illustrated the liver, the male and female reproductive organs, as well as the arterial and venous systems. Vesalius's *Tabulae* was groundbreaking in that it included a few – just a few – corrections to Galen's anatomy. For instance, he redrew Galen's description of the coccyx at the base of the spinal column (Galen had named this after the Greek for 'cuckoo', whose beak it seemed to resemble). He also radically revised Galen's assertion that the lower jaw was divided into two distinct sections.

Yet an indication of how far Vesalius still had to progress can be seen from the fact that he included in his drawings of humans the *rete mirabile* network of veins which Galen had found in sheep, while his depiction of the liver still had five lobes (like a pig's) and the heart was unmistakably that of an ape. These mistakes appear to be an indication of how he still respected the authority of Galen. Initially, before realizing his own errors, Vesalius is said to have attributed Galen's mistakes to two 'facts'. First, the human body must have 'changed' over the 1,300 years since Galen's time. Second, it was likely that different races, or customs, accounted for many of these alterations. For instance, the discrepancy between Galen's curvature of the femur (thigh bone) and his own version was probably due to the difference between the Ancient Romans' loose apparel, such as togas and tunics, and the modern fashion for wearing tight trousers. Only gradually did it begin to dawn on Vesalius that Galen's anatomical investigations were almost all limited to the characteristics of animals. In transposing these, Galen had made wide use of guesswork to interpret their place in the structure of human anatomy.

From now on, the more Vesalius continued with his investigations of the human body, the bolder he became. By this stage he had reached an agreement with the Paduan authorities, who allowed him to dissect the regular supply of cadavers of prisoners executed on the gallows. Vesalius's retelling of how he carried out his researches paints a vivid, if lurid, picture. He described how he 'would keep in my bedroom for several weeks bodies from graves or given me after public executions'. How did his neighbours put up with the appalling stench? To say nothing of their suspicions that he might be indulging in necromancy or demonology? The answer is that they may well have been unable to distinguish the stench from the general pervasive malodorousness.*

---

* During this era the waterways of Padua, like the canals of Venice and its nearby lagoon, emitted powerful smells, especially in the summer. This was hardly helped by the customary lack of bathing and personal hygiene which pervaded all classes throughout Europe. Indeed, such habits accounted for the constant use of sweet-smelling nosegays in genteel society. These consisted of flowers or herbs intended to mask the sense of smell. It is said that in Venice a certain type of nosegay evolved which went further, using citrus oil or extracts of resin intended to numb the olfactory sense altogether, rather than simply distracting it.

As for the suspicion that Vesalius might have been involved in occult practices – presumably he remained under the protection and good name of the university. This was still an era when a large majority of the population believed in demonology, witchcraft and the like – general superstition was rife. Here was one area where the power of the Church and its insistence on orthodoxy was beneficial: in its suppression of heretical practices and beliefs, it undoubtedly reduced the credulity which led to the outbreaks of mass hysteria that were prevalent during this period. An example of common credulity can be seen in the public reaction to the poet Dante and his *Divine Comedy*, in which he imaginatively described his journey through the underworld to Paradise. When passing through this region of Italy just two centuries previously he would be pointed out as the man who had actually visited Heaven and Hell and returned to the world to tell the tale of his exploits. Well into the Renaissance, and beyond, such myths remained persistent.

Vesalius now began assembling, together with Calcar, the large, precisely delineated drawings that would become the body of the masterpiece which assured his lasting place in medical history. Apart from Leonardo's, previous books containing anatomical illustrations had tended to be schematic, or cartoon-like, mostly drawn by their medical author – whose talent would often be amateurish at best. By contrast, Vesalius's *De Humani Corporis Fabrica* (The Apparatus of the Human Body) would not only be comprehensive and encyclopedic in its knowledge, but its precise illustrations would also be works of art as much as science. Calcar's large exact drawings, made under Vesalius's painstaking direction, would in their own distinctly different style be a match for the as-yet-unseen drawings of Leonardo.˙ Meanwhile Vesalius's text would set medicine free from the stranglehold of Galen.

---

* Such artistry did not come cheap. Indeed, Vesalius was unable to pay Calcar, and in lieu of a fee he signed over to the artist any future profits the *Fabrica* would make. This may appear absurdly generous, but it is revelatory of Vesalius's ultimate motives. He knew that this work would ensure him immortal fame, and he also felt certain that it would attract the attention of the one person he had in mind. Namely, Charles V. Vesalius's ambition was to emulate his grandfather and become Royal Physician to the Holy Roman Emperor. Such fame and the accompanying salary would surely provide him with financial security for life.

The *Fabrica*, as it is usually called, represented a colossal undertaking. Begun in 1539, it would not be completed until 1543. It would consist of seven books, covering 700 pages, filled with 200 illustrations and explicatory text. Vesalius makes his intentions clear from the outset. According to the twentieth-century historian of medicine Roy Porter, the frontispiece of the *Fabrica* 'presents the dreams, the programme, the agenda, of the new medicine'. In fact, it portrays Vesalius standing beside a cadaver with its skin peeled back to reveal its inner organs. Standing above them is a skeleton with a staff, taking on the role of the barber-surgeon at a university lecture, indicating the exposed innards. Porter again: 'Medicine would thenceforth be about looking inside bodies for the truth of disease. The violation of the body would be the revelation of its truth.'

This scene takes place in a vast pillared hall. Crammed around Vesalius, many peering at the exposed cadaver, is a positively Hogarthian* profusion of characters: sages, sinners, monks, students, street characters, and even a monkey... All humanity is there. (Except, of course, any women: such was the propriety of the age.) But one should not be misled. This is the entry into a demonstrably serious work – though its prose would include more than a few jokes and amusing stories. Vesalius's intention was revolutionary and he knew it: here he was demonstrating that his findings would affect *everyone*.

Surprisingly, the success of this enterprise lay largely in the fact that Vesalius followed Aristotle's philosophy. When it came to describing a bone, a structure, an organ, he always viewed it through the eyes of Aristotle's teleology, which decreed that everything must have a purpose. (Not until Darwin would teleology be overturned and reversed. There is no purpose beyond survival of the fittest: evolution is blind. Despite this, we frequently regard anatomical features in teleological terms. For instance, we say that the purpose of the eye is to see, and so forth.)

---

* This may be anachronistic: Hogarth would not be describing such scenes for another two centuries. Perhaps a more consistent description would be 'Rabelaisian', though Rabelais would not have included so many courtly characters amongst the cram of humanity, and would undoubtedly have introduced a few women of varying appearance and virtue.

The originality of Vesalius's approach is clear from the outset. Book 1 of the *Fabrica* is devoted to the human skeleton. Here he showed that he had understood, as previous anatomists had not, that bones not only support the human body but also articulate and enable its movements. He went further, explaining how some bones 'such as the skull... the breastbone and the ribs, were constructed by nature for the protection of other parts'. Meanwhile, some bones 'were placed before joints to prevent them from being moved too freely or bent to an excessive angle'.

However, it has to be said that in this aspect Vesalius provided only a piecemeal beginning to the science of physiology and how the body worked. Here, in the general medical sense, Paracelsus was the true pioneer, providing an overall modus operandi with the chemistry of the digestive system, a process which applied to the whole body. Likewise his iatro-chemistry, which provided cures for bodily malfunctions. Yet there is no denying that Vesalius corrected many of Galen's misconceptions, which had persisted through the centuries. For instance, he gives the human sternum (breastbone) three parts, as distinct from the several mythical parts ascribed by Galen. But it is in Book 2 that the *Fabrica* comes into its own. This describes the human musculature and includes the justly celebrated depictions of '"muscle-men" at different stages of corporeal "undress"'.

Inevitably, during the course of this work, the relationship between the author and the artist became strained. At one point, Vesalius comments on 'the bad temper of artists and sculptors [meaning wood-block cutters] who made me miserable more than the bodies I was dissecting'. It is worth noting here how even Vesalius lets slip that on occasion his obsession could be a depressing business. He was no pathological ghoul. He had the same natural reactions and revulsions as any other who condemned himself to such a depressing task. This, if anything, makes his great work even more impressive. Often it was his scientific ambition alone, overcoming his natural revulsion, that drove him on.

Alas, Vesalius's perfectionism would result in an increasing number of quarrels with Calcar. Breaks in their collaboration now followed, and Vesalius began drawing a number of the anatomical illustrations in the *Fabrica* himself. These fall below the initial aesthetic standards, though

Vesalius did not allow his scientific rigour to lapse. Take, for instance, the 'venous man', which portrays the network of the veins permeating the entire body. This is definitive science, rather than art, inspiring wonder only on account of its filigree complexity: a wicker man, rather than a variant on a Leonardo. Further into the *Fabrica*, some of the illustrations are distinctly uninspired: adequate representations, rather than bravura works of scientific art. Though such niggling criticisms are only possible in the light of the preceding pages.

By now, it appears, Calcar had quit the project altogether. We must imagine him storming off in some indignation at Vesalius's tenacious insistence upon the minutest detail. (This was woodcut, remember, not drawing; erasure was no simple matter with a gouged wooden surface.) No matter – Vesalius persisted. The scientific veracity of the anatomical investigations remained undiminished. His discoveries likewise.

Vesalius's dissection of the heart had led him to doubt the orthodox Galenic view that the blood sweats from the left into the right ventricle through miniscule passages which elude human vision. Vesalius may have been sceptical of Galen's description but he could find no alternative process, and was thus unable to provide any alternative explanation of his own in the text. Despite this inadequacy, Vesalius's scepticism would prove inspirational. It was this doubt which would later motivate the English physician William Harvey to come up with the revolutionary idea that the blood circulated through the human body.

Ensuing books of the *Fabrica* would prove similarly perceptive – especially Vesalius's investigations of the human brain. Time and again, he was able to correct Galenic models. And his ever-increasing expertise in anatomy even led to him correcting his own errors, especially those he had made in his first work, the *Tabulae*. From now on, the *rete mirabile* was cast out from human anatomy. Likewise Galen's five-lobed liver was dismissed: 'The liver is not divided into fibres or lobes.'

Even so, some time-honoured errors persisted. In a rare lapse of physiological interpretation, Vesalius clung to Galen's theory that venous blood is produced by the liver. But where did the blood for the arterial system come from? Vesalius never fully investigated this anomaly.

As the work continues, the illustrations become less precise and their interpretation less exact. Many of the minor illustrations are undoubtedly by Vesalius himself. Though it is not lack of artistry which causes Vesalius to make a number of uncharacteristic and unnecessary blunders – such as, for instance, missing out on the pancreas altogether.* And the illustration of the pregnant uterus containing a foetus is undeniably medieval in its crudity – especially when compared with Leonardo's superb illustration of this feature in his notebooks. Indeed, Vesalius's description of specifically female anatomy and organs is decidedly weak. The reason for this is evident: the cadavers he received fresh from the scaffold were almost entirely male.

But these are mere quibbles, in the light of Vesalius's overall achievement and the immense trouble he took over the production of his masterpiece. He busied himself with every detail – choosing the typography, the paper it was printed on, and the binding of the book – with almost as much care as he had taken over its contents.

When he had completed the manuscript of *Fabrica*, he sent the text and illustrations north to Basel in Switzerland. This was the home of Johannes Oporinus, who sixteen years previously had worked as Paracelsus's long-suffering assistant. Oporinus had now succeeded Paracelsus as a rather more orthodox professor of medicine in Basel. He also happened to come from a family renowned for their printing and engraving skills, and combined his medical knowledge with an expert understanding of the entire printing process. This was the only man in Europe whom Vesalius could trust with the production of his masterwork.

Excusing himself from his academic duties in Padua, Vesalius travelled to Basel to supervise the printing of the *Fabrica*. He even went so far as to ensure that the illustrations of the first copy were coloured by hand. (The engraved and woodcut illustrations in later editions remain for the most part devoid of colour.) The first copy of the first edition was then bound in silk velvet of imperial purple and dedicated to the Holy Roman Emperor Charles V.

---

* Even Galen refers to 'the so-called pancreas', though he does assign it to the wrong place.

This copy of the *Fabrica* is known to have been completed by early 1543. Leaving Oporinus to continue with printing out the entire first edition, Vesalius left Basel bearing the first copy off the press. With this he travelled to the German city of Mainz, where Charles V was in residence with the powerful Archbishop of Mainz, one of the seven electors who chose the Holy Roman Emperor. On arrival, Vesalius duly presented the *Fabrica* to its dedicatee, who was more than delighted. With Vesalius at his side, Charles V pored through the pages with expressions of astonishment and delight as the author indicated the salient points of his discoveries.

In gratitude, Charles V appointed Vesalius Royal Physician to the Imperial Court. Vesalius was just twenty-seven years old and he had achieved his lifelong dream of emulating his illustrious grandfather. The publication of the *Fabrica* also established him as a leading medical authority, renowned throughout Europe for his anatomical expertise and knowledge.

Vesalius could afford to rest on his laurels... and this is precisely what he did. From now on, he would accompany Charles V on his regular travels. (Besides being Holy Roman Emperor, whose imperial realm stretched throughout many German and Flemish states as well as Bohemia, Charles V was also King of Spain and Naples.) Vesalius appeared to be uninterested in undertaking further anatomical research. He never returned to teach at Padua, or at any other university, despite many offers. Indeed his only contact with academic life was through his old anatomy professor at the University of Paris – Jacobus Sylvius. So outraged was Sylvius at his former student's desecration of Galen's teachings that he wrote directly to Charles V:

I implore his Imperial Majesty to punish severely, as he deserves, this monster born and bred in his own house, this worst example of ignorance, ingratitude, arrogance, and impiety, to suppress him so that he may not poison the rest of Europe with his pestilential breath.

Henceforth Sylvius would never mention the name Vesalius, referring to him only as *Vesanus*, Latin for 'madman' – the last two syllables of
which contain an added anatomical insult.

Undeterred by such calumnies, Vesalius continued in his post as Royal
Physician, with the evident approval of the emperor. Prior to Charles
V's abdication in 1555, he ensured that Vesalius was made a Spanish
count and granted him a generous pension for life. But when Philip II
succeeded Charles V as King of Spain, he insisted that the unorthodox
Vesalius should retain his post as Royal Physician. Spain was by now the
richest country in Europe, benefitting from the regular arrival of treasure
galleons bringing gold, silver and spices from the New World and the Far
East. (It was during this time that the Philippines was named after Philip
II.) On occasion Philip II would lend out his Royal Physician to distinguished peers, who were more interested in Vesalius's medical expertise
than his unorthodox academic reputation. Most notably Vesalius was sent
to France after Henry II was injured in a jousting accident. Vesalius also
attended Philip II's son when he fell down some stairs and cracked his
head.

By now, Vesalius had married Anne van Hamme, who came from
a distinguished Flemish family, and they had a daughter. During the
ensuing decade, Vesalius travelled extensively in the imperial entourage,
living a life of some luxury. His duties were light. Only occasionally would
he be called upon to perform an autopsy, or to patch up some aristocrat who had been injured while jousting or hunting. However, he still
had his enemies. Followers of Sylvius continued to wage a propaganda
war against the 'new anatomy' of the *Fabrica*, attempting to persuade the
Church of its heresy.

By the time Vesalius reached the age of forty-nine, his surgical skills
were beginning to grow rusty. In 1564 he performed an autopsy on a
nobleman, only to discover that his heart was still beating. The Spanish
Inquisition soon got wind of this, and Vesalius was lucky that Philip II
intervened on his behalf, countermanding the Inquisition's sentence to
death by torture. Instead, Vesalius was invited by his imperial patron to
undertake as a penance a pilgrimage to the Holy Land. Vesalius sent

his wife and daughter back to Brussels to take up residence in the large mansion he had built amidst gardens on the outskirts of the city, while he made preparations for his 'penance pilgrimage'.

Vesalius then travelled to Venice; here he joined a flotilla of Venetian galleys embarking for Cyprus and the Holy Land, where he journeyed to Jerusalem. On the return voyage, the galley in which he was sailing was caught in a storm and shipwrecked on the island of Zante (modern Zakynthos) off the west coast of Greece. Vesalius was rescued, but died a few days later. He was just forty-nine.

However, recent researchers have cast doubt on accounts of the latter part of Vesalius's life in the luxurious entourage of Philip II. According to this alternative reading, Vesalius had grown tired of the constricting life at the Spanish court. It is said that he longed to return to genuine medical practice and anatomical research, but Philip II refused to release him from his royal duties. In this version of events, Vesalius's pilgrimage to the Holy Land was a pretext for breaking free of his master, and if he had not been shipwrecked he would have returned to the University of Padua.

After Vesalius had abruptly absented himself from Padua, his post had been taken over by his most skilled student, Gabriele Fallopius, who was able to set right some of the omissions and shortcomings of the *Fabrica*. It was Fallopius who undertook a series of dissections of female cadavers, observing what is now known as the fallopian tube, after its discoverer. It was Fallopius who also named the vagina.

Over the coming years, many anatomists, prompted by Vesalius's *Fabrica*, sought immortal fame by discovering new human organs and naming these after themselves. Vesalius, despite his ambitious quest, never indulged in such a practice. Consequently, although he single-handedly invented modern anatomy, no part of the human body is named after him. Three centuries later, Charles Darwin would study the *Fabrica*, drawing on its vast store of anatomical knowledge to help construct his theory of evolution.

CHAPTER 15

CATHERINE DE' MEDICI

THE HISTORY OF EUROPE was by this time at a fundamental stage in its own evolution. Several decades had passed since Luther's dramatic proclamation of his *Ninety-Five Theses* in 1517. As we have seen, the majority of the north German states, including Prussia, soon became Lutheran, as did the Scandinavian countries and the Baltic states. Meanwhile the Dutch states tended towards the alternative form of Protestantism in the form of Calvinism, as did Switzerland and Scotland. And in 1534, Henry VIII would declare an independent Church of England. Eleven years later Pope Paul III would summon the Council of Trent, where the Catholic Counter-Reformation was launched. This would see the Inquisition granted extensive powers throughout Catholic territories, with the avowed aim of rooting out heresies and returning worshippers to the fold.

In 'most Catholic' France, the situation was particularly fraught. Initially the Protestant Huguenots had begun to flourish in southern and western France. They had largely favoured the ideas of the French-born John Calvin, who had lived in Picardy in northern France before fleeing the country. As we have seen, initially the humanistically inclined Francis

I took a more tolerant approach to the Huguenots. But this changed in the 1530s when Calvin became openly defiant after establishing himself in Switzerland, beyond the reach of the French authorities, with a number of powerful French figures taking a sympathetic view of his ideas.

Such was the volatile situation when the fourteen-year-old Catherine de' Medici travelled to France from her native Italy to marry Francis I's second son, Henry, Duke of Orléans. Just as her fellow Florentine Leonardo da Vinci had done several decades earlier, Catherine de'Medici's arrival in France would mark a further introduction of the southern Renaissance into northern Europe. But where Leonardo's influence had been benign, and indeed largely symbolic, Catherine's influence would be another matter altogether. None could have foreseen that this demure young maiden – who was not even an aristocrat, let alone of royal blood – would in time establish herself as the most powerful woman in French history since Joan of Arc. Yet where Joan of Arc's role had been brief, with her martyrdom leading to canonization, Catherine's power would extend over decades, and be characterized by her devious determination.

From the outset, Catherine's life was marred by tragedy and political intrigue. Within a month of her birth in Florence in 1519, both her parents had died. Catherine was brought up by relations amidst the luxurious surroundings of the Palazzo Medici. But by now the power of the Medici banking family in Florence was beginning to diminish. When Catherine was eight years old, the Medici were overthrown and fled the city. Amidst the turmoil Catherine was detained as a hostage and was from then on educated by nuns in a series of convents in the city. Ironically, within the peaceful confines of the convents Catherine thrived, and would look back on these years as 'the happiest of her entire life'. Meanwhile, beyond the convent walls the city was in disorder. By now her great-uncle, the profligate Pope Leo X, had been succeeded by his cousin Clement VII, who appealed to the Holy Roman Emperor Charles V for aid in retaking Florence for the Medici. In 1529 a vast imperial army began laying siege to the city. Members of the republican government suggested that the young Medici hostage should be murdered, and her naked body displayed in chains on the city walls. Others called for her to be removed from the convent and handed over to the city barracks for the pleasure of the soldiery. The school-girl Catherine seems to have been blissfully unaware of this at the time, but her later discovery of her near-fate may well account for the element of ruthlessness in her character.

After Florence fell to the troops of Charles V, Catherine was transported to Rome where she was welcomed with open arms by a tearful Clement VII. The second Medici pope was a man of light and darkness. The bastard nephew of Lorenzo the Magnificent, he was generally disliked and sported a dark beard (unusual amongst popes of the period). His openness to humanistic ideas and the new sciences was undermined by his indecisive caution and the unfortunate events which marred his reign.* Clement VII had inherited a weak papacy, and his acceptance of help from Charles V left him at a disadvantage. So when Charles V's enemy the French king Francis I proposed that Catherine should marry his second son, Henry, Clement VII was overjoyed. He would be able to play off the power of France against the might of Charles V and the Holy Roman Empire.

Clement VII had access to both papal and Medici money,† and he was determined that no expense should be spared for the wedding. In the autumn of 1533, Catherine set sail for Marseille from Italy accompanied by a flotilla bearing extravagant gifts. The wedding celebrations in Marseille lasted several days, with the young bridegroom displaying great valour in several bouts of (staged) jousting matches.

The adolescent Henry had if anything suffered an even more perilous childhood than his bride. Though unlike his bride he had been all too aware of what was happening. After his father, Francis I, had been defeated and captured by the forces of Charles V at the Battle of Pavia in

---

* Clement VII was the first pope to understand and accept the Copernican view of the solar system, yet his reign descended into impotence when Rome was sacked by anarchic German *landsknecht* (mercenaries).

† The latter no longer came from the Medici Bank, which had been dissolved in 1494. By now the Medici relied upon money they could embezzle from the Florentine exchequer, as well as the large personal fortune accumulated by Pope Leo X.

1525, the six-year-old Henry and his older brother had been despatched to Spain as hostages in exchange for their father. For four years the frightened young brothers were imprisoned in a remote Spanish castle in the mountains, guarded by rough Spanish soldiers. Their mother was dead, so it was the thirty-five-year-old lady-in-waiting Diane of Poitiers who had bade them farewell in France, and it was Diane who lovingly welcomed them home after their ordeal.

In truth, the fourteen-year-old Catherine de' Medici who arrived in Marseille was an intelligent, self-possessed but rather dull girl. She was certainly innocent, and the obligatory nuptials – witnessed by Francis I in customary fashion to ensure that the marriage was properly consummated – must have been something of a trial for her. Though this certainly would not have been the case for her husband, who had already received considerable coaching in such matters from the affectionate Diane of Poitiers.

Catherine's arrival at the French court caused little stir. An unimpressive personality, she was somewhat overwhelmed by the grandeur of it all. Francis I chose to reside mainly at Chambord, the largest and most grandiose of the Loire chateaux, which as we have seen incorporated a number of Leonardo's suggestions – most notably his skilfully designed double staircase. Initially, the aristocrats and court functionaries tended to look down on the insignificant Catherine – to such an extent that Francis I felt it necessary to take her under his wing, acting as her paternal mentor during the early days of her bewilderment and homesickness.

Catherine saw little of her husband, who spent much of his time elsewhere – hunting, jousting and womanizing with his circle of aristocratic friends. Diane of Poitiers was but one of many conquests, though she did remain Henry's main mistress, despite being nineteen years older than her royal lover.* Consequently, there was no sign of Catherine

---

* Such was the penchant amongst French royalty for taking on mistresses that, besides having an official wife, whose purpose was to bear him an heir, the king also had a *maîtresse-en-titre*, an official mistress. This tradition began in the late 1300s with Charles V (of France); by the time of Francis I the king had two *maîtresses-en-titre*. The following century would see French monarchs taking on as many as half a dozen or more *maîtresses-en-titre*. And it should be remembered that these were only the official mistresses.

producing an heir. Catherine's position was further undermined when Clement VII died just a year after her marriage. As part of the dowry agreement, he had promised to despatch a lavish annual sum from the papal purse to Francis I. However, the new pope, Paul III, immediately reneged on this arrangement, causing even the sympathetic Francis I to lament: 'The girl has been given to me stark naked.'

Despite such setbacks, Catherine retained the high regard of the French king. He was certainly impressed by her willingness to join him in the hunting field. It remains something of a mystery how Catherine became such an adept horse-rider, but she early outshone the few other ladies of the court who chose to join the royal hunts. This may well have been due to Catherine's Italian side-saddle, which she introduced to France. The other noble ladies of the court rode on 'a cumbersome apparatus that resembled a sideways armchair (called the *sambue*) perched on the horse's back'. Thus seated, the ladies of the court were only capable of a 'decorous amble', falling far behind the main hunt, while Catherine was capable of keeping up with the others. The side-saddle also enabled her 'to display one of her few physical strong points' – her well-shaped calves. She showed a willingness to jump any fence or hedge in order to stay alongside His Majesty, and even when she was dismounted she fell to the ground 'gracefully and bravely'. Catherine's physical and courtly daring were much appreciated by Francis I and the noblemen who made up his fellow hunters.

Similarly appreciated was Catherine's enthusiasm for dancing. Such an activity was very much a decorous, courtly affair, with the lines of ladies moving opposite, or occasionally encircled by, the lines of male dancers. Movements of side-steps were interspersed with hops, in time with the music. Such routines were incorporated into formal celebrations, but also served as pastimes at court. Sometimes when the men were away hunting, these were entirely female affairs, with a succession of different dances lasting for as long as the musicians could play. Dancing was as much a form of courtly exercise as it was entertainment. Although the lines did not join, their passing provided much opportunity for mock-flirtatious glances. Encouraged by Francis I, Catherine's enthusiasm enabled her to introduce lively Italian dances she had learned at the Palazzo Medici into the more staid French routine.[*]

Despite Catherine's comparatively junior position in the court hierarchy at this early stage, she was also responsible for an even more dramatic transformation of life at Château Chambord. As part of her entourage, she had brought to France some Italian chefs. At the time, 'Italian cooks were light years ahead of French culinary specialists'. French cuisine still languished in lumpen medieval fare, where *service en confusion* ensured that all dishes for an entire banquet were placed on the table at the same time. The aim was to impress His Majesty and his guests with the profusion of the fare: display was the order of the day, rather than taste. Roast swans were served stuffed back into their white-feathered skins, complete with beaks and webbed feet (often adorned with gold rings or other ornaments). Whole wild boars from the hunt were roasted on spits and formed centrepieces (with some being similarly reclad in their furry skins, along with their tusks). Beside this, a variety of meats – in the form of haunches and legs and heads – were similarly arranged in colourful displays. All meats were stuffed, salted and heavily spiced, in order to mask the taste of any tainted flesh. Heavy and pungent sauces were prepared with a similar aim. Vegetables were also heavily salted, having been preserved and pickled in jugs since they were picked in an earlier season. Sweet and savoury elements were mixed as a matter of course. Portions of meat were hacked off at will from joints by the diners with their carving knives, who then used their fingers to convey the food to their plates and mouths. Here indeed was a *confusion*.

By contrast, Italian dining was a more mannerly affair. Forks, unknown in France, were used instead of fingers. Meanwhile the cuisine itself was cooked and prepared with the aim of bringing out its specific flavours,

---

* Many years later, Catherine would send for the Italian musician Baldassare de Belgiojoso (whose name was Frenchified to Balthasar de Beaujoyeulx). He would mount a series of choreographed dances for the French court, including the *Ballet Comique de la Reine*. In this, sixteen female dancers in full-length gowns representing each of the provinces of France enacted a mythical theme. This is widely regarded as the first publicly staged ballet north of the Alps.

rather than masking them in heavily spiced dressings. When richness was required this was provided by subtle use of truffles, mushrooms or garlic. Vegetables were served separately, and freshly cooked. Ironically, it was this Italian influence – introduced by Catherine de' Medici – which marked the beginning of the classic French cuisine that would in time come to be regarded as the finest in Europe. In this way, the Renaissance even penetrated the kitchen. And more was to come.

Hitherto, French royal banquets had been very much male affairs, often accompanied by boisterous behaviour, proud declamations and grandiose toasts. Catherine's influence on the cuisine soon extended to her presence at the royal banquets – if only to demonstrate to the clumsy royal diners how to use their forks. Naturally, someone as junior as Catherine could not be the only female present. Others, such as the queen and her attendants, took precedence over Catherine and thus also had to be invited to the royal table. Within a surprisingly short span, royal dining evolved from uncouth male occasions to more decorous dining in the Italian style.

Just three years after Catherine's arrival in France, her husband's older brother Francis, the Dauphin (official title of the heir to the French throne), collapsed with a chill after a game of tennis. This quickly deteriorated into a fever, and within days he was dead. His Italian secretary, Sebastiano de Montecuccoli, who was suspected of links with Charles V, was immediately accused of poisoning the Dauphin, and soon confessed to this under torture. Although it was widely recognized that Montecuccoli was blameless, he was nonetheless condemned to be executed in the manner reserved for regicides – his chained body was torn to pieces by four horses galloping in four different directions.

Catherine's husband now succeeded as Dauphin, and it became imperative that she produce an heir. One of Henry's mistresses was known to have produced a child, so it was clear that the new Dauphin was fertile. However, despite his renewed attempts in the marriage bed, Catherine remained childless. Gossip spread through the court that she was barren. In the words of the court chronicler: 'many people advised the king and the Dauphin to repudiate her, since it was necessary to continue the line of France'.

Even Catherine's mentor, Francis I, was now forced to consider the possibility of her divorce. Fearful of being sent home in disgrace, Catherine sought the advice of her Italian maids. Soon she began resorting to all manner of outlandish folk remedies that promised to induce pregnancy, including such magical 'cures' as powdering her loins with ground-up stags' horns, and even drinking mule's urine. At last, after ten years of marriage, Catherine became pregnant, giving birth to a son in January 1544. The child was named Francis after his delighted grandfather. Unexpectedly, after this change of fortune Catherine would now prove to be exceptionally fecund, going on to produce no less than ten children, a circumstance which would prove decisive both for the history of France and her own personal destiny. Amongst Catherine's children would be no less than three future kings of France.

Three years later, news reached the Dauphin that his father had died at Château de Rambouillet, his summer residence outside Paris. Francis I had passed away on 31 March 1547, which happened to be the new Henry II's twenty-eighth birthday. Catherine's husband was crowned King of France, and she duly became his Queen Consort. However, despite Catherine continuing to provide a regular succession of children, her marriage remained as problematic as ever. The new king installed his *maîtresse-en-titre* Diane of Poitiers in the Château de Chenonceaux, the most romantic of all the chateaux along the Loire – the very residence where Catherine herself had expected to live. Henry II remained besotted with Diane. During royal audiences he was wont to sit on her lap, fondling her breasts, playfully asking her advice on matters of state. He trusted her to write many of his official letters, which were signed 'HenriDiane'. And in the evenings he would serenade her with his lute. Ironically, it was Diane who persuaded Henry II that he should spend time with his queen. These infrequent visits would be the cause of Catherine's continuing fecundity.

Throughout this period Catherine's position as Queen Consort of France was totally undermined. Even when Henry II was abroad, leaving her as regent in his absence, her authority was largely titular, with little say in the day-to-day running of the country. And it was quickly made clear that larger matters of state, such as foreign policy, were none of her concern. Despite such inauspicious circumstances, Catherine remained observant of royal protocol, familiarizing herself with the mechanics of power over which she merely presided. In retrospect, it appears Catherine felt that her humiliating role would not be permanent. She was, after all, Queen Consort of France. Diane of Poitiers was now well into her fifties, her appeal unmistakably beginning to fade, despite cosmetics and corsets. Catherine was sure her day would come.

Such confidence was not misplaced. Catherine's change of fortune was both swift and dramatic. During Henry II's absences she may have been a mere figurehead, but this did not stop her from apprising herself of matters of state.

Henry II followed his father in trying to combat creeping Huguenot influence, as Protestantism continued to spread through northern Europe. (Nearby England had broken with Rome in the very year Catherine arrived in France.) At the same time, Henry II was determined to avenge the humiliation he had suffered as a young hostage in Spain. However, it would soon become clear that such a policy was futile, as well as being dangerous to France's interests. Spain threatened from the south but also still retained the Spanish Netherlands, which bordered French territory in the north-east.

For the comprehensive protection of France, Henry decided in 1559 to sign the Treaty of Cateau-Cambrésis. This not only made peace with Spain, but also nullified the other threat from the north by making peace with England. To celebrate this double treaty, a great tournament was held. The forty-year-old Henry II was determined to take a leading role in the celebrations, and would not be deterred from jousting. He rode valiantly to the joust sporting the black-and-white colours of his mistress, Diane of Poitiers, but was wounded when his opponent's splintered lance penetrated the visor of his helmet, passing through his eye and into his skull. As the king lay unconscious, the Royal Physician Ambroise Paré sent word summoning the finest surgeons throughout Europe, including the great Vesalius.

Through the following fraught days, Catherine remained at her husband's bedside. As the court chronicler recorded: 'Madame [Diane of Poitiers] has not entered the bedchamber since the day of the wound, for fear of being expelled by the Queen.' Catherine had taken full charge, and even sent an officer to Diane demanding the return of the many royal jewels Henry II had bestowed upon his grasping mistress. The more Diane aged, the more she had insisted upon proof of his continuing affection.

In many ways, Catherine had long been prepared for this moment. Since leaving Italy for the alien culture of France she had taken increasing solace in consulting with seers and astrologers. In 1552 word had reached her from Italy of a prediction made by Luca Guorico, the astrologer favoured by the Medici family. Guorico was said to have successfully predicted that her great-uncle would become pope (Leo X), and even hinted that his cousin would follow in his footsteps (becoming Clement VII). Now he was warning that when Catherine's husband reached his fortieth year he should take particular care 'to avoid all single combat in an enclosed space' lest he risk a wound that could blind or even kill him. Three years later such forebodings had been strengthened, when the renowned French seer Nostradamus published the first volume of *Les Prophéties* (The Prophecies). In this Catherine had read:

> The young lion will overcome the old, in
> A field of combat in a single fight. He will
> Pierce his eyes in a golden cage, two
> Wounds in one, he then dies a cruel death.

Now her fears had materialized: as she had long feared, the 'old lion' was Henry II. On hearing that during the treaty celebrations her husband wished to take part in the jousting, she had implored him not to – even going so far as to cite the prophecies. But Henry II had brushed aside her fears. According to Catherine's biographer Leonie Frieda, Henry II is even said to have remarked to his opponent prior to the fatal joust: 'I care not if my death be in that manner... I would even prefer it, to die by the hand of whoever he might be, so long as he was brave and valiant and that I kept my honour.'

When Vesalius arrived at the king's bedside, he made a thorough inspection of Henry II's wounds. Paré had ordered the decapitated heads of some recently executed criminals, and 'had tried with jagged shards of wood to reproduce the wound on the skulls of the corpses'. Meanwhile Vesalius recorded in meticulous detail the nature of Henry II's wounds and his treatment:

> After about half a dozen splinters from the lance, which surrounded the eye, especially on the outer side, had been picked from the wound by hand, he vomited his dinner, and also later a small portion of the mixture of rhubarb… which had been given to him. Thereafter a large quantity of pituitous blood flowed from the wound…

While Paré and Vesalius pondered on any possible course of action, Henry II drifted in and out of consciousness. At one point he attempted to dictate a letter to Pope Paul III in Rome, promising that he would continue the struggle against the heretics as soon as he was recovered.

On 8 July, just over a week since Henry II had received his wounds, he once again regained lucidity, and spoke to Catherine. According to his secretary Carloix, 'he commended to her his kingdom and his children'. Two days later he finally died.

These long intense days at the centre of attention by her husband's deathbed would have an indelible and formative effect on Catherine. In certain ways, they were the making of her. Many of the often-inexplicable actions she would take during the coming years of her life would be informed by the impressions this vigil made upon her: the reserve of inner strength she had not realized that she possessed, the weakness of her enemies (as indicated by Diane of Poitiers), to say nothing of her superstitious belief in her own destiny.

Upon the death of Henry II, the sickly fifteen-year-old Dauphin, Catherine's firstborn son, became King Francis II. Under normal circumstances, Catherine would have expected to become the power behind the throne, guiding her inexperienced and somewhat feeble son in his royal duties. However, Catherine quickly found herself sidelined by a well-prepared *coup d'état*. The previous year the powerful Guise brothers – the Cardinal of Lorraine and the Duke of Guise – had engineered the marriage of Francis II to their niece Mary, Queen of Scots, who was at the time living in France. The day after Henry II's death, the Guise brothers quickly installed themselves, along with Francis II and his young wife, in the Louvre Palace, the royal residence in Paris. In the words of the English ambassador: 'the house of Guise ruleth and doth all about the French king'.

Understanding that she had been outmanoeuvred, Catherine chose to bide her time, only going so far as to evict Diane of Poitiers from the Château de Chenonceaux. Meanwhile the Guise brothers divided the power between them: Cardinal Charles Guise took control of foreign affairs, and the Duke of Guise commanded the army. The brothers were strongly anti-Protestant, and began conducting a fierce campaign against the Huguenots, supported by both Spain and the papacy.

The position of the Huguenots had now begun to undergo a subtle shift. Initially, this form of Lutheran Protestantism in France had mainly found favour amongst the downtrodden peasantry, who still largely lived in conditions of feudal poverty – particularly in southern and western France. The peasant class had experienced a spiritual renaissance with the coming of Luther and the Reformation. But increasingly the peasantry were now being joined by the lower-middle classes in the form of the overtaxed shopkeepers and tradesmen. The religious divide in France was beginning to split the country along political lines. Then, in 1559, this took on a more threatening aspect when a number of disaffected members of the aristocracy emerged on the Huguenot side. Secret congregations in the households of the lower classes now emerged into open political disaffection, with Huguenot noblemen addressing large crowds in provincial town squares. In the face of persecution by the Guise brothers, the Huguenot nobility appealed to Catherine de' Medici,* as Queen Mother,

---

* Catherine de' Medici had of course been born Caterina de' Medici. Upon her entry into France she had been known as Catherine de' Medici. Around this time, following the death of her husband, her name had become further Frenchified to Catherine de Médicis. In the interests of consistency, I have referred to her as Catherine de' Medici throughout.

to restrain the Guise brothers, who claimed to be acting in the name of her son Francis II.

However, before Catherine could even attempt to act, Francis II died and was succeeded by his ten-year-old brother, Charles IX. Like his older brother, he was physically weak, but worse still he exhibited signs of mental unbalance. This had almost certainly been inherited from the Medici side of the family, as Catherine's father, Lorenzo di Piero de' Medici,* had shown signs of instability before his death, 'worn out by disease and excess', just weeks after Catherine's birth. (This was the man to whom Niccolò Machiavelli had dedicated his notorious political treatise *The Prince*.)

This time Catherine was better prepared for the transition of power, and ensured that immediately following the death of Francis II she was officially appointed regent (*gouvernante de France*), taking charge of the young Charles IX's affairs. Catherine had also made up her own mind as to how she would act in this role. By now she was well aware that her idyllic childhood behind convent walls in Florence had been something of an illusion. Amidst civil disorder, she had been extremely lucky to escape a fate she could hardly bear to imagine. Consequently, Catherine was determined that France should not descend into the atrocities of civil war.

By now the Huguenots were gaining certain civil rights, a course further encouraged by Catherine. However, although these rights were written into law, in practice they were largely ignored by the Catholic authorities. Catherine may have had the power to create laws, but she did not have the power to enforce them. In 1562, despite all Catherine's efforts (and perhaps even in part provoked by them), France was plunged into civil war.

In a last-ditch attempt to restore peace, Catherine de' Medici summoned an official meeting, now known as the Colloquy de Poissy, so that the opposing leaders could meet face to face and iron out their differences. However, in part because she was Italian, Catherine did not understand the true nature and depth of the division between the two

---

* Not to be mistaken for his grandfather, the illustrious Lorenzo de'Medici, known as Lorenzo the Magnificent.

parties. What she regarded as merely political differences, which could be solved by discussion and compromise, were in fact based on much deeper religious principles. (In Italy there could be violent conflicts, as between the Medici and the people of Florence, but all believed in the same God, and worshipped him in the same manner.) Catherine watched helplessly as the religious leaders at the Colloquy broke off their meeting regardless of not having received royal assent to do so.

The following year, while besieging the Huguenots at Orléans, the Duke of Guise was assassinated by a twenty-two-year-old member of his entourage called Jean de Poltrot de Méré, who shot him dead with an arquebus.* While attempting to flee across the lines to the besieged city, Poltrot de Méré was apprehended and brought back to the camp. In the words of Catherine's biographer Frieda, 'one look at the half-witted creature satisfied everyone that this was not the work of a clever man, but a fool possibly operating under orders from others'. It soon emerged that Poltrot de Méré had been hired by Admiral Gaspard de Coligny, the Huguenot leader, which prompted a widespread call for vengeance amongst the Catholic leaders.

Despite such setbacks, Catherine's advisers managed to broker a peace in March 1463. Five months later, Charles IX was declared of sufficient age to rule on his own. Despite this move, he showed little inclination to take up the reins of power. At the same time, the Guise faction remained hell-bent on revenge. Civil war broke out again in 1567 and in 1568, with Spain urging the annihilation of the Huguenots. Catherine conducted talks with the Guise faction, and invited the dashing Huguenot leader Coligny to meet with Charles IX. However, before the meeting could take place she was called away to tend to her sick daughter. While Catherine was away, Coligny used all his charms to beguile the young and inexperienced Charles IX. It appeared that he was bent on usurping Catherine's power over her son. Catherine quickly returned to Paris to reinstate herself.

In a last-ditch attempt to secure peace, Catherine arranged for her daughter Marguerite to marry the young Protestant leader of Bourbon

---

* An early form of musket, resembling a blunderbuss.

The Tower of Babel by Pieter Bruegel the Elder, c. 1563.

The Peasant Wedding by Pieter Bruegel the Elder, 1567.

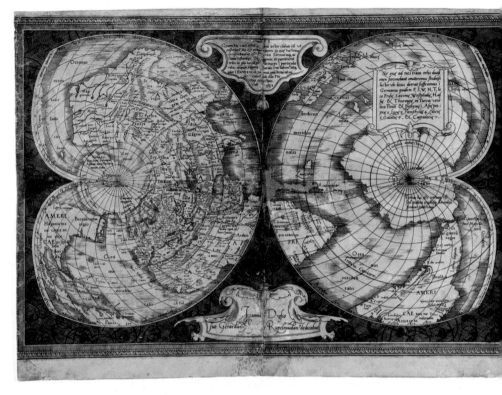

(*Above*) Mercator's first map of the world, 1538. (*Below*) His map from 1569 contained much more detail.

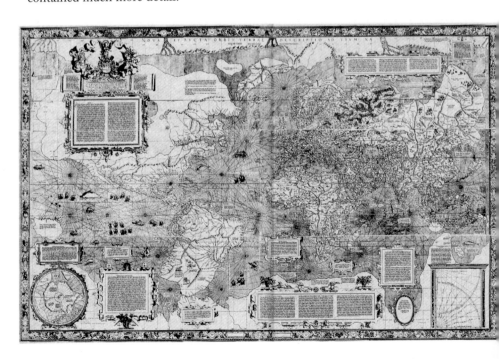

(*Right*) Portrait of Vesalius from *De Humani Corporis Fabrica*, 1543. (*Below*) Vesalius's 'muscle men', in various stages of 'undress', drawn by Jan von Calcar under the close supervision of Vesalius.

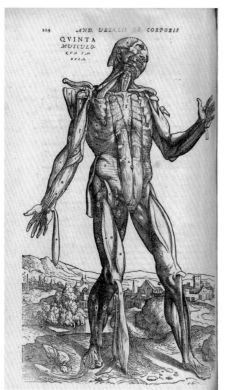

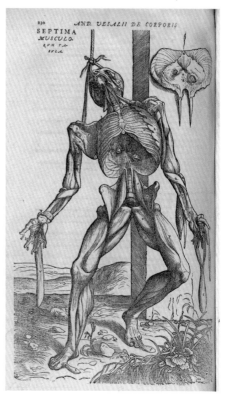

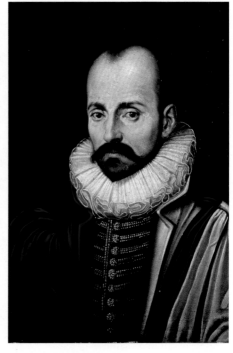

Catherine de' Medici, c. 1580.   Michel de Montaigne.

St Bartholomew's Day Massacre, Paris, 1572

'The Armada Portrait' of Elizabeth I, c. 1588.

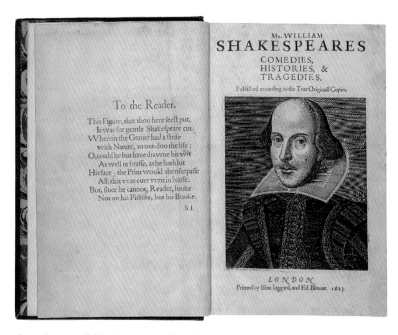

An edition of Shakespeare's First Folio, 1623.

Above right:
Posthumous
engraving of
Tycho Brahe, 1644.

Above: Johannes
Kepler, 1610.

Right: Johannes
Kepler's model of
the solar system as
nesting platonic
solids. Line engraving
from his *Mysterium
Cosmographicum*,
1596.

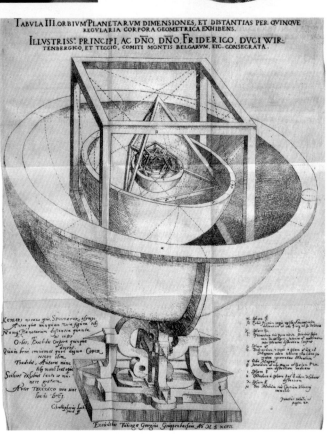

Map of Muscovy by Anthony Jenkinson and Gerard de Jode, 1593.

The Battle of White Mountain by Peter Snayers, 1630s. A key battle in the Thirty Years' War, which began by pitting Catholics against Protestants across the whole of Europe.

Triple Portrait of Cardinal de Richelieu by Philippe de Champaigne, c. 1642.

royal blood, Henry of Navarre. In August 1572 the Catholic and Huguenot leaders gathered in Paris to celebrate the marriage.

The foregoing is in fact a simplification of the constant back-and-forth of the Huguenot and Catholic causes which were splitting France. However, the northern Renaissance continued to flourish regardless. Once again, one is reminded of the constant warring between the city-states of Ancient Greece, which formed the background to the first great cultural flowering in European history. France was far from being the only northern European country to be involved in internecine Catholic–Protestant conflicts. The situation in nearby England was similarly fraught. Here the Protestant Queen Elizabeth I faced covert internal opposition from Catholic recusants secretly practising their outlawed religion. And later King Philip II of Spain would launch an armada in the vain attempt to assert what he claimed was his right to the throne of England. At the same time Elizabeth I faced a rival claim from the Catholic Mary, Queen of Scots.

Similar complex conflicts were either brewing or erupting across Europe, from Bohemia and Hungary, through the Netherlands and the German states, to Sweden. Virtually the only exception was the Grand Duchy of Lithuania, briefly one of the largest states in Europe.*

---

* During the fifteenth century, the Grand Duchy of Lithuania was for a time the largest country in Europe, stretching from the Baltic to the Black Sea. It covered parts of modern Russia, Belarus, Lithuania, Poland and Ukraine. From 1569 it became the remarkable Polish–Lithuanian Commonwealth. This state embodied many of the more advanced Renaissance political concepts. The Polish–Lithuanian Commonwealth was arguably the first large state in Europe since Ancient Rome to become a republic. Anomalously, it was ruled by an elected king, but he remained answerable to parliament. In 1573, Henry of Valois, the son of Henry II of France and Catherine de' Medici, was elected king, a position he would hold for two years. This commonwealth contained a mixed population of Prussians, Balts, Rus, Poles and various other Slavs; its tolerant polity would also contain and attract a large number of Jews. (It is claimed that anything between 85 to 70 per cent of modern Jews are descended from one-time members of this state.) Members of the Orthodox Church, Catholics, Protestants and practitioners of Judaism were all permitted to worship freely, despite the wars of religion taking place over much of the rest of Europe. This was the prosperous territory where Copernicus grew up, was educated and became a canon.

The various European wars of religion resulted in constant sporadic conflicts, civil wars and numerous massacres. Indeed, perhaps the most notorious of the latter would take place in France in August 1572, when Catherine de' Medici was presiding over the Catholic and Huguenot gathering in Paris to celebrate the marriage of her daughter Marguerite.

Initially the many signs of public rejoicing, with the bells ringing out from Notre-Dame and church towers all over Paris, provided a festive background to the streets, which were decorated with arches of flowers. Paris may have been 'the ultra-Catholic city', yet the arriving Huguenot leaders and their entourages were pleasantly surprised at their welcome. One of the visitors wrote: 'This populace, which has always been described as so terrible, would like nothing better than to live in peace, if only the great, in their ambition and disloyalty, did not exploit its excitability.'

Paris was sweltering in a mid-August heatwave, and soldiery of the Duke de Montmorency, governor of Paris, managed to ensure public order amongst the celebrating populace, despite the free-flowing wine in the taverns. News now came through that Pope Gregory XIII had condemned the marriage, but regardless of this setback Catherine managed to persuade the Cardinal de Bourbon (Henry's uncle, who remained nonetheless a Catholic) to conduct the marriage ceremony itself. Owing to the papal ban this could not now take place in Notre-Dame, as planned, but Cardinal de Bourbon was happy to perform the marriage in the square immediately in front of the cathedral. All went well until the cardinal began conducting the celebratory mass for the newlywed couple. At this point the Huguenot leaders ostentatiously rose and 'went for a walk'.

By Wednesday 20 August, as the wedding celebrations reached their climax, a series of violent incidents broke out between the Catholic supporters of the Guise brothers and the Huguenot supporters of Admiral Gaspard de Coligny. Two days later, as Coligny was riding home from the Louvre Palace, an attempt was made on his life. A man fired an arquebus from an upper window as he was passing down the Rue de Béthisy (now the Rue de Rivoli). The buckshot blasted a finger from Coligny's hand and shattered his left shoulder. Coligny survived, but it soon became known that the house from which the arquebus had been fired belonged to a retainer of the Guise family, evidently seeking to avenge the murder of the Duke of Guise.

Historians through the centuries have disagreed over who was responsible for this pivotal action. There are three main suspects. The first is the Guise faction, led by Cardinal Guise (who was conveniently absent in Rome at the time). It has been suggested that he hired the would-be assassin. A second, closer suspect is the Duke of Alba, who had been appointed by Philip II as governor of the Spanish Netherlands. Alba was at the time attempting to put down a Protestant revolt that Coligny was secretly backing with Huguenot troops. The third suspect is Catherine de' Medici herself, who is said to have feared Coligny's influence over her son Charles IX, suspecting that he was trying to drag France into war with Spain over the Netherlands revolt.

Shortly after the attack on Coligny, Catherine and Charles IX hastened to his bedside. Coligny indicated that he wished to speak alone with the young king. On their way back to the Louvre, Catherine pressed her son into revealing that Coligny had warned him not to trust his mother.

By now Paris was on the brink. An armed band of 200 Huguenots had occupied the Guise house on Rue de Béthisy. Meanwhile the shops had been boarded up and the markets were deserted, as bands of armed Huguenots roamed the streets.

It looked as if another civil war was inevitable, this time breaking out in the capital itself – the stronghold of Catholic power. The following day, purported evidence came into the possession of Charles IX that Coligny had intended to assassinate him. Never mentally stable at the best of times, the twenty-two-year-old king became unhinged at this news of his betrayal by his friend. It is unclear whether Charles IX now acted on his own or was persuaded to act by his mother.

Either way, in the early hours of 24 August (the Feast of St Bartholomew), members of the Royal Guard burst into the house where Admiral Gaspard de Coligny lay in bed, and stabbed him to death, throwing his mutilated body out of the window into the street below. This was said to be the sign for Parisians to rise up and attack all Huguenots within the city. The city gates were locked in order to prevent any Huguenot forces from entering Paris, and the Catholic forces, along with many citizens, set about slaughtering every Huguenot they could find. Estimates of the death toll vary wildly, but it seems certain that at least 2,500 lost their lives. Catherine's responsibility for this and the ensuing events remains hotly disputed. When news of the massacre reached the provinces, many other cities followed suit – and another 10,000 Huguenots may well have been killed.

In Paris, the Protestant bridegroom of Catherine's daughter, Henry of Navarre, was spared – but only on condition that he convert to Catholicism. Later, he would escape and renounce his Catholicism. Yet by this stage such was the distrust of Catherine de' Medici that many suspected this was what she had planned all along – so that Henry of Navarre would counterbalance the ever-growing influence of the Guise brothers.

The evidence suggests that Catherine de' Medici was at least partly responsible for the St Bartholomew's Day massacre. Did she panic? Was this the only option left open to her? Were she and her son in danger of losing their lives? Or did she simply let things follow their seemingly inevitable course?

The effect of these events on Catherine is equally difficult to assess. One view is that she never really recovered from her shock at what had taken place. By now she was in her fifties but would still continue her active role in French politics. Her involvement in manipulation and intrigue became more cynical, and as she aged her appearance is said to have deteriorated along with her lack of principles. It is claimed that she became grossly overweight, and made little attempt to disguise this fact, by wearing unshapely dark clothes. These may well have been nothing more than widow's weeds, a continuing mark of respect for her dead husband – but they certainly contributed to her reputation as the 'Black Queen', a legend she did little to discourage.

Other reports insist that Catherine remained a lively figure, mentally and physically active well into her old age – dancing, hunting and engaging in witty conversation. France remained as divided as ever, even in the way it regarded its de facto ruling monarch – the power behind the throne.

Two years after the St Bartholomew's Day massacre, Charles IX died – and Catherine's third son was recalled from the Polish–Lithuanian Commonwealth, where he had been elected king, to become Henry III of France. He had always been his mother's favourite – her nickname for him was *chers yeux* (precious eyes) – and she had high hopes for his reign as king.

The twenty-two-year-old Henry III had always kept himself aloof at court, forming a circle of his own friends widely known as *les mignons* (the cuties). Catherine accepted his homosexuality, but made sure that the day after his coronation he married Louise of Lorraine, with the aim of securing the succession with a son. Catherine remained the effective ruler of France until the last days of Henry III's nineteen-year reign. Thus, in all she can be said to have ruled Europe's leading Catholic nation for over four decades.

Any final assessment of her 'reign' remains problematic. It is clear that some of Catherine de' Medici's methods bear an uncanny resemblance to the advice proffered by Machiavelli in *The Prince*, his so-called textbook for tyrants. As we have seen, this work was in fact dedicated to her father, which suggests that she must at least have been aware of it. Indeed, two of her biographers (R. J. Knecht and Leonie Frieda) have claimed that she certainly read Machiavelli's masterwork. Frieda even goes so far as to suggest 'that each of Catherine's children carried a volume with them at all times'. This may be something of an exaggeration; however, there is no denying the fact that Catherine de' Medici employed many of the 'pragmatic' methods proposed by Machiavelli. 'Whosoever desires constant success must change his conduct with the times' certainly applies to Catherine, in all but the gender chosen by Machiavelli. Another piece of advice is also relevant: 'Never attempt to win by force what can be achieved by deception.' As such, Catherine can be said to have introduced a new humanistic realism into the politics of northern Europe. This realpolitik was well suited to the ever-shifting, often violent history which formed the background to the northern Renaissance.

Yet these are but the mechanics of her decades-long rule. As to the de facto rule itself: Catherine's hold on power was often contentious and often contended, yet she managed to survive – and thrive. While France was in danger of tearing itself apart through dynastic and religious rivalries, she managed to hold the kingdom together. Given the power of France and its geographical centrality, it comes as little surprise that at least one modern historian has judged her to be 'the most important woman in Europe'. Without her, France would have destroyed itself, and during the ensuing pan-European struggle to take over France's mantle, to say nothing of chunks of its territory, the northern European Renaissance would certainly not have survived – at least in the form that we know it. Catherine de' Medici's main contribution to the Other Renaissance was nothing less than ensuring its continued existence.

CHAPTER 16

MONTAIGNE

I T MIGHT WELL COME as a surprise that in the midst of France's bitter and often fanatical wars of religion, and the decades-long devious, manipulative rule of Catherine de' Medici, there flourished in France as fine a philosophical thinker as the country had produced up to this point in its history. Or should we be surprised? As we have seen, such civil turmoil has frequently been accompanied by historic transformations.

So who was this French philosopher who shone like a beacon through the storms of an age characterized by its prejudice and conflict? The man we know as Michel de Montaigne was born in 1533, fourteen years before Catherine de' Medici first became Queen Consort of France, and died at the age of fifty-nine in 1592, just three years after her death. Montaigne was a profound thinker and humanist, as well read as his predecessor Erasmus, and the inventor of a new literary-philosophical form – yet many in his own time, and even today, question whether he was a philosopher at all. In his major work, his *Essays*, he would claim 'I am myself the subject matter of my book' – regardless of the fact that such subjectivism was regarded as a somewhat trivial pursuit. He would also ask (all but despairing of an answer): '*Que sçay-je?*' ('What do I know?') And the form that he invented, and chose to write in, he called the 'essay' – from the French word *essai*, meaning 'a trial', 'a test', or 'an attempt'. In other words, anything but an answer or a conclusion. Here was a philosopher without an answer, whose thought was undeniably systematic in its pursuit of the truth – yet he neither produced nor adhered to any system. As Bertrand Russell put it, Montaigne was 'content with confusion: discovery is delightful and system is its enemy'. Perhaps he did reflect his age, in spite of himself.

The Renaissance may have brought about a rebirth of classical knowledge and thought, but as we have seen it was also very much an age of discovery: from the New World to Copernicus's heliocentric system; from the new realism of its subtle oil painting to Vesalius's intricate examination of human anatomy. Trying to impose a system on this profusion of new knowledge would only have limited it; indeed, the entire Renaissance can be seen as bursting free from the constraint of systematic medieval thought.

Montaigne's philosophy insisted upon adhering to this subjective ethos. Best to be overwhelmed by the flood of new knowledge and let it wash over us, rather than try to contain it and direct its flow. Or better still, to wait and see what effect it had on us as human beings, on our humanity; to question, to look, to examine. We should experience as much as we can, and let this knowledge inform our judgement. In this way we will become aware of what we are. And we should not shrink from any frank assessment of ourselves which this knowledge provokes.

This, if anything, is Montaigne's missing conclusion, his non-existent system, his philosophy which was not a philosophy.

Despite such seemingly free-wheeling thought and a lack of answers, Montaigne's thinking led him to two important conclusions: his belief in God, and his conviction concerning the nature of true knowledge. He believed firstly that we require faith in God and divine revelation in order to overcome what we discover to be the limitations of human reason. And secondly, that we should act 'according to the opinion of Plato, who says that steadfastness, faith and sincerity are real philosophy, and the other sciences which aim at other things are only powder and rouge'. His essays (attempts at thinking properly) led him to increase his faith in God. And, following in the footsteps of Erasmus, he regarded science as superficial – mere make-up on the true body of knowledge. Natural philosophy was not real philosophy, as far as Montaigne was concerned.

Here again we come to one of the central anomalies of the Renaissance. Science was being shaken back into life after its long slumber. The seed of the modern idea of progress had begun to germinate. Many of the greatest advances which took place during the Renaissance were scientific – in fields ranging from astronomy, medicine and cartography, to mathematics, architecture and engineering. But for many of its finest thinkers it was the humanities that remained central – science was a mere sideshow, irrelevant to what it meant to be human. Yet it was this very sideshow that was opening up the world, and expanding the vision of humanity as it did so.*

Montaigne came from a moneyed family. His great-grandfather Raymond Eyquem had made a fortune in the herring trade during the 1300s, and bought 'two noble houses and accompanying vineyards, woods, other lands and mills'. This chateau estate lay some thirty miles east of Bordeaux, and with it came the title 'de Montaigne'. Montaigne's father, Pierre, fought with the French army of Francis I in Italy; on his return at the age of thirty-three he made an arranged marriage to Antoinette de Louppes, who came from a wealthy family. Antoinette was half Jewish and of Spanish descent; her family were *conversos*, Jews who had converted to Christianity in order to remain in Spain. She was also a highly practical woman, and appears to have run the family estate.

Montaigne himself records that he was born 'between eleven o'clock and noon on the last day of February, 1533'. Montaigne's father was not a learned man, but according to his son he became 'inflamed with that new ardour with which King Francis I embraced letters and brought them into credit, sought with great diligence and expense the acquaintance of scholarly men, receiving them at his house like holy persons'.

---

* Another similar anomaly at the heart of the Renaissance can be seen in the fact that banking was regarded as being based on a sin (breaking the biblical prohibition against usury). Yet it was this very banking which funded much of Renaissance art – and with it some of the finest expressions of the human spirit.

Montaigne appears to have been very close to his father, who was a great influence. He has a lot to say about him in his writings:

> He scarcely ever found a man of his condition who was his equal in any bodily exercise... I have even seen some canes filled with lead, with which they say he exercised his arms... and some shoes with leaded soles to train him to be lighter in running and jumping.

Of his father's character, Montaigne comments: 'His bearing was one of humble, gentle and very modest gravity. A singular care for neatness and propriety of person and dress, whether afoot or on horseback. A prodigious fidelity in keeping his word...'

An indication of the local regard for Montaigne's father can be seen in the fact that he was elected mayor of Bordeaux. As the local chronicler Jean Darnal put it, the mayor of Bordeaux was invariably elected 'from the most noble, valiant, and capable lords of the region'. Such was the man who would organize Montaigne's education, drawing up a pedagogical plan on the advice of his humanist friends. Despite this, for the first three years of Montaigne's life he was farmed out to a nearby peasant family. According to his father, this was intended to 'draw the boy close to the people, and to the life conditions of those, who need our help'.

Upon his return to the family chateau, the young Montaigne was put under the charge of a German tutor who spoke Latin but no French. Similarly, the servants and other family members were only permitted to speak to him in Latin. Not surprisingly, he became fluent at an early age. As part of his father's pedagogical regime, Montaigne was woken by a musician every morning, and besides learning Latin his educational curriculum also included games, exercises, and periods given up to solitary meditation. This strict education does not appear to have been onerous to Montaigne, who spoke of its 'liberty and delight'.

At the age of six, Montaigne was sent to board at the College of Guienne in Bordeaux, an establishment famed for its schooling in the liberal arts. The headmaster was the renowned Scottish humanist George Buchanan, a skilled Latin poet and tragedian who had been exiled from Scotland for his opposition to the king. By the age of thirteen Montaigne had completed the curriculum and left the college. Where precisely he went after this remains unclear, but it is known that he studied law.

The law school at the University of Bordeaux was not highly esteemed at the time, and there is speculation that he studied at Toulouse and then Paris – for according to his biographer Donald Frame he claimed that 'Paris had his heart since childhood'. After serving in various legal positions, he returned to Bordeaux and was appointed counsellor to the Parlement, a high court post where he acted as magistrate in numerous cases. This introduced him to a wide range of human experience which would later inform his writings. Though his heart was not in the enforcement of justice: 'I am so squeamish about hurting that for the service of reason itself I cannot do it. And when occasions have summoned me to sentencing criminals, I have tended to fall short of justice.'

As he remarked to himself: 'How many condemnations I have seen more criminal than the crime.' He could find no philosophical backing to the law:

> Now laws remain in credit not because they are just, but because they are laws. That is the mystic foundation of their authority... They are often made by fools, more often by people who, in their hatred of equality, are wanting in equity; but always by men, vain and irresolute authors.

Living amidst such violent times, he was witness to many 'reminders of man's cruelty, courage, anger, and folly'. In one essay he tells of seeing a peasant:

> left for dead stark naked in a ditch, his neck all bruised and swollen from a halter that was still hanging from it, by which he had been dragged along all night at a horse's tail, his body pierced in a hundred places with stabs from daggers... who had endured all that... rather than promise anything.

It was during these years that he formed a close friendship with the humanist, poet and political theorist Étienne de La Boétie, whose best-known work was his *Discourse on Voluntary Servitude* (or *Anti-Dictator*). La Boétie's emphasis on liberty was far ahead of his time. The twentieth-century political theorist Murray Rothbard best sums up La Boétie's position:

> To him, the great mystery of politics was obedience to rulers. Why in the world do people agree to be looted and otherwise oppressed by government overlords? It is not just fear, Boétie explains in the *Discourse on Voluntary Servitude*, for our consent is required. And that consent can be non-violently withdrawn.

Despite the inspiring, indeed incendiary anti-authoritarian ideas of his friend, Montaigne served for two years as a courtier at the court of Charles IX. He would be with the king at the vital siege of Rouen in 1562, which lasted for five months at the port closest to Paris before the defending Huguenots were overrun and Paris was once again opened up to overseas trade.

On the other side of the coin, it was at Rouen, after it had been taken by royalist forces, that Montaigne accompanied Charles IX when they encountered three cannibals recently shipped from Brazil. Montaigne learned from the cannibals that 'they have an idiom in their language which calls all men "halves" of one another'. When the cannibals 'were shown our manners, our ceremonial and the layout of a fair city... someone asked them what they thought of all this and wanted to know what they had been most amazed by'. Montaigne noted how 'they had noticed that there were men among us fully bloated with all sorts of comforts while their halves were begging at their doors, emaciated with poverty and hunger: they found it odd that those destitute halves should put up with such injustice and did not take the others by the throat or set fire to their houses'. Later, Montaigne would come to see these cannibals as exemplars of the honesty which he strove to achieve in his writing: 'Had I been placed among those nations which are said to live still in the sweet freedom of nature's first laws, I assure you I should very gladly have portrayed myself here entire and wholly naked.'

Montaigne ends the story of his meeting with the cannibals by describing how he had a long conversation with one of them '[using] a stupid interpreter who was so bad at grasping my meaning' and learned how they lived and behaved towards one another – before concluding with heavy sarcasm: 'Not at all bad, that. – Ah! but they wear no breeches...'

Around this time, Montaigne was awarded the collar of the Order of Saint Michael, thus becoming a member of the most exclusive chivalric order of French nobility, 'a distinction all the more exceptional as Montaigne's lineage was from recent nobility'. Montaigne's biographer Donald Frame sees this as an instance of Montaigne's 'love of glory', remarking on his 'ostentation in his youthful studies and certain purchases of books'. Frame goes on to characterize Montaigne as 'neither gregarious nor withdrawn, he dislikes small talk and thrives on candid communication. He is keen to enjoy life... relishes all wines and sauces – he follows his natural love of pleasure. One of his favourite pleasures is the pursuit of women.'

It seems unlikely that Montaigne curtailed these pursuits when at the age of thirty-three he entered into an arranged marriage with a rich merchant's daughter named Françoise de La Chassaigne, whose father was the president of the Parlement of Bordeaux. This appears to have been a conventional French marriage of the period. Françoise would produce six daughters, only one of whom survived infancy.

Montaigne's wife and child are barely mentioned in his free-ranging writings, which cover almost everything else in his life. Though he does comment on marriage in general:

In marriage, alliances and money rightly weigh at least as much as attractiveness and beauty. No matter what people say, a man does not get married for his own sake... I know no marriages which fail and come to grief more quickly than those which are set on foot by beauty and amorous desire.

On the other hand, Montaigne's father receives frequent loving mention – as does his close friend La Boétie, who besides being an accomplished poet and political writer was also a fellow magistrate at the Bordeaux Parlement. Montaigne's conversations with the idealistic La Boétie were undoubtedly a major feature of his early manhood. As he wrote of their friendship, 'I think it was by some ordinance of heaven.' Indeed, the intensity of their friendship has led some to speculate that it may have contained an element of homosexual love.

However, the consensus is that the relationship between Montaigne and La Boétie was one of brotherly love. La Boétie was three years older than Montaigne, and may well have fulfilled the role of the older brother that Montaigne never had. Similarly, La Boétie was orphaned at an early age, 'and may have welcomed such a link with the brilliant but still somewhat rudderless Montaigne'.

La Boétie's writings were not all as idealistic as his *Discourse on Voluntary Servitude*. In reply to Catherine de' Medici's Edict of 1562, which attempted to appease the Huguenots by allowing them more freedom of worship, La Boétie wrote a detailed analysis warning against the country tearing itself apart. Two religions in the one country could only lead to anarchy, he said. 'The Church has much to answer for; the Indulgences of 1517 should have been condemned when Luther pointed them out.' Such hindsight is of no more practical value than the anarchic implications of his *Discourse*. Likewise his remedies for the situation, which end up suggesting that 'Protestants must return to the religion of their ancestors or leave the country', seem equally drastic. As advice this was of little help – even though it was pretty much what would happen in the end.

Montaigne remained very much of the Catholic persuasion, while his friend was more inclined to even-handedness. However, such disagreements were not divisive between La Boétie and Montaigne; if anything, their intense discussions drew them closer together. As Montaigne would later write of their friendship: 'If you press me to tell why I loved him, I feel that this cannot be expressed, except by answering: Because it was he, because it was I.'

Inevitably, it came as a profound shock to Montaigne when in August 1563 La Boétie suddenly fell ill, and died ten days later. Montaigne was at his friend's bedside and described La Boétie's death in a long, detailed letter to his father. This appears to have been somewhat revised before its publication, which brings out resemblances to the death of Socrates, including 'equable discussions on death, comforts to the weeping wife, and friends'.

La Boétie's death would leave a vast absence in Montaigne's life, and it has been suggested that the tone of his later essays, in their frankness and honesty, is an echo of his conversations with La Boétie.

Five years later, Montaigne's beloved father would die. This marked a turning point in his life. Montaigne resigned from his legal duties at the Parlement of Bordeaux and prepared himself for the second half of his life. He would retire to the tower in the grounds of his chateau and begin setting down his thoughts in the form of his essays.

Montaigne had almost certainly had this idea in mind for some years beforehand. He definitely went about his preparations for his retirement in a thorough fashion. He had the tower completely refurbished, installing a private chapel, a bedroom, and most important of all a library and study. These were all furnished according to his precise requirements. The walls featured murals of classical scenes, while the library included over a thousand books which he had acquired during his life so far.* The beams, joists and sideboards of the library were adorned with some sixty-seven maxims, mostly taken from the Bible and classical authors – especially the Roman playwright Horace, the materialist poet Lucretius, the Ancient Greek tragedian Sophocles and the Roman philosopher Sextus Empiricus, whose works contain the surviving remnants of the fourth-century Greek philosopher Pyrrhus, the founder of Pyrrhonism (a form of scepticism). Pyrrhus advocated that we should withhold our judgement and not become involved in controversies regarding the

---

* Many of these Montaigne had bought himself, but he did also inherit La Boétie's library – as well as the few books his father had collected on the recommendation of his humanist friends (even if he did not, or could not properly, read them).

possibility of certain undeniable knowledge. Indeed, we should accept things as they are without indulging in superfluous analysis. This philosophical outlook is perhaps best summed up in the maxim by the Ancient Roman dramatist Terence: 'Nothing human is alien to me' – which takes pride of place in Montaigne's attitude to life.

The bravery and honesty inherent in this remark would inform all of Montaigne's essays. Not for him the easy dismissal of human actions or monstrous behaviour as simply 'evil', 'barbarous', 'depraved' or the like. It is by means of these words of disapproval that we distance ourselves from such acts. Montaigne insisted that we instead *identify* ourselves with such acts, and try to understand how we ourselves might have committed them. This Renaissance idea marks nothing less than a tectonic shift in human self-understanding – one which remains far from being fulfilled to this day.*

Such is the bedrock beneath Montaigne's pleasant, discursive, informative and often highly entertaining essays. They are not horror stories. To repeat: as Montaigne said, the subject matter of his work is 'I... myself'. And as such he meant *all* human beings. A list of the titles of his essays gives an indication of the quotidian nature of their content: 'On Idleness', 'On Educating Children', 'On Solitude', 'On Friendship' (a detached examination in the light of his friendship with La Boétie). Yet his essays are also informed with his knowledge of all aspects of life: 'On the Lame', 'On Drunkenness', 'On Fear', 'On Cruelty'...

---

* Identifying with humanity's failings is a comparatively simple exercise when we look back on the savageries of history, relating them to the circumstances of their time. To bring such an attitude up to date is another matter altogether. But only by doing this can we expose ourselves to the full thrust of Montaigne's argument. We should not simply condemn Hitler, Stalin, Mao, Pol Pot et al. Instead we should seek to understand what animated their behaviour, and thus imagine how we too might be possessed of similar human impulses. It is not difficult for us to see such behaviour as the background in France to Montaigne's solitary, thoughtful life in his tower. During the lawlessness of the religious wars in France, similar unspeakable figures roamed the land performing their acts in the name of religion. But Montaigne insisted that we should not recognize them and their acts as simply 'unspeakable'. We should discover what in us is capable of such 'speech'.

Montaigne's tower was no ivory tower. Even the life he led during this period was not that of a saintly hermit, removed from the world. His wife gave birth to five of his six children after he 'retired' to his tower. Their births (and deaths) are recorded in Montaigne's copy of *Ephemeris* by the contemporary German humanist Michael Beuther. For instance:

> May 16 1577. There was born to Françoise de La Chassaigne, my wife, the fifth child of our marriage. It was a girl, who died one month later. My brother... and my sister... baptized her without ceremony.

Montaigne's laconic style here, and the absence of the child's name – to say nothing of the title in which he chose to record these events – would seem to indicate a lack of feeling on his behalf. Does this indicate that Montaigne did not always practise, at least at home, the much-vaunted empathy he preaches in his essays? His biographer Frame offers an original defence of Montaigne here – one whose ingenuity does not necessarily detract from its possible truth:

> It seems likely that Montaigne and his wife reacted quite differently to all these losses; his expressions of relative unconcern may well be responses to what he considered her excessive distress. If so, they had a share in pushing the two spiritually apart.

On the other hand, Frame also records Montaigne's occasional descriptions of quiet contented domestic life at the chateau, such as the regular card games he played with his wife and daughter: 'I handle the cards and keep score for a couple of pennies just as for double doubloons; when winning or losing, against my wife and daughter, is indifferent to me, just as when playing for keeps.'

Far from living the sedentary, contemplative life during these years, Frame points out that: 'His best ideas never came to him [in his tower], but at table, in bed, and mostly "on horseback, where my thoughts range most widely'". But even horseback riding on his estate was no easy matter in those days. As Montaigne described it:

> I went riding one day about a league from my house, which is situated at the very hub of all the turmoil of the civil wars of France. Thinking myself perfectly safe... I took a very easy, but not very strong horse. On my return... one of my men, big and strong, riding a powerful work horse... to show his daring and get ahead of his companions, spurred his horse at full speed up the path behind me, came down like a colossus on the little man and little horse, and hit us like a thunderbolt with all his strength and weight, sending us both head over heels. So that there lay the horse bowled over and stunned, and I ten or twelve paces beyond, dead, stretched out on my back, my face all bruised and skinned, my sword, which I had had in my hand, more than ten paces away, my belt in pieces, having no more motion and feeling than a log. It is the only swoon that I have experienced to this day.

Despite such rough-and-tumble violence, Montaigne professed a deep distaste for hunting and all cruelty to animals – a rarity in his time and amongst his class. His love of animals and his insight into their behaviour led him to subtle psychical intuition. When his dog enticed him, he could never refuse to play games with it. Similarly: 'When I play with my cat, who knows if I am not a pastime to her more than she is to me?' It seems that nothing animal was alien to him.

Montaigne had long suffered from kidney stones, an ailment he inherited from his father. By 1578, this affliction had begun to incapacitate Montaigne. In an attempt to discover a cure he set out on travels which would lead him through France, southern Germany, Austria and Italy. Naturally he kept a diary, recording all he saw and discovered – from steep hillsides in Germany covered with rows of vines, to ingenious fountains in northern Italy 'gushing of an infinite of jets... launched by a single spring, that can be worked from far off'; as well as a powerful water organ in a cave and the pleasure gardens of the Fuggers at Augsburg. He questioned priests about their beliefs, and did not refrain from making similar spiritual enquiries when he visited Protestant territories. Frame mentions how: 'he is especially curious about other faiths... attending synagogues and describing a circumcision sympathetically and at length'.

In Italy, Montaigne took the waters at Bagni di Lucca: 'For about ten days the stone, together with stomach trouble, headaches, and toothaches, gave him pain that rose to agony.' Montaigne described how he treated his ailment:

> I pushed down a stone that stopped in the passage. I remained from that moment until dinnertime without urinating, in order to increase my desire to do so. Then I got my stone out, not without pain and bleeding, both before and after: as big and long as a pine nut, but as thick as a bean at one end, and having, to tell the truth, exactly the shape of a prick.

He was fully aware of the seriousness of his condition, chiding himself:

> There would be too much weakness and cowardice on my part if, finding myself every day in a position to die in this manner, and with every hour bringing death nearer, I did not make every effort toward being able to bear death lightly as soon as it surprises me. And in the meantime it would be wise to accept joyously the good that it pleases God to send us.

As Frame points out: 'This is Montaigne's final philosophy, balanced and receptive'.

On entering Rome, Montaigne's books, along with the text of the essays he had so far completed, were confiscated by customs so that they could be scrutinized by the papal censor. This might well have ended in disaster. Montaigne learned that recently some German books had been condemned 'for mentioning the Protestant heresies they were combatting'. Fortunately, the examination of Montaigne's essays was similarly ludicrous. The censor was 'able to judge them only by the report of some

French friar, since he did not understand our language at all; and he was so content with the excuses I offered on each objection that this Frenchman had left him, that he referred it to my conscience to redress what I should see was in bad taste'. Just one of his books was seized: 'a Swiss History, simply because the anonymous author was a heretic and the preface condemned'.

In the midst of Montaigne's second sojourn at Lucca, he received a message informing him that he had been elected mayor of Bordeaux. He immediately returned home, where he took up the post once held by his father. Montaigne would remain in this position for two two-year periods of office, during which he was called upon to moderate the conflicting calls of the local Catholic and Huguenot factions. In 1586 there was an outbreak of plague in the region. This, along with the continuing wars of religion in France, forced him to leave his chateau for two years, during which he once again became a royal courtier. He joined Henry III as he fled Paris to avoid the clutches of the Catholic League and the increasingly fanatical Guise faction.

In 1588 Montaigne returned to Paris, where he was laid low with an attack of gout. Consequently he was seized by Guise's men and confined in the Bastille. Fortunately news of this reached Catherine de' Medici, and as Montaigne put it: 'I was released by an unheard-of favour.'

The following year, when Henry III was assassinated, Montaigne was back in Bordeaux. Here he managed to rally the city to support Catherine de' Medici's son-in-law Henry of Navarre, who would succeed as Henry IV.

Astonishingly, in the midst of all this, Montaigne managed to oversee the publication of his *Essais*. These attracted favourable attention. He had no taste for personal fame; in fact, his wish was to return to his beloved tower and write further essays. Even so, he felt it his duty to contact the newly crowned Henry IV and offer his services as a personal adviser. Turbulent circumstances, along with Montaigne's increasing illness, kept them apart. However, Montaigne did manage to write, advising the king 'that you may be rather loved than feared by your people'. These words echo the personal sentiment expressed by Montaigne in his essays: 'Even if I could make myself feared, I would much rather make myself loved.'

This was a controversial position to maintain amidst such bitter national conflict. Indeed, it was precisely the opposite of the realpolitik advised by Machiavelli in *The Prince*, which as we have seen was very much in favour at the time. The religious wars would continue for some years to come, but it was not until both sides adopted a position similar to the one advised by Montaigne that the conflict was resolved.

For the next four years, Montaigne continued to write. Some of this takes on a more confessional – or at least, self-revelatory – tone. Frankly, he reveals his personal weaknesses – as seen by himself, and others: 'idle; cool in the duties of friendship and kinship, and in public duties; too self-centred.' This may smack of a strict headmaster's end-of-term report; but judgement was not Montaigne's intention. Far from it. As we continue reading we find that his remarks are frequently comic, often obscene – yet invariably such intimacies are at his own expense. Of his penis, he writes in 'On Some Verses of Virgil':

> the unruly liberty of this member, obtruding so importunately when we have no use for it, and failing so importunately when we have the most use for it, and struggling for mastery so imperiously with our will, refusing with so much pride and obstinacy our solicitations, both mental and manual.

He insists upon expressing the needs and behaviour of the whole man, penis and all: 'Each one of my parts makes me myself just as much as every other. And no other makes me more properly a man than this one.' He concludes, piercing all hypocrisy: 'On the loftiest throne in the world we are still sitting on our own rump.' Now that he is old and ailing, he remarks how: 'I would run from one end of the world to the other to seek a single twelve-month of gay and pleasant tranquillity: I have no other end but to live and enjoy myself.' He points out the stupidity of the ancient philosophers, whose idea of decency boils down to advising us 'not to dare to do openly what it is decent for us to do in private'. He concludes with his aim and obligation: 'I owe a complete portrait of myself to the public. The wisdom of my lesson is wholly in truth, in freedom, in reality... of which propriety and ceremony are daughters, but bastard daughters.'

Montaigne died at home in his chateau in 1592, just a few months short of his sixtieth birthday. Three centuries later, the essayist Ralph Emerson, in many ways his American counterpart, would observe: 'Montaigne is the frankest and honestest of all writers. His French freedom runs into grossness; but he has anticipated all censure by the bounty of his own confessions.'

In his day Montaigne was a new voice – a man expanding into the fullness of his character. While his inspiration may be found in classical writers from Plato to the Sceptics, his words are very much related to the time in which he lived. He absorbed both Rabelais and Erasmus. Here indeed was the Renaissance in body and soul. For once, it is no cliché to say that he managed to embody the spirit of his age, and his influence would reflect this. By the time Montaigne died, the young Shakespeare had arrived in London and was beginning to spread his wings as a dramatist. When the first English translation of Montaigne's essays was published in 1603, it would be read by Shakespeare just as he was embarking upon his mature tragedies. It is possible to glimpse the ghost of Montaigne in the hollow grandeur and absurdities of *King Lear*.

CHAPTER 17

ELIZABETHAN ENGLAND

THE NORTHERN RENAISSANCE WOULD reach an apogee in the Elizabethan England that produced William Shakespeare. The resemblance between Montaigne and Shakespeare is striking. Montaigne's breadth of interests and understanding are matched by Shakespeare's breadth of imagery and insight. Both men raised a wealth of questions concerning the human condition – questions which explored and expanded what it meant to be a complete human being. Montaigne philosophized in his essays but reached no conclusion. Shakespeare philosophized in his dramas, but felt compelled to abjure any revealing conclusions. In Elizabethan England, the expression of beliefs, either original or simply unorthodox, could place their author in mortal danger.

When the twenty-five-year-old Elizabeth I ascended to the throne of England in 1558, she was a pale red-haired virgin, already well into womanhood by the standards of the time. A portrait of her from this period depicts a woman of unexceptional appearance yet whose face has the hallmarks of an apparent self-possession that belied her years and her unsettling upbringing. She may not have been as intellectually and physically gifted as her father Henry VIII during his youth, but she was imbued with the same ruthless streak that had enabled her father to have her mother Anne Boleyn beheaded before Elizabeth was three years old.

Yet it was from this very mother whom she never knew that she inherited the psychological mix of ambition and uncertainty which informed her political acumen. Elizabeth I was well aware of the hazardous complexity of her position as a Protestant monarch. As such, she was the secular and religious leader of a nation still disturbed by undercurrents of religious intransigence. She wisely recognized her limitations and relied upon a close-knit group of skilled advisers led by William Cecil, a loyal statesman who chose to identify himself with the fortunes and destiny of his nation.

Elizabeth I's father had impelled England from the periphery of European nations to a force to be reckoned with. The pretensions exhibited by Henry VIII at the Field of the Cloth of Gold remained central to Elizabethan England's self-conception. But in Europe such overweening ambition was covertly viewed as laughable by the likes of Catholic France and Habsburg Spain. France may have had its internal divisions with the Huguenots, but its sheer size, history and national pride informed its superiority. Meanwhile Spain, enriched by its influx of gold from the New World, viewed England as ripe for addition to the territorial empire that stretched from the Pacific to the Netherlands. Philip II had refused to recognize Henry VIII's divorce, and regarded Elizabeth I as the mere illegitimate offspring of this maverick apostate monarch. In his eyes, Elizabeth I's cousin the Catholic Mary, Queen of Scots remained the true heir to England's throne.

England was in many ways an anomaly, especially in its political structure. Although the monarch ruled, the power of the throne was curtailed, saddled with its upstart parliament whose consent was required for royal taxes.* In European eyes its makeshift national church – the so-called

---

* Elizabeth I would summon parliament just thirteen times during her forty-five-year reign. William Cecil and the privy council ruled on an everyday basis. However, England had since 1215 had the Magna Carta, which guaranteed certain personal liberties that were unheard of in most European nations.

Church of England – barely commanded the respect of its people. Catholic recusants continued to worship in secret throughout the land, while Puritans and other Protestant non-conformists sought the erasure of all traces of Catholic worship. Henry VIII had ensured that this island nation was protected by a strong navy. Yet now this defensive force had given birth to semi-condoned 'privateers' whose sole purpose appeared to be raiding Spanish treasure galleons on their way back from the New World. Both at sea and on land, both in religion and governance, the citizens of England appeared to answer to no coherent authority. Indeed, the consensus of opinion in Europe increasingly regarded England as politically incomprehensible and virtually a failed state.

As it happened, there was more than a little truth to this jaundiced view. Protestant England was ripe for invasion, surrounded as it was by Catholic countries. To the north, independent Scotland was ruled by the Catholic Mary, and allied itself with France. England continued with its struggle to conquer Ireland, whose Catholic population provided ample opportunity for a 'back door' invasion of England. Across the Channel, France had now ousted England from its last foothold in Europe at Calais. And further along the coast was the Spanish Netherlands, to say nothing of powerful Spain itself over the south-western horizon.

The main events of Elizabeth's life feature a succession of near misses or lucky escapes; throughout her reign the very existence of England was afflicted by uncertainty. A brief summary of her life and reign gives an indication of these circumstances, providing an instructive narrative of the nation's affairs.

From the outset, Elizabeth was a neglected child; her governess was even forced to write to her father, the king, for the provision of new clothes. Elizabeth's early life was beset by the political manoeuvring which swirled around her. How much she was aware of this is difficult to tell.

When Henry VIII died in 1547, Elizabeth's nine-year-old half-brother, Edward VI, succeeded to the throne. Within months, Henry VIII's widow Katherine Parr married the Lord High Admiral, Sir Thomas Seymour, Baron Seymour of Sudeley – an ambitious man of considerable charm and charisma who also happened to be the brother of the Lord Protector of the young king.

The thirteen-year-old Elizabeth now found herself living at Chelsea with the newly wedded couple, supposedly under their protection. What took place in this house would play a formative role in Elizabeth's emotional psychology, and may well have been a contributing factor to her later self-image as the 'Virgin Queen'.

The young Elizabeth soon warmed to the playful charms of her half-brother, Edward. Together they would romp and run about the house, with much chasing, giggling and horseplay. Sir Thomas took to creeping into Elizabeth's bedroom of a morning in his nightgown, playing boisterous games of tickling and bottom-slapping. Rather than chide her husband, Katherine Parr chose to join in. On one occasion she even held down the squealing Elizabeth as her husband removed her gown and tore it into pieces.

But such days were not to last. In 1548 Katherine Parr died in childbirth. Within months Sir Thomas was arrested for treason and imprisoned in the Tower of London. According to the charge, he had sought to depose his brother as Lord Protector and marry Elizabeth, putting him in line to inherit the throne. Two months later, he was beheaded.

In 1553, Edward VI died and was soon succeeded by his Catholic half-sister, Mary I, who was also an older half-sister of Elizabeth. The following year, Mary I's intention to marry Philip II of Spain provoked an uprising intended to depose her and place the Protestant Elizabeth on the throne. Whether or not the twenty-one-year-old Elizabeth was aware of this plan remains unclear. Either way, Mary I ordered Elizabeth to be imprisoned in the Tower of London. This must have been a traumatic experience: those who were confined to the Tower were liable to be executed. Fortunately, after two months Elizabeth was released, but had to spend a further year under house arrest at Woodstock, some sixty miles north-west of London.

In 1558 Mary I died amidst an outbreak of influenza in London, and Elizabeth eventually ascended to the throne to begin her forty-five-year reign. From the outset, Elizabeth I was the most eligible royal female in Europe. However, prompted by William Cecil, her chief adviser, she spurned all offers of marriage – angering many ambitious suitors, not least Philip II of Spain.

In 1567, Mary, Queen of Scots was forced to abdicate her throne by a cabal of rebellious Scottish noblemen, whereupon she fled south across the Scottish border into England, seeking the protection of her cousin Elizabeth I. This was granted, but Elizabeth was advised to keep Mary isolated, because many Catholics regarded her as the legitimate heir to the throne of England. Mary ended up in comfortable isolation at Tutbury Castle, a safe distance from Scotland, far enough from the coast to prevent her escape by sea, and over a hundred miles from London.

However, Elizabeth I's act of familial generosity would eventually turn sour, curdled by the acrid winds of religious differences. In the early 1580s, Elizabeth's spymaster, Sir Francis Walsingham, began intercepting and decoding secret letters which indicated that Mary was involved in a plot to assassinate Elizabeth and place herself on the throne of England. Not without mixed feelings, Elizabeth ordered that Mary be beheaded.

By now the Protestants in the Spanish Netherlands had begun the long struggle to rid themselves of rule by Philip II. Elizabeth despatched an army to aid the Dutch rebels, aware that their revolt was distracting Philip from invading England. By now English naval privateers* were stepping up their attacks on Spanish shipping. In 1587, Elizabeth appointed Sir Francis Drake to lead an English fleet in a daring raid on the Spanish navy in Cádiz. Having destroyed what was almost certainly a fleet preparing to sail on England, Drake continued laying waste to Spanish ships and ports on his return home. This successful naval expedition became popularly known in England as Singeing the King of Spain's Beard.

This was too much for Philip II, who began assembling a vast Spanish fleet to invade England. With 130 ships containing 8,000 sailors and

---

* These privateers were armed ships of the English navy allegedly acting on their own private initiative. In essence they were often little more than licensed pirates. Indeed, many never returned to service, but continued to ply their trade – often in the Caribbean.

more than 18,000 soldiers, the fleet was of such a size that it took no less than two days to clear port. The *Grande y Felicisima Armada* (Great and Most Fortunate Navy) set sail in 1588 under the command of the Duke of Medina Sidonia with orders to destroy the English fleet and transport the Spanish army of the Netherlands to occupy England.

This proved an unexpected, and indeed unprecedented, disaster for Spain. When the large ships of the Spanish fleet entered the English Channel they were attacked by the smaller and more manoeuvrable ships of the English navy. As the Armada made its way up the Channel, it suffered considerable losses before ending up off the coast of the Spanish Netherlands, where it expected to pick up the army. Here the Armada was attacked by Dutch coastal ships; meanwhile Drake set alight fireships and aimed them at the heart of the anchored Armada, where the flames and exploding gunpowder wreaked further havoc. Abandoning their planned invasion, sizeable remnants of the Spanish fleet set sail north with the aim of rounding Scotland and returning to Spain. En route they ran into a fierce Atlantic storm, which caused many of them to be wrecked on the rocky western coast of Ireland. Of the vast Armada that embarked from Cádiz, only 67 ships returned – with just 10,000 men, many laid low by disease and starvation.

This catastrophic Spanish defeat was due to a combination of circumstances – including the weather, superior English seamanship, the intervention of the Dutch, but most of all incompetent Spanish leadership. The Duke of Medina Sidonia lacked any military experience, either on land or sea. Philip II had appointed him purely on account of his aristocratic seniority and 'his reputation as a good Catholic'.

In the midst of these events, while England stood in greatest danger with the apparently invincible Spanish Armada sailing up the English Channel, Elizabeth I had travelled down the River Thames to address her troops at Tilbury. England faced being overrun by its first major invasion since 1066. Elizabeth I was now fifty-five years old, an ageing figure of increasing frailty and vanity. The bloom of her youth had vanished some decades previously when she suffered a bout of disfiguring smallpox. Now her visible face was but a mask. Her high ruff covered her mottled neck;

the curls of the dyed red wig ringing her high forehead contrasted starkly with her white-chalk-powdered face, its lines and pockmarks disguised by her caked make-up. Her wrinkled lips, smeared with rouge, parted to reveal her remaining discoloured teeth. Standing alone above her assembled soldiers, her shrill voice rang out:

> I know I have the body of a weak and feeble woman; but I have the heart and stomach of a king – and of a King of England too, and think foul scorn that… Spain, or any prince of Europe, should dare to invade the borders of my realm; to which, rather than any dishonour should grow by me, I myself will take up arms.

Ten years later, Shakespeare would pen a similarly rousing patriotic speech, as he imagined it delivered by Henry V on St Crispin's Day (25 October) before the Battle of Agincourt in 1415:

> He that outlives this day, and comes safe home,
> Will stand a tip-toe when this day is nam'd, […]
> He that shall live this day, and see old age,
> Will yearly on the vigil feast his neighbours, […]
>
> Then will he strip his sleeve and show his scars,
> And say 'These wounds I had on Crispin's day.'
> Old men forget: yet all shall be forgot,
> But he'll remember with advantages,
> What feats he did that day.

The artist in Shakespeare could not refrain from that final human touch, 'with advantages', i.e. exaggerations.

Many of Shakespeare's earlier plays depict historic English kings. The events which take place in these plays echo the turmoil of his time – vainglory, betrayal, murder, love – yet they always take place in a distant age. When he wrote *Henry V*, this involved events from nearly two centuries previously. His more daring *Richard II*, which features the downfall of a monarch, was generally considered too far in the past for any relevant parallels to be drawn. (Imagine a present-day play depicting events which took place some two decades before Queen Victoria ascended the throne.) These were dangerous times, and any drama even suspected of political content would never have been performed, its author liable to a charge of treason.

Shakespeare grew up in an England transformed. Thirty years before his birth, Henry VIII had broken with Rome, and in the decade following this the king had launched the dissolution of the monasteries. Some 800 or so establishments – including monasteries, priories, convents, nunneries and other religious institutions, many housed in some of the finest medieval buildings in the land – had been destroyed and pillaged, their treasures looted, their communities scattered. These had been centres of learning as well as hubs of artisanal life.

Perhaps most significantly of all, the dispossessed monks and nuns had spoken Latin. In adapting to secular life, they were forced to revert to the English language, the remnants of their learning introducing a new richness of vocabulary and usage. Such was the evolving language into which William Shakespeare was born in 1564. Little wonder that his fertile imagination would coin so many words we still use to this day. 'Hot-blooded' (and 'cold-blooded'), 'swagger', 'unaware' and 'unreal'... these are but a few of the neologisms Shakespeare inserted into his plays. The use of onomatopoeia, mellifluous phraseology, as well as countless prefixes (un-) and suffixes (-less), meant that they were easily understood by their audiences. Likewise references to current notions: 'Am I a Machiavel?' (Machiavelli), and the desert island which is the setting for *The Tempest*. The strange half-human creatures who inhabit this latter location – the innocent sprite Ariel and the uncouth monster Caliban – are recognizable from the references in maps to 'Here be dragons' and other mythical beings. Their quasi-human aspect indicates that Shakespeare seems to have concurred with Montaigne's attitude towards human arrivals from distant continents. And as we shall see, Shakespeare's contact with such unfamiliar examples of the human race probably involved more than an interview conducted through a wonky interpreter.

What else would have been immediately recognizable to Shakespeare's rowdy audiences? Certainly they would have warmed to mention of the drunkard Falstaff's favourite 'Malmsey... sack' (wine originally from Monemvasia in Greece; ironically it was sickly sweet, despite 'sack' possibly originating from the French *sec* or 'dry'). The reference to Machiavelli would have been aimed at the educated amongst the audience; the naming of Falstaff's favourite tipple would have been understood by any who frequented the taverns and 'stews' (bordellos) in the unlicensed district of Southwark across the Thames from the City of London.

So who was this audience? Many may have been descendants of the monks and nuns dispossessed by Henry VIII, their learning or artisanal skills urbanized. The theatres in which Elizabethan plays were performed were round, with a large area in front of the stage. This common space, open to the heavens (and rain) was occupied by the rowdy groundlings, who gobbled their nuts and apples, and drank their ale, pissing it into the sawdust or sand on which they stood. These were the porters, servants and brawling apprentice boys, the odiferous mob who cheered the heroes and booed the villains, taking an interactive part in the performances. They each would have paid for their admission by dropping their penny into the box at the entrance (the box office); a penny was the cost of a loaf of bread. The 'better sort', who paid anything from two pennies to six pennies, or more, to occupy the circular upper balconies, were members of the merchant class or minor nobility, or even on occasion personages of some import in the land. (Initially, when a court wished to watch a play, the actors' company would be summoned to the grandee's palace to stage a private performance. The company to which Shakespeare belonged was the Lord Chamberlain's Men – later the King's Men, as they would be called after King James I ascended to the throne.)

There were several competing theatres, and these accommodated as many spectators as could be crammed in, which meant that the audiences used up popular plays at a prodigious rate. Besides acting in minor roles in his own plays, Shakespeare was often expected to produce more than one play for a 'season' – many tailored especially for the leading actor of the company so he could show off his talents. In Shakespeare's case this

was Richard Burbage, the finest actor of his age, who owned the Globe
Theatre and would welcome the successful Shakespeare as a part-owner
of his company the Lord Chamberlain's Men.

William Shakespeare was a country boy, born in 1564 in the provincial town of Stratford-upon-Avon, a hundred miles from London. Little
is known for certain of Shakespeare's personal life, let alone his interior
life, which makes it all but impossible to account in any meaningful way
for the full range of his prodigious originality. This has led some – even
including Sigmund Freud – to claim that the minor actor Shakespeare was
no more than a front for the brilliant courtier, scholar, politician, essayist
and scientist Sir Francis Bacon. However, such theories are undone by
evidence of the uncharacteristic ineptitude of Bacon as a playwright.
More intriguing is the possibility that Shakespeare was brought up a
secret Catholic. There is convincing evidence that his father, a Stratford
glove-maker, and his mother, daughter of a propertied family, were both
covertly practising Catholics. This might in part account for the verbal
pyrotechnics with which Shakespeare succeeded in obscuring any trace
of his true beliefs.

Shakespeare grew up in a town where rural England was never far
distant. At night, the darkness amongst the eaves of Stratford would
have resounded with the hoots of owls in the nearby Forest of Arden, the
baby-like yowling of fighting foxes, and the sudden hissing of disturbed
swans on the banks of the Avon. At dawn the local farmers would drive
their sheep and pigs into the market, their wives milking cows for the
servants queueing with their pails, their daughters carrying twisted shawls
of duck eggs or wooden buckets of watercress. Markets, harvests, old wives'
tales and the passage of the seasons must have coloured Shakespeare's
childhood as much as they do his works. (The surprise missing element is
nautical imagery, whose paucity is curious in a member of such a proud
island race who lived in London when it was very much a port: one has
to dig hard to find lacunae in Shakespeare.)

Shakespeare went to the local grammar school, where he would have
received a sound education in grammar, rhetoric and classical authors –
especially Aristotle – such as he might have received at any time during

the preceding century or so. The northern European Renaissance would barely have penetrated Stratford.

When Shakespeare was eighteen he was obliged to marry Anne Hathaway before she produced his daughter. His son Hamnet was born two years later, but would die aged eleven. (Two years after this, by now in his thirties, Shakespeare would write *Hamlet*, the finest – if not the most finely constructed – of his plays.)

Shortly after the birth of Hamnet, Shakespeare left Stratford to take up a post as tutor to the children of a wealthy Lancashire landowner, Alexander Hoghton, who is known to have had Catholic sympathies. This large household and its intellectual visitors appears to have functioned as Shakespeare's university, introducing him to a wide range of knowledge and literature that he would not ordinarily have encountered. It was here that he would have first come across Plutarch's *Lives*, comparing famous Ancient Greek and Roman figures – which would provide material for such plays as *Julius Caesar* and *Antony and Cleopatra*. At this time he may also have read Raphael Holinshed's *Chronicles of England, Scotland and Ireland* – which inspired such works as *Macbeth* and *King Lear*. But while Shakespeare may have borrowed the stories, it was his language and insight into the psychology of the characters which informed their transcendent qualities.

He would have begun writing his first sonnets here, a habit which persisted throughout his life and came closest to revealing his raw feelings concerning love, jealousy, loneliness, mortality and a wide range of traditional poetic subjects. Though he did not treat these in the traditional manner of the troubadour and courtly love. The mysterious 'dark lady' who features in several sonnets seems to have caused Shakespeare some anguish. And she was certainly no beauteous maiden such as would have attracted a troubadour's platonic blandishments. Her wiry black hair, 'dun breasts' and 'eyes... raven-black' have led some to speculate that she may have been of African, or at least Moorish, origin. Either way, she certainly inspired in him a sexual passion as well as 'green-eyed' jealousy. Other poems suggest homoerotic love, as well as all manner of clues and mysteries alluding to identities that would have been recognizable only to a few insiders.

The Hoghton household probably introduced Shakespeare to the delights of Italy, at least in literary form. Shakespeare would never travel to the birthplace of the Renaissance, though he would set several of his plays in this country.

Sometime before 1592, when Shakespeare turned twenty-eight, he is known to have arrived in London. By that year, he had become successful enough to be lampooned by a jealous competitor, Robert Greene, who referred to him as 'an upstart Crow, beautified with our feathers' (i.e. plagiarizing our works), adding that Shakespeare was 'in his conceit the only Shakescene in a country'. In other words, Shakespeare was getting above himself in attempting to compete with university-educated writers such as Christopher Marlowe and of course Robert Greene himself.

As had been the case with the Ancient Greek tragedians, competition spurred on excellence. Shakespeare was but one of a generation of inspired playwrights who would ride the crest of the breaking wave of the new English language which came into being in Elizabethan England.* Amongst these were Shakespeare's friend Ben Jonson; the tragedian John Webster, who famously saw 'the skull beneath the skin'; John Fletcher, who would later collaborate with Shakespeare; and Thomas Kyd, tortured into betraying his friend Marlowe, who was consequently murdered in a tavern brawl in Deptford. Marlowe, whose life was cut short at just twenty-nine, had been born in the same year as Shakespeare, and his *Doctor Faustus* was so accomplished that later some suspected it had been written by Shakespeare.

At the time of Marlowe's mysterious demise in 1593,† Shakespeare's oeuvre consisted of comedies, such as *The Comedy of Errors*,

---

* A similar transformation had occurred in Italy two centuries earlier when Dante formalized the Italian language in the Florentine dialect. Meanwhile, French acquired a new form and plasticity with Rabelais, Montaigne and the court poet Pierre de Ronsard. The Renaissance of the Spanish language would occur with Shakespeare's contemporary Cervantes.

† With the lack of any hard evidence to explain this event, scholarly speculation abounds. Was he working as a spy? Was he homosexual? Was he guilty of blasphemy?...

historical works such as *Richard III*, and the grotesque early tragedy *Titus Andronicus*. Not until the turn of the century would his talent begin to evolve with such accomplished works as the comedy *Twelfth Night*, the rousing *Henry V*, and tragedies such as *Romeo and Juliet* and *Julius Caesar*. These were followed by *Hamlet*, whose stylistic and rhetorical devices lifted it beyond the limits of classic tragedy. In this work, the young bewildered Prince of Denmark begins to struggle with his own thoughts, standing on stage speaking to himself. In his soliloquies we hear a consciousness debating its future, its options, talking to itself in philosophical monologue: 'To be or not to be, that is the question...' This voice was utterly new – humanity evolving into a novel form of consciousness and self-consciousness. This is sixteenth-century existentialism, no less.

Here, if anywhere, we hear Shakespeare speaking in his true voice, the voice of a recognizable modern humanity: impetuous in its youth, its certainties undermined by doubt, prompted by his oedipal vision of his father's ghost. Here is a spirit coming into its own, sinuous in its deviousness and so utterly alone... Is it too trivial, or fanciful, to see Shakespeare mourning Hamnet? The father who realizes that he will have no son to carry on his name. The writer, emerging into the glory of his talent, in which he will revel – but who could not, even in his greatest conceit, have ever envisaged what place his name would come to occupy in the world through the coming centuries. The 'upstart Crow' who will still be croaking his honeyed cacophony four centuries after his words are first inked, crossed out, inserted onto a blank page. Words filled with 'sound and fury' but certainly signifying something – what, precisely, remains mysterious, remains to be explored and explained by each generation anew – but such is their power that they could well continue to involve us 'to the last syllable of recorded time'.

Indeed, Shakespeare has been as well served by posterity as he has served it. His works remain the joint property of both meticulous scholars and demonstrative actors, and it is the dialectic between these two strange bedfellows which has been responsible for keeping his words very much alive. Before these words can be desiccated by over-interpretation, some rash actor's voice breathes new life into them. Thus they are still capable of taking their place, centre stage, in the drama of our time.

In the twentieth century, during the midst of the Second World War, when Britain stood alone against Nazi-occupied Europe, the British government would finance a film version of Shakespeare's *Henry V*, starring Laurence Olivier, in which Henry V addresses his troops before the Battle of Agincourt:

> We few, we happy few, we band of brothers;
> For he to-day that sheds his blood with me
> Shall be my brother; be he ne'er so vile,
> This day shall gentle his condition:
> And gentlemen in England now a-bed
> Shall think themselves accurs'd they were not here,
> And hold their manhoods cheap whiles any speaks
> That fought with us upon Saint Crispin's day.

All who watched Olivier deliver these words in the film well understood their stirring patriotic message.

Indeed, from the very outset Shakespeare's words were capable of embodying a message – despite the fact that he did so much to obfuscate any relevant political interpretation that might be put upon his works. On 7 February 1601, Robert Devereux, Earl of Essex, paid the Lord Chamberlain's Men handsomely to stage a performance of *Richard II*. Unwittingly, Shakespeare and his fellow actors obliged. Only afterwards did they discover the earl's intentions concerning the play, in which Richard II is overthrown and murdered. The next day, Devereux, a rejected suitor of Elizabeth I, staged a rebellion. Fortunately this was unsuccessful, and Elizabeth I's advisers managed to convince her of the actors' innocence. But Elizabeth was not above using Shakespeare and his actors for her own purposes, either. On the day before the Earl of Essex was publicly beheaded, Elizabeth I commanded the actors from the Globe to stage a performance of the same play at her residence, Whitehall Palace. Later, she was said to have remarked: 'I am Richard II, know ye not that?'

Some claim that Elizabeth I's vanity led her to see an image of herself in Shakespeare's Cleopatra, who attracts the love of both Caesar and Mark Antony. On a slightly more ambiguous note, the American critic Helen Morris claims: 'I believe that in certain aspects of Shakespeare's Cleopatra we find a reflection or "shadow" of Queen Elizabeth.' This is unlikely, given Shakespeare's aversion to any such contemporary identifications in his dramas. But it is not impossible, for a man whose font of inspiration appeared to flow so freely from his unconscious mind. As we have seen, even before the end of his life Shakespeare's words had already escaped his grasp and begun to take on a life of their own. Here, arguably, was the voice of the northern Renaissance in all its glory and tragedy.

CHAPTER 18

BRAHE AND KEPLER

S OMETIME DURING THE 1590s, Richard Burbage and his players were invited by the King of Denmark to perform a lucrative summer season at the royal castle at Elsinore (Helsingør). Shakespeare was not amongst these players, but would later be regaled with tales of their foreign adventure. These would provide the background for the play he had in mind, whose full title would be *Hamlet, Prince of Denmark*.

It is at night on the battlements of Elsinore Castle that Hamlet encounters his father's ghost, whose revelations sow the seeds of the ensuing tragedy. Coincidentally, some years earlier, while pacing these same battlements, the King of Denmark had suddenly seen the solution to a problem that was troubling him.

King Frederick II had taken under his wing an aristocratic young astronomer called Tycho Brahe, whose behaviour was as eccentric as his appearance: he wore a false metal nose and his awkward paranoid character inclined him to flamboyant cantankerous outbursts. Brahe's most recent astronomical observations had made him famous throughout Europe, and the king knew that Brahe was planning to leave Denmark. Brahe had received an offer to set up in Basel, one of the leading intellectual centres in Europe: home of the artistic Holbeins; where Paracelsus had briefly been professor; location of the skilled printer Oporinus to whom Vesalius had entrusted his masterwork. Looking out over the sea, Frederick II's eye happened to alight on the remote island of Hven, in the middle of the Øresund (Sound) between Denmark and Sweden. Hven was royal territory, occupied only by a small village of fisherfolk and smallholders. If he offered Brahe this island, where the astronomer could build his own private residence, perhaps this would tempt him to remain in Denmark.

Tycho Brahe was amongst the more exotic characters to have contributed to the northern Renaissance. He came from a high-flying but dysfunctional noble family. His father, Otte, was the resident governor of a succession of royal castles (and may even have been a temporary governor of Elsinore). Tycho's uncle Jørgen, who had inherited the considerable family fortune, was a royal counsellor, naval hero and hard-drinking pal of Frederick II. When Jørgen discovered that he could not have children, he decided that he would select his own heir. In pursuance of this aim, he bullied his younger brother Otte into promising that he would present him with his firstborn son.

Otte's disappointment with this arrangement was allayed when his wife gave birth to twin boys. Unfortunately, the other twin died in infancy, and Uncle Jørgen turned up to collect Tycho when he was just two years old. (Some reports claim that Tycho was kidnapped.) Tycho's father threatened to murder his older brother, but nothing came of this. Tycho's childhood was passed in a succession of cold draughty castles on the Baltic coast, dining at long wooden tables crammed with innumerable relatives. At the head of the table sat the intimidating figure of Uncle Jørgen; topics of mealtime conversation were 'warfare, politics and court gossip'.

Otte wished his son to be educated in Latin, but Jørgen did not believe in such fripperies. Ten years before Tycho's birth, in 1536, Denmark had broken definitively from the Roman Catholic Church and converted to Lutheranism. Despite this, Tycho received a traditional education in accord with the Aristotelian beliefs which still prevailed in Denmark. He would look back on his childhood as a boring, vacuous period of aristocratic neglect, consisting mainly of 'horses, dogs and luxury'. Upon finishing his primary education, Tycho entered the University of Copenhagen to study rhetoric, philosophy and law at the age of twelve, a seemingly normal practice at the time.

The following year, the adolescent Tycho witnessed a partial eclipse of the sun. Although this eclipse arrived a day after it had been predicted, the very fact of its prediction was what most impressed Tycho. Here at last he had a glimpse of something certain in his life. He immediately began purchasing books on astronomy, including one by Regiomontanus, a map of the constellations drawn by Dürer and *De Sphaera Mundi* (The Sphere of the World) written by the thirteenth-century monastic scholar Johannes de Sacrobosco, which was regarded as the classic exposition of the Ptolemaic earth-centred astronomical system. Subsequently, Uncle Jørgen despatched the fifteen-year-old Tycho on a tour of German universities, accompanied by a nineteen-year-old tutor who was instructed to cure him of this astronomy nonsense and make sure he equipped himself with the type of education expected of a court counsellor. Within months the young Tycho's enthusiasm had convinced his tutor to disobey his instructions, and together the two of them embarked upon the study of astronomy at the safe distance of the University of Leipzig.

Here Brahe gained a thorough knowledge of both the Ptolemaic and the Copernican systems. Together, he and his tutor observed a close conjunction of the planets Jupiter and Saturn. Brahe was perplexed to discover that the tables drawn up using both the Ptolemaic system and the Copernican system contained minor inaccuracies in their predictions of the conjunction. This led him to start making astronomical observations of his own. He decided that the only way to create correct tables was to make meticulous personal observations, night after night, using the most accurate astronomical instruments available. (The telescope had yet to be invented.) Meanwhile he checked the accuracy of his observations by using them to draw up the horoscopes of various famous historical figures, and seeing whether these chimed with recorded history. This was not necessarily an aberration: at the time, the drawing-up of horoscopes was the only way an astronomer could hope to earn a living, and the accuracy of such characterizations was considered vital. The fortunate difference here was due to Brahe's arrogance: he refused to believe that his observations were incorrect, regardless of the astrological anomalies they threw up. It was Brahe's supreme self-confidence and unshakeable belief in (his) factual observations which would result in him becoming the finest astronomer of his time.

Tycho returned to Denmark in 1565 at the age of eighteen. By now Denmark had once again been plunged into war with its neighbour Sweden. (The sixteenth century had already witnessed three such wars of varying duration; during the previous century there had been no less than eight wars between the two countries.) Uncle Jørgen had become a national hero after the defeat of the Swedish fleet at Öland the previous year. But it was shortly after this that Brahe's larger-than-life 'stepfather' had performed his most heroic, but alas fatal, deed. Frederick II and Jørgen were returning home one night after a long night's carousing in Copenhagen, when the king suddenly fell off his horse into a canal. Jørgen heroically dived into the canal and rescued the king, but unfortunately died some days later of pneumonia.

Using the inheritance he received from his stepfather, Brahe set off to study at the historic University of Rostock, on the north German coast of the Baltic. Here Brahe became involved in an altercation with a Danish cousin who was also studying at the university. Their dispute originated over which of them was the finest mathematician. However, rather than settle this in the obvious mathematical manner, the two of them ended up having a duel. It was during the course of this that Brahe lost his nose, which was sliced off at the bridge by his opponent's sword. According to historical accounts, Brahe had a new nose made out of a gold and silver alloy, and is said to have carried a small box, similar to a snuff box, 'containing some ointment or glutinous composition which he frequently rubbed on his nose'.*

---

* In 2010 Brahe's remains were exhumed and subjected to chemical analysis. According to science writer Meghan Gannon: 'Though the prosthesis has not been found, greenish stains around the nasal area of Brahe's corpse contained traces of copper and zinc, indicating that his fake nose was made of brass.' However, alternative sources stoutly maintain that this was caused by Brahe's everyday nose: 'The prosthetics made of gold and silver were mostly worn for special occasions, rather than everyday wear.'

Brahe would continue with his studies at various German universities until he was twenty-six years old, by which time he had accumulated a superb collection of observational instruments – including 'a large
quadrant of brass and oak, thirty-eight feet in diameter and turned by
four handles'. This enabled him to measure with precision the angle of
elevation of a star above the horizon. Brahe was the first to insist upon
the central importance of precise astronomical observation.* As recognized by the twentieth-century American philosopher of science E. A.
Burtt, Brahe was 'the first competent mind in modern astronomy to feel
ardently the passion for exact empirical facts'. It was this empiricism, and
his reliance upon mathematical calculation, which makes him a truly
modern scientist – one of the first to emerge in the Renaissance era. Not
until the third decade of the ensuing century would Galileo famously
proclaim: 'The book of nature is written in the language of mathematics.' Brahe may not have said this, and he certainly would not have
fully realized its implications, but his practice undeniably chimed with
Galileo's later remark.

In 1570 Brahe received a communication from a powerful uncle on
his mother's side, named Steen Bille, inviting him to come and set up a
laboratory on his estate at Herrevad Abbey, in southern Scania on the
Swedish mainland (which was at the time Danish territory). Herrevad
had formerly been a large Cistercian monastery, but had been taken
over by the Danish Crown and was being administered by Uncle Steen.
Together, he and Brahe set about converting one of the large old monastery buildings into a laboratory and manufactory. This would soon begin
producing glassware, and became the first paper factory in Scandinavia.

Despite such distractions, Brahe was able to continue with his unrelenting
schedule of nightly observations. On the night of 11 November 1572 he
noticed a new star, 'brighter than Venus', which had suddenly become visible
in the constellation of Cassiopeia. (This group of stars, visible to the naked

---

* As Arthur Koestler pointed out, during the course of his life Copernicus would
just make twenty-seven astronomical observations. The remainder of his astronomical data was reliant upon observations made by the likes of Ptolemy and
Hipparchus in the second century AD.

eye, lay in the northern sector of the sky, and had been named by Ptolemy in the second century AD.) Brahe called in others to confirm the existence of the star he had discovered, which he named a 'nova' (new) star. According to the orthodox Aristotelian view of the universe, the region beyond the moon's orbit was eternal and immutable. Only sublunar phenomena such as comets could exhibit any degree of change. But Brahe was able to show that this nova star displayed no parallax against the unchanging background of the fixed stars. That is, it showed no displacement when viewed from different positions; also, when observed over a period of weeks the nova still did not change position relative to the fixed stars. This meant that the nova was not sublunar, and not even a planet. It was a fixed star in the stellar sphere beyond the planets.* Brahe's observations caused much controversy amongst orthodox Aristotelian astronomers, who continued to insist any changing astronomical phenomena must exist in the sublunar realm. But Brahe was equally convinced that he was right. His observations presaged the end of the Aristotelian view of the heavens.

Brahe set down his observations and their implications in a book entitled *De Stella Nova* (About the New Star). The preface to this work begins in characteristic fashion, addressing his detractors: *O crassa ingenia. O caecos coeli spactatores* (Oh dimwits! Oh blind spectators of the sky). The publication of this work would make Brahe's name known in universities throughout Europe. He had done for the universe something similar to what Copernicus had done for the Ptolemaic geocentric solar system. Astronomy was now a new science, released from the constrictions of a false Aristotelian orthodoxy. Brahe was invited on a tour of European universities, and the metal-nosed Danish wonder with the huge, drooping, sausage-like moustache delivered lectures in halls from Heidelberg to Basel, and even as far afield as Venice, where he prolonged his stay for some weeks.

It was now that Frederick II learned of Brahe's plans to take up

---

* Such a star is today classified as a supernova, and is known to be at least 7,500 light years from earth. What we see as a supernova is in fact the powerful light produced by a large exploding star in the last stages of nuclear fusion.

residence in Basel, and offered him the island of Hven if he would remain in Denmark. Brahe was initially reluctant to take up the king's offer, writing to a friend: 'I am displeased with society here [in Denmark]. I have had enough of all this rubbish.' But Brahe was by this time married, with children, and decided against inflicting upon his own sons the peripatetic life he had suffered in his own childhood. Brahe took up the king's offer, and was soon at work constructing a large castle on Hven. In this he was inspired by the Italian Renaissance architect Andrea Palladio, with whose work he had been favourably impressed during his stay in Venice. Palladio's villas sought to emulate the work of Ancient Greek and Roman architects, notably Vitruvius.*

Brahe's castle was named Uraniborg after Urania, the ancient classical muse of astronomy, mathematics and the exact sciences. The islanders were conscripted as building labourers, and 100 students were brought on board – to learn from the master, as well as assist him in his building project. Uraniborg was soon envisaged as far more than a castle, or even a scientific laboratory (though it would fulfil both these purposes); it was to be a Renaissance palace, fit for entertaining visiting scholars from all over Europe.

But this was not all. Quite apart from the castle, Brahe was determined to build himself the finest observatory in Europe. This Stjerneborg (City of the Stars) would be constructed in the grounds of the castle, and would consist of no less than six chambers, placed underground so as 'not to be exposed to the disturbing influence of the wind'.

Such was the cost of Brahe's project on Hven that Frederick II was soon diverting no less than 1 per cent of the entire national budget in order to keep it going, while many of the students and all of the locals were declared 'indentured' labour, i.e. unpaid. Uraniborg would become

---

* Vitruvius is best remembered today in the drawing by Leonardo da Vinci of 'Vitruvian Man', which portrays a naked figure whose navel is the centre of a circle. The enclosed man's arms and legs reach out to the edges of the circle and a square. This has been seen by many as the epitome of the humanistic adage: 'Man is the measure of all things.' This claim was in fact first set down by the Ancient Greek philosopher Protagoras of Abdera in the fifth century BC.

renowned on the scholarly circuit throughout Europe, attracting scientists and dignitaries of all kinds, including James VI of Scotland (who would succeed Elizabeth I, becoming James I of England). The host's banquets became the stuff of legend, 'presided over by the indefatigable, hard-drinking, gargantuan host'. According to Brahe's biographer Kitty Ferguson, a typical winter (Martinmas) feast enjoyed by scholars during this period consisted of 'sugar, almonds, chestnuts, a goose, a suckling pig and eighty bottles of wine'. As Ferguson wryly points out: 'Clearly they were going to drink more than they were going to eat.'

Between toasts, Brahe would be moved to deliver speeches on such matters as eccentricities in the orbit of Mars, the latest stars whose location he had identified, and so forth – at the same time tossing aside scraps of food for his dwarf jester, Jepp, 'who sat at the master's feet under the table chattering incessantly amidst the general noise'. According to Brahe, Jepp was gifted with second sight 'of which he seemed to give spectacular proof on several occasions'. As we have already seen, Brahe remained susceptible to the scientific misapprehensions of his age. (The basement of Uraniborg also contained a number of furnaces, which were used for alchemy.)

It was during these years that Brahe observed the Great Comet which was visible throughout Europe from November 1577 to January 1578. Brahe managed to calculate the distance of this comet from earth, and also its direction of flight. He was thus able to show that its orbit lay far beyond that of the moon. This disproved once and for all the Aristotelian contention that all stars beyond the moon were 'immutable and eternal'. Comets had long been supposed to presage apocalyptic events, and the Lutherans of Denmark were soon issuing their predictions of doom. Not to be outdone, Brahe issued his own prophecies: tumultuous events would soon be seen in Russia, culminating in the overthrow of Ivan the Terrible in 1583. (In fact, Ivan the Terrible would be overthrown in 1584.)

Brahe also kept a moose at Uraniborg, allegedly for the purposes of biological observation. In order to facilitate this, the moose was allowed to wander at will through the chambers of the castle. Unfortunately one day the moose wandered into the pantry, where it slaked its thirst by drinking copious amounts from an open vat of beer. It then staggered about in a drunken state, before finally falling down the stairs into the cellar, suffering mortal injuries.

Yet amidst all this, Brahe continued with his dogged research into what was indisputably genuine science. His meticulous map of the night sky had now progressed well beyond 500 stars. In this he was aided by his students, as well as his long-time assistant Sophie, his younger sister, who since the age of fourteen had clocked up a series of remarkable triumphs. These included a precise observation of the eclipse of the moon, as well as many adjustments to the Copernican tables.

Indeed it was the sheer accuracy of Brahe and his indefatigable team of observers and checkers which would prove their worth in both the quantity and the quality of their mapping of the night sky. Nothing before, or since, matched the accuracy of his observations reliant upon the naked eye, using early theodolites and such, unaided by lenses or telescopes. Using the metal measuring instruments he had designed for the purpose, Brahe was able to make observations precise to within two minutes of an arc – now acknowledged as the very limit of the human eye's capability. Ptolemy and the Ancient Greeks, even aided by the supreme clarity of the Mediterranean night sky, could only manage an accuracy of ten minutes of an arc.* Such was the accuracy of Brahe's observations of the motion of the sun that he was able to calculate the length of a year to within less than a second. As a result, Brahe's readings would play a decisive role in the reformation of the calendar which took place under Pope Gregory XIII in 1582.

---

* For the purposes of celestial measurement, the sky can be viewed as a dome. A perfectly flat horizon is like a circle and can be divided into 360 degrees. A line from the centre of the circle can also be drawn to the zenith of the dome, directly overhead. Thus the overall structure of the sky can be mapped in much the same way as the upper half of the globe. A line from a point on the horizon to the centre of this circle, and a second line from the centre of the circle to the zenith of the dome above, makes an angle of 90 degrees. For more precise measurements, 1 degree is divided into 60 arc-minutes. For instance, the average width of a full moon is ½ degree, or 30 arc-minutes. Thus the Ancient Greeks managed an accuracy of a third of the size of an average full moon, whereas Brahe was managing an accuracy of one-fifteenth of the size of a full moon.

On the other hand, Brahe's observations did not prevent him from making certain mistakes. For instance, he concluded that the distance from the earth of the planet Saturn (the furthest known planet at the time) was 48 million miles. As Asimov observed, this 'seemed an enormous distance for the astronomers of the age but was only one-eighteenth of the real figure'.

Another oddity in Brahe's thinking was his overall conception of the universe – the so-called Tychonic system. Although Brahe was well aware of the Copernican heliocentric system, he refused to jettison all the workings of the Ptolemaic geocentric system. His view of the universe was essentially a compromise between the two. For Brahe the earth remained at the centre of the universe. The sun and the moon circled the earth. However, all other planetary bodies revolved around the sun. This lopsided picture found little favour with either camp in the growing Copernican–Ptolemaic debate.

In 1588 Frederick II unexpectedly died at the age of fifty-three. He was succeeded on the throne of Denmark by his eleven-year-old son, Christian IV. Owing to the new king being underage, for the time being a regency council ruled in his stead. Brahe's headstrong behaviour had already outraged several aristocratic members of the royal council, and it soon became clear that the flow of funds from the royal coffer to finance Brahe's extravagant projects on Hven was unlikely to continue as before.

After a long struggle, Brahe finally set off into exile in 1597. By now he had completed his star catalogue, which gave the positions of some 1,000 stars. In fact, Brahe had definitively mapped the positions of 777 stars, but added a further 223 whose positions were not yet fully confirmed because he wished to emulate the fabled thousand-starred charts of the ancients. He also felt that the idea of a large round number would appear more impressive to any potential sponsor. And this indeed proved to be the case. In 1599 Brahe accepted the invitation of the Holy Roman Emperor Rudolf II, and moved to Prague to take up the post of Imperial Court Astronomer. He was given a castle in which to set up an observatory, and a young German assistant named Johannes Kepler. Brahe gave Kepler access to his star catalogue, and together they began working on the planetary motions, with the aim of drawing up a complete chart of these.

In October 1601 Brahe fell ill during a royal banquet, and died some days later. Poison was suspected, as Brahe's high-handed manner had already antagonized several important figures at the imperial court. However, according to the first-hand report by Kepler, Brahe refused to leave the banquet to urinate, as this would have been a breach of etiquette. This exacerbated problems that Brahe was experiencing with his bladder, causing it to burst – leading Kepler to suspect that this was the cause of his death.*

Brahe was fifty-four years old and feared that he had not fully accomplished his life's mission. His last words to Kepler were: 'Let me not seem to have lived in vain.' But already Brahe had justified himself. In the eyes of Asimov, and other historians, 'the crowning act of [Brahe's] life' was placing his star catalogue into the hands of his young assistant Kepler. By now this did indeed record the verified position of almost 1,000 stars. Using Brahe's work, Kepler would lay the foundations for the seventeenth-century Scientific Revolution, which culminated in Newton's law of universal gravitation.

Johannes Kepler had been born some thirty years before Brahe's death, in the small historic town of Weil der Stadt on the edge of the Black Forest in south-west Germany. Like Brahe, he had a conflicted family background. His grandfather, who was still alive when Johannes was born, had been the mayor of Weil. According to Kepler, his seventy-five-year-old grandfather was 'remarkably arrogant and proudly dressed... short-tempered and obstinate, and his face betrays his licentious past'.

---

* When Brahe's body was exhumed in 2010, both the poison and the burst bladder theories were disproved. Samples of hair from Brahe's beard were found to contain 'a gold content of 20 to 100 times higher than what one would expect to find in a typical person today'. This led a number of researchers to conclude that the build-up of gold had resulted from his imbibing 'elixirs of life', which frequently contained large amounts of gold leaf.

This may account for why Johannes's father, Heinrich, spent so many years away from home, earning a precarious living as a mercenary soldier. According to his son, Heinrich was 'vicious, inflexible, quarrelsome, and doomed to a bad end'. Over the limited period when Johannes knew his father, he seems to have been both in awe and afraid of this flawed yet charismatic character. Johannes's father would finally die fighting for the imperial army during the war in which the Spanish Netherlands gained its independence. Johannes's mother, Katherina, was an innkeeper's daughter, and was described by her son as 'small, thin, swarthy, gossiping and quarrelsome, of a bad disposition'. She was a 'healer' and probably practised witchcraft. These descriptions come from what Kepler's biographer Arthur Koestler called 'a kind of genealogical horoscope' which Kepler wrote when he was twenty-six.

From the outset, it was clear that the young Kepler was a mathematical prodigy. The most significant event of his early life occurred when he was six years old and his mother took him to a nearby hilltop to view the Great Comet of 1577 (whose course was being traced by Brahe at Uraniborg). Three years later, Kepler would be called out of the house to see an eclipse of the moon. These two events made a deep impression on Kepler – both in a scientific sense and in a mystical sense. This double legacy would influence him throughout his life. His thought would retain a mathematical precision which coexisted with a pervasive belief in esoteric symbolism. Here was a mind far more typical of the general view held during the Renaissance era than we are comfortable with.

The advances Kepler would make were often as deeply prompted by his pervasive mystical view of the cosmos as they were by his scientific-mathematical viewpoint. Fortunately, he did not allow the former to warp the exactitude of the latter: if anything, his religious viewpoint informed the rigid structure of his scientific investigations, lending them a wider apprehension of the universe as a whole. Even so, the victory of his science over his divine world view was not always assured, and was in many instances a close-run thing. Not for nothing would his most characteristic work be entitled *Harmonice Mundi* (The Harmony of the World), which sought to bridge what we – with hindsight – see as the chasm between his scientific and pseudo-scientific thought. Here Kepler referenced musical harmony – his ideas harking back to Pythagorean mysticism. According to these ancient ideas, the individual soul is attuned to the movements of the heavens, reacting to the light emanating from the planets 'according to the angles they form with each other, and the geometrical harmonies or disharmonies that result'. This is compared with the way the ear hears harmonies in music, and the eye sees harmonies in colour: 'The capacity of the soul to act as a cosmic resonator has a mystic and a causal aspect: on the one hand it affirms the soul's affinity with the *anima mundi* [world spirit], on the other, it makes it subject to strictly mathematical laws.'

At this point, Koestler points out: 'Kepler's particular brand of astrology merges into his all-embracing and unifying Pythagorean vision of the Harmony of the Spheres.' Yet alongside this metaphysical mumbo-jumbo, Kepler also included in this work his revolutionary third law of planetary motion, which laid the foundation for the solar system as we know it today.* This division between sense and nonsense may appear schizoid to the modern view, but it must nonetheless be borne in mind from the outset when following the life and exceptional penetration of Kepler's thought.

After excelling at school, Kepler gained a scholarship to attend the nearby University of Tübingen. Kepler had been a sickly child, and it was expected that he would enter the Church, as his physique was thought incapable of surviving a more strenuous occupation. At university, Kepler studied theology. Fortunately, during this period theology was so all-pervasive that it included what we would call philosophy. And in doing so, it also included natural philosophy or science. All this was comprehended in the study of Aristotle – the most wide-ranging of the ancient philosophers. Aristotle's theology predated Christianity; but as we have seen, over time this had been skilfully elided to enable his natural philosophy to become that most unscientific of entities – namely, the Holy Writ. Thus

---

* Just over half a century later, when Isaac Newton was asked how he had come up with his transformative idea of the universe, he replied that he had done this 'by standing on the shoulders of giants'. One of the giants which Newton indubitably had in mind here was Kepler.

Kepler's theological studies certainly catered to his scientific interest, even if they were presented in what contemporary progressive thought was increasingly recognizing as an outmoded form.

In the context of such convoluted thought, it should come as no surprise that at Tübingen Kepler 'proved himself to be a superb mathematician and earned a reputation as a skilful astrologer, casting horoscopes for fellow students'. One step backwards, one step forwards: at Tübingen Kepler also embraced the Copernican view of the universe, yet with an unusual mystical twist. In student debate, 'he defended *heliocentrism* from both a theoretical and theological perspective, maintaining that the *Sun* was the principal source of motive power in the universe'.

Kepler's frail health persisted as he grew into manhood, and this was further exacerbated by his obsessive mathematical (and other, extracurricular) studies. In times of extreme stress he was liable to succumb to fits of all but uncontrollable rage. It is difficult to speculate on this pathology, though from what we know of his physical and mental condition such 'episodes' could have been a manifestation of anything from sheer mental stress to epilepsy.

Kepler would not finish his studies at Tübingen. Possibly due to financial constraints, during his last year he accepted a post as a teacher of mathematics and astronomy at the Protestant school in Graz (in modern-day Austria). Here he continued to develop his mystic-scientific ideas along Aristotelian lines of teleology: the idea that everything in the universe has been created according to a divine purpose.

A year after arriving in Graz, Kepler met and fell in love with Barbara Müller, the daughter of a prosperous local mill-owner. Although she was only twenty-three, Barbara had already outlived two husbands, and had thus accumulated a small fortune. Her father was not in favour of Kepler, on the grounds of his poverty, but was eventually won over by Kepler's social standing as the grandson of a former mayor. In 1597, at the age of twenty-five, Kepler married Barbara, and they soon had children.

One day while teaching at Graz, Kepler experienced a sudden insight into his understanding of the cosmos. He saw the sun as the centre of the solar system, with each of the planets orbiting about it according to a complex mathematical system. This involved an ingenious nesting of the five platonic solids, one within the other.* Each of these solids was encased within a sphere, and these expanding spheres described the circular orbits of the planets about the sun. Though based on Greek mathematics, this shows a medieval ingenuity in its abstraction and symbolism. However, empirical science it is not.

Kepler would publish these ideas in his first work, which he characteristically entitled *Mysterium Cosmographicum* (loosely, The Mystery of the Cosmos). This again has a distinctly medieval resonance: the Renaissance was very much an age of *de*-mystifying.† On the other hand, Kepler's work was undoubtedly revolutionary – making, as it did, a strong contribution to the advancement of science. This was indeed the first work which publicly endorsed the Copernican heliocentric system. On top of this, it also gave a mathematical (if mystical) explanation of the orbits of the planets. This question had for some time bothered those who had come to believe in the Copernican system. If the planets did in fact orbit the sun, what accounted for their different orbits? Kepler may have provided an unscientific answer, but he did at least see the need for an answer to this question.

As we shall see, such a harsh scrutiny of Kepler's world view should not detract from the major contributions which this pre-Newtonian giant would make. Perhaps it is best to take him at his own (mystical) word, when he modestly declared: 'I am merely thinking God's thoughts after Him.' It is worth comparing this with the declared intention of the great Islamic scientists of the Golden Age, who made advances which would inspire the European Renaissance in the first place. These dedicated Islamic pioneers, who carried the torch of Ancient Greek knowledge

---

* The five Platonic solids have faces which are identical in shape and size, such as a triangular pyramid, a cube or an octahedron.

† One only has to compare Kepler's 'mystery' with the plain-speaking titles of his fellow participants in the Scientific Revolution. See, for instance: Copernicus's *On the Revolution of Celestial Spheres*, Mercator's *Atlas*, Vesalius's *The Apparatus of the Human Body*, and especially Galileo's titles, such as *Dialogue Concerning the Two World Systems*, *The Assayer* and so forth.

before passing it back once more to Europe, believed that in learning how the world worked they were discovering the mind of God. Such a sentiment is easily recognizable in Kepler's attempts to read 'God's thoughts'.

Despite his otherworldly views, Kepler was ambitious and determined that his work should be recognized. With this in mind he sent copies of his *Mysterium* to the finest astronomers he knew – including Galileo and Brahe. Galileo rejected Kepler's mystical approach, but in so doing he overlooked the importance of the questions which Kepler's work posed – especially with regard to the mechanics of the solar system and its orbits. Brahe, on the other hand, recognized a kindred spirit. Although he dismissed Kepler's Copernican view in favour of his own, he was sufficiently impressed to enter into a correspondence with Kepler. As a result, when Brahe arrived in Prague in 1599 he invited Kepler to visit him. By now Kepler's Copernican views were beginning to attract the attention of the Catholic authorities of the Counter-Reformation, which was becoming a force to be reckoned with in Graz. Kepler travelled to Prague and was more than pleased when Brahe offered him the post of his assistant, under the auspices of the Holy Roman Emperor Rudolf II.

Kepler went to live at Benátky Castle, in the wooded hills some fifty miles north-east of Prague – the residence which had been placed at Brahe's disposal by the emperor. From the outset, it was evident that the talents of Brahe and Kepler were a perfect match. Brahe's comprehensive and meticulous observations were just the discipline which Kepler's supreme mathematical imagination required. Meanwhile Kepler's creative insights were precisely what Brahe's endless tables of observations needed to extend their scope to a wider view of the universe.

Kepler had left his family behind in Graz, and was worried about the increasing persecution of Protestants which had begun taking place in the city. He wanted to bring them to Benátky, but first he insisted upon formalizing his position with Brahe. He drew up a detailed document, specifying the precise conditions he expected Brahe to arrange for him with the emperor. He expected to be paid 'fifty florins a quarter' (no mean sum), and on top of this specified the details of his domestic needs, right down to the 'quantities of firewood, meat, fish, beer, bread, and wine' with which he would be supplied. He also required 'a detached apartment, because the noise and disorder of the household were having a terrible effect on [his] gall, and provoked him to violent outbursts of temper'. Evidently Brahe's roistering dining habits were not to Kepler's liking.

Brahe was not interested in such petty-minded demands from his assistant, and his habitual arrogance and high-handed treatment of Kepler hardly helped matters. The result was an explosive falling-out between Brahe and Kepler. Various attempts by third parties to patch up their differences proved in vain.

In the end it was Kepler who came to the realization of what was at stake. He wrote a letter to Brahe, a curious mix of abject apology, perceptive understanding of what they could do together, and general philosophical reflection: 'What shall I mention first? My lack of self-control, which I can only remember with the greatest pain... But since the ways of men are slippery, I ask you... to remind me of myself... I pray that God may help [me] to fulfil this promise...'

Once again, Koestler provides psychological insight: 'These turns of phrase do not seem to come from a scholar of repute, but from a tortured adolescent, begging to be forgiven by a father whom he hates and loves... At the base of his iridescent, complex character, Kepler always remained a waif and stray.'

When Brahe died in 1601, Kepler was left to fulfil Brahe's injunction that he had not 'lived in vain'. Kepler would more than fulfil this. Brahe had specifically set him the task of calculating the orbit of Mars, using his observations. Kepler had bragged that he would complete this within a week. In the end it took him eight years of ceaseless calculation. And it was during the course of this work that he discovered his first two laws of planetary motion. The first improves upon Copernicus's description of the planets' circular motion about the sun. Kepler was able to calculate that instead each planet describes an elliptic orbit (like a squashed circle), with the sun at one focus of the ellipse. The second law asserts that a line drawn between the planet and the sun sweeps out an equal area in equal amounts of time.

Despite these momentous discoveries, Kepler was never a physicist. In explaining the movement of the planets he resorted to a curious mixture of metaphysics and mathematics. At first he accepted the religious development of Aristotelian thought, assigning all movement to a Prime Mover. But he quickly realized that a single force could not explain the oval orbits of the planets, or the variations in their speed as they swept out equal segments of space. This could only be attained by two opposing forces. Kepler ascribed these to the force of the sun and the 'laziness' of the planets. If we transmute these metaphysical ideas into some physical equivalent, the opposing ideas of the sun's 'force' and the planets' 'laziness' come uncannily close to the mechanics of what would later be described by Newton as gravity (a force overcoming inertia).

Kepler continued in the employ of Rudolf II, painstakingly seeking to complete Brahe's map of the stars. In 1607 he observed the passage of the comet which would later be known as Halley's Comet (after Halley correctly predicted its orbit). Kepler's life then took a turn for the worse. In 1611 Bohemian Protestants rose against Rudolf II, and he was forced to abdicate in favour of his brother Matthias. Both parties in the dispute turned to Kepler for astrological advice. He did his best to produce conciliatory interpretations of the movements of the heavens, but to no avail. Amidst the deteriorating situation Kepler and his family fled Prague. While travelling, his wife Barbara and three sons contracted smallpox. In the year that followed, Barbara and one of his sons died. Eventually Kepler returned to Austria, this time settling in Linz, where he would later remarry. It was here that he learned that back in Württemberg his mother had been put on trial as a witch. Using all the influence at his disposal, he managed to secure her release after three years.

Despite his troubles, Kepler persisted with his astronomical work, completing Brahe's catalogue of the stars, along with his own additions, in 1617. Owing to the political situation it would be another ten years before it was published as the *Rudolphine Tables*, named after his former benefactor Rudolf II. Despite the advent of the telescope, these would become the standard work of reference for many decades to come. Despite their differences, Kepler and Galileo would continue to correspond on surprisingly amicable terms. Galileo even sent Kepler one of his telescopes. This enabled Kepler to see for himself the moons of Jupiter, whose existence he had previously dismissed. His knowledge of optics even enabled him to make considerable improvements to Galileo's telescope, introducing two convex lenses, which were capable of higher magnification than Galileo's combination of convex and concave lenses.

Kepler continued with his observations of the planets, and his calculations enabled him to predict that the planets Venus and Mercury would pass across the sun and be visible from earth as they made this 'transit'. Kepler died in 1630 at the age of fifty-eight, while travelling back through Germany. The following year the first 'transit' of Mercury across the face of the sun was observed, just as Kepler had predicted.

Kepler's legacy is difficult to underestimate. Despite his mystical inclinations, his mathematical descriptions of the solar system were novel, revolutionary in scope, and precise. Such innovations proved so difficult to accept, let alone understand, that many astronomers refused to accept his elliptical-orbit version of the Copernican solar system, with the planets altering speed as they swept through their orbits. But the confirmation in 1631 of his prediction of the transit of Mercury would prove a tipping point. Kepler's laws of planetary motion would lead directly to Newton's law of universal gravitation, which he formulated just thirty-five years after Kepler's death.

CHAPTER 19

EUROPE EXPANDS

T HE MAPPING OF THE stars was but an extension of the mapping of the globe which continued to be inspired by Renaissance explorers. (These two enterprises were intimately linked, as the earliest explorers relied upon accurate star charts for navigation.) As we have seen, the first European exploration of the globe had been by sailors of the southern Renaissance – such as Dias, Columbus and Vespucci – sponsored by Spain and Portugal. England, and later France, had staked claims in the northern regions of North America. However, for the most part the northern Renaissance was very much following in the footsteps of the southern Renaissance in this aspect.

A telling illustration of this can be seen in the respective circum-navigations achieved by these regions. After the exploration and circum-navigation of the globe undertaken by Magellan's Spanish-sponsored expedition in 1519–21, it would be more than half a century before Elizabeth I of England sponsored a similar voyage, by Francis Drake. Tellingly, neither of these two voyages was wholly interested in explora-tion. Magellan's expedition was sponsored by the Holy Roman Emperor Charles V, King of Spain, with the intention of discovering an eastern route to the lucrative Spice Islands. These had been the sole preserve of Portugal after Pope Alexander VI drew a line down the centre of the Atlantic, giving territory east of this line to Portugal and west of it to Spain. Magellan's voyage was intended to circumvent the line by finding a western route.

Drake's voyage, on the other hand, was intended as an act of aggression against Spanish interests in the Americas. Elizabeth I ordered Drake to capture any Spanish treasure galleons he encountered, and to conduct raids on Spanish settlements – especially along the western coast of the New World. It was this which led Drake to sail around Cape Horn and head north up the west coast of America, as far as what is now Oregon. On his return he also laid claim to territory he called Nova Albion (New Britain), which the Spanish had named California. Only then did he sail west across the Pacific to the Spice Islands (modern Indonesia), then across the Indian Ocean and round the Cape of Good Hope back to England.

The role played by the northern Renaissance in the exploration of North America has already been mentioned. Here it was England, and later France, who were responsible for mapping the territory now known as Canada, with the English later pressing south along the eastern seaboard of North America. Here they explored such locations as Virginia (named after Elizabeth I, the Virgin Queen), and eventually in 1607 established a settlement at Jamestown (named after Elizabeth I's successor James I).

Around the same time, the English explorer Henry Hudson led four expeditions, one sponsored by the Dutch, in an attempt to discover the elusive Northwest Passage. This legendary route around the top of America to the Pacific would open up a way for northern Renaissance traders to sail across the Pacific to the Spice Islands. During Hudson's fourth expedition, he reached the large stretch of open water now known as Hudson Bay. He was convinced that he had now discovered the Northwest Passage, and began mapping the shores of the bay before becoming trapped in winter ice. When the ice broke up in the spring of 1611, Hudson was determined to press on, but his crew mutinied. Eventually he and his son, along with loyal crew members, were cast adrift in an open boat with a few provisions. They were never seen again, and no trace has been found of them to this day.

When the mutineers returned to England they were put on trial, though they were not given the customary sentence of death by hanging. It is generally assumed that they were spared because they were the only ones who had first-hand knowledge of a possible Northwest Passage. However, no further English expeditions were mounted in search of this elusive sea route for several years to come.

Ironically, English optimism concerning the existence of the Northwest Passage had been inspired by an unsuccessful attempt to discover a Northeast Passage around Siberia to the Pacific during the previous century. Despite the failure of this earlier ambitious expedition into the unknown, its far-reaching potential would remain largely overlooked. It is no exaggeration to claim that the lessons learned from this expedition would not only extend the geographical reach of the northern Renaissance, but also revolutionize its economic expertise and ultimately lay the foundations for the northern European empires that would one day straddle the globe.

The first English expedition to attempt to discover a Northeast Passage around Siberia to China was set up by three remarkable men. The first of these was Sebastian Cabot, son of the John Cabot who had staked England's claim to North America in 1497. Sebastian had accompanied his father on one of his early expeditions to the New World, and had later led the first English expedition in search of a Northwest Passage to the Pacific, some years prior to Hudson's expedition. In 'high latitudes' Cabot 'encountered fields of icebergs and reported an open passage of water but was forced to turn back'.

When his sailing days were over, Sebastian Cabot took to cartography, encouraging the study of maps amongst English sailors. Prior to this, the English had relied upon foreign navigators such as John Cabot and Amerigo Vespucci (both experienced Italian explorers) to lead their voyages of discovery. Before making use of these foreign experts, English sailors had tended to hug coastlines and then rely upon local pilots when entering unknown waters. According to contemporary British historian

James Evans: 'It was no wonder that English seamen and merchants did not aspire to sail to distant lands, without the maps to fire their imaginations and their ambitions.' Cabot's insistence upon English sailors learning to extend their navigation and seamanship beyond their own coast, along with Henry VIII's building-up of a large defensive navy, would be instrumental in making England a naval power, culminating in saving the country from the Spanish Armada. This would mark the emergence of the likes of Francis Drake and Walter Raleigh: the first stage in England's growth towards becoming the world's greatest sea power.

The second instigator of the search for a Northeast Passage was Richard Chancellor, now in his early thirties and one of the first to benefit from Cabot's influence. While still a young man he had sailed the Mediterranean as an apprentice navigator, and was eager to put his skills to the test.

In classic English fashion, the chief of the expedition was a soldier named Sir Hugh Willoughby, who had proved his military capabilities defending northern English castles against the Scots but had no nautical experience whatsoever. However, 'it was hoped he would transition into naval life with the same aplomb he showed on land'.

In 1551, Willoughby, Cabot and Chancellor came together to found the 'Mystery and Company of Merchant Adventurers for the Discovery of Regions, Dominions, Islands, and Places unknown', later to become better known as the Muscovy Company. This was a joint-stock company – a comparatively new financial organization which was financed by outsiders purchasing shares of the company stock.* The full title of the company expresses all aspects of its intention – its essential secrecy (to protect it from competitors), its commercial aims, as well as exploration.

---

* This was of course a development of the 'bourse' that was founded more than a century previously in Bruges – which was in turn based on the Venetian method of purchasing a share in merchant voyages. Such financial institutions remained in their infancy in London, but were on the brink of widespread expansion in northern Europe as commercial fortunes waxed and waned, and financial expertise sought how to deal with such fluctuations.

The commercial aspect was needed to attract investors, but also had a particular national purpose. The increasing religious conflicts in Europe had led to a slump in the English wool trade with Italy, one of the nation's main sources of foreign income. As well as searching for a trade route to China, the merchant adventurers were seeking to establish trade links with little-known Muscovy, which was said to be rich in furs while being much in need of woollen cloth.

On 10 May 1553, an expedition set sail from London consisting of three newly fitted-out merchant ships: the *Bona Esperanza*, the *Bona Confidentia* and the *Edward Bonaventure*. The flotilla was under the command of Sir Hugh Willoughby, with Richard Chancellor second-in-command and chief navigator. They were seen off by the eighty-two-year-old Sebastian Cabot. Contrary winds and inaccurate navigation ('it was not generally known whether Willoughby and Chancellor intended to lead their expedition North-east, North-west or over the Pole') meant that the expedition got off to a somewhat farcical start. Initially it made landfall several times in East Anglia, before keeling off towards the islands of northern Norway. Eighty-four days after embarking from London, on 2 August, the three ships finally approached 'high rugged mountains rising hard up from the sea'. By now it was approaching the end of summer and the weather had begun to deteriorate. A small skiff manned by local Norwegian fishermen came out to meet the English ships, and offered to guide them through gaps in the jagged cliffs. As Willoughby noted in his log, 'The land [was] very high on either side.' By now the wind was blowing hard, gusting in various directions between the rock faces. By the time the ships emerged into open water, a full storm had blown up. Attempts to communicate between ships by shouting were in vain. In the ensuing tumultuous seas they became separated as they rounded the north of Norway (during which passage Stephen Borough, the captain of Chancellor's ship *Edward Bonaventure*, found time to bestow upon the northernmost tip of land the name 'North Cape').

The *Bona Esperanza* and the *Bona Confidentia*, with Willoughby in command, managed to regain contact with each other; but there was no sign of the *Edward Bonaventure*. Willoughby now faced a difficult decision.

With no sightings of the *Edward Bonaventure* he decided to strike out on his own. Continuous cloud cover, to say nothing of mist and fog, made star navigation impossible. When Willoughby's men first let out their 100-foot plumb line into the heaving seas they found it did not reach the seabed. After extending their line they found that they were sailing through waters 160 feet deep. A few days later, they found that even when their plumb line was extended to 200 feet it still did not reach the bottom. They appeared to be sailing further from land. The only map they had to rely upon was one drawn up by Mercator, which in this region was 'speculatively drawn'. Indeed, there was no sign of a certain landmass which Mercator had marked, and 'no amount of staring at Mercator's globe could make it align with the geography they were experiencing'. And to make matters worse, their compass needle had begun to behave erratically. (The entire notion of the North Pole was speculative at this point. Also, navigators remained unaware of any difference between the putative pole and the magnetic pole, the one which attracted the compass needle. All this produced larger variations the further north they travelled.)*

Willoughby and his two ships continued sailing north-east into the open sea for some 200 miles. Encountering no land, they then turned south-east for a hundred miles or so. Still no land. After zigzagging in a generally eastern direction for well over 200 miles they eventually sighted land in the form of 'inhospitable ice-fronted mountains'. But passage to the shore was blocked by an 'expanse of sandbanks and shallows'. Willoughby and his men had in fact reached the south-west tip of what is now known as Novaya Zemlya, the large island which curves 500 miles north above Siberia into the Arctic Ocean. They were the first Europeans to have seen this land.

---

* For centuries the magnetic compass had proved sufficiently accurate for sailors in the Mediterranean. North was the direction of the Pole Star, east was understood to be the direction of the Holy Land. Indeed, compasses were not marked with 'E' for east, but with a cross, symbolising Jerusalem or the Holy Land. However, as navigators extended their explorations into the Atlantic it was observed that the compass needle no longer pointed north to the Pole Star but often deviated significantly to the east or west of this star depending upon one's position.

Willoughby decided to head back south-west in the hope of reaching Scandinavia. After 400 miles the *Bona Esperanza* and the *Bona Confidentia* reached the Kola Peninsula above the entrance to the White Sea. It was by now mid-September. The nights were closing in, the temperature was beginning to drop, and storms were becoming more frequent. Willoughby put ashore a party to search for signs of human habitation, but they returned after a few days having found nothing amidst the Arctic tundra. In the end, Willoughby anchored offshore in the lee of a river estuary (now known to be that of the River Varzina). The men collected sea coal which was plentifully scattered along the shore, and prepared to sit out the winter. Soon, the two ships became trapped in the ice. The crew had enough coal for heat, a good supply of warm clothing for the winter, and sufficient provisions to last until they rounded Asia and entered the Pacific Ocean – which still remained, at least theoretically, the main object of the expedition.

Two years later, some Russian fishermen came across the *Bona Esperanza* and the *Bona Confidentia* trapped in the ice. Hailing the ships, they received no reply. After clambering aboard the *Bona Esperanza* they broke into the cabin. Pushing aside the wooden door, they came across an eerie sight. Willoughby and the members of his crew were frozen solid, as if suddenly petrified in ice. Some were sitting at the table, others were lying in their bunks and hammocks, their bodies stiff and glazed. There was frozen food on the pewter plates on the table, frozen drink in the tankards. Also on the table, beside the slumped form of Willoughby himself, was the open journal in which he had been writing. Its last entry was for January 1554.

When news of their fate eventually reached England, at first it was thought that Willoughby and his men had succumbed to the bitter cold, which could dip to as low as −15°C – with the wind chill factor sinking it even lower during the howling winds of the Arctic winter. Now it is known that the opposite was the case. In order to keep warm, all cracks allowing draughts into the cabin had been meticulously caulked and sealed. Even the stove chimney had been blocked to keep out the cold. Insulated against the outer air, the carbon monoxide from the burning coal had gradually built up, until the men had succumbed to the poisonous fumes.

Meanwhile Richard Chancellor and the *Edward Bonaventure* were now back in England, having completed their mission with some success. After becoming separated from Willoughby and his ships, Chancellor had sailed east around the Kola Peninsula and into the White Sea, where he had anchored at the mouth of the River Dvina (now the port of Archangel).

The sheer size of the *Edward Bonaventure* had been a cause of great wonder amongst the local people. When Chancellor came ashore he found the population wearing clothes 'as ours had been' some centuries earlier. Many fishermen lived out the winter in upturned boats, and the local church was 'full of painted images, tapers and candles'. When the river iced over, the fishermen ventured out and clubbed to death the seals which lay in their thousands upon the frozen sea. These supplied oil for their lamps and fresh meat to supplement their diet of salted fish.

News of Chancellor's arrival quickly spread down the 600-mile trade route to Moscow. Here Tsar Ivan IV, more generally known as Ivan the Terrible, was intrigued by the news and invited these foreign visitors to Moscow. After journeying by horse-drawn sleigh through the snow-covered countryside, stopping at sixty-four staging posts, Chancellor and his party eventually arrived in Moscow. This they found to their surprise was much larger than London, though its winding lanes and simple wooden dwellings gave it a comparatively primitive air. Here was a city that appeared trapped in a past which to Chancellor and his men existed as little more than a folk memory.

But when they were led into the Kremlin palace of Ivan the Terrible, all this changed. The court and its furnishings were both sumptuous and archaic. One of Chancellor's men described a Russian nobleman in his winter clothes:

> His upper garment is of cloth of gold... long, down to the foot,
> and buttoned with great buttons of silver... set on with brooches,
> the sleeves thereof very long, which he weareth on his arm, ruffed
> up... On his head he weareth a white Colpeck, with buttons of

silver, gold, pearl or stone, and under it a black Fox cap, turned up very broad.

Beneath this he wore high leather boots, stained yellow. Others in similar attire wore red boots. But this was the clothing of mere noblemen courtiers... Resplendent beneath a canopy in the corner of the room was the tsar himself, Ivan the Terrible, seated on his gilt throne studded with jewels, on a carpeted dais approached by four silver steps. The tsar was wearing layers of finest fur garments, and fastened around his shoulders was a cape of beaten gold. On his head he wore the celebrated Cap of Monomakh, an item of pointed headgear studded with precious stones, its circular rim bordered with the finest sable fur. (This headgear was based on the skullcap crown worn by the ancient khans of the Russian steppes.) As one of Chancellor's party later remarked: 'There was a majesty in his countenance proportionable with the excellency of his estate.' And though he greeted his visitors with regal friendliness 'his eyes were cold and penetrating – a sign of the unpredictable cruelty to which he was already prone'.

Ivan the Terrible had initially been ruler of the Grand Duchy of Muscovy, which had centred on Moscow, but now ruled over central Russia. Its territory extended north to the Arctic Sea at Archangel and east to the Ural mountains, but remained cut off from the Black Sea and virtually excluded from the Baltic. Despite Moscow's isolation it regarded itself as the 'Third Rome'.* But this proud isolation was more than just geographical and spiritual, it was also cultural. Russia's feudal system of serfs 'owned' by their landowners remained intact – as it would for another three centuries. Its culture too belonged to another age.

---

* With the fall of Ancient Rome, Constantinople had become capital of the eastern Roman Empire. After adopting Orthodox Christianity as its official religion, the emperor had also become 'God's representative on Earth'. Then in 1453 Constantinople had fallen to the Ottoman Turks, and Moscow had laid claim to the title of the 'Third Rome'. The word 'tsar' derives from the Ancient Roman Caesar, and as such he too was God's representative on earth. Ivan the Terrible had assumed these powers, and believed in exercising them. To contradict the tsar was blasphemy, and was punished as such.

Russia's art consisted of stylized golden icons; its literature was made up largely of anonymous ancient folk tales and hagiographies written in monasteries. Russia remained (and would remain) untouched by any Renaissance: realistic art, scientific enquiry, humanistic thought and the like were not only unknown but quite simply unthinkable. And the effect of this permeated all levels of society, from the serfs to the tsar. Indeed, to paraphrase the modern Slavonic scholar Faith Wigzell: in Muscovite Russia, superstition was a fundamental part of everyday life.

This isolation was not entirely Russia's fault. Its contact with eastern and central Europe was blocked by the Swedish Empire and the Polish–Lithuanian Commonwealth, which reached from the Baltic to the Black Sea. Russia's only commercial contact was through the monopoly exercised by the Hanseatic League, which jealously guarded its access to the lucrative Russian fur trade via the Baltic.

Ivan the Terrible saw these new English visitors to his court as a golden opportunity. If a trade link to England could be established via the White Sea, this could break the monopoly of the Hanseatic League and prove to be of great advantage to both nations. Chancellor and his party were subjected to a strenuous bout of customary Russian hospitality. Winter fare at Kremlin banquets was more than bizarre to English tastes. The almost total absence of bread was 'made up by consumption of lichens, of roots like those of the bog arum, and of the ground bark of the fir tree'. Main courses consisted of ill-preserved haunches of game (bear, buffalo, wolf), and according to Chancellor these were accompanied by 'the pickle of Herring and other stinking Fish'. All this would be washed down with frequent obligatory toasts of vodka, over which Ivan the Terrible maintained a nationwide royal monopoly.*

---

* For Ivan the Terrible, vodka was an instrument of both imperial and state policy. The government ran all taverns. Landlords were ordered to lead their customers in regular toasts to the tsar's good health, and all profits accrued to Ivan himself. Likewise, he insisted that all his close advisers and courtiers drank with him each evening to ensure that they were too drunk to oppose him, and too hungover in the morning to plot against him. (Some 400 years later, this policy was also adopted by Stalin to ensure the loyalty of his aides.)

Despite such hazards, Chancellor managed to come to an agreement with Ivan the Terrible. When Chancellor and his mission returned to England in 1554 he carried with him a letter from the tsar inviting English traders to Russia and personally guaranteeing that they would be granted trading privileges.

So successful was this venture that the Muscovy Company sponsored Chancellor to undertake another trip to Russia the following year, and when he set sail back to England in 1556 he carried aboard his ship a wide-ranging cargo. This included the coffin of Sir Hugh Willoughby, whose body had not been embalmed so the smell of his decaying corpse pervaded the entire *Edward Bonaventure*. Also on board the accompanying two ships was much Russian merchandise to sell in England, including: 'wax, train oil [extracted from whale or seal blubber], tallow, furs, felts, yarn "and such-like"'. The *Edward Bonaventure* alone carried goods worth £20,000 (equivalent to £5 million in modern terms), and the combined cargoes of the other two ships came to a similar amount. All this was before profit on sales.

Perhaps most significant of all was the presence on board the *Edward Bonaventure* of a Russian nobleman named Osip Nepeya, whom Ivan the Terrible had designated as the first Russian ambassador to England. For the English, this was an initial step in relations between the two countries. As we shall see, this was a serious misjudgement by England. For Ivan the Terrible and Russia this was much more: it was the first move towards Russia becoming part of Europe.

Unfortunately, Chancellor and his ships were caught in a storm off the coast of Scotland, where Chancellor was drowned. Nepeya made it ashore but was immediately held hostage by his local Scottish rescuers. After lengthy negotiations between the English and the Scots concerning the nature of diplomatic immunity, Nepeya was reluctantly freed and carried south to England, where he was greeted at the gates of London by the Lord Mayor.

Chancellor's position as go-between with Ivan the Terrible was taken over by the Leicestershire-born Anthony Jenkinson, a wealthy member of the landed gentry. Jenkinson was commissioned by the Muscovy

Company to lead a four-ship expedition to Russia in 1558. On board his flagship he carried a 'very tenderly and friendly written' message addressed by the English monarch to Ivan the Terrible, with the Great Seal of England attached. Jenkinson was accompanied by the Russian ambassador Nepeya, who had been loaded with gifts – including a heavy gold chain and various pieces of ornate silverware. However, these were quite outshone by the gifts he was instructed to convey to Ivan the Terrible. Amongst these were 'fine samples of cloth, an ornate breastplate "covered with crimson velvet and gilt nails", and a pair of lions'.

Jenkinson was a far-sighted man and he intended to revive the original purpose of the Muscovy Company's expedition: the discovery of a route to China. He rightly discounted any attempt to achieve this by sailing around Siberia, and had in mind an overland journey, possibly linking up with the ancient Silk Routes across central Asia.

Following negotiations with Ivan the Terrible, Jenkinson and his party set off from Moscow, travelling down the River Oka and then the River Volga as far as Astrakhan on the upper Volga Delta. This was at the very limit of Russia's new territories, and had only been conquered two years previously. From here Jenkinson chartered a ship to sail his party down the Caspian Sea to its south-east coast, landing in what is now Turkmenistan. They then joined a trading caravan travelling east. After several months they eventually reached Bokhara (in modern-day Uzbekistan). Jenkinson and his party had already been forced to repel ambush by bandits, but they were now informed that the Old Silk Road to China was no longer passable, owing to local wars and further bandits.

Jenkinson reluctantly decided to return to Moscow. This was a fortunate decision, for no sooner had he left Bokhara than it was besieged by an army from Samarkand. After many further adventures, Jenkinson managed to find his way back to the shores of the Caspian. Here he and his party were forced to construct a boat of their own, before retracing their route up the Volga and back to Moscow.

Jenkinson would undertake a second attempt to reach India and China in 1561. He managed to negotiate various trade deals en route, and even had an audience with the Shah of Iran, Tahmasp I. But after pressing on he found his way barred by a fortified Portuguese trading post that had been established at Ormuz, overlooking the mouth of the Persian Gulf.

Meanwhile Ivan the Terrible was more than pleased with the Muscovy Company, which he saw as Russia's one reliable link to western Europe. In 1558, Russia was plunged into the Livonian War. A coalition of the Swedish Empire, the Polish–Lithuanian Commonwealth and their Scandinavian allies invaded Russia with the intention of taking over Livonia, a confederation of Baltic territories. The Russian army was driven into retreat and it looked as if Ivan the Terrible might be forced to flee his country. In desperation he despatched Jenkinson to England bearing a proposal of marriage to Elizabeth I, whom he had heard was still an unmarried virgin. He let it be known that he was prepared to take over as King of England if it meant his survival.

This offer was diplomatically turned down, but by now Ivan had agreed a ceasefire. Following this near-disaster, Ivan was more determined than ever to forge strong links with western Europe. Unfortunately, the Muscovy Company saw their connection somewhat differently. As far as they were concerned, this was purely a trading link between England and Russia. When the tsar learned that England was excluding other European countries from trade with Russia, insisting upon its monopoly rights, he reacted angrily. All English trading rights were summarily revoked. Although England would soon manage to patch up this disagreement, Ivan the Terrible would never again fully trust the English traders, who continued to operate a covert monopoly.

This can be seen as one of the great lost opportunities of history. Had the English retained the trust of the tsar, Russia would perhaps have been drawn into the sphere of European civilization. It would have been a powerful 'player' on the European scene (some two centuries or so before this became the case). Trade with northern Europeans during the Renaissance era would have overcome Russian isolation (and its consequent instinctive *isolationism*). Commercial intercourse would not only have diluted its absolutist form of government, but would almost certainly have introduced ideas of reform and 'Europeanization' in the arts, sciences and literature. The ingrained romantic yet essentially backward notion of 'Holy Russia' would have been leavened by the European norms, and a Renaissance of sorts would almost certainly have taken place. (The absence of such an event in Russian history retains a fundamental effect to this day.)

Ivan the Terrible was the first 'tsar of all the Russias', 'God's representative on earth', ruler of 'the Third Rome', etc. This idea, and all it stood for, would become ingrained over the centuries as tsar followed tsar. (Although European rulers of the Renaissance era adhered to the similar 'divine right of kings', mostly this was in practice tempered by powerful aristocracies, competing 'royal lines', and in many cases the growing power of parliaments.)

The activities of the Muscovy Company introduced – with more or less success – three elements into the northern European Renaissance: namely, geographical reach, mercantile expertise, and the foundation of a financial structure which would lead to the creation of northern European global empires. It certainly extended the eastern geographical reach of Europe, though to little avail: no Northeast Passage, or even an overland route, was extended to China. Nonetheless, a seed was sown.*

The second and third elements of change exemplified by the Muscovy Company are basically intertwined. History had already seen empires, as well as the development of economic expertise (usually in the form of naked exploitation and slavery). Yet the northern Renaissance would see the evolution of these elements on a global scale.

The partial success of the Muscovy Company brought to the fore two concepts whose power had not yet been fully realized. The Muscovy

---

* When Napoleon invaded Russia some 250 years later, his ultimate aim was to circumvent English naval power by establishing an overland link – of trade and conquest – to India and ultimately China. Contemporary China's Belt and Road overland link to Europe is but the latest incarnation of this idea. Had England and Russia established such a revival of the old Silk Routes in the 1500s, it is no exaggeration to claim that this would have changed the entire course of world history. How it would have done this can only be a matter of speculation; but there can be no doubting that the modern world would be very different.

Company opened the way for private enterprise and the global scale of such endeavour. It may have required a 'royal charter', but this was soon reduced to little more than a nominal aspect, a mere formality. As for the global aspect: the joint-stock company, with its private investors and exclusive trading territories, was categorically different from the 'Crown colonies' that European nations were establishing elsewhere.

But this was just the beginning. Around 1600, merchants in the City of London set up the East India Company, which was originally chartered as the 'Governor and Company of Merchants of London, Trading into the East-Indies'. The 'East-Indies' initially referred to the Indian subcontinent, but would extend to include China. Like the Muscovy Company, the East India Company was a joint-stock company, whose shares were traded on the embryonic London stock exchange, and as such it was nominally a capitalist entity. Yet in so far as capitalism involved an element of free trade, it was definitely not capitalist. The company was founded with the explicit aim of establishing a trade monopoly in these regions. It began with trading posts, which soon expanded to take control of hinterland territory in order to 'protect' land upon which this trade depended. As these hinterlands expanded, they became 'policed' by the company's own private army. This modus operandi proved so phenomenally successful that within the span of two centuries, the company's operations in India and China would 'account for half the world's trade'.

Ironically, the East India Company's only serious competition was from another east India company: *Vereenigde Oostindische Compagnie* (VOC), better known to us as the Dutch East India Company. This was founded in Amsterdam around the same time as its English counterpart, and was also a joint-stock company. (In fact it issued its first shares before the English company.) And it also was essentially unhampered by its national government. As with the English company, the VOC would soon establish its own 'empire', with 'trading territories' (i.e. colonies) encompassing South Africa, southern India and Ceylon (Sri Lanka), but mostly in the spice-rich Indonesia archipelago – from which it expelled the Portuguese.

Both the English and the Dutch East India Companies were founded towards the end of the northern European Renaissance, and their full history does in fact belong to a later age. However, they are included here because their origins are intimately linked to the Europe-wide Renaissance which developed banking (the Medici of Florence), conglomerate companies (the Fuggers of Augsburg), enforced trade monopolies (the Hanseatic League),* and the spread of joint-stock companies (such as the Muscovy Company). Here were the beginnings of capitalism as we know it in its modern form. And as can be seen from the preceding examples, this may have originated in Italy, but was more fully developed when it spread across the Alps to the northern Renaissance.

---

* During the medieval era, guilds were established in cities, each devoted to a particular craft or trade – from goldsmiths to carpenters and artists. First, one had to serve an apprenticeship with a member of the guild; having achieved proficiency in the guild's particular skill, one then qualified as a member of the guild and was able to practise this trade or skill within the jurisdiction of the guild, or in other cities which recognized this guild's qualification. This ensured a certain level of competence, but it also limited the market to members of the guild, and was thus a monopoly. Interestingly, this also led to the founding of the earliest universities. When the University of Bologna was founded in 1088, it was originally a guild of students. A few years later, Oxford University too began in this fashion. In the following century the University of Paris was established as a guild of masters. During the Renaissance era, guilds continued to maintain professional and artisanal standards, but their monopolistic element proved too restrictive to contain many new elements of economic activity, such as free trade, technological innovations and new commercial developments (e.g. the joint-stock companies).

CONCLUSION

A LAST LEGACY

D URING THE CENTURY FOLLOWING Luther's dramatic nailing of his *Ninety-Five Theses* to the door of Wittenberg Castle Church in 1517, Europe was transformed. The Protestant Reformation began, and quickly spread through the continent. The Church responded by launching a Counter-Reformation. In the south of Europe any hint of Protestantism was largely quelled by the Inquisition, while in the north and east of the continent Protestantism took deeper roots. From England to Denmark, from Bohemia to Switzerland and Sweden, worshippers began adopting their own versions of Protestantism. In the process, nations became divided, particularly amongst the small German states which had previously been part of the Catholic Holy Roman Empire. Not all these divisions were prompted by purely religious motives. Many feudal lords opportunistically embraced Protestantism in order to bolster their own authority, either internally or externally. Protestantism was on occasion imposed on unwilling citizens, while their masters seized valuable Church properties and estates. At the same time, borders were ignored as princes sought to take over neighbouring territories, either in the name of their new religion or to defend the authority of the Roman Catholic Church.

Inevitably, the division between Protestant and Catholic territories remained fatally blurred in several regions. One of these was Bohemia, which stood between the Catholic strongholds of Bavaria and Austria. In Bohemia the Catholic King Ferdinand ruled over a majority Protestant population championed by their local nobility. At the same time, the Habsburg Holy Roman Emperor Matthias was dying, and next in line for the succession was none other than his cousin King Ferdinand of Bohemia (also King of Hungary, King of Croatia, Duke of Styria, and other lesser titles). However, the powerful Bohemian nobles were now planning to oust King Ferdinand in favour of a Protestant German prince. This would at a stroke have presented the Holy Roman Empire with the possibility of an intolerable anomaly: a wholly Catholic organization ruled by a Protestant prince.

Things came to a head in 1618 with an event which became known as the Defenestration of Prague. Catholic regents arrived at the city's castle bearing a letter from the Holy Roman Emperor that forbade the building of Protestant chapels in Bohemia, which was claimed to be imperial land. Whereupon the outraged Protestant leaders manhandled two of the regents out of the third-floor window of the castle. Despite falling seventy feet, the two men survived. The Catholics declared this to be a miracle, claiming that they had been borne down by angels. The Protestants pointed out that the falling regents had been saved by a soft landing on the local dunghill. This event marked the beginning of the Thirty Years' War, the most bitter, destructive and complex conflict which Europe had yet witnessed.

The war initially divided the whole of Europe into two camps, Protestants against Catholics. In 1620, at the Battle of White Mountain in Bohemia, 25,000 troops of the Holy Roman Emperor, under the leadership of the French Count of Bucquoy, defeated an army of 30,000 troops formed from an alliance of German Protestants. As the war progressed, with hostilities taking place from German Brandenburg in the east to the Iberian Peninsula, from the Spanish Netherlands in the north to Italy and Hungary, it soon became clear that the Catholic Holy Roman Empire was gaining the upper hand. Powerful France had as a matter of course joined forces with its co-religionists the Holy Roman Empire. Yet France's chief minister, the Duc de Richelieu, now began to suspect that if the Protestant forces were crushed, the Holy Roman Empire would then move against France and assert once and for all its superiority in Europe.

Cardinal Armand Jean du Plessis, Duc de Richelieu, would be responsible for an entirely new concept of statecraft and the politics involved in this enterprise. Machiavelli, who had drawn on his experiences as an envoy to inform his political theory, was essentially a perceptive observer. Richelieu, on the other hand, was a participator, a leading player in the practice of politics. But he shared Machiavelli's amoral outlook, and is known to have read *The Prince* several times – understanding its historical lessons, and the principles required to achieve covert aims. A chilling indication of Richelieu's modus operandi can be seen in his memorable observation: 'If you give me six lines written by the hand of the most honest of men, I will find something in them which will hang him.'

Cardinal Richelieu, as he is known to history, was born in Paris in September 1585 to a family of minor nobility from Poitou, in western France. When he was just five his father died fighting for the Catholic cause in the French Wars of Religion between the Catholics and the Huguenots. This left the family in debt, but they were rescued by a royal grant in recognition of the loyal military service by the head of the family. The nine-year-old Richelieu began his education at the University of Paris, where he was sent to study philosophy, prior to embarking upon a career in the army. Henry III had rewarded Richelieu's father with the Bishopric of Luçon, and the family lived off the generous revenues this provided. Richelieu's older brother Alphonse was destined to become Bishop of Luçon, in order to protect the family income from the hands of the local clergy – who wished to use this money for ecclesiastical purposes. But Alphonse had no wish to become a bishop, and instead elected to enter a Carthusian monastery, adopting a life of silent contemplation and prayer. Consequently Richelieu was chosen to take his place, whereupon he abandoned the army to study theology. A highly intelligent student, he excelled at his new studies. There was only one snag: at twenty-one, he

was too young to be appointed a bishop. So he travelled to Rome, where
he had an audience with the pope, lied about his age, and was appointed
a bishop with the pope's blessing.

In 1614, the clergy of Poitou persuaded Richelieu to become their
representative at the Estates-General, France's central legislative assembly.
Here Richelieu presented himself as a reformer, while simultaneously
arguing that the Church should be exempt from taxes and that bishops
should be ceded greater power. When the Estates-General was dissolved
by royal decree, Richelieu entered the royal court. Here he thrived amidst
the intrigue and politicking, and soon attached himself to the Florentine-
born Concino Concini, the favourite of Marie de Médicis, who ruled
France as regent.*

Concini had established himself as the most powerful minister in the
land, and at the same time as one of the most reviled men at court. As well
as being disliked for being Italian, he made himself unpopular through his
habit of diverting funds from the treasury for his own personal use. In 1616,
Richelieu was appointed by Concini as minister of state for foreign affairs.

The leader of the faction opposed to Concini was the powerful Henri
II de Bourbon, Prince de Condé. On Richelieu's advice, Concini had
Condé arrested. The following year, the sixteen-year-old Louis XIII was
induced to order the arrest of Concini, who was inadvertently murdered
during the course of his detention. Louis XIII then stripped his mother,
Marie de Médicis, of her power, ordering her to retire to her chateau at
Blois and refrain from any further political activity. In the course of this
palace revolution, Richelieu too fell from power.

---

* Marie de Médicis (who had adopted the French version of her family name) was
a distant cousin of Catherine de' Medici, who had died twenty-five years earlier.
Like Catherine, Marie had been born in Florence, a scion of the other branch
of the Medici family who had inherited the rule of Florence and become Grand
Dukes. Much like her cousin, Marie's French royal husband, Henry IV, had died
(by assassination) and she had become regent to his underage successor, Louis
XIII. Even when he came of age in 1614, she insisted upon retaining her power.
Unlike her strong-willed cousin, Marie was indecisive, extravagant, and tended to
rely upon her untrustworthy Italian favourite, Concini, who ensured that she never
fully comprehended the complexities of French politics.

Two years later, Marie de Médicis escaped from Blois and became the focus of aristocratic opposition to Louis XIII. Richelieu was immediately recalled by Louis XIII in the hope that he could reason with Marie and persuade her to desist from her activities. The Cardinal launched into complex negotiations, which to the surprise of many resulted in Marie de Médicis being allowed her freedom, restored to the royal council and reconciled with her son. Richelieu was now appointed by the grateful Louis XIII as his chief minister. Neither Louis XIII nor Marie de Médicis, nor any other senior figure at court, trusted Richelieu, but all recognized his supreme political skills. And these were now much in demand, as France had entered the Thirty Years' War in support of the new Holy Roman Emperor Ferdinand. However, France's support for the Catholic cause was hampered by a Huguenot uprising.

Over the coming years it looked increasingly probable that the Holy Roman Empire would eventually emerge from the war victorious, with the likelihood that it would later turn on France. Then in 1630, the Protestant King Gustav II Adolf of Sweden launched an invasion south across the Baltic into the German duchy of Pomerania. Despite his comparatively small army, the Swedish king was soon pushing south into the heart of Holy Roman Empire territory, proving himself one of the greatest military leaders of all time (a supreme estimation which over the centuries would be backed by figures as disparate as von Clausewitz, Napoleon and Patton). In 1632, Gustav II Adolf won a famous victory over Holy Roman Empire forces at the Battle of Lützen, during the course of which he was killed. This loss led to a lack of leadership amongst the Protestant forces.

Richelieu had been watching intently from Paris as the Swedish army pushed back the forces of the Holy Roman Empire, even going so far as to afford covert assistance to Gustav II Adolf. Richelieu had by now consolidated his power in France in both the religious and the secular sphere. In 1622 he had been appointed a cardinal by the pope, at the recommendation of Louis XIII, in part to encourage his continued efforts to subjugate the Huguenots; then in 1629 he had been made a duke of the realm, mainly to reinforce his position as chief minister. With Protestant forces in some disarray after the death of the Swedish king, Richelieu now made a decision which would be greeted with astonishment and outrage throughout Europe: he switched French support to the Protestant cause. For centuries the pope had traditionally recognized the French king as *Rex Christianissimus* (the Most Christian King), and now France had gone over to the enemy!

Having noted the increasing complexity of the political situation faced by Richelieu, as well as the expertise and duplicity with which he handled it, we can now examine the principles which established Richelieu as the father of modern statecraft. Admittedly, it may be difficult to comprehend the wider notion of 'principles' in such a context; but as we have learned from Machiavelli, moral rectitude is hardly a required ingredient for the practice of effective statecraft.

One of Richelieu's first moves on his appointment as first minister was to consolidate his position at home. This involved the centralization of power in France. No longer would feudal lords and provincial aristocrats be able to rule their own lands as semi-autonomous fiefdoms. No longer would they be allowed sufficient power to rebel and champion their own favourite candidate for the monarchy, as had so long been the case. The king would rule from Paris, and his word would be law throughout the land. To reinforce this measure, Richelieu ordered the razing of all fortified castles, apart from those deemed necessary to defend the borders against any invading enemy. This earned him the undying hatred of dukes, princes and minor nobility throughout the land. Yet it also meant that he was able to project royal authority to the furthest corners of France. And thus the gathering of taxes became more efficient, accruing further power to the king as well as enabling the more efficient running of his kingdom.

This would have made the king all-powerful, but for the establishment of an abstract concept that would over the centuries come to transform political thinking. Richelieu all but invented the idea of the state existing as a continuous historical entity in its own right. This entity – the sovereign state – was not to be guided by any whim or wish of the ruler's personality. The ruler would not be guided by either family interests or the wider interests of the Catholic religion. His only guiding principle had to be that of national interest: *raison d'état*.

Such a policy could only be followed by adhering to definite principles and cold calculation. Richelieu sought nothing less than to turn the
art of statecraft into a logical quasi-scientific enterprise. His axiomatic
principle was simple in the extreme. Before embarking upon any course of
action he asked himself: Was such an endeavour in the national interest?
Did it outweigh any possible repercussions?*

As a result of Richelieu's decision, France would continue to play a
pivotal role in the balance of power in Europe. This would allow Europe
to continue the progressive development instigated by the Renaissance –
rather than lapsing into the repression of a Counter-Reformation under
the hegemony of the Holy Roman Empire.

Richelieu died in 1642, some six years before the end of the Thirty Years'
War. Yet when hostilities finally came to a close it was Richelieu's principles
that prevailed at the ensuing comprehensive pan-European treaty known as
the Peace of Westphalia. In many ways, this was the last embodiment of the
humanist ideals of the Renaissance. And it would long outlive its era. This
embodiment of humanist ideals would lay the foundations of the modern
world and international politics. Its two central principles – namely, the idea
of the nation state, and international law – remain central to this day. The
idea that a sovereign nation has a right to pursue its own internal politics
without interference from its neighbours, and the international law that
ensures this – as well as adherence to a mutually recognized civilised norm –
are certainly the most lasting political legacies of the northern Renaissance.
It is to the northern Renaissance that we owe the nation state – the formative concept within which we continue to live to this day.

The Renaissance was very much an age of discovery – in fields ranging
from geography to anatomy, from oil painting to innovations of commerce.

---

* Unlike the history-changing opportunity squandered by the English in Russia,
Richelieu's bold volte-face in the Thirty Years' War would ensure that the power
of France was not relegated to some 'alternative history'. Had Richelieu not taken
this bold decision in line with his principles of statesmanship, the power of France
would have become as much a chimera as an early 'Europeanized Russia'.

The analogies between many of the discoveries (or rediscoveries of ancient knowledge) which came about during the Renaissance, both north and south of the Alps, suggest that these were the external manifestation of an internal mental transformation taking place in western European humanity. Evolution may be a gradual widespread process, but at certain periods tipping points appear to occur, bringing about a more abrupt overall metamorphosis.

The twentieth-century American philosopher Thomas Kuhn conceived of such a process with regard to the basic concepts and conduct of science, resulting in a fundamental 'paradigm shift' in a particular field. There are many obvious examples of this. In the Renaissance, Copernicus's conception of the solar system springs to mind. Later, Newton's conception of gravity would bring about a similarly drastic paradigm shift. And in the modern era, Einstein's conception of relativity would have its own revolutionary effect.

Where Kuhn saw the paradigm shift in terms of scientific revolutions, it could be said that the Renaissance experienced such an event across an entire culture. This may, at least in some part, account for the analogous transformations that took place in such a wide range of fields. The self-understanding implicit in humanism, the realism of art, the understanding of human anatomy, the mapping of the globe, the attempted standardization of symbols in mathematics, the host of rationalisations and interlocking processes involved in printing, and more... many of the transformations in these different fields exhibit an unmistakable resemblance to each other. And it is only a short step to recognizing this as the evolution in western European humanity of an entirely new mental vision, or concept of life.

One coherent world view was being replaced by another. As the overall standardization, spirituality and Church hegemony of medieval life began to crumble, a new – more realistic, more scientific – network of standardizations appeared to take its place. The very novelty of this emerging world enabled it to avoid the restrictions of the previous world view. For implicit in this new world view was the possibility of further change. The era of progress had begun.

ACKNOWLEDGEMENTS

As with so many of my previous works, assistance, guidance and encouragement while researching, writing and rewriting *The Other Renaissance* have come from many sources, of which I can mention but a few. My apologies to those who feel left out. First of all I wish to thank my *agent extraordinaire*, Julian Alexander, of The Soho Agency, who was instrumental in making it all happen. Also, a special thanks to my editor James Nightingale, who as usual provided many suggestions and insights which played a significant role in improving my original manuscript. Sterling, meticulous and knowledgeable work was done on the manuscript of this work by Gemma Wain, whose informative advice and suggestions were invaluable.

I have consulted sources in many record offices and libraries. I have also received help and advice from a number of academic experts. Any mistakes which remain in the text are entirely my own.

Particularly useful, especially during Covid restrictions, have been the London Library and the British Library. As ever, in the latter my particular thanks go to the kind and friendly staff of the Humanities 2 Reading Room.

My partner, Amanda Bush, supplied several suggestions, and helped me avoid certain blunders. As usual, I received encouragement and hospitality from my family, especially Oona and Matthias. My competitor Tristan provided a useful stimulus (except with the title), and Julian added some expert opinion. This work is dedicated to my brother Mark.

P.S.

NOTES AND
FURTHER READING

PROLOGUE: LIFTING THE LID

p. 2 'If you will not hear the mysteries…': Cited by P. D. Smith in 'The Ragged-Trousered Alchemist', *Guardian*, 28 January 2006, https://www.theguardian.com/books/2006/jan/28/featuresreviews.guardianreview4. Also see Arthur Edward Waite, *The Hermetic and Alchemical Writings of Paracelsus* (London: James Elliott and Co., 1894), https://archive.org/details/hermeticalchemic00para/page/n9/mode/2up [accessed 19 November 2022].

p. 4 'Knowledge is experience': John G. Hargrave, 'Paracelsus', *Encyclopedia Britannica*, https://www.britannica.com/biography/Paracelsus [accessed 20 January 2021].

p. 4 'The patients are your…': Waite, *Paracelsus*.

p. 5 'beggar's garb' et seq.: Franz Hartmann, *The Life and Doctrines of Paracelsus* (New York: Macoy Publishing, 1932). Additional material from Henry M. Pachter, *Paracelsus: Magic into Science* (New York: Henry Schuman, 1951).

p. 8 'from each point of every coloured…': David C. Lindberg, *Theories of Vision from Al-Kindi to Kepler* (Chicago: University of Chicago Press, 1976), p. 73.

p. 8 A good summary of Dietrich's study of the rainbow can be found in Carl B. Boyer, *The Rainbow: From Myth to Mathematics* (New York: Thomas Yoseloff, 1959), pp. 110-24.

p. 10 'probably the most dramatic…': Edward Grant, *A Source Book in Medieval Science* (Cambridge, MA: Harvard University Press, 1974), p. 864.

CHAPTER 1: GUTENBERG

p. 15 'although the concept of printing…': Isaac Asimov, *Asimov's Biographical Encyclopedia of Science and Technology* (London: Pan Macmillan, 1975), p. 105.

p. 16 'capture holy light…': 'Charlemagne', https://en.wikipedia.org/wiki/ Charlemagne [accessed 26 January 2021].

CHAPTER 2: JAN VAN EYCK

Much material in this chapter has been influenced, both for and against, by Till-Holger Borchert (ed.), *Van Eyck to Dürer: The Influence of Early Netherlandish Art* (London: Thames & Hudson, 2011) and Jenny Graham, *Inventing Van Eyck: The Remaking of an Artist for the Modern Age* (Oxford: Berg, 2007).

p. 26 'secret… in certain distant lands': Till-Holger Borchert, *Van Eyck* (London: Taschen, 2008), p. 8.

p. 31 'The only fifteenth-century Northern panel…': Craig Harbison, 'Sexuality and Social Standing in Jan van Eyck's Arnolfini Double Portrait', *Renaissance Quarterly*, vol. 43, no. 2 (Summer 1990), pp. 249–91.

CHAPTER 3: NICHOLAS OF CUSA

p. 33 'a prosperous boatman…': Donald F. Duclow, 'Life and Works', in Christopher M. Bellitto, Thomas M. Izbicki and Gerald Christianson (eds), *Introducing Nicholas of Cusa: A Guide to a Renaissance Man* (New York: Paulist Press, 2004), p. 25.

p. 35 'Mathematics is the mind of God' et seq.: H. Lawrence Bond (ed.), *Nicholas of Cusa: Selected Spiritual Writings* (New York: Paulist Press, 1997). This also contains translations of major works such as *On Learned Ignorance*, *Dialogue on the Hidden God* and *On the Summit of Contemplation*.

p. 37 'Since, then, the earth cannot…': Arthur Koestler, *The Sleepwalkers* (London: Penguin Books, 2014), pp. 182–3, citing Karl von Gebler, *Galileo and the Roman Curia*, trans. G. Sturge (London: C. Kegan Paul & Co., 1879), p. 161.

p. 37 'The earth is a noble star…': George Sarton, *The History of Science and the New Humanism* (Cambridge, MA: Harvard University Press, 1937), p. 241.

p. 37 'It does not seem that…': Ibid., p. 252; see also Koestler, *Sleepwalkers*, p. 183.

p. 39 fn. 'To know the world…': See for instance the Quran, 14.52.

p. 39 fn. 'He believed that God…': See for instance Alice Calaprice, *The Ultimate Quotable Einstein* (Princeton, NJ: Princeton University Press, 2010), p. 325; also Denis Brian, *Einstein: A Life* (New York: John Wiley & Sons, 1996), pp. 4, 266.

p. 39 'since by nature…': George Holland Sabine, *A History of Political Theory* (New York: H. Holt & Co., 1937), p. 319.

p. 42 'I cannot get over my amazement…' et seq.: Cited in Koestler, *Sleepwalkers*, pp. 184–5.

p. 42 'comets were dry exhalations…': Paul Weissman, 'Comet: History', *Encyclopedia Britannica*, https://www.britannica.com/science/comet-astronomy/History [accessed 16 February 2021].

p. 43 'These values, of course…': David A. J. Seargent, *The Greatest Comets in History* (London: Springer, 2009), p. 104.

p. 43 'His boyhood lasted one sixth of his life…' Original source: Metrodorus, The Greek Anthology (5th century BC). See also Wolfram, MathWorld: Diophantus' Riddle, https://mathworld.wolfram.com/DiophantussRiddle.html [accessed 3 November 2022].

p. 43 fn. 'This was the first time…': 'Nicholas of Cusa', Asimov, *Encyclopedia of Science and Technology*.

CHAPTER 4: FRANCIS I AND THE FRENCH RENAISSANCE

p. 48 'we can discern a distorted…': Michael White, *Leonardo: The First Scientist* (London: Little, Brown, 2000), p. 257.

p. 48 'How many changes of state…': Leonardo, *Codex Atlanticus* (Milan: Ambrosiana Library, 2006), 244r.

p. 48 'Thereupon [Leonardo] was seized…': Giorgio Vasari, *Lives of the Painters, Sculptors and Artists*, trans. Gaston du C. de Vere (London: Everyman's Library, 1996), p. 639.

p. 48 fn. '*de par le roi*': Cited in Serge Bramly, *Leonardo: The Artist and the Man*, trans. Sian Reynolds (London: Michael Joseph, 1991), p. 408.

p. 50 'since he was by nature…': Ascanio Condivi, *The Life of Michelangelo*, trans. Alice Sedgwick (Oxford: Phaidon, 1976), p. 102.

p. 55 'discover certain islands…': 'Jacques Cartier', https://en.wikipedia.org/wiki/Jacques_Cartier [accessed 4 November 2022].

p. 56 'out of the 110 that we were…' et seq.: H. P. Biggar, *The Voyages of Jacques Cartier*, no. 11 (Ottawa: Public Archives of Canada, 1924), p. 204.

p. 57 'the Country of Canadas': W. J. Eccles, 'Jacques Cartier', *Encyclopedia Britannica*, https://www.britannica.com/biography/Jacques-Cartier [accessed 24 February 2021].

p. 60 'It is devised…': Cited in Martin Garrett, *The Loire: A Cultural History* (Oxford: Oxford University Press, 2010), p. 78.

CHAPTER 5: A NEW LITERATURE: RABELAIS

p. 65 fn. 'to do no harm' et seq.: Hippocrates of Cos, *Hippocrates: Volume 1*, trans. W. H. S. Jones, Loeb Classical Library, No. 147 (Cambridge, MA: Harvard University Press, 1923), pp. 298–9.

p. 65 'Most illustrious drinkers…' et seq.: Guy Demerson and Genevieve Demerson (eds), François Rabelais, *Œuvres complètes* (Paris: Seuil, 1995), p. 50.

p. 66 'hypocrites, bigots, the pox-ridden…': Ibid., p. 272.

p. 67 'such idle tales and amusing…' et seq.: François Rabelais, *Gargantua and Pantagruel*, trans. M. A. Screech (London: Penguin Books, 2006), pp. 163–4.

p. 68 'drink for the thirst…': This and ensuing sayings can be found in any anthology of Rabelais quotes. To sample his works, see *The Portable Rabelais* (London: Penguin Books, 1977).

p. 68 'a revolutionary who attacked…': Georges Bertrin, 'François Rabelais', in *The Catholic Encyclopedia* (New York: Robert Appleton Company, 1911), https://www.newadvent.org/cathen/12619b.htm [accessed 17 November 2022].

p. 69 'an exceptionally perverse, morbid writer…': George Orwell, 'Review of Landfall by Nevil Shute and Nailcruncher by Albert Cohen', *The Collected Essays, Journalism and Letters of George Orwell*, vol 2 (London: Martin Secker & Warburg Ltd, 1968).

p. 70 'Those whom the gods…': Sophocles, Antigone, v 620–3.

CHAPTER 6: MARTIN LUTHER AND THE PROTESTANT REFORMATION

p. 74 'purgatory and hell' et seq.: Martin Marty, *Martin Luther* (London: Penguin Books, 2008), pp. 2–4.

p. 75 'Help! *Saint Anna…*': Martin Brecht, *Martin Luther: Road to Reformation*, trans. James L. Schaaf (Philadelphia: Fortress Press, 1985).

p. 76 'these included a thumb…': Marty, *Martin Luther*, p. 18.

p. 77 'If it had not been…': See Reformation 500, http://reformation500.csl.edu/bio/johann-von-staupitz [accessed 31 March 2021].

p. 78 'The city, which [Luther] had greeted as holy…': George Wolfgang Forell, *The Luther Legacy: An Introduction to Luther's Life and Thought* (Minneapolis: Augsburg Publishing House, 1983), pp. 15–6.

p. 79 'As soon as the gold…': Henry George Ganss, 'Johann Tetzel', *Catholic Encyclopedia*, Vol. 14 (New York: Robert Appleton Company, 1912), pp. 539-41, https://en.wikisource.org/wiki/Catholic_Encyclopedia_(1913)/Johann_Tetzel [accessed 17 November 2022].

p. 80 'a very good example…': Cited in Billy Perrigo, 'Martin Luther's 95 Theses Are 500 Years Old', *Time*, 31 October 2017, https://time.com/4997128/martin-luther-95-theses-controversy/ [accessed 1 April 2021].

p. 80 'When our Lord and Master…': Brecht, *Martin Luther*, p. 192.

p. 80 'Why does the pope…': Ibid., p. 197.

p. 81 'in just two months…': Lyndal Roper, *Martin Luther: Renegade and Prophet* (London: Bodley Head, 2016), p. 96.

p. 82 'And I say to thee...': King James Bible, Matthew 16:18–19.

p. 82 'That is why faith alone...': From the Introduction to the Gospel of St Paul in Luther's German translation of the Bible (1522).

p. 83 'Every Christian is ...': Luther, 'On Confession', see Brecht, *Martin Luther*.

p. 83 'During my absence, Satan...': Letter of 7 March 1522, Philip Schaff, *History of the Christian Church*, Vol. VII, Chap. IV, https://www.ccel.org/s/schaff/history/7_ch04.htm [accessed 17 November 2022].

p. 84 'Therefore let everyone...': Jaroslav J. Pelikan and Hilton C. Oswald, *Luther's Works*, 55 vols (St. Louis: Concordia, 1955–1986), vol. 46, pp. 50-1.

p. 84 'I, Martin Luther...': *Luther's Works*, vol. 59 (St. Louis: Concordia, 2012), p. 284.

p. 85 'Suddenly, and while I was...': Schaff, *History of the Christian Church*.

p. 85 'his mildewed bed...': Marty, *Martin Luther*, p. 109.

CHAPTER 7: THE RISE OF ENGLAND

p. 90 'Henry VII was diligent...': Paraphrased from Francis Bacon, *History of the Reign of King Henry VII* (1622); more readily accessible in Markku Peltonen, *The Cambridge Companion to Bacon* (Cambridge: Cambridge University Press, 1996). See also 'Henry VII of England', https://en.wikipedia.org/wiki/Henry_VII_of_England [accessed 11 April 2021].

p. 90 'whatsoever islands...': 'First Letters Patent granted by Henry VII to John Cabot, 5 March 1496', in H. B. Biggar (ed.), *The Precursors of Jacques Cartier, 1497–1534* (Ottawa: Government Printing Bureau, 1911), pp. 8–10, http://www.bris.ac.uk/Depts/History/Maritime/Sources/1496cabotpatent.htm [accessed 17 November 2022].

p. 91 'he went with one...': 'John Day letter to the Lord Grand Admiral, Winter 1497/8', in L. A. Vigneras, 'The Cape Breton Landfall: 1494 or 1497', *Canadian Historical Review*, vol. 38 (1957), pp. 219–28, http://www.bris.ac.uk/Depts/History/Maritime/Sources/1497johnday.htm [accessed 17 November 2022].

p. 92 fn. 'ten feet tall or even...': Robert Silverberg, 'The Strange Case of the Patagonian Giants', *Asimov's Science Fiction*, vol. 35, no. 12 (December 2011), pp. 6–9.

p. 93 'the finest Renaissance tomb...': Michael Wyatt, *The Italian Encounter with Tudor England: A Cultural Politics of Translation* (Cambridge: Cambridge University Press, 2005), p. 47.

p. 94 'untrained in the...': J. J. Scarisbrick, *Henry VIII* (New Haven, CT: Yale University Press, 1997), p. 6.

p. 95 'sole protector and Supreme Head…': J. R. Tanner, *Tudor Constitutional Documents A.D. 1485–1603: With an Historical Commentary* (Cambridge: Cambridge University Press, 1930).

p. 96 'honey clarified and coloured…': Peter Marshall, *Heretics and Believers: A History of the English Reformation* (New Haven, CT: Yale University Press, 2017), p. 269.

p. 99 'fat Flanders mare': Appears in various unattributed sources, a few of which doubt its provenance. The earliest source is Gilbert Burnett in his 1679 *History of the Reformation*. See Claire Ridgway, 'Anne of Cleves – Flanders Mare?', The Anne Boleyn Files, 10 February 2011, https://www.theanneboleynfiles.com/anne-of-cleves-flanders-mare/ [accessed 19 April 2021].

p. 99 'very evil smell…' et seq.: Cited in Alison Weir, *Henry VIII: The King and His Court* (London: Random House, 2007), p. 382.

p. 99 'the king's beloved sister': Elizabeth Norton, *Anne of Cleves: Henry VIII's Discarded Bride* (Stroud: Amberley Publishing, 2010), p. 108.

p. 101 'The apparently splendid world…': Stephanie Buck, *Hans Holbein* (Cologne: Konermann, 1999), pp. 88–95.

CHAPTER 8: THE RISE AND RISE OF THE FUGGERS

p. 107 'Fucker': Greg Steinmetz, *The Richest Man Who Ever Lived* (New York: Simon & Schuster, 2015).

p. 108 'property assessment' et seq.: Mark Häberlein, *The Fuggers of Augsburg: Pursuing Wealth and Honor in Renaissance Germany* (Charlottesville: University of Virginia Press, 2012), pp. 12–13.

p. 110 'The Romans had dug canals…': Steinmetz, *Richest Man*, p. 7.

p. 111 'the social centre of gravity…': Cited in Häberlein, *The Fuggers*, p. 28.

p. 117 '543,585 florins': Ibid., p. 64.

p. 117 fn. 'they lived on oats…': Steinmetz, *Richest Man*, p. 19.

p. 120 'German money for a German church': Roland H. Bainton, *Here I Stand: A Life of Martin Luther* (Nashville: Abingdon Press, 1978), p. 76.

p. 121 'more drunken…' et seq.: Cited Ernest Belfort Bax, *The Peasants' War in Germany* (London: Swan Sonnerschein, 1899), p. 164.

p. 121 'If someone wants to properly…' et seq.: Steinmetz, *Richest Man*, p. 207.

p. 121 'All things are to be held…': Peter Matheson (ed), *Thomas Müntzer, The Collected Works of Thomas Müntzer* (Edinburgh: T & T Clark, 1988), p. 437.

p. 121 'own 2.2%…' et seq.: Steinmetz, cited in Scott Smith, 'Jacob Fugger Banked On Being The Richest Man Ever', *Investor's Business Daily*, 12 January 2015, https://www.investors.com/news/management/leaders-and-success/banker-jacob-fugger-made-renaissance-fortune/ [accessed 17 November 2022].

p. 122 'The new priests…': Steinmetz, *Richest Man*, p. 218.

p. 122 'total assets' et seq.: These are taken from Richard Ehrenberg, *Das Zeitalter der Fugger, Geldkapital und Creditverkehr im 16. Jahrhundert* (Jena: G. Fischer, 1896).

p. 123 'Anton Fugger's abandonment…': Häberlein, *The Fuggers*, p. 80.

CHAPTER 9: COPERNICUS

p. 125 'His hypotheses are that…': Archimedes, *Arenarius*, 4–5, trans. Thomas Heath (Cambridge: Cambridge University Press, 1913), p. 302.

p. 126 'enjoyed almost the authority…': H. Darrel Rutkin, 'The Use and Abuse of Ptolemy's *Tetrabiblos* in Renaissance and Early Modern Europe', in *Ptolemy in Perspective* (New York: Springer, 2010), pp. 135–49.

p. 126 'Of all discoveries and opinions…': Johann Wolfgang von Goethe (1808), cited in Jack Repcheck, *Copernicus' Secret* (London: JR Books, 2009), frontispiece.

p. 131 'the remotest corner…': Cited ibid., p. 8.

p. 131 'He was a retiring hermitlike…': Ibid., p. 4.

p.132 'was undoubtedly the first…' et seq.: Koestler, *Sleepwalkers*, p. 186.

p. 133 'by standing on…': Isaac Newton, in a letter to fellow English scientist Robert Hooke, 5 February 1675.

p. 133 'defects' et seq.: Edward Rosen, *Three Copernican Treatises* (New York: Dover, 2004), pp. 57–90.

p. 134 'mathematical demonstrations' et seq.: Koestler, *Sleepwalkers*, p. 125.

p. 135 'We in our sluggishness do not…': Cited in Murray N. Rothbard, 'Copernicus and the Quantity Theory of Money', in *An Austrian Perspective on the History of Economic Thought, Volume 1: Economic Thought Before Adam Smith* (Auburn: Ludwig von Mises Institute, 1995), https://mises.org/library/austrian-perspective-history-economic-thought [accessed 17 November 2022].

p. 137 'In his old age he…': Edward Rosen, *Copernicus and the Scientific Revolution* (London: 1984), pp. 158–9.

p. 138 'I have no doubt that some learned…' et seq.: For full text of Osiander's Preface, see Koestler, *Sleepwalkers*, pp. 529–33.

p. 139 'For many days he…': Ibid., p. 163, citing L. Prowe *Niccolaus Copernicus* (1883–4), vol. I, part II, p. 554.

CHAPTER 10: ERASMUS

p. 141 '10–20 per cent of [the] books in circulation…': Mark Galli and Ted Olsen, *131 Christians Everyone Should Know* (Nashville: Holman Reference, 2000), p. 343.

p. 141 'The greatest danger…': Nicholas of Cusa, *De Docta Ignorantia* (On Learned Ignorance), cited in *Selected Spiritual Writings*.

p. 142 'Human affairs are so obscure...': Erasmus, *In Praise of Folly*, trans. Leonard Dean (Chicago: Packard & Co., 1946), p. 84.

p. 142 'In humility alone lies true greatness...': See, for instance, Bellitto et al., *Introducing Nicholas of Cusa*.

p. 142 'In no kind of verse have I had...': *Collected Works of Erasmus* (Toronto: University of Toronto Press, 2004), vol. 9, pp. 293–363.

p. 142 'Prevention is better...' et seq.: See various internet sites devoted to collections of quotes, e.g. azquotes.com, brainyquote.com, and https://quotes. thefamouspeople.com/desiderius-erasmus-3781.php [accessed 16 June 2021].

p. 143 'a stain, and [it] cast a pall...': 'Erasmus', https://en.wikipedia.org/wiki/ Erasmus [accessed 15 June 2021], citing Cornelis Augustijn, *Erasmus: His Life, Work and Influence* (Toronto: University of Toronto Press, 1991).

p. 143 'the bewilderment of an...': Léon-Ernest Halkin, *Erasmus: A Critical Biography* (London: John Wiley & Sons, 1991), p. 2.

p. 144 'Life without a friend I think...': P. S. & H. M. Allen (eds), *Opus Epistolarum Des. Erasmi Roterdami*, 12 vols (Oxford: 1906–58), Ep. 187 A, III, xxix.

p. 145 'His letters...': Halkin, *Erasmus*, p. 23.

p. 145 'a second homeland': Ibid., p. 50.

p. 145 'ever susceptible...': Thomas Penn, *Winter King: The Dawn of Tudor England* (London: Allen Lane, 2011).

p. 146 'no personal...': Paraphrasing Erika Rummel, *Erasmus* (London: Continuum, 2004).

p. 146 'For since young children...': Cited in Halkin, *Erasmus*, p. 40.

p. 147 'I have not come to...': Allen, *Opus Epistolarum*, vol. 1, Ep. 118 (December 1499), p. 273.

p. 147 'In Erasmus's life...': See Halkin, *Erasmus*, p. 267.

p. 148 'Not wanting to waste all...': From the Introduction to Erasmus, *In Praise of Folly*.

p. 149 'I am myself wherever I am...' et seq.: *Collected Works of Erasmus*, vol. 27, pp. 138–47. Some of the material I have used can be accessed more easily in Halkin, *Erasmus*, pp. 76–80.

p. 152 'Although Erasmus himself would...': Hunt Janin, *The University in Medieval Life, 1179–1499* (London: McFarland & Company, 2008), p. 160.

p. 152 'Classical humanism, championed by....': Harold Grimm, *The Reformation Era: 1500–1650* (New York: Macmillan, 1973), p. 71.

p. 153 'There are some things...': Erasmus, 'On the Freedom of the Will: A Diatribe or Discourse', in Gordon Rupp and Philip Watson (eds), *Luther and Erasmus: Free Will and Salvation*, (Philadelphia: Westminster Press, 1969), pp. 39–40.

p. 153 'God has caused…': Brian Flamme, 'Luther and Erasmus', LutherReformation.org, 8 June 2017, https://lutheranreformation.org/theology/luther-and-erasmus/ [accessed 17 November 2022].

p. 153 'You are not…': Cited in Halkin, *Erasmus*, p. 221.

p. 154 'It is much safer for a prince…' et seq.: Machiavelli, *The Prince* (1532), chapter 17.

p. 154 'Am I a Machiavel?': Shakespeare, *Merry Wives of Windsor*, Act 3, Scene 1, ll. 92–3.

p. 155 'test everything against…': Erasmus, *The Education of a Christian Prince* (Cambridge: Cambridge University Press, 1997), p. 60.

p. 156 'Diversity is essential…': Bertrand Russell, *History of Western Philosophy* (London: Allen & Unwin, 1979), p. 508.

CHAPTER 11: DÜRER

p. 159 'The work is a tour de force…' et seq.: Jane Campbell Hutchison, *Albrecht Dürer: A Biography* (Princeton, NJ: Princeton University Press, 1990), pp. 24, 25.

p. 160 'Still wearing her hair…': Ibid., p. 24.

p. 161 'You stink so much of…': Nuremberg Stadtbibliothek, Pirckheimer-Papiere 394, p. 7.

p. 162 'handsome Italian…': Hutchison, *Albrecht Dürer*, p. 92.

p. 162 'troubling wondrous image…': Jonathan Jones, 'Divine Inspiration', *Guardian*, 30 November 2002, https://www.theguardian.com/artanddesign/2002/nov/30/art.artsfeatures1 [accessed 17 November 2022].

p. 164 'one of those brushes…': This anecdote is cited in Alastair Smith, *'Germania' and 'Italia': Albrecht Dürer and Venetian Art*, Fred Cook Memorial Lecture, 24 May 1978.

p. 165 'In the context of the Renaissance…': 'Albrecht Dürer', https://en.wikipedia.org/wiki/Albrecht_Dürer [accessed 29 June 2021].

p. 166 'a mistake of purpose…': Aristotle, *Physics*, II, 8, trans. R. P. Hardie and R. K. Gaye, in Richard McKeon (ed.), *The Basic Works of Aristotle* (New York: Random House, 1941).

p. 166 'This same Jesus…': Acts 1:11.

p. 167 'So the old woman…': Cited in Hutchison, *Albrecht Dürer*, p. 75.

p. 168 'She feared death…': Ibid., p. 122.

p. 168 'losing my sight…': See letter to Elector of Saxony, cited in Giulia Bartrum et al. (eds), *Albrecht Dürer and His Legacy* (London: British Museum Press, 2002), p. 204.

p. 169 'a lyric confession…' et seq.: See Iván Fenyő, *Albrecht Dürer* (Budapest: Corvina Press, 1956), p. 52.

p. 170 'Dürer is in bad…': Letter from Pirckheimer to his friend Venatorius, 18 January 1519.

p. 170 'And God help me…': David Hotchkiss Price, *Albrecht Dürer's Renaissance: Humanism, Reformation and the Art of Faith* (Ann Arbor: University of Michigan Press, 2003), p. 225.

p. 171 'the great bed…': Cited Hutchison, *Albrecht Dürer*, p. 127.

p. 171 'Then the skipper tore his…': Ibid., p. 155.

CHAPTER 12: STRADDLING TWO AGES: PARACELSUS AND BRUEGEL THE ELDER

p. 177 'astral body' et seq.: Hartmann, *Life and Doctrines of Paracelsus*, p. 10.

p. 179 'sought a universal …': Nicholas Goodrick-Clarke, *Paracelsus: Essential Readings* (Berkeley: North Atlantic Books, 1999), p. 16.

p. 179 'I leave it to Luther…': Paracelsus, *Paragranum* (1530); see Philip Ball, *The Devil's Doctor: Paracelsus* (London: William Heinemann, 2006), p. 105.

p. 179 'The simple reason for this is…': ibid.

p. 180 'What is a poison if…': Cited in ibid., p. 236.

p. 183 'There is, in fact, every reason…': Alexander Wied and Hans J. Van Miegroet, 'Bruegel', *Grove Art Online* [accessed 13 July 2021].

p. 184 'he had not mastered…': Nadine M. Orenstein (ed.), *Pieter Bruegel the Elder: Drawings and Prints* (New York: Met Museum of Art, 2001), p. 64.

p. 186 'The decision on how to engage…': Julian Horx, *Beings and Their World* (London: UAL, 2021), p. 26.

p. 187 'spent more attention to making…' et seq.: Peter Frankopan, 'Antwerp: The Glory Years by Michael Pye Review – The Medieval Mammon', *Observer*, 8 August 2021, https://www.theguardian.com/books/2021/aug/08/antwerp-the-glory-years-by-michael-pye-review-the-medieval-mammon [accessed 17 November 2022].

p. 192 'essentially a comic…': Paraphrasing James Snyder, *Northern Renaissance Art* (New York: Prentice Hall, 1985), p. 484.

CHAPTER 13: VERSIONS OF THE TRUE: MERCATOR AND VIÈTE

p. 195 'In one of the more raucous…': Nicholas Crane, *Mercator: The Man Who Mapped the Planet* (London: Phoenix, 2002), p. 30.

p. 195 'images of debauchery…': Ibid., paraphrasing Macropedius.

p. 195 '*pauperes ex castro*': Ibid., p. 40.

p. 196 'Since my youth, geography has been…': Ibid., (2003 ed.), p. 54.

p. 197 fn. 'Dagroians' et seq.: B. F. De Costa, 'The Lenox Globe', *The Magazine of American History*, vol. 3, no. 9 (1879).

p. 198 'an ingenious all-in-one...' et seq.: Crane, *Mercator*, p. 54.

p. 200 'the daughter of an eminently...': Andrew Taylor, *The World of Gerard Mercator* (London: Walker & Co., 2004), p. 80.

p. 201 'More dangerous than...': Macropedius, *The Rebels* (1535), Act 3 chorus, in Yehudi Lindeman, *Two Comedies of Macropedius* (1983), pp. 64–5.

p. 203 'It is no great matter...': For details of the persecutions, see Geeraert Brandt, *The History of the Reformation and Other Ecclesiastical Transactions in and about the Low-Countries*, trans. John Chamberlayne (London: Timothy Childe, 1720), Vol. 1, Book 3, p. 80.

p. 204 'unjust persecution': Maurice Van Durme, *Correspondance mercatorienne* (Antwerp: Nederlandsche Boekhandel, 1959), p. 15, Letter to Antoine Perrenot.

p. 208 'archfiend in league...': Cited in Simon Singh, *The Code Book: The Secret History of Codes and Code-breaking* (London: Fourth Estate, 1999), p. 28.

CHAPTER 14: VESALIUS

p. 212 'windows into the body': Nutton Vivian, 'The Chronology of Galen's Early Career', *Classical Quarterly*, vol. 23, no. 1 (1973), pp. 158–71.

p. 212 'With his left-handed curved...': Walter Isaacson, *Leonardo da Vinci* (London: Simon & Schuster, 2017), p. 395.

p. 212 'One should place...': Edward MacCurdy, *The Notebooks of Leonardo da Vinci* (London: Jonathan Cape, 1938), p. 253.

p. 213 'I made an autopsy in order...': Royal Collection, Windsor Castle: Inventory No. 9, 19027v.

p. 214 'some 13,000 pages...': White, *Leonardo*, p. 1.

p. 216 'it was considered degrading...': 'Andreas Vesalius', Famous Scientists, 22 December 2015, https://www.famousscientists.org/andreas-vesalius/ [accessed 9 September 2021].

p. 217 'spent long hours in...' et seq.: Cited in C. D. O'Malley, *Andreas Vesalius of Brussels* (Berkeley: University of California Press, 1964), p. 59.

p. 218 'a young man... of great promise...': Preface of Johann Günter von Andernach, *Institutiones Anatomicae* (1538), cited in O'Malley, *Andreas Vesalius*, p. 62.

p. 218 'locked out of...': Vesalius, *Fabrica* (1543), cited ibid., p. 64.

p. 218 'In the course of a dissection...': Vesalius, *Fabrica* (1555) p. 658, cited ibid., p. 63.

p. 220 'would keep in my bedroom...': ibid.

p. 222 'presents the dreams, the programme...' et seq.: Roy Porter, *The Greatest Benefit to Mankind: A Medical History of Humanity* (London: HarperCollins, 1999), p. 181.

p. 223 'such as the skull...' et seq.: Vesalius, *Fabrica,* see O'Malley, *Andreas Vesalius,* p. 62.

p. 223 '"muscle-men" at different stages...': Porter, *Greatest Benefit,* p. 180.

p. 223 'the bad temper...' : see Brian S. Baigrie, *Scientific Revolutions,* which includes a translation of Vesalius's preface.

p. 224 'the blood sweats...' George Sarton, *Galen of Pergamon* (Lawrence: University of Kansas Press, 1954), cited in O'Malley, *Andreas Vesalius,* p. 35.

p. 224 'The liver is not divided...' : Cited in O'Malley, ibid.

p. 225 fn. 'the so-called pancreas': Ryochi Tsuchiya, 'The Pancreas from Aristotle to Galen', *Pancreatology,* vol. 15, no. 1, pp. 2–3.

p. 226 'I implore his Imperial Majesty...': Cited in O'Malley, *Andreas Vesalius,* p. 239.

CHAPTER 15: CATHERINE DE' MEDICI

p. 230 'the happiest of her entire life': Mark Strage, *Women of Power: The Life and Times of Catherine de' Medici* (London: Harcourt, 1976) pp. 13, 15.

p. 233 'The girl has been...': Ivan Cloulas, *Catherine de Médicis: Le destin d'une reine* (Paris: 1979), p. 57.

p. 233 'a cumbersome apparatus that...' et seq.: Leonie Frieda, *Catherine de' Medici* (London: Weidenfeld & Nicolson, 2003), p. 56.

p. 234 'Italian cooks were...': 'A Brief History of French Cuisine', ECPT University [blog], https://www.ecpi.edu/blog/a-brief-history-of-french-cuisine [accessed 29 September 2021].

p. 235 'many people advised the king...': Court chronicler Brantôme, cited in R. J. Knecht, *Catherine de' Medici* (London: Routledge, 1998), p. 24.

p. 238 'Madame... has not entered the bedchamber...': Cited in Ralph Roederer, *Catherine de' Medici and The Lost Revolution* (London: Harrap, 1937), p. 146.

p. 238 'to avoid all single...': Cited in Frieda, *Catherine de' Medici,* p. 3.

p. 238 'The young lion will overcome...': Nostradamus, *Prophecies,* quatrain 1, XXXXV.

p. 238 'I care not if my death...': Cited in Frieda, *Catherine de' Medici,* p. 4.

p. 239 'had tried with jagged shards...': Cited in Frieda, *Catherine de' Medici,* p. 6.

p. 239 'After about half a dozen splinters...': O'Malley, *Andreas Vesalius,* p. 396.

p. 239 'he commended...': Vincent Carloix, *Mémoires de Vieilleville,* Frieda, *Catherine de' Medici,* p. 7.

p. 240 'the house of Guise ruleth...': Cited in Knecht, *Catherine de' Medici,* p. 60.

p. 241 'worn out by disease...': 'Lorenzo di Piero de' Medici', *Encyclopedia Britannica,* https://www.britannica.com/biography/Lorenzo-di-Piero-de-Medici-duca-di-Urbino [accessed 4 October 2011].

p. 242 'One look at the half-witted creature…': Frieda, *Catherine de' Medici*, p. 195.

p. 243 fn. '85 to 70 per cent…': See www.arrse.co.uk [accessed 20 December 2021]; also Nancy Sinkoff, *Out of the Shtetl: Making Jews Modern in the Polish Borderlands* (Providence, RI: Brown Judaic Studies, 2020).

p. 244 'the ultra-Catholic city': Frieda, *Catherine de' Medici*, p. 291.

p. 244 'This populace, which has…': Roederer, *Catherine de' Medici*, p. 444.

p. 247 'textbook for tyrants' et seq.: Frieda, *Catherine de' Medici*, p. 325; Knecht, *Catherine de' Medici*, p. 164. The Machiavelli quotes are from *The Prince*.

p. 247 'the most important…': Strage, *Women of Power*, p. xi.

CHAPTER 16: MONTAIGNE

p. 249 'I am myself…': Michel de Montaigne, 'Apology for Raymond Sebond', in *The Essays: A Selection*, trans. M. A. Screech (London: Penguin Classics, 2004).

p. 249 '*Que sçay-je*': Middle French; see Montaigne, *Essais* (1580).

p. 250 'content with confusion…': Russell, *History of Western Philosophy*, p. 503.

p. 250 'according to the opinion of Plato…': Michel de Montaigne, *The Complete Essays of Montaigne*, trans. Donald Frame (New York: Harcourt, 1948), p. 136.

p. 251 'two noble houses and…': Donald Frame, *Montaigne: A Biography* (London: Hamish Hamilton, 1965), p. 8.

p. 251 'between eleven o'clock…': Cited in ibid., p. 29.

p. 251 'inflamed with that new ardour…': Montaigne, *Complete Essays*, p. 319.

p. 252 'He scarcely ever found a man…': Ibid., p. 486.

p. 252 'His bearing was one…': Ibid., pp. 247–8.

p. 252 'from the most noble…': Jean Darnal, cited Frame, *Montaigne*, p. 227.

p. 252 'draw the boy close…': Montaigne, *Complete Essays*, p. vii.

p. 252 'liberty and delight': Cited in 'Michel de Montaigne', https://en.wikipedia.org/wiki/Michel_de_Montaigne [accessed 13 October 2021].

p. 253 'I am so squeamish…' et seq.: Ibid., p. 61.

p. 253 'reminders of man's cruelty…': Ibid., p. 129.

p. 253 'left for dead…': Cited in ibid.

p. 254 'To him, the great mystery of…': Murray Rothbard, 'Ending Tyranny Without Violence', *An Austrian Perspective*.

p. 254 'they have an idiom in their…' et seq.: See Montaigne, *Essays: A Selection*, p. 91.

p. 255 'a distinction all the more exceptional…': 'Michel de Montaigne: Life', *Stanford Encyclopedia of Philosophy*, https://plato.stanford.edu/entries/montaigne/ [accessed 15 October 2021].

p. 255 'love of glory' et seq.: Frame, *Montaigne*, p. 66.

p. 255 'In marriage, alliances…': Montaigne, *Essays: A Selection*, p. 272.

p. 256 'I think it was by some ordinance...': Montaigne, *Complete Essays*, p. 139.

p. 256 'and may have welcomed...': Frame, *Montaigne*, p. 69.

p. 256 'The Church has much to...' et seq.: Paraphrase of Frame, *Montaigne*, pp. 72, 73.

p. 256 'If you press me to tell...': Montaigne, *On Friendship*.

p. 257 'equable discussions on...': Frame, *Montaigne*, p. 79.

p. 259 'May 16 1577. There was born...': Montaigne, *Oeuvres Complètes* (Paris: 1962), pp. 61–2.

p. 259 'It seems likely that...': Frame, *Montaigne*, p. 95.

p. 259 'I handle the cards and...': Montaigne, *Essays: A Selection*, p. 79.

p. 259 'His best ideas never came...': Frame, *Montaigne*, p. 95.

p. 260 'I went riding one day...': Montaigne, *On Some Lines By Virgil*.

p. 260 'When I play with my cat...': Montaigne, *Complete Essays*, p. 331.

p. 260 'gushing of an infinite of jets...': Montaigne, *Essays: A Selection*, pp. 962–4.

p. 261 'he is especially curious about other...': Frame, *Montaigne*, p. 213.

p. 261 'For about ten days...': Ibid., p. 221.

p. 261 'I pushed down a stone...' et seq.: Montaigne's *Travel Journal*, see *Essays: A Selection*, p. 1018.

p. 261 'This is Montaigne's final philosophy...': Frame, *Montaigne*, p. 221.

p. 261 'for mentioning the Protestant...': Ibid.

p. 261 'able to judge them only by...': Montaigne, *Essays: A Selection*, p. 937.

p. 262 'a Swiss History, simply...': Frame, *Montaigne*, p. 217.

p. 262 'I was released...': Montaigne, *Essays: A Selection*, p. 973.

p. 262 'that you may be rather...' et seq.: Frame, *Montaigne*, pp. 286–7.

p. 263 'the unruly liberty of this member...' et seq.: Montaigne, 'On Some Verses of Virgil', *Essays*.

p. 264 'Montaigne is the frankest...': See Emerson, *Address Delivered At Harvard, 1837*.

CHAPTER 17: ELIZABETHAN ENGLAND

p. 270 'his reputation as a...': 'Alonso Pérez de Guzmán y Sotomayor, 7th Duke of Medina Sidonia', https://en.wikipedia.org/wiki/Alonso_de_Guzmán_y_Sotomayor,_7th_Duke_of_Medina_Sidonia [accessed 22 October 2021].

p. 271 'I know I have the body...': See Elizabeth I Tilbury Speech, delivered July 1588.

p. 271 'He that outlives this day...': *Henry V*, Act IV, Scene 3.

p. 276 'an upstart Crow...' et seq.: Stephen Greenblatt, *Will in the World: How Shakespeare Became Shakespeare* (New York: W. W. Norton, 2005), p. 213.

p. 276 'the skull beneath the skin': T. S. Eliot, 'Whispers of Immortality' (1919), https://poets.org/poem/whispers-immortality [accessed 17 November 2022].

p. 277 'to be or not ...': *Hamlet*, Act 3, Scene 1.

p. 277 'sound and fury': *Macbeth*, Act V, Scene 5.

p. 277 'to the last syllable...': ibid.

p. 278 'We few, we happy few...': *Henry V*, Act 4, Scene 3, ll. 18–67.

p. 278 'I am Richard II...': Queen Elizabeth I to the keeper of records on the tower; see E. K. Chambers, *William Shakespeare*, Vol. II (Oxford: Clarendon Press, 1930), pp. 323–7.

p. 279 'I believe that in certain aspects...': Helen Morris, 'Queen Elizabeth I "Shadowed" in Cleopatra', *Huntington Library Quarterly*, vol. 22, no. 1 (May 1969).

CHAPTER 18: BRAHE AND KEPLER

p. 282 'warfare, politics and...': Kitty Ferguson, *The Nobleman and His House Dog: Tycho Brahe and Johannes Kepler* (London: Headline, 2002), p. 11.

p. 282 'horses, dogs and luxury': Koestler, *Sleepwalkers*, p. 257.

p. 284 'containing some ointment or...': Ibid., p. 256.

p. 284 fn. 'Though the prosthesis has...': Meghan Gannon, 'Tycho Brahe Died of Pee not Poison', Live Science, 16 November 2012, https://www.livescience.com/24835-astronomer-tycho-brahe-death.html [accessed 2 November 2021].

p. 284 'The prosthetics made of gold...': 'Tycho Brahe', https://en.wikipedia.org/wiki/Tycho_Brahe [accessed 2 November 2021].

p. 285 'a large quadrant of brass...': Koestler, *Sleepwalkers*, p. 257.

p. 285 'the first competent mind...': Edwin Arthur Burtt, *The Metaphysical Foundations of Modern Physical Science: A Historical and Critical Essay* (New York: Doubleday, 1925).

p. 285 'The book of nature...': Galileo Galilei, *The Assayer* (1623).

p. 285 'brighter than Venus': See Koestler, *Sleepwalkers*, p. 260.

p. 286 '*O crassa ingenia*...': My paraphrase; also see J. R. Christianson, *On Tycho's Island: Tycho Brahe and His Assistants, 1570–1601* (Cambridge: Cambridge University Press, 2000), pp. 17–8.

p. 287 'I am displeased...': My paraphrase; see ibid., p. 8.

p. 287 'not to be exposed...': Tycho Brahe, *Astronomiæ Instauratæ Mechanica* (Wandsbek: 1598) pp. 82–3.

p. 288 'presided over by the indefatigable...': Koestler, *Sleepwalkers*, p. 265.

p. 288 'sugar, almonds, chestnuts...' et seq.: See Ferguson, *The Nobleman*, p. 57.

p. 288 'who sat at the...' et seq.: Koestler, *Sleepwalkers*, p. 265.

p. 290 'seemed an enormous distance...': 'Tycho Brahe', *Asimov's Encyclopedia*, p. 85.

p. 291 fn. 'a gold content of 20…': American Association for the Advancement of Science, EurekAlert! [news release], 1 December 2016 [accessed 8 November 2021].

p. 291'Let me not seem to…': Cited in 'Tycho Brahe', *Oxford Dictionary of Scientists*, p. 71.

p. 291 'the crowning act of…': *Asimov's Encyclopedia*, p. 86.

p. 291 'remarkably arrogant and proudly…' et seq.: Cited in Arthur Koestler, *The Watershed: A Biography of Johannes Kepler* (New York: Doubleday, 1960), pp. 19–22.

p. 293 'according to the angles they…' et seq.: See Koestler, *Sleepwalkers*, pp. 218–9, which paraphrases Kepler's ideas.

p. 293 fn. 'standing on the shoulders…': Letter from Isaac Newton to Robert Hooke, 5 February 1675.

p. 294 'proved himself to be a superb…' et seq: 'Johannes Kepler', https://en.wikipedia.org/wiki/Johannes_Kepler [accessed 8 November 2021].

p. 295 'I am merely thinking God's…': Kepler, *Harmonice Mundi* (1619).

p. 296 'fifty florins a quarter' et seq.: See Koestler, *Watershed*, p. 112.

p. 297 'What shall I mention first?…': Letter, Kepler to Brahe, April 1600; cited in full Koestler, *Watershed*, pp. 114–5.

p. 297 'These turns of phrase do not seem…': Ibid., p. 115.

CHAPTER 19: EUROPE EXPANDS

p. 303 'high latitudes' et seq.: 'Sebastian Cabot', https://en.wikipedia.org/wiki/Sebastian_Cabot_(explorer) [accessed 12 November 2021].

p. 304 'It was no wonder that English…': James Evans, *Merchant Adventurers: The Voyage of Discovery that Transformed Tudor England* (London: Orion, 2013), pp. 47–8.

p. 304 'it was hoped he would…' et seq.: 'Muscovy Company', https://en.wikipedia.org/wiki/Muscovy_Company, which is a paraphrased summary of Evans, *Merchant Adventurers*, pp. 79–80 [accessed 17 November 2021].

p. 305 'it was not generally known…' et seq.: See Evans, *Merchant Adventurers*, pp. 114, 129.

p. 305 'North Cape': R. Hakluyt, *The Principal Navigations, Voyages, Traffiques and Discoveries of the English Nation*, vol. 1 (London: Viking, 1927), p. 336.

p. 306 'speculatively drawn' et seq.: See Evans, *Merchant Adventurers*, pp. 147–8, 206, 264.

p. 308 'as ours had been' et seq.: See ibid–., (ibid.,) pp. 184–5. My description depends heavily upon that of Evans, who in turn draws on S. Bogatyrev, *The Sovereign and His Counsellors; Ritualised Consultations in Muscovite Political*

Culture, 1350s to 1570s (Helsinki: Annales Academiae Scientiarum Fennicae, 2000), pp. 39-41, 75–6.

p. 308 'His upper garment is of cloth…': Anthony Jenkinson in Hakluyt . *Navigations*, pp. 413–14.

p. 309 'There was a majesty…' et seq: See Evans, *Merchant Adventurers*, p. 185.

p. 310 'In Muscovite Russia…': Valerie A. Kivelson and Robert H. Greene (eds), Orthodox Russia: Belief and Practice under the Tsars', *Folklorica* vol. 9, no. 2, pp. 169–71.

p. 310 'made up by concumption of lichens…': Hakluyt Vol. 1, p. 437.

p. 310 'the pickle of Herring…': Cited in Evans, *Merchant Adventurers*, p. 171.

p. 311 'wax, train oil…': Cited in ibid, p. 282.

p. 312 'very tenderly…' Evans, *Merchant Adventurers*, p. 299.

p. 312 'fine samples of cloth…': Ibid..

p. 315 'Governor and Company of Merchants…': Parliament of England, 'Charter Granted by Queen Elizabeth to the East India Company', 31 December 1600, https://en.wikisource.org/wiki/Charter_Granted_by_Queen_Elizabeth_to_the_East_India_Company [accessed 17 November 2021].

p. 315 'account for half the world's trade…': Anthony Farrington, *Trading Places: The East India Company and Asia 1600–1834* (London: British Library, 2002).

CONCLUSION: A LAST LEGACY

p. 319 'If you give me six lines…': David Hackett Fischer, *Champlain's Dream* (New York: Simon & Schuster, 2009), p. 704, n. 14. Fischer does not wholly accept the attribution to Richelieu, though he mentions an early source in Françoise Bertaut, *Mémoires pour servir à l'histoire d'Anne d'Autriche*. True or otherwise, this *bon mot* is undeniably characteristic of Richelieu.

ILLUSTRATIONS

Section two

The Tower of Babel by Pieter Bruegel the Elder, c. 1563 (*Wikimedia Commons*)

The Peasant Wedding by Pieter Bruegel the Elder, 1567 (*Wikimedia Commons*)

Mercator's first map of the world, 1538 (*Wikimedia Commons*)

Mercator's map of the world, 1569 (*The History Collection/Alamy Stock Photo*)

Portrait of Vesalius from *De Humani Corporis Fabrica*, 1543 (*Wikimedia Commons*)

Two illustrations by Jan von Calcar from *De Humani Corporis Fabrica* (*The Metropolitan Museum of Art, New York*)

Catherine de' Medici, c. 1580 (*IanDagnall Computing/Alamy Stock Photo*)

Michel de Montaigne (*Archivart/Alamy Stock Photo*)

St Bartholomew's Day Massacre, Paris, 1572 (*Science History Images/Alamy Stock Photo*)

'The Armada Portrait' of Elizabeth I, c. 1588 (*Pictures From History/Alamy Stock Photo*)

An edition of Shakespeare's First Folio, 1623 (*Folger Shakespeare Library*)

Johannes Kepler, 1610 (*GL Archive/Alamy Stock Photo*)

Engraving of Tycho Brahe by Jeremias Falck, 1644 (*Rijksmuseum, Amsterdam*)

Illustration from Kepler's *Mysterium Cosmographicum*, 1596 (*Granger, NYC/Alamy Stock Photo*)

Map of Muscovy by Anthony Jenkinson and Gerard de Jode, 1593 (*Wikimedia Commons*)

The Battle of White Mountain by Peter Snayers, 1630s (*Wikimedia Commons*)

Triple Portrait of Cardinal de Richelieu by Philippe de Champaigne, c. 1642 (*Wikimedia Commons*)

INDEX

A NOTE ABOUT
THE AUTHOR

Paul Strathern studied philosophy at Trinity College, Dublin, and has lectured in philosophy and mathematics. He is a Somerset Maugham Award-winning novelist, and is author of two series of books – *Philosophers in 90 Minutes* and *The Big Idea: Scientists who Changed the World* – as well as several works of non-fiction, including *The Borgias* and *The Florentines*